Laos

a Lonely Planet
travel survival kit

Joe Cummings

Laos

2nd edition

Published by

Lonely Planet Publications
Head Office: PO Box 617, Hawthorn, Vic 3122, Australia
Branches: 155 Filbert St, Suite 251, Oakland, CA 94607, USA
10 Barley Mow Passage, Chiswick, London W4 4PH, UK
71 bis rue du Cardinal Lemoine, 75005 Paris, France

Printed by
Colorcraft Ltd, Hong Kong

Script Typeset by
Ratry Chanty

Photographs by
Joe Cummings
Glenn Beanland
Mark Downey
Oliver Hargreave

Front cover: Sitting Buddha at Haw Pha Kaew, Vientiane (Joe Cummings)

First Published
January 1994

This Edition
August 1996

Although the authors and publisher have tried to make the information as accurate as possible, they accept no responsibility for any loss, injury or inconvenience sustained by any person using this book.

National Library of Australia Cataloguing in Publication Data

Cummings, Joe
Laos

2nd ed.
Includes index.
ISBN 0 86442 381 0.

1. Laos – Guidebooks. I. Title (Series : Lonely Planet
travel survival kit).

915.94044

text & maps © Lonely Planet 1996
photos © photographers as indicated 1996
climate charts compiled from information supplied by Patrick J Tyson, © Patrick J Tyson, 1996

Joe Cummings
Joe Cummings first became involved in South-East Asian Studies while a political science student at Guilford College, a Quaker school in North Carolina, and then later as a Peace Corps volunteer in Thailand. Since then he has worked as a translator/interpreter of Thai in San Francisco, completed a master's degree in Thai language and Asian art history at the University of California, Berkeley, has been an East-West Center Scholar in Hawaii, taught university English in Malaysia, served as a Lao bilingual studies consultant in Oakland, California, and led one of the first American group tours to Laos.

Fluent in Thai and Lao, Joe is the author of Lonely Planet's popular guidebook to *Thailand* (winner of the 1995 Lowell Thomas Best Guidebook award) and our *Thai* and *Lao* phrasebooks, along with LP travel atlases for these two countries. He occasionally writes for *Geographical, Outside, Worldview, Earth Journal, World & I, BBC Holidays, The Independent* and other periodicals.

Acknowledgements
Many people gave generously of their time and spirit in the researching and writing of this guide. Special thanks to Santi Inthavong, Thaan Thongsa, Xa Thepvongsa, Burapha Development Consultants, Claude Vincent, Yoi Soumpholphakdy, Somdith Somphonxay, Walter & Petra, Somphone & Mayulee, Ron Gluckman, Maja Wallengren, James Wolstencroft, Carol Perks, Michel Somsanuk, Micha Möller, Angus Pringle, Pierre Perrot, Michael Hodgson, Hu Li Cheng, John Wroe, Crescent Press Agency, l'Ecole Française d'Extrême-Orient, UNDP, research assistant/travel companion John Demodena and all the LP readers who took the time to write with comments and suggestions.

From the Publisher
This second edition of *Laos – travel survival kit* was edited and indexed by Ian Ward, and proofread by Greg Alford. The maps were drawn by Glenn Beanland, who was responsible for the overall layout and illustrations. Thanks to Simon Bracken and David Kemp for front cover design and Adam McCrow for the back cover. Dan Levin generated the software for the Lao romanisation. Thanks also to Cathy Lanigan for checking the Health section and Trudi Canavan for her illustrations.

Author's Note to Readers
The Lao are inclined to open their country to tourism cautiously, step by step, not only to maintain economic and political control but

also because they want to keep their precious natural and cultural resources intact. They may not always do everything the way you'd like to see it done, but please grant them the right to choose their own way. You'll be doing future generations of visitors a big favour if you tread lightly while in Laos and leave the Lao people with a favourable impression of the outside world, one that will lead to a further loosening of travel restrictions rather than vice versa.

Thanks

Thanks to the following people and other travellers who took the time and trouble to write to us about their experiences in Laos:

Vic Adams, Karen Agate-Hilton, Danny Brook, Peter Callaghan, Toby Charnaud, Patrick D'Haese, Martin Fritze, Anne Froger, Don Geramom, Lorne Goldman, David Gowlett, David Grossman, Richard Harnetty, Chris Hilburn, MJ & HG Humphreys, John Hyde, Jeff Kaye, JA Kraushoar, Karen Lapsley, David Mullett, Taka Muraoka, Tony Orr, Diana Porter, Tina & Kevin Shirley, Henrik Simon, Gerard Snowball, Burt Sutherland, Melita Tickner, Frans Verbruggen and Russell & Barbara Wiemers.

Warning & Request

Things change – prices go up, schedules change, good places go bad and bad places go bankrupt – nothing stays the same. So if you find things better or worse, recently opened or long since closed, please write and tell us and help make the next edition better.

Your letters will be used to help update future editions and, where possible, important changes will also be included in an Update section in reprints.

We greatly appreciate all information that is sent to us by travellers. Back at Lonely Planet a hard-working readers' letters team of Julie Young and Shelley Preston (Australia), Sarah Long (UK), Marina Bonnamy (France) and Beth Eisler (USA) sort through the many letters we receive. The best ones will be rewarded with a free copy of the next edition or another Lonely Planet guide if you prefer. We give away lots of books, but, unfortunately, not every letter/postcard receives one.

Contents

INTRODUCTION 9

FACTS ABOUT THE COUNTRY 10

History 10
Geography 23
Climate 24
Ecology &
Environment 25
Flora & Fauna 27
Government & Politics 30
Economy 34
Population 40
People 41
Education 44
Arts 44
Society & Conduct 50
Religion 52
Language 58

FACTS FOR THE VISITOR 66

Planning 66
Highlights 67
Suggested Itineraries 69
Tourist Offices 70
Visas & Documents 71
Embassies 76
Customs 76
Money 77
Post & Communications 80
Books 81
Newspapers & Magazines 83
Radio 84
Television 84
Film & Photography 84
Time 85
Electricity 85
Weights & Measures 85
Health 85
Toilets & Showers 96
Women Travellers 97
Gay & Lesbian
Travellers 97
Disabled Travellers 97
Travel with Children 98
Dangers & Annoyances 98
Business Hours 101
Holidays & Festivals 101
Activities 101
Courses 104
Work 104
Accommodation 105
Food 105
Drinks 110
Entertainment 112
Spectator Sports 112
Things to Buy 113

GETTING THERE & AWAY 116

Air 116
Land 118
River 120
Leaving Laos 121

GETTING AROUND 122

Air 122
Road 123
Train 124
River 124
Local Transport 125
Organised Tours 127

VIENTIANE PROVINCE 129

Vientiane 129
History 129
Orientation 129
Information 131
Things to See & Do 134
Pha That Luang 144
Places to Stay 146
Places to Eat 151
Entertainment 157
Things to Buy 158
Getting There & Away 161
Getting Around 163
**Around Vientiane
Province 164**
Vientiane to Ang
Nam Ngum 164
Ang Nam Ngum 165
Phu Khao Khuai NBCA 166
Lao Pako 166
Vang Vieng 167
Kasi 168

NORTHERN LAOS 169

**Luang Prabang
Province 169**
Luang Prabang 170
Around Luang Prabang 186
Nong Khiaw
(Muang Ngoi) 187
**Xieng Khuang
Province 188**
Phonsavan 189
Plain of Jars 192
Phonsavan to Nong Haet 193
Old Xieng Khuang
(Muang Khun) 195
Muang Sui 195
Hua Phan Province 196
Sam Neua (Xam Neua) 197
Around Sam Neua 198
Sam Neua to Vieng Xai 198
Vieng Xai 199
Phongsali Province 200
Phongsali 200
Muang Khua 202
Udomxai Province 202
Muang Xai 203
Around Muang Xai 206
Luang Prabang to Muang Xai
Via Pakbeng 207
Pakbeng 207
**Luang Nam
Tha Province 208**
Luang Nam Tha 209
Muang Sing 211
Xieng Kok 213

Boten....................................214
Bokeo Province................214

Huay Xai.................................215
Sainyabuli Province 218

Sainyabuli 219
Pak Lai 221

SOUTHERN LAOS 222

Bolikhamsai &
Khammuan Provinces 222
Pakxan 224
Around Pakxan 225
Tha Khaek 225
Around Tha Kaek 229
Savannakhet
Province............................ 229
Savannakhet............................ 230
Around Savannakhet 234

Sepon (Xepon) & the Ho Chi
Minh Trail 235
Salavan Province............. 236
Salavan...................................236
Around Salavan 237
Champasak Province 237
Pakse.....................................238
Bolaven Plateau 242
Champasak...............................243
Wat Phu Champasak...............245

Um Muang 247
Ban Phapho & Kiet Nyong.... 248
Si Phan Don (Four Thousand
Islands).................................. 248
Sekong Province 255
Sekong (Muang Lamam)....... 256
Attapeu Province............ 256
Attapeu................................... 257
Around Attapeu...................... 258

GLOSSARY 260

INDEX 262

Maps 262   Text 262

Map Legend

BOUNDARIES

—··—··—··—··—··— ....International Boundary

—··—··—··—··—··— ....Regional Boundary

ROUTES

.... Freeway

.... Highway

.... Major Road

— — — — — — — — —.... Unsealed Road or Track

..............................City Road

..............................City Street

++++++++++++++—........................Railway

.... Underground Railway

....Tram

— — — — — — — — —............. Walking Track

• • • • • • • • • • • • • • • • • • ....Walking Tour

— — — — — — — — — — — —.............................Ferry Route

+‐+‐+‐+‐+‐+‐+‐+‐+‐+‐+.................Cable Car or Chairlift

AREA FEATURES

....................................Parks

.... Built-Up Area

.... Pédestrian Mall

.... Market

+   +   +   +   +   + ...Cemetery

.... Reef

.... Beach or Desert

.... Rocks

HYDROGRAPHIC FEATURES

.... Coastline

.... River, Creek

.... Intermittent River or Creek

.... Rapids, Waterfalls

.... Lake, Intermittent Lake

....................................Canal

.... Swamp

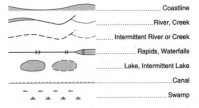

SYMBOLS

✪ CAPITAL	◔ ▯	..........Embassy, Petrol Station
◉ Capital	✈ ✝	........................Airport, Airfield
🌐 CITY	▭ ✿	..........Swimming Pool, Gardens
● City	❖ 🐘	...............Shopping Centre, Zoo
● Town	⚜ 🖼	...Winery or Vineyard, Picnic Site
● Village	← A25	One Way Street, Route Number
▪ ▼	🏛 ⚓	..........Stately Home, Monument
✠ 🍷	🏰 ◩	..............................Castle, Tomb
✉ ☎	⌂ ⌂	..................Cave, Hut or Chalet
❶ ❷	▲ ☀	..........Mountain or Hill, Lookout
◒ ℗	🗼 ⚓	...............Lighthouse, Shipwreck
🏛 ⌂	)(◎	...........................Pass, Spring
◫ ⛺	🏖 ⚡	....................Beach, Surf Beach
✚ ➕	∴	...... Archaeological Site or Ruins
☪ ✡		.... Ancient or City Wall
▣ 卍	⟶ ⟸	.... Cliff or Escarpment, Tunnel
✛ ★	+++++++	.... Railway Station

National Capital

Regional Capital

Major City

City

Town

Village

.........Place to Stay, Place to Eat

.... Cafe, Pub or Bar

...............Post Office, Telephone

.... Tourist Information, Bank

.... Transport, Parking

..............Museum, Youth Hostel

Caravan Park, Camping Ground

.... Church, Cathedral

.... Mosque, Synagogue

Buddhist Temple, Hindu Temple

.... Hospital, Police Station

Note: not all symbols displayed above appear in this book

Introduction

Known in antiquity as Lan Xang (Million Elephants), and by Indochinese War-era journalists as the Land of a Million Irrelevants, this sparsely populated country is finally enjoying peace after nearly 300 years of war with Annam, China, Siam, France and the USA.

Traditionally the least developed and most enigmatic of the three former French Indochina states, Laos has recently emerged as the front runner in economic and political reform. Free markets and private foreign investment have been the norm since 1989, and in 1991 the hammer and sickle were removed from the national seal. While Thailand speeds headlong into the 21st century, Cambodia suffers from deep internal divisions and Vietnam rapidly industrialises to provide work for its teeming population, Laos seems content to remain an Asian backwater while gradually developing one of the most stable, low-profile economic and political systems in the region.

After its 14 years of virtual isolation, landlocked Laos has in the '90s become more open towards the outside world, though the numbers of foreign visitors are kept down by a sometimes confounding tangle of red tape and a general deficiency of infrastructure. More a blessing than a curse, the overall lack of foreign influence offers travellers an unparalleled glimpse of old South-East Asia. From the fertile lowlands of the Mekong River valley to the rugged Annam-

ite highlands, travellers who have made it to Laos – even if only for a few days in transit to/from Vietnam – are unanimous in their admiration of the country. Many have found it to be a major highlight of their South-East Asian journeys.

Facts about the Country

HISTORY
Prehistory

The Mekong river valley and Khorat plateau areas which today encompass significant parts of Laos, Cambodia and Thailand were inhabited as far back as 10,000 years ago. Virtually all ethnic groups in these areas, both indigenous and immigrant, belong to the Austro-Thai ethno-linguistic family. In Laos, historically speaking, these are mostly subgroups identified with the Thai-Kadai and Miao-Yao, or Hmong-Mien, language families.

The Thai-Kadai is the most significant ethno-linguistic group in all of South-East Asia, with 72 million speakers extending from the Brahmaputra river in India's Assam state to the Gulf of Tonkin and China's Hainan island. To the north, there are Thai-Kadai speakers well into the Chinese

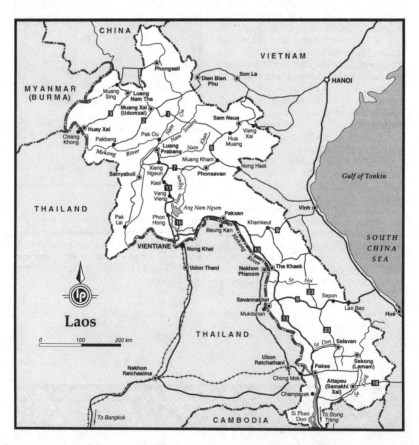

provinces of Yunnan and Guangxi, and to the south they extend as far as the northern Malaysian state of Kedah. In Thailand and Laos they are the majority populations, and in China, Vietnam and Myanmar (Burma) they are the largest minorities. The major Thai-Kadai groups are the Ahom (Assam), the Siamese (Thailand), the Black Thai (Laos and Thailand), the Shan (Myanmar and Thailand), the Thai Neua (Laos, Thailand and China), the Lü (Laos, Thailand and China) and the Yuan (Laos and Thailand). All of these groups belong to the Thai half of Thai-Kadai; the Kadai groups are relatively small (numbering less than a million) and include such comparatively obscure languages in Southern China as Kelao, Lati, Laha, Laqua and Li.

When trying to trace the origins of the current inhabitants of Laos, one must consider the fact that their predecessors belonged to a vast, nonunified zone of Austro-Thai influence that involved periodic migrations along several different geographic lines.

Austro-Thai Migration

A linguistic map of southern China, north-western India and South-East Asia clearly shows that the preferred zones of occupation by the Austro-Thai – collectively called 'Tai' by many scholars – have been river valleys, from the Red river (Hong river) in southern China and Vietnam to the Brahmaputra river in Assam. At one time, the main access points into what is now Thailand and Laos were the Yuan Jiang and other river areas in Yunnan and Guangxi and the Chao Phraya river in Thailand. These are areas where the populations remain quite concentrated today. Areas in mainland South-East Asia lying between these points were intermediate migrational zones and have always been far less populated.

The Mekong river valley between Thailand and Laos was one such intermediate zone, as were river valleys along the Nam Ou, Nam Seuang and other rivers in modern Laos (Myanmar's Shan States also fall into this category). As far as historians have been able to piece together from scant linguistic and anthropological evidence, significant numbers of Austro-Thai peoples in southern China or north Vietnam began migrating southward and westward in small groups as early as the 8th century AD, but most certainly by the 10th century. These groups established local polities along traditional Tai lines according to *meuang* (roughly principality or district) under the hereditary rule of chieftains or sovereigns called *jao meuang*.

Each meuang was based in a river valley or section of a valley. Some meuang were loosely collected under one jao meuang or an alliance of several. One of the largest collections of meuang (though not necessarily united) is thought to have emanated from southern China's Guangxi Province and/or Vietnam's Dien Bien Phu area, a theory favoured by pronunciation patterns today found along the Guangxi-Vietnam-Laos-Thailand-Myanmar axis.

In the mid-13th century, the rise to power of the Mongols under Kublai Khan in caused a more dramatic southward migration of Austro-Thai peoples. Wherever the Tai met indigenous populations of Tibeto-Burmans and Mon-Khmers in the move south (into what is now Myanmar, Thailand, Laos and Cambodia), they were somehow able to displace, assimilate or coopt them without force. This seems to puzzle many historians, but the most simple reason is probably that there were already Tai peoples in the area. This supposition finds considerable support in current research on the development of Austro-Thai language and culture.

In Lao legend, the mythic figure Khun Bulom cut open a gourd somewhere in the vicinity of Dien Bien Phu (north-western Vietnam) and out came seven sons who spread the Austro-Thai family from east to west. Although previous theory has placed the original centre of Austro-Thai culture in south-western China or even Indonesia, recent evidence suggests the possibility they may originally have emanated from the Dongson/Tonkin culture in northern Vietnam – a theory perhaps confirmed in the

Khun Bulom myth. Among tribal Thais, Dien Bien Phu is known as Muang Theng.

Southern Laos, on the other hand, was early on a centre of the Mon-Khmer Funan Kingdom (1st to 6th centuries) and the Chenla Kingdom (6th to 8th centuries), both of which extended from Champasak into north-western Cambodia. Further north two Mon kingdoms called Sri Gotapura (centred at present-day Tha Khaek) and Meuang Sawa (at Luang Prabang) flourished from the 8th to 12th centuries. These kingdoms were superseded by the Angkor Empire and later by Lao and Siamese principalities.

Lan Na Thai & Lan Xang

Until the 13th century, there were several small, independent Tai and Mon meuang in what is today northern Thailand and Laos. In the mid-13th century, a Tai rebellion against the Khmers resulted in the consolidation of several meuang to create the famous Sukhothai Kingdom in northern Thailand. Sukhothai's King Ram Khamhaeng supported Chao Mengrai of Chiang Mai and Chao Khun Ngam Muang of Phayao (Chiang Mai and Phayao were both meuang in northern Thailand) in the formation of Lan Na Thai (Million Thai Rice Fields), sometimes written simply as Lanna. Lanna extended across north-central Thailand to include the meuang of Wieng Chan (Vientiane).

Debate about whether Lanna was essentially Lao or Thai – or whether such a distinction even existed at the time – has become a hot topic in Laos today. There is evidence that both 'Lao' and 'Thai' were terms used by the people of this kingdom to describe themselves; nationalistic citizens of Thailand and Laos today make it a point to emphasise one over the other when writing and re-writing the history of the era.

In the 14th century, Wieng Chan was taken from Lanna by Chao Fa Ngum (also spelt Fa Ngoum) under Khmer sponsorship. As a child Fa Ngum had been expelled from Meuang Sawa along with his father, Chao Phi Fa, because the latter had seduced one of his father's (Fa Ngum's grandfather's) wives. The pair took refuge at the Angkor

In 1353 the territories of which modern Laos is now part was named Lan Xang Hom Khao (Million elephants & white parasol).

court, where Fa Ngum eventually married a Khmer princess named Nang Kaew Kaeng Nya. With a Khmer army behind him, Chao Fa Ngum took Wieng Chan, the Phuan kingdom of Xieng Khuang, the Khorat Plateau (in north-eastern Thailand) and finally Meuang Sawa. In 1353 he declared himself king of these territories, which he named Lan Xang Hom Khao (Million Elephants & White Parasol). Geographically, it was one of the largest kingdoms in mainland South-East Asia, although then, as now, it was sparsely populated. Although Lan Xang is considered by many present-day Lao to have been the first truly Lao nation, it was originally created as a Khmer client state; surviving inscriptions from the era most frequently refer to inhabitants of the state as 'Thai'.

Fa Ngum made Theravada Buddhism the state religion and accepted the Pha Bang, a gold Buddha image said to have been cast in Sri Lanka, from the Khmers. The Pha Bang became a talismanic symbol for the sovereignty of the Lao kingdom of Lan Xang and has remained so in the Lao People's Democratic Republic (LPDR) today. The image was kept in Meuang Sawa, which is how the city's name later became changed to Luang Phabang (Great Pha Bang), more commonly spelt 'Luang Prabang' following standard Thai pronunciation.

Within 20 years of its founding, Lan Xang's frontiers had expanded eastward to Champa and along the Annamite mountains in Vietnam. Fa Ngum became known as 'the

Conqueror' because of his constant preoccupation with warfare. Unable to tolerate his ruthlessness any longer, Fa Ngum's ministers finally drove him into exile – to the current Thai province of Nan – in 1373.

Fa Ngum's eldest son, Phaya Samsenthai (Lord of 300,000 Thai – derived from a census of adult males living in Lan Xang in 1376) succeeded Fa Ngum. Samsenthai reorganised and consolidated the royal administration of Lan Xang along Siamese lines, building many *wat* (temple-monasteries) and schools. He also developed the economy and during his 43-year reign Lan Xang became an important trade centre.

After his death at the age of 60, Lan Xang lapsed into warring factions for another century. Twelve rulers succeeded one another during this period, none ruling more than 20 years, most lasting only a year or two.

In 1520 King Photisarat came to the throne and moved the capital to Wieng Chan to avoid Burmese aggression from the west. In 1545, he subdued the kingdom of Lanna and gained the throne of that kingdom for his son, Setthathirat. When Setthathirat inherited the kingship of Lan Xang three years later, he brought with him the Pha Kaew or so-called Emerald Buddha from Lanna (the

Lan Xang Monarchs

During the first two centuries of Lan Xang history the royal seat was in Luang Prabang, after which it was moved to Vientiane (during the reign of King Sai Setthathirat).

Fa Ngum	1353-73
Samsenthai	1373-1416
Lan Kham Deng	1416-27
Phommathat	1428-29
Mun Sai	1430
Fa Khai	1430-33
Kong Kham	1433-34
Yukhon	1434-35
Kham Keut	1435-38
Sao Tiakaphat	1438-79
Theng Kham	1479-86
Lasenthai	1486-96
Som Phu	1496-1501
Wisunalat	1501-20
Phothisarat	1520-48
Sai Setthathirat	1548-71
Sensulinthara	1571-75
Maha Upahat	1575-80
Sensulinthara	1580-81
Nakhon Noi	1582-83
interregnum	*1583-91*
Nokeo Kumman	1591-96
Thammikrat	1596-1622
Upanyuvarat	1622-23
Phothisarat	1623-27
Mon Keo	1627
Upanyuvarat	-*
Ton Kham	-*
Visai	-*
Sulinya Vongsa	1637-94

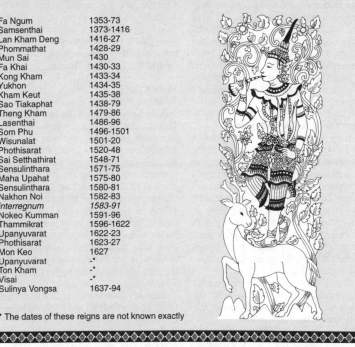

* The dates of these reigns are not known exactly

Lanna equivalent to Lan Xang's Pha Bang). He had Wat Pha Kaew built in Wieng Chan to house the Pha Kaew (the image was later taken back by the Thais) and also ordered the construction of That Luang, the country's largest Buddhist stupa.

Although Lan Xang was a large and powerful kingdom, its rulers were never able to fully subjugate the highland tribes of mountain Laos. States in north-eastern Laos, such as Xieng Khuang and Sam Neua, remained independent of Lan Xang rule and subject to Chinese or Annamese influence. In 1571, King Setthathirat disappeared somewhere in the mountains on the way back from a military expedition into Cambodia, and it is thought that his troops may have met with rebellious highlanders on an excursion into southern Laos.

Leaderless, Lan Xang declined rapidly over the next 60 years, dissolving into warring factions and subject to intermittent Burmese domination. Finally, in 1637 King Sulinya Vongsa ascended the throne following a dynastic war. He ruled for 57 years, the longest reign of any Lao monarch, and was able to further expand Lan Xang's frontiers. These years are regarded as Laos' 'golden age' – a historic pinnacle in terms of territory and power.

Fragmentation & War with Siam

When King Sulinya Vongsa died without an heir in 1694, there was a three-way struggle for the throne that led to the break-up of Lan Xang. By the early 18th century, Sulinya's nephew, under the stewardship of Annam (Vietnam), had taken control of the middle Mekong river valley around Wieng Chan. A second, independent kingdom emerged in Luang Prabang under Sulinya's grandsons. A prince in the lower Mekong river area established a third kingdom, Champasak, under Siamese influence.

Between 1763 and 1769 Burmese armies overran northern Laos and annexed the kingdom of Luang Prabang, while the Siamese took Champasak in 1778.

By the end of the 18th century, the Siamese had expanded their influence to

include the kingdom of Wieng Chan and were also exacting tribute from Luang Prabang. Wieng Chan was further pressured by the Vietnamese into paying tribute to Emperor Gia Long's Annamite Empire. Unable or unwilling to serve two masters, Wieng Chan's Prince Anou went to war with Siam in the 1820s, an unsuccessful challenge that resulted in the virtual razing of the Wieng Chan capital and the resettlement of many of its residents to Siam. Eventually the same fate overtook Luang Prabang and Champasak. By the late 1800s, practically the entire region between the Mekong and the Annamite Chain had been defeated and depopulated (which is one reason there are more Lao in Thailand today than in Laos).

Wieng Chan, Luang Prabang and Champasak then became Siamese satellite states by the late 19th century. In 1885, after successive invasions by the Annamese and the Chinese Ho, the neutral states of Xieng Khuang and Hua Phan also agreed to Siamese protection, a service the Siamese were glad to provide since they desired these states as buffers against the expanding influence of the French in Vietnam.

French Rule

In the late 19th century, the French were busy making inroads toward the establishment of French Indochina. After creating French protectorates in Tonkin and Annam, France secured a consulate at Luang Prabang (with Siamese permission) and was soon able to convince that state to ask for protectorate status as well. In current Lao histories, Luang Prabang monarch Oun Kham is painted as a villain for having agreed to French protectorship, but the bare truth is that his only feasible choice at the time was between French or Siamese rule; some historians claim there would be no Laos today had the territory been carved up by the Chinese and Vietnamese.

Through a succession of Siamese-French treaties between 1893 and 1907, the Siamese eventually relinquished control of all territory east of the Mekong river, keeping everything to the west for themselves. The

French united all of the remaining Lao principalities as one colonial territory according to the Western custom of territorial boundaries – before French rule none of the Lao kingdoms had ever been surveyed or mapped. Like the British, they assumed they had little to fear from uniting separate entities that had never been able to integrate successfully. The nation's present boundaries took shape in 1896-97 through joint commissions with China, Britain (for the Lao-Burmese border) and Siam. In retrospect France's disregard for differences between cultures west and east of the Annamite Chain – the historic dividing line between the Indianised and Sinicised cultures of South-East Asia – was a major blunder, for almost as soon as the French left the country was at war.

It was the French who gave the country its modern name, Laos, an apparent misapprehension of *le Laos* for *les Laos*, the plural of Lao, in reference to the several Lao kingdoms that existed side by side (in the Lao language, the country and people are both simply 'Lao'). Laos was never very important to France except as a buffer between British-influenced Thailand (and British-occupied Burma) and the more economically important Annam and Tonkin. An 1866 French survey concluded that the Mekong was useless for commercial navigation, that no precious metals were readily available and that the country was too mountainous for large-scale plantations.

In spite of producing small amounts of tin, rubber and coffee, Laos never accounted for more than 1% of French Indochina's exports (opium was by far the most lucrative) and by 1940 only 600 French citizens lived in Laos. Throughout the Francophone world Laos was known as the land of the lotus-eaters, and resident *fonctionnaires* (civil servants) were regarded as among the most dissolute in the French Empire for their adoption of native mores. But the presence of the French undermined the traditional flexibility of Lao interstate relations and severed the most populous part of the Champasak Kingdom by conceding Isan (north-eastern Thailand, predominantly Lao in population) to Siam. Hence the French involvement in Laos, however benign it may have initially appeared (there was never any French military action against the Lao people until 1964), resulted in a weakening of Lao states that probably could not have been achieved even by warfare.

The French also stifled the indigenous modernisation of Laos by imposing a Vietnamese-staffed civil service (just as the British did in Burma with their Indian-staffed civil service). Even the present-day Lao government labours under the influences of French and Vietnamese administrative styles.

WW II & Independence

In 1941, the Japanese occupied French Indochina with the support of the Vichy regime. The Lao mounted very little resistance against the occupation but were able to gain more local autonomy than they enjoyed under the French.

Towards the end of the war, the Japanese forced the French-installed King Sisavang Vong to declare independence in spite of his loyalty to France. The prime minister and viceroy, Prince Phetsarat, didn't trust the King and formed a resistance movement called Lao Issara (Free Lao) to ensure that the country remained free of French colonial rule once the Japanese left.

When French paratroopers landed in Vientiane and Luang Prabang in 1945, they had King Sisavang Vong relieve Prince Phetsarat of his official positions and once again declared Laos to be a French protectorate. Phetsarat and the Lao Issara formed the Committee of the People and in October 1945 drew up a new constitution proclaiming Laos independent of French rule. When the King at first refused to recognise the new document, he was deposed by the National Assembly.

Eventually Sisavang Vong came around to the Lao Issara view of things and was reinstated as king in April 1946 (the first time any Lao monarch actually ruled all of Laos). Two days after his coronation, French and

Lao guerrillas who called themselves the 'Free French' took Vientiane and smashed Lao Issara forces (as well as resistance forces sent by Ho Chi Minh from Vietnam). Phetsarat and many of the Lao Issara fled to Thailand, where they set up a government-in-exile with Phetsarat as regent. This brutal suppression of the Lao Issara sent many recruits in Ho Chi Minh's direction.

By late 1946, the French were willing to concede autonomy to Laos and invited the Lao Issara to enter into formal negotiations. But the Lao Issara split into three factions in response to the offer. One faction, under Phetsarat, refused to negotiate with the French, insisting on immediate independence according to Lao Issara terms only. The second was headed by Phetsarat's half-brother, Prince Souvanna Phouma, who wanted to negotiate with the French in forming an independent Laos. The third faction was led by another half-brother, Prince Souphanouvong, who wanted to work out a deal with the Viet Minh under Ho Chi Minh.

The French proceeded without the cooperation of the Lao Issara and in 1949 held a French-Lao convention in which Laos was recognised as an 'independent associate state' that remained part of the French Union. The treaty gave Laos the right to become an independent member of the United Nations and for the first time Laos was recognised by the West as a separate nation. The Lao Issara dissolved, but Phetsarat remained in Thailand.

Four years later, France granted full sovereignty to Laos via the Franco-Laotian Treaty of October 1953. By this time, the French were heavily preoccupied with the Viet Minh offensives in Vietnam and were looking to reduce their colonial burden in an attempt to preserve what little remained of the French Empire.

Rise of the Pathet Lao

Prior to the late '40s and early '50s, the only Lao association with the communist liberation movement had been through the membership of Prince Souphanouvong and Viet Minh organiser Kaysone Phomvihane in Ho Chi Minh's Indochinese Communist Party (ICP). In 1948, Prince Souphanouvong went to Hanoi to gain support from the Viet Minh for a Lao communist movement. At about the same time, Kaysone Phomvihane (who later became Secretary-General of the Lao People's Revolutionary Party and Prime Minister of the LPDR) was making headway among tribal minorities in the mountain districts of eastern Laos on behalf of the ICP.

In 1950, the Viet Minh-supported Free Lao Front (Neo Lao Issara, often incorrectly translated as Lao Freedom Front) and the Lao Resistance Government under Prince Souphanouvong were founded in eastern Laos to fight French colonial influences in Laos.

The 25 years that led to the Lao communist takeover in 1975 encompassed a somewhat bewildering succession of political changes – just keeping track of all the name changes requires an almost prodigious memory. First, the ICP reconstituted itself as the Vietnamese Workers Party in 1951, with plans to organise separate covert parties in Laos (the Lao People's Party) and Cambodia (the Cambodian People's Party) as well. The first use of the term Pathet Lao (Land of the Lao) came in an international communiqué released by the Free Lao Front in 1954 and referred specifically to the tactical forces of the FLF (and later the Patriotic Lao Front). In 1965, the name was changed to the Lao People's Liberation Army (LPLA) but, for the international media, the term Pathet Lao (PL) became generally applied to the Vietnamese-supported liberation movement in Laos.

In 1953-54, the kingdom of Laos was governed by a constitutional monarchy along European lines. A French-educated elite ran the government, while the Lao resistance in the countryside increased. The US government, anxious to counter the Viet Minh influence in South-East Asia, began pouring aid into Laos to ensure loyalty to the 'democratic cause'. During this same period, Viet Minh and PL troops claimed the north-eastern Lao provinces of Hua Phan and

Phongsali following the Geneva Conference of 1954, which sanctioned the takeover 'pending political settlement'.

In 1955, a clandestine communist party was officially formed in Sam Neua (Hua Phan Province) under the name Lao People's Party (LPP), consisting of 25 former ICP members. In reality, this group had existed since 1951 when the ICP split into three groups representing Vietnam, Laos and Cambodia. The LPP set up a national front in early '56 called the Lao Patriotic Front (LPF, known in Lao as Neo Lao Hak Sat or NLHS – which ought really to be translated as Patriotic Lao Front). The LPP, like its counterpart in Cambodia, was a member of the Indochinese United Front, which was led by the Vietnamese Workers Party.

Coalition & Dissolution

In 1957, the participants at the Geneva Conference had finally reached a settlement. The LPF and the Royal Lao Government agreed to a coalition government (under the RLG's Prince Souvanna Phouma) called the Government of National Union. Two LPF ministers and their deputies were admitted at the national level.

According to the Geneva agreement, the 1500 PL troops in the north-east were supposed to be absorbed into the Royal Lao Army, but disagreements over rank precluded a successful merger. When a 1958 National Assembly election in the two north-eastern provinces demonstrated unexpected LPF support among the general populace (13 out of 21 seats), there was a right-wing reaction that led to the arrest of LPF ministers and deputies, and the re-entrenchment of PL troops in the countryside. This government action was undoubtedly fuelled by the US government's withdrawal of all aid to Laos (which by this point made up the bulk of the Lao national budget) following the electoral results.

The fall of the Government of National Union left the Vientiane government under the dominance of the Committee for the Defence of National Interests (CDNI), which was made up of extreme right-wing military

officers and French-educated elites. The CDNI had strong US backing. Phoui Sananikone was installed as prime minister and Prince Souvanna Phouma was made the Lao ambassador to France. But within a year of their arrest, Prince Souphanouvong and his LPF colleagues had escaped and were again leading the resistance in the countryside.

When a 1959 UN investigation declared that the PL were not using regular North Vietnamese troops, the Vientiane government was strongly advised to adopt a more neutral policy toward the LPF.

The PL was definitely receiving North Vietnamese support in the form of resident political and military advisors throughout this period, however. The North Vietnamese, in fact, took virtual control of sparsely populated eastern Laos to use as a supply route (the 'Ho Chi Minh Trail') to the Viet Cong in South Vietnam. In the north and northeast, the North Vietnamese assisted the PL in gaining control over the tribal mountain-dwellers. Once again, to counter the North Vietnamese presence, the USA began pouring aid into Laos – this time mostly for direct military use.

Coup & Counter-Coup

In August 1960, a neutralist military faction led by Kong Le seized Vientiane in a coup d'état and recalled Prince Souvanna Phouma from France to serve as prime minister. Rightist General Phoumi Novasan (cousin to Thailand's Marshal Sarit) at first agreed to support the new government and to allow LPF participation, but in a few months changed his mind and withdrew with his troops to southern Laos. In December he launched an attack on Vientiane and wrested control from the neutralists in a CIA-rigged election. Kong Le and his troops retreated to Xieng Khuang, where they joined forces with the PL and North Vietnamese. The USSR supplied this new coalition with armaments and by 1961 they held virtually all of northern and eastern Laos.

A superpower confrontation threatened to erupt when the USA announced that it would

The Secret War & Its Legacy

From 1964 to 1973 Laos was a battlefield in a war that most of the Western world didn't know about. Basically a continuation of a struggle whose roots extended back centuries, the historic antagonists were the relatively peaceful Indianised cultures west of the Annamite Chain and the more expansionist Sinicised Vietnamese. These enemies were superseded by modern opponents playing native pawns – the Hmong and the Pathet Lao – against one another while committing thousands of their own troops in support.

Both the USA and North Vietnam acted in direct contravention of the Geneva Accord of 1962, which recognised the neutrality of Laos and forbade the presence of all foreign military personnel. To evade the Geneva agreement, the USA placed CIA agents in foreign aid posts and temporarily turned air force officers into civilian pilots. The war was so secret that the name of the country was banished from all official communications; participants simply referred to operations in Laos as 'The Other Theatre'.

As Christopher Robbins, in his well-researched book *The Ravens* (a code name for US pilots in Laos), has described:

The pilots in the Other Theater were military men, but flew into battle in civilian clothes: denim cutoffs, T-shirts, cowboy hats and dark glasses...They fought with obsolete aircraft...and suffered the highest casualty rate of the Indochina War, as high as 50%...Each pilot was obliged to carry a small pill of lethal shellfish toxin, especially created by the CIA, which he had sworn to take if he ever fell into the hands of the enemy.

US military 'technicians', however, were in Laos as early as 1959, when they began training the Royal Lao Army (RLA) as well as Hmong hill-tribe guerrillas under the charismatic Vang Pao. First used as anti-insurgent armies by the French in Vietnam (a CIA case officer was sent to study French methodology while the French were still embroiled in Indochina), the Hmong became perhaps the most important human component of the US-financed Secret War. The so-called Armée Clandestine grew to 9000 troops by mid-1961 with nine CIA specialists, nine Special Forces officers ('Green Berets') and 99 CIA-trained Thai 'special service' officers in command of a force of Hmong, Lao and Thai footsoldiers.

Long Tieng (or Long Chen), a name which didn't appear on any maps even though with the American-Hmong military presence it became the second-largest city in the country, was the clandestine headquarters for the Other Theatre. Located about halfway between Vientiane and the Plain of Jars, Long Tieng was never referred to by its geographic name but by the code name 'Alternate'; other towns around the country with military landing strips were called 'Lima Sites' and numbered (eg, LS 20). Today Long Tieng is surrounded by the Saisombun Special Zone, a new administrative unit carved out of Luang Prabang and Xieng Khuang provinces by the Lao military due to continuing 'security problems' related to Hmong army remnants in the area.

The American presence was so thick when travel writer Paul Theroux passed through while writing *The Great Railway Bazaar* he called Laos 'one of America's expensive practical jokes'. Of the hundreds of Americans who volunteered to serve in Laos as pilots, intelligence operatives or reconnaissance troops, an estimated 400 died in combat while over 400 others have been classified as 'missing in action' (MIA).

Combat planes and bombers used regularly in the Secret War included the Douglas A-1 Skyraider, Vought A-7 Corsair II, Boeing B-52 Stratofortress, McDonnell Douglas F-4 Phantom II and Republic F-105 Thunderchief.

On the other side of the battlefield headquartered in the Plain of Jars (Xieng Khuang), Hua Phan and other northern provinces were thousands of Vietnamese-trained Pathet Lao, backed by equal numbers of North Vietnamese regulars, who didn't bother to disguise themselves as civilians. The illegal Vietnamese occupation was far greater than the US presence from beginning to end. By 1969 the entire North Vietnamese 316th Division was deployed in Laos, fielding a total of 34,000 combat

intervene with US troops to prevent what was perceived as a communist takeover of Laos. A 14-nation conference convened in Geneva in May 1961 to try and halt the crisis. Both sides held their ground, awaiting the outcome of the conference. In May 1962, after long internal and international negotiations, a set of agreements were signed which provided for an independent, neutral Laos. The observance of these agreements was to troops, 18,000 support troops, 13,000 army engineers and 6,000 advisors for the purpose of placing Long Tieng under siege.

Outnumbered and outmanoeuvred, the US-Hmong-Thai forces lost Long Tieng and scored few strategic victories during the nine-year Secret War, in spite of the fact that they had superior firepower. They also had the opportunity to ignore virtually all the 'rules of engagement' (aka ROEs, nicknamed 'Romeos') that had to be observed in Vietnam (where they were often cited as an excuse for the US defeat). In Vietnam, for example, the ROEs prohibited bombing within 500 metres of a temple while in Cambodia there was a one km limit. In Laos, bombardiers were free to decimate temples, hospitals and any other building that came into their sights.

In support of Vang Pao's army alone, the Ravens and their native cohorts flew 1.5 times the number of air sorties flown in all of Vietnam. Totalling 580,944 sorties by 1973, the secret air force dropped an average of one planeload of bombs every eight minutes, 24 hours a day, for nine years! This cost US taxpayers around US$2 million per day, a figure that equals the total foreign aid Laos received in the entire year of 1988 from donor countries, the United Nations and non-governmental organisations.

After US President Johnson halted all bombing raids on North Vietnam in November 1968, the bombing of Laos increased as more air power became available. An American pilot quoted in *The Ravens* recollects:

Many times we got so much air we couldn't handle it all. Even before the bombing halt there were times when the weather was so bad over North Vietnam that they would come back [to Laos] in waves. They were damn near out of gas and they wanted to make one pass and get rid of their bombs...[O]ften you ended up doing saturation bombing in the area you happened to be at the time the first flight got in [to Laos].

In 1970 US President Richard Nixon, on the advice of Henry Kissinger, authorised massive B-52 air strikes in Laos, all of which remained highly classified until years later. Between 1964 and 1969 about 450,000 tons of ordnance had been let loose on the country, but afterwards that amount was fielded every year through the end of 1972. By the war's end the bombing amounted to approximately 1.9 million metric tons in all, equalling 10 tons per sq km, or over a half-tonne for every man, woman and child living in Laos.

Defoliants and herbicides were also dropped on Laos by the secret air force. During 1965-66, 200,000 gallons of herbicides were deposited along the Ho Chi Minh Trail near Xepon, laying bare all vegetation, poisoning civilian crops and rendering the water system unusable even for irrigation, much less drinking. Dubbed 'Agent Orange' and 'yellow rain' in the modern media, the toxic substance is still responsible for a large number of infirmities suffered by the inhabitants of eastern Laos. ∎

A Boeing B-52 Stratofortress on a bombing sortie over Laos

be monitored by the International Commission for Supervision & Control (ICSC). A second Government of National Union was formed the following month, a coalition of Prince Boun Oum (representing the rightist military), Prince Souphanouvong (for the PL) and Prince Souvanna Phouma (for the neutralist military).

This second attempt at a coalition government didn't last long. Minor skirmishes occurred between PL and neutralist troops over the administration of the north-east. The PL seriously upset the tripartite balance of power by attacking Kong Le's neutralist headquarters in Xieng Khuang, thus forcing Kong Le into an alliance with the rightists to avoid defeat.

In 1964, there was a rapid series of coups and counter-coups that resulted in the final alignment of the PL on the one side and the neutralist and right-wing factions on the other. From this point on, the PL leadership refused to participate in any offers of coalition or national elections, quite justifiably believing that they would never be given a voice in governing the country as long as either of the other two factions were in power.

War of Resistance

From 1964 to 1973, the war in Indochina heated up. US air bases were established in Thailand, and US bombers were soon criss-crossing eastern and north-eastern Laos on their way to and from bombing missions in North Vietnam and along the Ho Chi Minh trail. Secret saturation bombing of PL and NVA strongholds was carried out, but the PL simply moved their headquarters into caves near Sam Neua. Even without specific targets, B-52 captains would empty their bomb bays over civilian centres in eastern Laos when returning from Vietnamese air strikes so that their orders to release all bombs would be fulfilled. The USA, in fact, dropped more bombs on Laos than they did worldwide during WW II; Laos has thus earned the distinction of being the most heavily bombed nation, on a per capita basis, in the history of warfare.

As guerrilla resistance in South Vietnam increased, the US military leadership feared that bombing Laos wasn't enough, so they began forming a special CIA-trained army in the country to counter the growing influence of the Pathet Lao. This army of 10,000 was largely made up of Hmong tribesmen under the direct command of the Royal Lao Army General Vang Pao, himself a Hmong. These troops were a division of the RLA that was trained for mountain warfare and were not, as has been claimed, mercenaries in the true sense of the term. Like the South Vietnamese army, however, they were US-trained (in the case of Laos, also Thai-trained) and US-paid. By the end of the '60s, there were more Thais and Lao Theung than Hmong in the RLA.

In addition, a rotating number of USAF pilots, stationed in Long Tieng and Savannakhet, flew missions in northern and eastern Laos as forward air controllers (FACs), spotting PL and NVA targets for Lao and Thai-piloted tactical bombers.

By 1971 Chinese troops were also engaged in Laos with an air defence force of 6000 to 7000, mostly concentrated along the 'Chinese Road' – actually a complex of roads the Chinese were building in the provinces of Luang Nam Tha, Udomxai and Phongsali. Along with anti-aircraft personnel the Chinese maintained as many as 16,000 Chinese road workers in Laos throughout the war.

Revolution & Reform

In 1973, as the USA began negotiating its way out of Vietnam, a cease-fire agreement was reached in Laos. The country was effectively divided into PL and non-PL zones, just as it had been in 1954. Only this time the communists controlled eleven of thirteen provinces instead of two. A Provisional Government of National Union (PGNU) was formed after long negotiations and the two sides began trying to form yet another coalition government. Popular support for the PL grew as the non-PL Vientiane leadership showed increasing signs of corruption and US manipulation.

The unexpectedly rapid fall of Saigon and Phnom Penh following US withdrawal in April 1975 led the PL to seize Sala Phu Khun, a strategic crossroads between Luang Prabang and Vientiane. The LPP applied political pressure to non-PL ministers and generals as well, urging them to resign. Luang Prabang and Vientiane were papered over with threatening PL posters that left little to the imagination as to what the alternative to resignation might be.

On 4 May 1975, four ministers and seven generals resigned and an exodus of the Lao political and commercial elite across the Mekong into Thailand began. PL forces then seized the southern provincial capitals of Pakse, Champasak and Savannakhet without opposition and on 23 August they took Vientiane in a similar manner.

Over the following months, the PGNU was quietly dismantled and in December the Lao People's Revolutionary Party (LPRP) was declared the ruling party of the newly christened Lao People's Democratic Republic (LPDR). The takeover was totally bloodless; even the US embassy closed down for only a day. Kaysone Phomvihane, a long-time protégé of the North Vietnamese, served as the Prime Minister of the LPDR until his death in November 1992 at the age of 71. Born Cai Song ('Kaysone' is a Lao approximation of this name) to a Vietnamese father and Lao mother in Savannakhet in 1920, Kaysone spent much of his early life in Hanoi, where he studied law. Assisted by the Viet Minh, he helped organise the Lao Issara resistance movement in the '40s. His role in modern Lao politics cannot be overestimated; he was fluent in Lao, Vietnamese, Thai, Shan, French and English, and was considered a highly pragmatic ruler who learned from his mistakes. He was succeeded by former deputy prime minister and defence minister Khamtay Siphandone in the position of prime minister. In 1996 Khamtay was elected president.

Observers of East European politics may notice a close similarity between the 1975 Revolution in Laos and the communist takeover in Czechoslovakia in 1948. Both involved national fronts, supported by covert Marxist-Leninist parties, which effected semi-legal changes of power through a combination of popular support and armed threats. Furthermore, both countries were in the shadow of intimidating foreign armies stationed at nearby borders, ready to intervene at any moment (the Soviets in the case of Czechoslovakia, the Vietnamese in the case of Laos).

During the first two years of LPRP rule,

harsh political and economic policies caused thousands of refugees to leave the country. The government followed the Vietnamese policy of 'accelerated socialisation' through a rapid reduction of the private sector and a steep increase in agricultural collectivisation.

The practice of the traditional Lao religion, Buddhism, was also severely curtailed (see the Religion section later in this chapter for more detail).

At first King Savang Vatthana was given a figurehead role in the new government. But, in early 1977, anti-communist rebels briefly seized Muang Non, 50 km south of Luang Prabang. When government forces regained the village, the captured rebels supposedly implicated the monarchy. Immediately thereafter, the king and his family were banished to Vieng Xai, a village in northern Laos on the Vietnamese border. Although it was announced that the King would be attending a *samana* (re-education camp), he and his wife reportedly died a few years ago in their cave prison in northern Laos.

By mid-1979, this repression had resulted in widespread unrest among the peasants, the traditional power base for Lao communism. As in Vietnam, liberal reforms were undertaken, but in Laos the liberalisation went further (see the Economics & Religion sections later in this chapter). Unfortunately, the gradual reforms were too little and too late to prevent the further reduction of an already small population. By the end of the '70s, Lao refugees (including hill tribes) in Thailand constituted 85% of all Indochinese with official refugee status. Unlike the Vietnamese, who had to undertake perilous sea journeys, or the Cambodians, who braved the equally perilous Dang Rek mountains and the 'killing fields' of the Khmer Rouge, Lao refugees had but to cross the Mekong to escape the change of governments.

After 1975 around 300,000 Lao citizens officially resettled abroad. Countless others simply blended into largely Lao-speaking north-eastern Thailand. By 1992, approximately 53,000 Lao refugees still resided in

six camps in Thailand, and the Thai government set a deadline for all Lao living in
Thailand to return to their homeland or leave
for a third country by 1 January 1995. All
Lao refugee camps in Thailand are now
officially closed, although there remain
'holding centres' for a few thousand mostly
Hmong refugees in Thailand's Nakhon
Phanom, Loei, Chonburi and Phayao provinces. Total repatriation is expected within
the next three years.

Laos in the '80s and '90s

As many as 40,000 people were sent to re-
education camps – known as samana in Lao
– and 30,000 imprisoned for 'political
crimes' following the 1975 PL takeover.
One's position in the old regime's hierarchy
determined the length of stay; the higher the
position, the longer you were subjected to
manual labour and daily lectures on the
glories of communism. Since 1989 most of
the camps have reportedly closed and most
political prisoners have been released. At
least 30 officials from the former royal government are believed to remain in custody.
Amnesty International, in its 1995 report on
Laos, noted the continued existence of a
re-education camp – or political prison – in
Hua Phan Province where three prisoners of
conscience were recently sentenced to 14
years imprisonment for peacefully advocat-
ing a multi-party political system. Two
former RLG officials were reportedly
released only in 1994.

The influence of the former USSR's
glasnost and perestroika policies undoubtedly contributed to further reform in the
LPDR during the '80s in the form of
jintanakan mai (new thinking). As in other
socialist nations, there has been an on-going
power struggle between the old hardliners
and the younger Party and non-Party leadership, who seek further liberalisation.

In Laos, this is compounded by two con-
flicting tendencies for policy development.
One tendency has been for the Lao leadership to follow the Vietnamese example, the
other to implement policies that are developed specifically for the Lao situation. The
second tendency has appeared to gain
more and more strength during recent
years. But the flourishing of a truly Lao
socialism, if such is possible, is still ham-
pered by the direct and unavoidable
Vietnamese ideological influence on Lao
affairs via high-ranking hardliners in the Lao
government who received their military and
political training in Hanoi. Younger pragmatists who push for liberalisation always run
the risk of being labelled pátíkąn (reaction-
aries).

Another very significant influence on
modern Laos is its relationship with Thailand. Immediately following the Revolution
the Lao government banned practically all
things Thai, including Thai university and
Buddhist texts – previously central compo-
nents of educational and religious literature
in Laos. Friction grew as Thailand provided
resources for huge camps housing thousands
of Lao refugees. The conflict culminated in
a three-month border war in 1987-88
between the Lao and Thai armies in which
over a hundred Lao and Thai soldiers died in
combat (the Thai government denies Lao
reports that 500 Thai were killed).

The battle seemed to clear the air and the
two neighbours have been closer than ever
throughout the 1990s; Thai investment is
now by far the largest component of the
country's foreign portfolio. Some worry that
Laos will be overwhelmed by Thai culture
and by the Thais' business acumen, and that
Laos will eventually become an 'economic
province' of Thailand. Others say they would
prefer living under Thai economic hege-
mony to remaining a political vassal of
Vietnam.

As greater regional economic integration
draws Laos into the greater South-East Asian
marketplace, the dual influences of Vietnam
and Thailand should become more diffuse.
Exhibiting their readiness to combine forces
with other market economies, government
representatives from Laos have been invited
as observers at Association of South-East
Asian Nations (ASEAN) meetings since
1992. The country looks forward to becoming a full ASEAN member in 1997, the

eighth participant in an economically-oriented organisation that includes Thailand, Indonesia, Malaysia, the Philippines, Brunei, Vietnam and Singapore. As a member of the Mekong River Commission, Laos has also signed the 1995 Chiang Rai Accord, an agreement which creates joint regulatory roles and mechanisms for settling international disputes with regard to Mekong river use.

Historically, virtually all Lao polities from the early meuang to the LPDR have been dependent on some greater Asian power, whether it be the Siamese, Burmese, Khmer or Vietnamese. Sometimes as many as three of these at one time have exacted tribute, as in the case of 16th-century Lan Xang – a vassal of Siam, Myanmar and Vietnam. Add to this the fact that three Western powers (France, the USA and the USSR) have contributed greatly to the destabilisation of the Asian balance of power, and the result has been a Laos that has until recently never been able to establish a stable, separate national entity.

When compared with the country's long history of civil and international war, the current state of Lao affairs seems relatively peaceful and stable. Vietnamese and Lao party officials continue to maintain that absolutely no non-communist Party members will ever be allowed a share in governing any part of Vietnam or Laos. It remains to be seen whether the Lao will continue to tolerate a Soviet-modelled, one-party system.

GEOGRAPHY

Landlocked Laos shares borders with Thailand, Cambodia, Vietnam, China and Myanmar. It covers 235,000 sq km, an area slightly larger than Great Britain. All of Laos is within the tropics, between latitudes 14°N and 23°N and longitudes 100°E and 108°E. Two main physical features, rivers and mountains, dominate the topography, and their interaction accounts for most of the country's geographic variation. Four biogeographic zones are recognised: the northern Indochina hilly sub-tropical sector

(most of the north); the Annam Trung Son mountain chain (bordering Vietnam from Bolikhamsai Province in the north to Attapeu in the south), the central Indochina tropical lowland plains (along the Mekong river floodplain from Sainyabuli to Champasak), and a small section forming the Indochina transition zone (at the northern tip of Phongsali Province).

Sourced 4350 km from the sea, 5000 m up on the Tibetan Plateau, the Mekong River is known as Lancang Jiang (Turbulent River) in China, Mae Nam Khong (Khong, Mother of Waters) in Thailand, Myanmar and Laos, Tonle Thom (Great Water) in Cambodia and Cuu Long (Nine Dragons) in Vietnam. Half its length runs through China, after which more of the river courses through Laos than through any other South-East Asian country. At its widest, near Si Phan Don, the river can measure 14 km across during the the rainy season. During the high-water season (July to November) barge trade from China's Yunnan Province brings machinery downriver to Huay Xai and ships timber back up to China. The Mekong's 549-km middle reach, what the French colonists called *le bief de Vientiane*, is navigable year-round, from Heuan Hin (north of the Khemmarat Rapids in Savannakhet) to Kok Phong, Luang Prabang, 1074 and 1623 km respectively from the sea.

The Mekong Committee (Committee for Coordination of Investigations of the Lower Mekong Basin), set up in 1957 under UN auspices to coordinate development of irrigation, electricity, flood control, fishing and navigation, has recently been revived under the name Mekong River Commission. Member states Thailand, Cambodia, Laos and Vietnam have allowed representatives from China and Myanmar to participate in talks since mid-1993.

Although the six countries each have their own set of priorities, the Chiang Rai Accord signed by the Commission members in 1995 now allows them the means to settle disputes, an important step in coordinating regional development. Cambodia and Vietnam have the most to lose from exploitation of the Mekong, since they are last in line for its resources. In China, the river's relative remoteness protects it from helter-skelter development. In Thailand a growing environmental movement should temper commercial expansion (though at the same time some Thai companies are looking northward for an escape from conservationist pressures at home). Laos has the most to gain by exploiting the river in ways potentially harmful to the environment, so ultimately it is the key to the river's future.

All rivers and tributaries west of the Annamite Chain drain into the Mekong. Waterways east of the Annamites (in the provinces of Hua Phan and Xieng Khuang only), eventually flow into the Gulf of Tonkin off the coast of Vietnam.

The Mekong river valley and its fertile floodplains form the country's primary agricultural zones as well, including virtually all of the country's wet-rice lands. The two largest valley sections surround Vientiane and Savannakhet, and these are, as a result, the major population centres. The Mekong and its tributaries are also an important source of fish, a mainstay of the Lao diet.

Major tributaries of the great river include the Nam Ou and the Nam Tha, both of which flow through deep, narrow limestone valleys from the north, and the Nam Ngum, which flows into the Mekong across a broad alluvial plain in Vientiane Province. The latter river is the site of a large hydroelectric plant that is a primary source of power for Vientiane area towns. Electricity generated at the plant is also sold to Thailand and is an important source of revenue for the country. At least 20 other hydroelectric facilities are 'under development' – a term referring to everything from pre-feasibility studies to construction design – for other points along the rivers of Laos.

Mountains and plateaus cover well over 70% of the country. Running about half the length of Laos, parallel to the course of the Mekong river, is the Annamite Chain, a rugged mountain range with peaks averaging 1500 to 2500m in height. Roughly in the centre of the range is the Khammuan plateau,

an area of striking limestone grottoes and gorges. At the southern end of the Annamite Chain is the 10,000 sq km Bolaven plateau, an important area for the cultivation of high-yield mountain rice, coffee, tea and other crops that flourish at higher altitudes.

The larger, northern half of Laos is made up almost entirely of broken, steep-sloped mountain ranges. The highest mountains are found in Xieng Khuang Province, where peaks exceeding 2000m are not unusual. Phu Bia, the country's highest peak at 2820m, is found in Xieng Khuang. Just north of Phu Bia stands the country's largest mountain plateau, the Xieng Khuang plateau, which rises 1200m above sea level. The most famous part of the plateau is the Plain of Jars, an area dotted with huge prehistoric stone jars of unknown origin.

CLIMATE
Rainfall

The annual Asian monsoon cycles that affect all of mainland South-East Asia produce a 'dry and wet monsoon climate' with three basic seasons. The south-west monsoon arrives between May and July and lasts into November. Average precipitation varies considerably according to latitude and altitude, with the central highlands of Vientiane, Bolikhamsai, Khammuan and eastern Champasak province getting the most rain overall. The southern peaks of the Annamite Chain receive the heaviest rainfall, over 300 cm annually. The provinces of Luang Prabang, Sainyabuli and Xieng Khuang, for the most part, receive only 100 to 150 cm a year. Vientiane and Savannakhet get about 150 to 200 cm, as do Phongsali, Luang Nam Tha and Bokeo.

The monsoon is followed by a dry period from November to May, a period that begins with lower relative temperatures (because of the influences of Asia's north-east monsoon, which bypasses Laos but creates cool breezes) through mid-February. Once the cooling influence of the north-east monsoon has passed, the country experiences much higher relative temperatures from March to May.

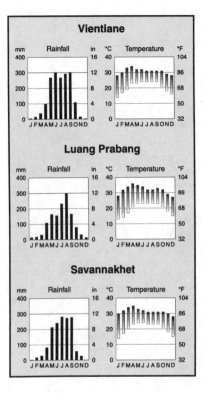

Vientiane

Rainfall

Temperature

Luang Prabang

Rainfall

Temperature

Savannakhet

Rainfall

Temperature

Temperatures

As with precipitation, temperatures vary according to altitude. In the low-lying Mekong river valley from Bokeo Province to Champasak Province, as in most of Thailand and Myanmar, the highest temperatures occur in March and April (with temperatures approaching 38°C), and the lowest in December and January (dropping as low as 15°C). In the mountains of Xieng Khuang, however, December to January temperatures can easily drop to 0°C at night; in mountainous provinces of lesser elevation, temperatures may be 5 to 10°C higher. During most of the rainy season, daytime temperatures average around 29°C in the lowlands and around 25°C in mountain valleys.

ECOLOGY & ENVIRONMENT

Although major disruptions were wreaked on the eastern section of the country along the Ho Chi Minh Trail (where herbicides and defoliants – not to mention bombs – were used in abundance during the war), Laos as a whole has one of the most pristine ecologies in mainland South-East Asia. Along with Cambodia, it is also the most understudied country in the region in terms of zoological and botanical research.

Because Laos contains the least exploited, least damaged ecological system in South-East Asia, it's a country of major importance for world wildlife conservation. Many of the plant and animal species found within its borders, though decreasing in numbers, face less risk of extinction than in neighbouring countries.

In 1993 the Lao government conferred legal protection upon 17 national biodiversity conservation areas (NBCAs), for a total of 24,600 sq km, or just over 10% of the country's land mass. Most of them are located in southern Laos, which bears a higher percentage of natural forest cover than the north. One of the consulting agencies involved in surveying these areas, the Wildlife Conservation Society, has recommended that an additional 11 sites be added to the list. These NBCA units aren't preserves; forests encompassed by this designation, for example, are divided into production forests for timber, protection forests for watershed and conservation forests for pure conservation. The largest of the NBCAs, Nakai-Nam Theun, covers 3710 sq km and is home to the newly discovered saola or Vu Quang ox.

As in many developing countries, one of the biggest obstacles facing environmental protection is corruption among those in charge of enforcing conservation regulations. Illegal timber felling and the smuggling of exotic wildlife species would decrease sharply if all officials were held accountable for their civil duties. Fortunately there is at least some awareness of, and concern for, this type of corruption in Laos; the former governor of Attapeu Prov-

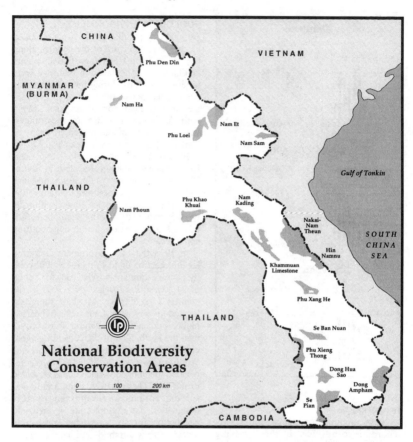

National Biodiversity Conservation Areas

ince was recently sentenced to 15 years in prison for timber smuggling.

Most Lao still lead their lives at or just above a subsistence level, consuming comparatively much less of their own natural resources than the people of any 'developed' country. The frugal country ranks 99th in the world with regard to per-capita energy consumption by the kg-oil-equivalent measure.

Thus the major challenges facing natural Laos today are the internal pressures of economic growth and the external pressures of Laos' more populated and affluent neighbours – particularly China, Vietnam and Thailand – who would like to exploit the country's abundant resources as much as possible. Over 20 hydroelectric projects, some of which would be contained in the NBCAs, are on the boards for development in the near future. It would be over-optimistic to expect that none of the dams will ever be built, but there is still time for the government to consider cancelling at least some of the projects intended for the more ecologically sensitive areas, eg the Nam Theun II plant scheduled for Nakai-Nam Theun NBCA.

One of the more disturbing aspects of the

hydroelectric industry is the way in which companies deliberately apply for concessions in areas zoned for dams, confident in the knowledge that – even if the facility is never constructed – they can usually stall for time long enough to log the valleys intended for inundation. Hence the main profit, whether or not the dams go through, comes from timber.

Tourism, in its infancy in post-1975 Laos, has thankfully had no major impact on the environment thus far. Until recently the government has wisely avoided granting contracts to companies wishing to develop large-scale resorts. A memorandum of agreement for a huge hotel-casino complex in Champasak Province, financed by a Lao-Thai joint venture, was recently signed; if constructed as intended the resort will be placed next to the beautiful Khon Phapheng Falls (see the Si Phan Don section in the Southern Laos chapter for more detail), heretofore undeveloped. Proponents of the hotel-casino project say it will provide job alternatives to local villagers who presently make their living cutting timber to make charcoal or over-fishing the Mekong river to the detriment of the rare Irrawaddy dolphin. Opponents claim it will increase overall human activity in the area and lead to environmental degradation. The World Bank recently issued a report that concluded the negative ecological consequences of this resort would outweigh any benefits gained; following this report the project developers should have difficulty finding the necessary financial support for the US$140 million resort.

Laos has not yet ratified the UN Convention on International Trade in Endangered Species of Wild Flora & Fauna (CITES) although the country is on the verge of becoming a signatory. A traditional trade in rare and endangered species continues unabated, especially in rural areas. While CITES has been somewhat effective in protecting species endangered as a direct result of international trade, the principal cause of species loss worldwide remains habitat destruction.

Doing Your Part
Visitors to Laos can contribute to environmental conservation in many ways, including: proper disposal of rubbish; avoidance of restaurants which serve threatened or endangered wildlife species; trekking only on established trails; patronising hotels, guest houses and restaurants which employ 'green' methods of construction and waste disposal as much as possible; and by reporting any illegal or unethical environmental practices to international watchdog groups such as the Wildlife Conservation Society, PO Box 6712, Vientiane (☎ (21) 313133) or the International Union for Conservation of Nature & Natural Resources, 15 Thanon Fa Ngum, Vientiane (☎ 216401).

FLORA & FAUNA
Vegetation
As in other parts of tropical mainland South-East Asia, with distinctive dry seasons of three months or more, most indigenous vegetation is associated with monsoon forests. Such forests are marked by deciduous tree varieties which shed their leaves during the dry season to conserve water. Rainforests – which are typically evergreen – don't exist in Laos, although imported rainforest species are commonly seen in the lower Mekong river valley.

Monsoon forests typically exhibit three vegetative layers. Dipterocarps – tall, pale-barked, single-trunked trees that reach as high as 30m – dominate the top canopy of the deciduous monsoon forest, while a middle canopy consists of teak, Asian rosewood and other hardwoods. Underneath are a variety of smaller trees, shrubs, grasses, and – along river habitats – bamboo. In certain plateau areas of the south are dry dipterocarp forests in which the forest canopies are more open, with less of a middle layer and more of a grass-and-bamboo undergrowth layer. Parts of the Annamite Chain are covered by tropical montane evergreen forest, while tropical pine forests can be found on the Nakai plateau and Sekong area to the south.

According to the International Union for

the Conservation of Nature & Natural Resources (IUCN), natural, unmanaged vegetation covers 85% of Laos. About half the country (47 to 56% depending on which source you believe) bears natural forest cover. Of these woodlands about half can be classified as primary forest – a very high proportion in this day and age – while another 30% or so represents secondary growth. The country's percentage of natural forest cover ranks 11th, ahead of Malaysia and just behind Indonesia. Although the official export of timber is tightly controlled, no one really knows how much teak and other hardwoods may be being smuggled out of the country into China, Vietnam and Thailand. During the Indochinese War, the Pathet Lao allowed the Chinese to take as much timber as they wanted from the Liberated Zone (11 provinces in all) in return for building roads.

Other pressures on the forest cover come from swidden (slash-and-burn) methods of cultivation, in which small plots of forest are cleared, then set afire for nitrogenation of the soil, and farmed intensively for two or three years, after which they are unfarmable. Land processed this way takes eight to 10 years to become fertile again. Environmental researchers are divided among those who believe swidden cultivation is a sustainable agricultural practice that is ultimately less destructive than other forest usages, and those who believe it is not sustainable. Considering the sparse population, swidden cultivation may not be a major threat in Laos – certainly not compared to logging.

In addition to teak and Asian rosewood, the country's flora include a toothsome array of fruit trees (see the Food section in the Facts for the Visitor chapter later in this book), bamboo (more species than any country outside Thailand and China) and an abundance of flowering species such as the orchid. In the high plateaus of the Annamite Chain, extensive grasslands or savanna are common.

Fauna

As in Cambodia, Vietnam, Myanmar and much of Thailand, most of the fauna in Laos belong to the Indochinese zoogeographic realm (as opposed to the Sundaic domain found south of the Isthmus of Kra in southern Thailand or the Palearctic to the north in China).

Around 45% of the animal species native to Thailand are shared by Laos, often in greater numbers due to higher forest cover and fewer hunters. Notable **mammals** endemic to Laos include the concolor gibbon, snub-nosed langur, lesser panda, raccoon dog, pygmy slow loris, giant muntjac, Lao marmoset rat and Owston's civet. Other exotic species common to an area that overlaps neighbouring countries in mainland South-East Asia are a number of macaques (pig-tailed, stump-tailed, Assamese and rhesus), Phayre's leaf monkey, François' leaf monkey, Douc langur, Malayan and Chinese pangolins, Siamese hare, six species of flying squirrel, 10 species of nonflying squirrel, 10 species of civet, marbled cat, Javan and crab-eating mongoose, spotted linsang, leopard cat, Asian golden cat, bamboo rat, yellow-throated marten, lesser mouse deer, serow (a goat-antelope sometimes called Asian mountain goat), goral (another goat-antelope) and 69 species of bats. Around 3000 wild Asiatic elephants roam open-canopy forest areas throughout the country, especially in Sainyabuli Province north-west of Vientiane and along the Nakai plateau in central eastern Laos.

More rare are the endangered Asiatic jackal, Asiatic black bear, Malayan sun bear, Malayan tapir, barking deer, sambar (a type of deer), gaur, banteng (both gaur and bantengs are types of wild cattle), leopard, tiger, clouded leopard and Irrawaddy dolphin (see the Si Phan Don section in the Southern Laos chapter later in this book for more detail on these freshwater dolphins).

The most exciting regional zoological discovery of recent years has been the detection of a heretofore-unknown mammal, the spindlehorn bovid – also known as the Vu Quang ox (saola in Vietnam, nyang in Laos), a horned animal found in the Annamite Chain along the Lao-Vietnamese border.

The endangered Malayan sun bear

A few Javan one-horned and/or Sumatran two-horned rhinos, probably extinct in neighbouring Thailand, are thought to survive in the Bolaven plateau area of southern Laos. Sightings of kouprey, a wild cattle extinct elsewhere in South-East Asia, have been reported in Attapeu and Champasak provinces as recently as 1993.

Herpetofauna include numerous snake varieties, of which six are venomous: the common cobra, king cobra (hamadryad), banded krait, Malayan viper, green viper and Russell's pit viper. The country's many lizard species include two commonly seen in homes and older buildings, the *túk-kąe* (a large gecko) and the *jî-jîan* (smaller house lizards), as well as larger species like the black jungle monitor.

The pristine forests and mountains of Laos harbour a rich selection of resident and migrating **bird** species. Surveys carried out by a British team of ornithologists in 1992-93 recorded 437 species, including eight globally threatened and 21 globally near-threatened species. Notable among these are Siamese fireback, green peafowl, red-collared woodpecker, brown hornbill, tawny fish-owl, Sarus crane, giant ibis and the Asian golden weaver. Urban bird populations are noticeably thin as a result of bird-hunting; in downtown Vientiane or

The Douc langur is common to a number of overlapping countries in mainland South-East Asia.

Savannakhet it's not uncommon to see someone pointing a long-barrelled musket at upper tree canopies – even on monastery grounds where killing is supposedly not permitted.

GOVERNMENT & POLITICS

Since 2 December 1975, the official name of the country has been the Lao People's Democratic Republic (Sathalanalat Pasathipatai Pasason Lao). Informally, it is acceptable to call the country Laos, which in the Lao language is Páthêt Lao – *páthêt* means land or country, from the Sanskrit *pradesha*. Among English-speakers there is a growing movement to drop the 's' added by the French and simply use 'Lao' as the country's shortened name. Even many Western expats in the country are now showing a preference for the word 'Lao'.

Following the 1975 takeover, the former pro-Western, monarchical regime was replaced by a government which espoused a Marxist-Leninist political philosophy in alignment with other communist states, most explicitly the Socialist Republic of Vietnam, the People's Republic of Kampuchea (now the State of Cambodia) and the USSR. The national motto – which appears on all official government stationery – is Peace, Independence, Democracy, Unity & Prosperity (the latter was substituted for 'Socialism' in 1991).

The Party

The central ruling body in Laos is the Lao People's Revolutionary Party (LPRP), which is modelled on the Vietnamese Communist Party. The LPRP is directed by the Party Congress, which meets every four or five years to elect Party leaders. Other important Party organs include the Political Bureau (Politburo), the Central Committee and the Permanent Secretariat.

The Party ideal is a 'proletarian dictatorship', as proclaimed by the late Secretary-General Kaysone Phomvihane in 1977:

To lead the revolution, the working class must act with the help of its general staff, that is to say the political party of the working class, the Marxist-Leninist Party. In our country it is the LPRP which is the sole authentic representative of the interests of the working class, of the working masses of all ethnic groups in the Lao nation.

Despite the claim to proletarianism, membership in the LPRP has consisted mainly of peasant farmers and tribespeople from various ethnic groups, though urban worker membership has increased since the 1975 Revolution. Before the Revolution, Party membership was about 60% Lao Theung (lower mountain dwellers, mostly of proto-Malay or Mon-Khmer descent), 36% Lao Loum (lowland Lao) and 4% Lao Sung (mostly Hmong and Mien hill tribes). Today's percentages are not known outside the Party.

The main seat of LPRP power, as in most communist parties, is the Politburo, which officially makes all policy decisions. In theory, members of the Politburo are selected by the Party Central Committee. In practice, since the Secretary-General of the Politburo, the Secretariat and the Central Committee are all one man, Khamtay Siphandone (who is also the President), virtually all members of these major Party organs are coopted by this lead position, which has enjoyed the full support of the Vietnamese since the '40s.

Administration

The LPDR government is structured along Socialist Republic of Vietnam (SRV) lines. The Council of Government, like the SRV's Council of Ministers, consists of twelve ministries (eg, the Ministry of Information & Culture). In addition to the Council of Government, there is the Office of the Prime Minister, the National Bank, the National Planning Committee and the Nationalities Committee.

The National Assembly (formerly the Supreme People's Assembly) serves as the government's legislative body and is modelled on the SRV's National Assembly and the former USSR's Supreme Soviet. Since the Revolution, total membership in the Assembly has varied between 40 and 45.

Corruption

The Lao have a saying which they may utter whenever they want to indicate to someone that they're not rich, or that they can't afford a high asking price: 'I'm (one of the) people, not (one of the) government'. In other words *phùu mii sii* – 'people with colour' (ie those in uniform) – are generally assumed to have access to wealth denied the average civilian. As in many developing countries, the low salaries paid to government employees understandably motivate some civil servants to seek other sources of income. Some moonlight by working other jobs outside government hours, while others take the easy money offered to them by private interests seeking to navigate the Lao government bureaucracy.

At the everyday level of the common bureaucrat, this takes the form of minor bribes or 'tips' of a few thousand kip here and there, accepted for faster or preferential service, or sometimes simply for doing one's job. At higher levels of government the sums can be vast. Virtually any foreign organisation – governmental or non-governmental, public or private – that wants to do business in Laos participates in the game in one way or another. Bids for government or foreign aid contracts – especially highway projects, energy programmes and other high-ticket items – face fierce competition in the development world and the deciding factor often comes down to which company pays the best kickback. Unfortunately this sometimes results in substandard project fulfillment since it's not always the best company that gets the contract. Foreign companies and aid organisations also usually have a 'fixer' on staff, a Lao whose job it is to arrange air tickets when the planes are full or to smooth over other inconveniences.

Considering that the Lao government is able to collect very little in income taxes from its own citizens, some corruption is understandable as a way to generate income for government works. Most bribes, after all, are a kind of luxury tax on the rich. Through minor corruption, a government uniform provides those who aren't very well educated or very ambitious with an earning potential they couldn't otherwise achieve.

But many Lao privately express the opinion that corruption in Laos is getting a little out of hand. Forty percent of all foreign aid goes directly to the government payroll and the more aid and investment funds come into the country, the richer the ministers and their cronies become. Huge mansions are springing up on the outskirts of Vientiane for high-ranking government officials and their relatives; a high-profile Lao architect recently completed the designs for a chateau-style estate for the president's son.

Meanwhile the government spends less than 20% of the national budget on social welfare. This mimics exactly the level of government corruption the Pathet Lao promised to wipe out when they wrested power away from the Royal Lao Government in 1975. For those citizens who believed in the socialist ideal of socio-economic equalisation and the redistribution of wealth the increasingly visible signs of corruption are disillusioning. ∎

About two-thirds of the members are drawn from the LPRP, the Lao Front for National Construction and the Alliance of Lao Patriotic Neutralist Forces (a group of military officers aligned with the Lao People's Revolutionary Army); the remaining third is drawn from groups sympathetic to the left. The Assembly's main function thus far has been to meet once a year to approve declarations of the prime minister. In February 1993 Samane Vignaket was elected President of the National Assembly. Vignaket was a member of the Politburo and former Minister of Sports & Education.

For 15 years following the Revolution, the LPDR had no constitution. The first official constitution was drafted in mid-1990 by the Party for the approval of the National Assembly. Interestingly enough, it contains no reference to socialism in the economy but formalises private trade and foreign investment. The constitution also removed the hammer-and-sickle and communist star from the official national seal to be used on government signs and stationery, replacing it with a likeness of Pha That Luang (see the section on Economy later in this chapter for more commentary on the Lao brand of communism). Red hammer-and-sickle flags are still commonly raised around the country on National Day (2 December).

The LPDR's first legal code wasn't

enacted until 1988, the same year that Vientiane began looking abroad for foreign capital. The new canon established a court system, prosecutor's office, criminal trial rules and one of the most liberal foreign investment codes in Asia. Although the Lao constitution guarantees property rights, the Pathet Lao still holds substantial amounts of private property seized in 1975. Only through direct military connections have many people begun to get their land and houses back.

Lao Front for National Construction

The Lao Front for National Construction (LFNC) was formed in 1979 to take the place of the old Lao Patriotic Front, which had been in existence since 1956 as a political cover for the clandestine Lao People's Party. Its new incarnation was intended to quell unrest among the general population by providing mass participation in a nationalistic effort, much like the Fatherland Front in the SRV. In other words, you don't have to be a Party member to join, as long as you follow Party principles.

The LFNC is comprised of the LPRP, the Federation of Lao Trade Unions, the Federation of Lao Peasants, the Association of Women and other groups originally organised by the Party. The Front is administered by a National Congress (the general membership), a Presidium (headed by President Khamtay Siphandone, elected by the National Assembly), a Secretariat, a Central Committee and local committees at the village, canton, district and provincial levels.

Like the National Assembly, the LFNC has no real power and appears mainly to serve as a rubber stamp apparatus for LPDR policies. There is a potential for pluralism in the Lao government structure, however, which may eventually be realised (assuming East European trends are paralleled).

National Symbols

Laos' national seal, often applied to official government publications, features a near-complete circle formed by curving rice stalks which enclose six component symbols of the productive proletarian state: Vientiane's Pha That Luang monument (representing religion); a checkerboard of rice fields (agriculture); gear cogs (industry); a dam (energy); a highway (transport); and a grove of trees (forestry). A label in Lao script at the bottom of the seal reads 'Lao People's Democratic Republic'.

The national flag consists of two horizontal bars of red (symbolising courage and heroism), above and below a bar of blue (nationhood) on which is centred a blank white sphere (the light of communism). This flag is flown in front of all government offices and by some private citizens on National Day (2 December). On the latter holiday the Lao national flag may be joined by a second flag featuring a yellow hammer and sickle centred on a field of red, the international symbol of communism. The latter's display is rather ironic given the fact that the word 'communism' doesn't appear in any government documents, not even the Lao constitution. Nor are there any public statues of Lenin or Marx anywhere in the country, save for one Lenin bust in Vientiane's Lao Revolutionary Museum.

The late Kaysone Phomvihane, founder of the Lao People's Revolutionary Party, has become the country's foremost national hero. In 1995 the government took delivery of 20 busts of Kaysone from North Korean sculptors who produced similar figures of the late Korean dictator Kim Il Sung. These busts are now being erected in newly constructed public memorial squares in every provincial capital as well as in other selected locations around the country. ∎

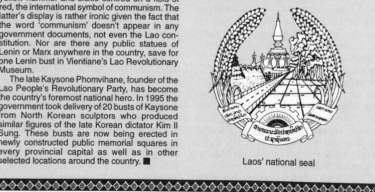

Laos' national seal

Political Divisions

Laos is divided into 16 *khwāeng* (provinces): Wieng Chan (Vientiane), Sainyabuli, Luang Prabang, Luang Nam Tha, Xieng Khuang, Hua Phan (Houa Phan), Phongsali, Bokeo, Udomxai, Bolikhamsai, Khammuan (Khammouane), Savannakhet, Salavan (Saravan), Sekong, Attapeu and Champasak. In addition, Vientiane (Kamphaeng Nakhon Wieng Chan) is an independent prefecture on an administrative parity with the provinces. The eastern half of Vientiane Province and part of south-western Xieng Khuang Province, chronically troubled by armed bandit and/or insurgent attacks, was recently converted into 'Saisombun Special Zone' and is administered by the Lao military.

Below the province is the *meúang* (district), which is comprised of two or more *tátséng* (subdistricts or cantons), which are in turn divided into *bâan* (villages).

Ties with Vietnam

The Vietnamese influence on Lao political affairs is still strong, thanks to continuing connections between aging hardliners educated in Vietnam and their ideological mentors. Several high-ranking party members with Vietnamese military and political training – including President Kaysone Phomvihane and former President Souphanouvong (the 'Red Prince') – died between 1992 and 1995, leading many observers to believe that Vietnamese influence will wane in the future as the hardliners are replaced by younger pragmatists. Current 69-year-old President Khamtay Siphandone, however, was trained in Hanoi and has close links with the Vietnamese military. Prime Minister Choummaly Sayasone, elected in early 1996, formerly served as the country's Defence Minister and is also considered a hardliner primarily influenced by Vietnamese political ideology.

Dissent & Insurgency

Unlike in Eastern Europe in 1988-90, where popular dissent led to massive political changes, or in China and Myanmar, where widespread dissent has met with harsh suppression, there is currently no significant 'democratic movement' or widespread spoken discontent in Laos. In part this can be explained by the Lao Buddhist tendency to say *'baw pen nyāng'* ('it doesn't matter') when faced with adversity, and in part because by and large the Lao seem satisfied with the post-Revolutionary political system, which has brought them the first extended period of secular peace they've known in three centuries. The threat of being sent to samana certainly silenced most protest during the late '70s and '80s.

But probably the most compelling reason dissent is noticeably absent is simply because dissenting Lao have a built-in escape hatch, the Mekong river border with Thailand. Dissenters can vote with their feet, easily crossing the river into north-eastern Thailand, where with little difficulty they blend in with their Lao-speaking Isaa brethren. Ten percent of the population has left Laos in this fashion since 1975, among them an estimated three-quarters of the country's intelligentsia – perhaps those most inclined to voice political dissatisfaction.

Still, a small insurgent movement – perhaps several – lurk in the forests and mountains. Some are Hmong warriors who seek to fulfill Vang Pao's dream of creating an independent Hmong district, or who are simply seeking revenge for Pathet Lao defeats or for long stints in re-education camps. Other factions may be armed groups financed by fanatical anti-communist Thais who had connections with the now-defunct Royal Lao Army, and by US POW/MIA groups hoping to gain information on US airmen lost in Laos during the war. In the early '90s the US National League of Families, a previously respected POW/MIA advocacy group, were discovered to have diverted US$700,000 to guerrilla training programmes, led by a retired USAF colonel, for Lao and Hmong living in Thailand.

Experts speculate there may be a few hundred (estimates vary from a conservative 200 to an absurd 10,000) armed insurgents in the outback. A 'Lao United Independence Front' occasionally issues messages to the

Thai media proclaiming a 'provisional government' somewhere in Laos, but if this group really exists at all it is probably on Thai soil. Other groups who have issued anti-government decrees include the Free Lao National Liberation Movement, the Free Democratic Lao National Salvation Force and the France-based Movement for Democracy in Laos.

For the most part these rebels – when active at all in Laos – operate sporadically. Nothing exists on the scale of insurgency that goes on, for example, in Cambodia, Myanmar or the Philippines. Meanwhile international support for any such movements steadily wanes as the Pathet Lao government continues to open the country to more political and economic freedoms. For more on armed rebel activity in Laos, see the Dangers & Annoyances section in the Facts for the Visitor chapter later in this book.

For its part, the Thai government is very sensitive to accusations that Thailand may be harbouring an insurgent movement, however small. In July 1992, the US Department of State received complaints from the governments of Thailand and Laos concerning the alleged conduct of US nationals and legal residents who were reportedly involved in efforts to overthrow or otherwise destabilise the Lao government, activities which allegedly took place in Thailand and Laos. That same month, three US citizens and one legal resident were arrested in Thailand for the possession of unauthorised weapons. All four were subsequently deported from Thailand. The Thai government has also issued an outstanding order to place Hmong General Vang Pao – currently residing in the US – under immediate arrest if he comes to Thailand.

ECONOMY
Pre-Revolutionary Economics
About 80% of the Lao population is engaged in agriculture, fishing and forestry; another 10% is employed in the armed forces or in the civil service. This breakdown remained virtually the same before and after the 1975 Revolution. Laos has been dependent on

foreign aid since the '50s, however, and the amounts and sources of aid have varied greatly over the intervening years.

Between 1968 and 1973, when US aid to the Royal Government of Laos (RLG) was at its peak (averaging about US$74.4 million a year), the Lao received as much aid per capita as almost anyone in the world. This aid, of course, was enjoyed by those in the RLG-controlled Vientiane/ Luang Prabang/ Savannakhet zone and not by those in the Pathet Lao 'liberated zone' (who got falling US bombs instead). During this period (and back as far as 1964, when the War of Resistance really began), the 11 provinces of the liberated zone existed on a subsistence economy supplemented by commodity assistance from the USSR, China and North Vietnam.

Post-Revolutionary Reforms
After the termination of US aid in 1975, the Vientiane economy collapsed and the new government found itself struggling to manage a virtually bankrupt state. Until 1979, policies of 'accelerated socialisation' (nationalisation of large private sector businesses and collectivisation of all agriculture) only made conditions worse. In July 1979, however, the government stopped the creation of new collectives and ordered the consolidation of existing ones, admitting that most Lao peasants were dissatisfied with the system.

Under the new policy, a certain amount of free enterprise was allowed at the village level. For example, families were given permission to cultivate individual rice fields, although major farming activities (clearing fields, planting, weeding and harvesting) were to be carried out cooperatively. Anyone familiar with rice farming in mainland South-East Asia knows that this is exactly how it's done traditionally, even in more capitalist countries like Thailand. Rice harvests in Laos are divided into three portions: one for the state, one for the village rice bank, and one for the family (according to a per capita ration system) for sale or consumption.

Lao Economic System

Laos' current economic system can perhaps best be described as a capitalist reality trimmed with socialist ideology. *Jntánakaan mai* (new thinking), the Lao version of perestroika, is another term for what the Lao rulership claims is a loyal rendering of Marxism, in which capitalist practices are a waystation on the road to full socialism. When will full socialism be achieved? 'When world conditions are ripe', according to government leaders.

As the Minister for Foreign Affairs told visiting reporters who gathered in Vientiane for the 20th anniversary of the 1975 revolution in December 1995: 'The Lao People's Revolutionary Party is still a party of Marxist-Leninist ideology and the new prosperity being enjoyed by many in the country exists as the product of that ideology not despite it'.

Observers who would criticise the leadership for what might appear to be hypocrisy should pause to remember that the Lao revolution was more motivated by nationalism than communist ideology. Because Ho Chi Minh and the North Vietnamese were the only party who would support their struggle, Lao nationalists walked and talked like their ideological masters, but in governing their new state followed a pragmatic path. When collectivisation didn't work, it was quickly abandoned; when the outright suppression of Buddhist monasticism violated the people's mandate, this policy too was relinquished.

One gets the impression that, for all its blunders, the Lao rulers really do have the general population's best interests at heart. Even the restrictive tourism policy – as wrongheaded as it may appear to outsiders – seems an expression of the government's preoccupation with dignity and security over money. ■

Government billboard in Vientiane

The LPRP has also made radical changes in monetary policy (allowing a free-floating currency) and commodity pricing (bringing prices closer to free market rates), with the result that by the end of the '80s the economy appeared to be relatively stable. Both consumer goods and agricultural products are widely available. The exception is in the rural areas of the south, where temporary rice shortages are still common.

In 1987, the government further loosened restrictions on private enterprise. Prior to that year, only about half of the shophouses along Vientiane's main commercial avenue, Thanon Samsenthai, were open. By the end of 1989, at least 75% had opened their doors and today the whole avenue is thriving again.

Foreign private investment is now welcome in Laos.

Private land ownership is now legal in Laos. Many farmers and householders (but by no means all) whose family lands had been collectivised since 1975 have been able to reclaim their property. Since 1991 even selected pre-1975 aristocrats – those who have the wherewithal to provide 'favours' to the political establishment – have been permitted to reclaim and re-inhabit their villas.

Current Income, Infrastructure & Inflation

But the credit for economic stabilisation can't all be ascribed to the liberalisation of the economy per se. Foreign aid has also greatly increased since 1980, making up as much as 78% of the national budget in certain years. Asian Development Bank (ADB) loans and other kinds of credit have also increased as the country's credit image has improved. UN agencies like UNESCO and the United Nations Development Programme (UNDP) are pouring funds and personnel into Laos as the country again becomes a player in the international development game. Several nongovernmental organisations such as Save the Children, Mines Advisory Group and World Concern are also present.

Foreign aid totalled US$145 million in 1994, 70% of which came from multilateral donors such as the ADB, UNDP and UNICEF, 25% from bilateral donors (mainly Japan, Sweden, Australia, France, Germany, Switzerland and the US) and 5% from NGOs. Russian aid fell by 60% in 1990 and virtually ceased in 1991; in 1995 the US Congress rescinded a 20-year ban on aid to Laos. All totalled, foreign aid comprises around 45% of the annual national budget, approximately 40% of which goes directly to the Lao government payroll.

Yet another reason the economy is doing comparatively well is due to the tolerance of the *talàat mèut* (free, or 'black', market). Markets everywhere in Laos trade freely in untaxed goods from Thailand, China and elsewhere and the changing of international currency (mostly US dollars and Thai baht) is quite open.

A small entrepreneurial class, along with members of the communist establishment who thrive on bribes and kickbacks, are flourishing in the cities, having attained a privileged economic status reminiscent of the French colonials. Lao and Thai architects are working overtime to design and build huge manors surrounded by gardens and swimming pools for the use of these groups.

On an international scale, however, Laos is still one of the poorest countries in the world. Agora Inc rated the country's infrastructure among the world's bottom 10 in 1993; others on the bottom-10 list included

Bhutan, Bangladesh and Rwanda. The annual per capita income in 1996 was US$325 (up from US$135 in 1989), which places Laos ahead of Vietnam (US$220) and Cambodia (US$215), but below China (US$435) and Bhutan (US$415). If measured using the 'purchasing power parity' method (which takes into account price differences between countries), the Lao average US$2071 per capita annually, compared to US$6816 in Thailand and US$1263 in Vietnam.

Gross National Product (GNP) growth in 1996 was estimated to be a strong 8% per annum. Further on the bright side, Laos has one of the lowest foreign debts in Asia – US$1.2 billion (compared with US$1.6 billion in Cambodia, US$5.3 billion in Myanmar, US$24.7 billion in Vietnam or US$62.1 billion in Thailand). According to World Bank figures, the country's foreign debt represents about four times its annual exports.

Inflation in Laos declined significantly in the early '90s, from 65% in 1989 to just 6 to 9% between 1992 and 1994. In 1995 the real-dollar inflation rate was holding steady at 6.7%. Inflation in Vientiane is somewhat higher – perhaps 10-12% per annum – due to the heavy influx of foreign aid specialists on expat salaries. The kip, the national currency, fell into a deflationary tailspin in mid-1995, however, due to a heavy influx of hard currency, especially the Thai baht. This devaluation somewhat stabilised real-dollar prices for the latter half of that year, but holders of kip are expected to see an inflation rate of 16% through 1996. All kip prices quoted in this book should be interpolated in the context of this predicted rate.

Economic Regionalisation
About 30% of the population live in dynamic zones along the Mekong river valley, where trade with Thailand is vital. Another 10% live in recently emerging economies in the extreme north (primarily Udomxai, Phongsali and Luang Nam Tha), where trade with China is dominant but where there has been little Lao government control since 1989. A

similar situation exists along the Savannakhet-Lao Bao corridor between the Thai and Vietnamese borders, where a three-way trade between Vietnam, Laos and Thailand goes on with little Lao government intervention.

A slim but significant 2% of all Lao participate in the insulated Luang Prabang economy, where production is growing but self-limited because of the area's isolation from exterior markets. Rising incomes in Luang Prabang are heavily infused with foreign aid money and tourism receipts. Once Route 13 between Vientiane and Luang Prabang is completely paved this area will probably boom, and after the highway is extended all the way to the Chinese border it will become a major trade crossroads (much to the chagrin of those who would like to keep the city quaint and charming).

An estimated 58% of the nation's population live at a subsistence level, largely autonomous from all government involvement, in small villages scattered throughout the country.

Agriculture & Forestry

Only around 10% of the total land area in Laos is considered suitable for agriculture. Cultivation is carried out according to dual patterns, one for the lowlands and one for the highlands. Lowland agriculture involves permanent farming communities which cultivate irrigated fields; in the highlands, farming communities are to some extent migrational, preferring to use swidden ('slash-and-burn') methods in which forest areas are cut to the ground and burned in preparation for planting. The Lao government is trying to discourage swidden agriculture among the highland peoples in order to prevent deforestation; current estimates indicate that around a million Lao farmers still practise this form of cultivation.

Important crops in the lowlands include wet rice, corn, wheat, cotton, tobacco, peanut, soybean, fruits and vegetables. In the mountains, dry rice, tobacco, tea, coffee, maize and opium (by far the country's most lucrative agricultural product) are the major cash crops.

Since about two-thirds of the country is forested, timber and wood products are also important products, making up about 23% of Laos' annual exports. Teak is the most important wood for export earnings, followed by secondary forest products like benzoin, a resin used to manufacture perfume, and cardamom, a spice.

Minerals

Laos' greatest economic potential lies in its rich mineral resources, which include tin, coal, oil, iron, copper, gold, phosphorite, gypsum, zinc and salt. Many of these are just starting to be exploited. Several international oil companies, including two of the country's largest investors, Lao Hunt Oil (American-owned) and Enterprise Oil (France/Britain), are currently engaged in petroleum exploration, mostly in southern Laos.

Hydroelectric Power

The Nam Ngum dam, 70 km north of Vientiane, generates most of the electricity used in the Vientiane Valley. In addition, Thailand buys about 850 million kilowatt-hours per year from Laos, via high power-lines that stretch across the Mekong to as far away as Udon Thani.

Once Route 13 is paved and the necessary equipment can be introduced along the way, Luang Prabang will join the Vientiane Valley power grid. Near Tha Khaek, the Nam Thuen dam project will export 100% of its 210-megawatt output to power-hungry Thailand by the year 2000, connected to Thailand's main grid via a 95 km transmission line to Sakon Nakhon Province. Nearly 20 other hydropower plants are also in the works. The country's top eight investment projects in 1995 were in fact all energy-related: Nam Theun 2 (Thai/Australian/French/Lao), Hongsa Lignite (Thai), Nam Ngiep 1 (USA) and Nam Ngum 2 (USA).

Fishing

The rivers in Laos yield a steady supply of fish, an important source of nutrition for the general population. The huge lake (370 sq

Opium & the Golden Triangle

The opium poppy, *Papaver somniferum*, has been cultivated and its resins extracted for use as a narcotic at least since the time of the early Greek Empire. The Chinese were introduced to the drug by Arab traders during the Kublai Khan era (1279-94). It was so highly valued for its medicinal properties that hill-tribe minorities in southern China began cultivating the opium poppy in order to raise money to pay taxes to their Han Chinese rulers. Easy to grow, opium became a way for the nomadic hill tribes to raise what cash they needed in transactions (willing and unwilling) with the lowland world. Many of the hill tribes that migrated to Thailand and Laos in the post-WW II era, in order to avoid persecution in Burma and China, took with them their one cash crop, the poppy. The tall flowering plant is well suited to hillside cultivation as it flourishes on steep slopes and in nutrient-poor soils.

Harvesting opium poppy in northern Laos

The opium trade became especially lucrative in South-East Asia during the '60s and early '70s when US armed forces were embroiled in Indochina. Alfred McCoy's *The Politics of Heroin in Southeast Asia* recounts how contact with the GI market not only expanded the immediate Asian market, but provided outlets to world markets. Before this time the source of most of the world's heroin was the Middle East. Soon everyone wanted a piece of the profits and various parties alternately quarrelled over and cooperated in illegal opium commerce. Most notable were the Nationalist Chinese Army refugees living in northern Burma and northern Thailand, and the Burmese anti-government rebels, in particular the Burmese Communist Party, the Shan States Army and the Shan United Army.

The American CIA eventually became involved in a big way, using profits from opium and heroin runs aboard US aircraft (the infamous Air America, a CIA front) from Laos to Vietnam and further afield to finance covert operations throughout Indochina. This of course led to an increase in the availability of heroin throughout the world, which in turn led to increased production in the remote northern areas of Thailand, Burma and Laos, where there was little government interference. This area came to be known as the 'Golden Triangle' because of local fortunes amassed by the 'opium warlords' – mostly Burmese and Chinese military-businessmen who controlled the movement of opium across three international borders.

As more opium was available, more was consumed and the demand increased along with the profits – so the cycle expanded. As a result, opium cultivation became a full-time job for some hill-tribe groups

km) created by the damming of the Nam Ngum is being used for a number of experimental fisheries. If these and other fishery projects are successful, Laos will probably begin exporting freshwater fish to Thailand in the future.

Manufacturing

This sector of the economy is expanding rapidly, with garments and motorcycle assembly capturing 18% and 11% respectively of the country's export market. Though most consumer goods used in the country are imported from Thailand or elsewhere, there are burgeoning factories in Vientiane that produce soft drinks, beer, cigarettes, bricks and cement. Foreign investment is beginning to move from raw materials to joint manufacturing ventures, though Laos doesn't have as large and skilled a labour force as Vietnam, which currently attracts such ventures.

In anticipation of the future, the government has plans to develop Khammuan Province in central Laos – an area rich in mineral and forest resources – as a major industrial centre.

within the Golden Triangle. Hill economies were thus destabilised to the point where opium production became a necessary means of survival for thousands of people.

Opium in Laos

Opium has been cultivated, processed and used in northern Laos for centuries but the country didn't become a major producer until the passing of the 1971 Anti-Narcotics Law by the Royal Lao Government (at the urging of the US government), a move which helped drive regional prices up steeply. This is turn resulted in an increase in criminal activity and in the increased use of heroin among former opium addicts (since heroin could be more easily transported and concealed). Licensed opium dens were permitted until the PL revolution. In 1975 there were over 60 licensed dens in Vientiane, and probably many other unlicensed ones; their current legal status is unclear though opium-smoking dens certainly still exist, even in Vientiane.

Today opium – until five years ago an official export in spite of objections from the USA and neighbouring countries – probably remains the country's biggest export earner. Worldwide the country ranks third in production after Myanmar (Burma) and Afghanistan, with annual crops yielding anywhere from 100 to 200 tons of refined opium, surpassing even the figures for colonial Laos under the French. Grown and collected by Hmong and Mien tribes – experts estimate around 60,000 families are directly involved – about half the product leaves the country along smuggling routes through Thailand, Cambodia and China. Some opium is also refined into heroin in clandestine laboratories in the north, and then smuggled out of the country.

Poppy is planted in 10 provinces, particularly throughout the north, although unlike in Myanmar it's not used to finance insurgent armies nor are there opium warlords per se. Instead it's mostly grown in small to medium-size plots, with planting beginning in October and harvesting taking place in January or February. Prices for processed (boiled) opium in Laos fluctuate from US$50 to US$120 per kg depending on the size of the annual harvest. Due to the country's rugged terrain and lack of roads, large-scale poppy cultivation is much tougher to combat here than in Thailand.

In 1987 the Lao and US governments signed an agreement to allow a Lao-American Counter-Narcotics Cooperation programme to be carried out in northern Laos. The UN Drug Control Programme also operates in the country; four UNDCP workers were killed in an ambush near Phalavek in 1995. The principal thrust of these programmes is to train poppy-growers in crop substitution. Experience with similar projects in Thailand indicate that success only occurs in areas where crop substitution is accompanied by a concentrated effort to indoctrinate minority ethnic groups into mainstream lowland culture.

For many ethnicities in Laos, opium plays an important role in traditional medicine. The Lao government doesn't discourage the latter use, instead concentrating on locating and destroying large fields. A recent French study concluded that in villages where opium was produced, only about 11% smoked it regularly and less than five per thousand were addicted to the point where they could no longer work. Among many ethnic groups, raw opium sap, pressed oil and/or poppyseeds also feature significantly in their villagers' daily food intake. ■

Tourism

Since the Lao government first began keeping tourism records, the number of annual visitor arrivals has increased from 14,400 in 1991 to 146,155 in 1994. The latter total includes 110,744 day-trippers from Thailand (82%), China (15%) and Vietnam (3%), a category the government terms 'regional tourists', plus 19,400 'visa extensions' (mostly Indians, Sri Lankans and Chinese who use Laos as a 'waiting room' while applying for Thai visa extensions).

Of the 16,000 'international tourists' (this includes regional visitors who stay at least one night) who visited Laos in 1994, half came from Europe (20% from France alone), 37% from Asia and the Pacific (10.6% from Japan, 9% from Thailand), and 9.8% from the USA. Only 58% of those classified by the government as international tourists actually reported tourism as the purpose of their visit; 17% came as international organisation experts, 14% on business and the remainder for private affairs or as official government invitees.

The total revenue earned from these arrivals in 1994 was estimated to be US$7.6

million, up from US$2.2 million in 1991. This makes tourism one of the country's most important sources of income, although Laos still lags far behind most of the countries surrounding it even if the entire 16,000 'international tourists' can be considered true leisure travellers.

Foreign Investment in Laos

Laos has one of the most liberal foreign investment codes in the world. Unlike in neighbouring Thailand, where foreign entities are limited to a maximum 49% ownership in any enterprise, the Lao government allows 100% foreign ownership in approved projects. Two major conditions apply: investors must operate through a broker to obtain all permits (including business visas) and 100% foreign ownership is limited to 15 years unless an extension is approved.

Working through a broker involves sometimes costly fees (the joke around Vientiane is that most of the country's foreign investment earnings accumulate from broker's fees) though some investment brokers are better than others. Many foreign investors claim that nothing happens after paying their fees and filing their applications with the appropriate ministries, while other investors have been quite happy with the results.

Standard profit taxes run at 35%, though a lower 20 to 30% rate is available in certain promoted sectors (mostly projects that build infrastructure). Personal income tax is limited to a low 10%. As of the end of 1994, the government had granted foreign investment licences totalling US$5 billion (nearly a tenfold increase since 1993), mostly in the areas of energy (76%), tourism (7%) and mining (5.6%), followed by smaller investments in garments/textiles, wood products, import/export and agribusiness.

Of the 31 countries with companies operating in Laos, the top five foreign investors by nationality are Thailand (42%), the USA (33%), South Korea (8.5%), France (6.7%) and Australia (3%).

POPULATION

A 1995 census of Laos taken by the government – with help from the Swedish International Development Agency – recorded a total population of 4.5 million, with an average annual growth rate of 2.4% since 1985. The nation's population density is one of the lowest in Asia, around 19 people per sq km – in other words Laos is roughly the same size as Great Britain with only 8% of Britain's population. By comparison, Vietnam suffers a density of 230 people per sq km, Thailand 120. Roughly 85% of the population lives in rural areas; according to the government's 1995 census, the population for the country's five largest cities and towns are: Vientiane 133,000; Savannakhet 124,000; Pakse 64,000; Luang Prabang 63,000; and Huay Xai 44,000.

Around 10% of the population left the country following the 1975 communist takeover, over half being lowland Lao and the remainder a mixture of minorities. Of those who emigrated, 66.5% have ended up in the USA, 14.5% in France, 8.7% in Canada, and 4.9% in Australia. The provinces of Vientiane and Luang Prabang lost the most people, with approximately 25% of the population of Luang Prabang going abroad. The emigration trend has recently reversed itself so that the influx of immigrants – mostly repatriated Lao, but also including Chinese, Vietnamese and other nationalities– now exceeds the number of emigres.

According to UNDP statistics, infant mortality in Laos runs at 125 per 1000 live births (about four times higher than in Thailand, twice as many as in Vietnam). The ratio of citizens to trained physicians is 4447; by comparison Vietnam has a ratio of 2298 people per doctor, Cambodia 9523.

On the UN Human Development Index – a complex matrix which integrates various statistics concerning income, health, education and living conditions – Laos ranks 133 out of the 173 countries surveyed. Only 20% of the annual national budget goes to the social sector, proportionately far less than in most non-communist countries in the west.

PEOPLE

Laos was once described as 'less a nation state than a conglomeration of tribes and languages...less a unified society than a multiplicity of feudal societies'. This is still borne out by the country's ethnic mix: Lao traditionally divide themselves into four categories – Lao Loum, Lao Thai, Lao Theung and Lao Sung – roughly classified according to the altitude at which they live.

About half the population are ethnic Lao or Lao Loum. Of the rest, 10 to 20% are tribal Thai, 20 to 30% are Lao Theung (lower mountain-dwellers, mostly of proto-Malay or Mon-Khmer descent) and 10 to 20% are Lao Sung (Hmong or Mien tribes who live higher up).The Lao government has an alternative three-way split, in which the Lao Thai are condensed into the Lao Loum group. Using that system, the percentages are 59.5% Lao Loum, 34% Lao Theung and 9% Lao Sung.

Ho woman wearing traditional dress

But which tribes belong to which category? There are officially 68 ethnic groups, classified by many factors – language, history, religion, customs, dress, etc. To divide these groups only by the height they live at (especially since many tribes have been 'invited' down since 1975) is somewhat ludicrous.

Recognising this complexity, ethnographer Laurent Chazee (see the Books section for details) has put forward a scheme of 119 ethnicities divided among Thai-Kadai, Austro-Asiatic (Mon-Khmer), Miao-Yao (Hmong-Mien), Sino-Tibetan and 'Others'. Several in the last category could go in one of the other four.

According to government statistics, the province with the highest number of ethnic groups is Luang Nam Tha. For all provinces the breakdown by number of resident ethnicities is as follows:

Vientiane	7	Xieng Khuang	22
Luang Prabang	12	Bolikhamsai	14
Phongsali	22	Khammuan	15
Luang Nam Tha	39	Savannakhet	12
Udomxai	23	Salavan	12
Bokeo	34	Champasak	21
Hua Phan	30	Attapeu	14
Sainyabuli	13	Sekong	14

Lao Loum The Lao Loum (Low Lao) are the ethnic Lao who have traditionally resided in the Mekong river alley or along lower tributaries of the Mekong, and who speak the Lao language. They are an ethnic subgroup of the Austro-Thai peoples who have proliferated throughout South-East Asia, southern China, and the north-eastern Indian subcontinent (see the History section earlier in this chapter for more detail on Thai migration routes). Under the official government classification they are supposed to be found at elevations between 200 and 400m above sea level.

The Lao Loum culture has traditionally consisted of a sedentary, subsistence lifestyle based on wet-rice (with *khào nǐaw* or glutinous rice the preferred variety) cultivation. The Lao, like all Austro-Thais, were originally animists (followers of earth spirit cults) who took on Theravada Buddhism as their main religion in the middle of the first millennium AD.

The distinction between 'Lao' and 'Thai' is a rather recent historical phenomenon, especially considering that 80% of all ethnic Lao (those speaking a language recognised as 'Lao') living in South-East Asia today reside in north-eastern Thailand. Even Lao living in Laos refer idiomatically to different Lao Loum groups as 'Thai', for example, Thai Luang Phabang (Lao from Luang Prabang), Thai Pakse (from Pakse), Thai Tai (from southern Lao) and Thai Neua (from northern Lao, which is especially confusing since there is also a Thai tribal group known to academics as Thai Neua).

Lao Thai These are Thai subgroups closely related to the Lao who are more 'tribal' in character; that is, they have resisted absorption into mainstream Lao culture and tend to subdivide themselves according to smaller group distinctions. Like the Lao Loum, they live along river valleys, but the Lao Thai have chosen to reside in upland valleys rather than in the lowlands of the Mekong floodplains.

The Lao Thai cultivate dry or mountain rice as well as wet, or irrigated, rice. Some still practise swidden agriculture. In general, they have maintained animist beliefs and eschewed conversion to Buddhism or Christianity.

Lao Loum & Lao Thai
Lao Theung
Lao Sung
Tibeto-Burman

Ethnic Groups in Laos

The various Lao Thai groups are distinguished from one another by the colour of their clothing or general area of habitation, for example, Black Thai, White Thai, Red Thai, Forest Thai, Northern Thai and so on.

To distinguish between the Siamese Thais and other Austro-Thai ethnic subgroups, a few English-speaking Lao scholars use the spelling 'Tai' to include them all, in spite of the fact that the origins and pronunciation for this word differs not in the slightest from the word 'Thai'. The spelling 'Tai' also poses potential confusion with the Lao-Thai word *tai* or 'south', as in the Lao Tai (or Thai Tai) of southern Laos.

Thai Dam The predominant Lao Thai tribe is the Thai Dam (Black Thai), who live in the upland valleys of north and eastern Laos, especially Xieng Khuang and Hua Phan provinces. As their name suggests, black is the preponderant colour of their traditional garb. A fairly large number of Thai Dam, 1950s refugees from North Vietnam's Dien Bien Phu, also live in Vientiane Province.

The Thai Dam have a caste system that divides them into three classes: the *phu tao* (nobility); the *phu noi* (commoners); and the *maw* (priests). Of all the Lao Thai groups, the Thai Dam are considered the most archetypical since their traditions have been so well preserved over the centuries. Among the Lao, they are known for their honesty and industriousness.

Lao Theung The Lao Theung (Upland Lao) are a loose affiliation of mostly Mon-Khmer peoples who live on mid-altitude mountain slopes (officially 300 to 900m) in northern and southern Laos. The most numerous group is the Khamu, followed by the Htin, Lamet and smaller numbers of Lavene, Katu, Katang, Alak and other Mon-Khmer groups in the south. The Lao Theung are also known by the pejorative term khàa, which means slave or servant in the Lao language. This is because they were used as indentured labour by migrating Austro-Thai peoples in earlier centuries and more recently by the Lao monarchy. Today, they still often work as labourers for the Lao Sung.

The Lao Theung have a much lower standard of living than any of the three other groups described here. Most trade between the Lao Theung and other Lao is carried out by barter. Metal tools are not common among the Khamu, Htin and Lamet, who rely mostly on wood, bamboo and stone implements.

Most of the Khamu – of whom there are eight subgroups – originally came from China's Xishuangbanna District (Sipsongpanna in Lao) in Yunnan Province and are now found in all nine northern provinces. For the most part they are swidden agriculturists who grow mountain rice, coffee, tobacco and cotton. Their villages are established near upland streams; their houses have dirt floors like those of the Hmong, but roofs sport crossed roof-beams similar to the northern Thai *kalae* (locally called *kapkri-aak*). Traditionally they are animists, though many of those living near Lao centres have converted to Theravada Buddhism and a few are Christians.

The Htin (pronounced 'Tin'), numerous in Sainyabuli Province, typically subsist by hunting for wild game, breeding domestic animals and farming small plots of land. Since metal is taboo in their culture, they are particularly skilled at manipulating bamboo to make everything needed around the house; for floor mats and baskets they interweave pared bamboo with a black-coloured grass to create bold geometric patterns. The Htin and Khamu languages are closely related.

Lao Sung The Lao Sung (High Lao) include those hill tribes who make their residence at altitudes greater than 1000m above sea level. Of all the peoples of Laos, they are the most recent immigrants, having come from Myanmar, Tibet and southern China within the last century.

The largest group are the Hmong, also called Miao or Meo, who probably number around 200,000 in four main subgroups, the White Hmong, Striped Hmong, Red Hmong and Black Hmong (the colours refer to predominant clothing), and are found in the nine provinces of the north plus Bolikhamsai in central Laos. The agricultural staples of the Hmong are dry rice and corn raised by the slash-and-burn method. They also raise cattle, pigs, water buffalo and chickens. For the most part, theirs is a barter economy in which iron is the medium of exchange. Iron is important for the crafting of machetes for land-clearing and flintlock rifles for hunting. Their one cash crop is opium, which they manufacture more of than any other group in Laos. The Hmong are numerous in the provinces of Hua Phan, Xieng Khuang and Luang Prabang.

The second-largest group are the Mien (also called Iu Mien, Yao and Man), who number 30,000 to 50,000 and live mainly in Luang Nam Tha, Luang Prabang, Bokeo, Udomxai and Phongsali. The Mien and Hmong have many ethnic and linguistic similarities, but intermarriage is rare. Both groups have a sophisticated social structure that extends beyond the village level, and both groups are predominantly animist. The Mien, like the Hmong, are poppy cultivators.

The Hmong are considered more aggressive and warlike, however, and as such were perfect for the CIA-trained special RLG forces under General Vang Pao in the '60s and early '70s. The anti-government resistance groups that still exist are mostly Hmong.

Girl from the riverine Lao Huay tribe

Large numbers of Hmong and Mien left Laos abroad following the 1975 Revolution. It is often claimed that this is because they were 'mercenaries' of the USA (see the History section earlier in this chapter for more detail). In fact the vast majority of Hmong and Mien who left Laos had no involvement in the war, but they may have expected reprisals because of those who did. Many were also simply following the example of their leader, Vang Pao, who now lives in California. It is estimated that 50,000 Hmong are living in the USA, with another 8000 in other countries. About 1000 to 2000 Hmong emigres have returned to Laos since 1991.

Other much smaller Tibeto-Burman hill-tribe groups in Laos include the Lisu, Lahu, Lolo, Iko (Akha) and Phu Noi. Sometimes these are classified as Lao Theung since they live at slightly lower elevations than the Hmong and Mien, but like the Hmong and the Mien they live in the mountains of northern Laos.

Other Asians As elsewhere in South-East Asia, the Chinese have been migrating to Laos for centuries to work as merchants and traders. Most come direct from Yunnan but more recently many have also been arriving from Vietnam. Estimates of their presence varies from 2 to 5% of the total population. At least half of all permanent Chinese residents in Laos are said to live in Vientiane and Savannakhet. Most businesses in these towns are owned by ethnic Chinese.

In just the last couple of years there has been an influx of Singaporeans and Taiwanese serving as managers or contractors for hotel projects. Thousands of temporary Chinese immigrants from Yunnan also work as skilled labourers in the far north.

Since the Thai-Lao rapprochement of the late '80s, Thais are coming in ever-increasing numbers. Unlike the Chinese, they only stay for short intervals engaging in business or aid and education projects.

In Vientiane, there is also a small but visible number of northern Indians and Pakistanis who run tailor and fabric shops. For some reason, they also seem to make up a good portion of FAO, WHO and UN teams working in Laos as well (along with Bangladeshis and Burmese).

In southern Laos, especially in Champasak Province, live small numbers of Cambodians. Most commonly they work as truck drivers and boatmen who are involved in legal and illegal trade between Laos, Cambodia and Thailand. A few Cambodians are stationed in Vientiane as members of Indochinese political committees.

Vietnamese can be found in substantial numbers in all the provinces bordering Vietnam and in the cities of Vientiane, Savannakhet and Pakse. For the most part Vietnamese residents in Laos work as traders and small businesspeople, though there continues to be a small Vietnamese military presence in Xieng Khuang and Hua Phan provinces. ■

EXPATRIATE COMMUNITY

Most of the expatriate Europeans living in Laos (less than a thousand in all) are temporary contract employees of multilateral and bilateral aid organisations or programmes such as UNESCO, UNDP, FAO, the Lao-Australian Irrigation Project, the Lao-Swedish Forestry Programme and so on. A smaller tally work for international companies, most numerously those concerned with mining, petroleum and hydropower. Virtually all of these groups inhabit huge mansions in eastern Vientiane, just like their compatriots did before 1975. Since the breakup of the USSR the Russian and Eastern European presence has shrunk to practically nil. There is also a growing number of foreign nongovernmental organisations (NGOs) – around 40 at last count – though their financial presence only comprises about 5% of total foreign aid to Laos.

Very few people of European descent, whether from the West or the East, have been allowed permanent residence in Laos, although quite a few expatriate business-owners are able to renew temporary residence permits on a yearly basis. About a dozen Europeans – including French and Americans – stayed right through the 1975 Revolution since small businesses were not nationalised. Up until 1990, the government enforced a quota on the number of Americans – including spouses and children – who could reside in Laos at any one time. All such quotas have since been lifted.

EDUCATION

Laos' public school system is organised around five years at the *pathom* (primary) level beginning at age six, followed by three years of *mathayom* (middle) and three years of *udom* (high) school. In reality less than three years of formal education is the national norm, and most teachers themselves have spent less than five years in school. Seventy percent of all Lao citizens enroll in primary school at some point in their youth,

but the dropout rate is 60%. These statistics don't take into account the education provided by the country's Buddhist wats; in rural areas, monastic schooling is the only formal education available, most commonly for boys only.

Private and international schools for the foreign and local elite abound in Vientiane, from a Montessori pre-school to the expanding Vientiane International School, which takes students through the ninth grade. The country has only two complete universities, Dong Dok University and Phaetsaat University in Vientiane, plus two technical colleges, all four of which are in Vientiane. Together they enrol a very small percentage of the school-age population.

Although the national literacy rate is 84%, if urban areas (representing only 15% of the population) aren't included, the reading rate drops to around 45%.

ARTS

Temple Architecture

Laos never really distinguished itself architecturally. Partially, this is because many structures were built of wood: fire, weather, invading armies and B-52 saturation bombing have left few wooden structures in Laos that hail from the pre-eminent 16th to 18th centuries.

The most emblematic edifice in Laos is the Pha That Luang (Great Sacred Stupa) in Vientiane (see the Vientiane chapter further on for more detail). A *thâat* (from the Pali-Sanskrit *dhatu*, meaning element or component part – usually a sacred relic) is a spire or dome-like structure that commemorates the life of the Buddha. The distinctive shape may have been inspired by the staff and begging bowl of the wandering Buddha. Many thâat are said to contain dhatu – parts of the Buddha's body, for example, a hair, nail or piece of bone. Considering the number of thâat throughout Buddhist Asia, it is very unlikely that all those which claim to contain Buddha relics actually do.

The curvilinear, four-cornered superstructure at That Luang is the Lao standard – most stupas of truly Lao origin are modelled on this one (you'll also see Lao stupas in north-eastern Thailand, which is mostly populated by ethnic Lao). Other types of stupas in Laos are either Siamese or Khmer-inspired. An exception is the That Mak Mo, or Water-melon Stupa, in Luang Prabang, which is hemispherical in shape – of possible Sinhal-ese influence, but still distinctive.

The *uposatha* (or in Lao, *sim*), the build-ing where new monks are ordained, is always the most important structure in any Thera-vada Buddhist wat. In Laos, there are basically three architectural styles for such buildings – the Vientiane, Luang Prabang, and Xieng Khuang styles. In Vientiane, sim are large rectangular buildings constructed of brick and covered with stucco, much like their counterparts in Thailand. The high-peaked roofs are layered to present several levels (always odd in number – three, five, or seven, occasionally nine) corresponding to various Buddhist doctrines which have been codified into groups of these numbers (the three characteristics of existence, the seven levels of enlightenment etc). The edges of the roofs almost always feature a repeated flame motif, with long, finger-like hooks at the corners called *jâo fâa* (sky lords). Legend has it that these hooks are for catching evil spirits that descend on the sim from above. The whole structure is mounted on a multilevel platform or pediment.

Vientiane Style The front of a Vientiane-style sim usually features a large veranda with heavy columns which support an ornamented, overhanging roof. Some Lao sim will also have a less-ornamented rear veranda, while those that have a full surrounding terrace are Bangkok-influenced. One of the best features of the Vientiane style is the carved wooden shade that often appears along the top portion of the front veranda. Usually the carving depicts a mythical figure such as the half-bird, half-human *kinnari*, or sometimes the Buddha himself, against a background of dense, stylised foliage. The artisans of Lan Xang were extremely adept at this type of wood-carving. Carved porticoes like these represent

one of the highlights of Lao art and provide links to sculptural and musical motifs that are seen throughout South-East Asia, from Myanmar to Bali.

Luang Prabang Style In Luang Prabang, the architectural style is akin to northern Siamese or Lanna style, which is hardly sur-prising as for several centuries Laos and northern Thailand shared the same king-doms. As in Vientiane, roofs are layered, but in Luang Prabang they sweep very low, almost reaching the ground in some instances. The overall effect is quite dra-matic, as if the sim were about to take flight. Luang Prabang temples are also admired for the gold relief on the doors and outside walls of some temple structures. Wat Xieng Thong is a prime example (see the Luang Prabang section in the Northern Laos chapter for more details). The building's foundation fea-tures a much more modest pediment than the Vientiane version.

Xieng Khuang Style Very little remains of the Xieng Khuang style of sim architecture simply because the province of Xieng Khuang was so heavily bombed during the war. Fortunately for admirers of temple art, a few examples of the Xieng Khuang style remain in Luang Prabang. As in the Vien-tiane style, the sim is raised on a multilevel platform; the roof sweeps wide and low, but as in the Luang Prabang style, but isn't usually tiered. Cantilevered roof supports play a much more prominent role in the building's overall aesthetics, giving the sim's front profile an almost pentagonal shape. The pediment is curved, adding a grace beyond that of the pediments of the typical Luang Prabang and Vientiane styles.

A fourth, less-seen style of temple archi-tecture in Laos has been supplied by the Thai Lü, who like the lowland Lao are Theravada Buddhists. Thai Lü temples are typified by thick, whitewashed stucco walls with small windows, two or three-tiered roofs, curved pediments and *naga* (mythic water serpent) lintels over the doors and steps. Stupas that accompany the Thai Lü style are typically octagonal and gilded, and are often swathed with Thai Lü fabrics embroidered with beads and bits of foil. Though there are examples of Thai Lü influence in a few Luang Prabang temples, their main location is in Sainyabuli Province, where road travel is rather difficult. Thai Lü temples can be seen in abundance in Thailand's Nan and Phrae provinces.

Modern Architecture Colonial architecture in turn-of-the-century urban Laos consisted largely of thick-walled buildings with shuttered windows and pitched tile roofs designed in the classic French provincial style. Although many of these structures were torn down or allowed to decay following Lao independence from France, today they are in much demand among foreign and local companies alike.

Shophouses throughout the country, whether 100 years or 100 days old, share the basic Chinese shophouse design in which the ground floor is reserved for trading purposes while the upper floors contain offices or residences. During most of the post-WW II era, the trend in modern Lao architecture – inspired by the European Bauhaus movement – was towards a boring functionalism in which the average building looked like a giant egg carton turned on its side. The Lao and French aesthetic, so vibrant in prewar eras, almost entirely disappeared in this characterless style of architecture.

Newer buildings erected in post-revolutionary Laos tended to follow the socialist realism school popular in the former Soviet Union and China. Cubistic towers with straight lines and sharp angles was the norm for much of the '70s and early '80s.

More recently a small trend toward integrating classic Lao architectural motifs with modern functions has taken hold. Prime examples of this movement include Vientiane's National Assembly hall and the new Luang Prabang airport, both of which were designed by Havana-and Moscow-trained architect Hongkad Souvannavong. Other design characteristics, such as those represented by the new Siam Commercial Bank on Thanon Lan Xang, seek to gracefully reincorporate French colonial features ignored for the last half century.

Sculpture

As in Thailand, Myanmar and Cambodia, the focus of most traditional art in Lao culture has been religious, specifically Buddhist. Unlike the art of these other three countries, Lao art never encompassed a broad range of styles and periods, mainly because Laos has had a much more modest history in terms of power and longevity. Furthermore, since Laos was intermittently dominated by its neighbours, much Lao art was destroyed or carried off by the Vietnamese, Siamese or Khmer. Influences from these steward states also left behind a very strong influence on local sculpture.

This doesn't mean, however, that what remains isn't worthy of admiration. Though limited in range, Lao art and architecture can be unique and expressive. Most impressive is Lao sculpture of the 16th to 18th centuries, the heyday of the kingdom of Lan Xang (Million Elephants). Lao sculptural media usually included bronze, stone or wood and the subject was invariably the Lord Buddha or figures associated with the *jataka* or life stories of the Buddha. Like other Buddhist sculptors, the Lao artisans emphasised features thought to be peculiar to the historical Buddha, including a beak-like nose, extended earlobes, tightly curled hair and so on.

Two types of standing Buddha images are distinctively Lao. The first is the 'Calling for Rain' posture, which depicts the Buddha standing with his hands held rigidly at his side, fingers pointing toward the ground. This posture is never seen in other South-East Asian Buddhist art traditions. The slightly rounded, 'boneless' look of the image recalls Thailand's Sukhothai style, and the way the lower robe is sculpted over the hips looks vaguely Khmer. But the flat, slab-like earlobes, arched eyebrows and very aquiline nose are uniquely Lao. The bottom of the figure's robe curls upward on both sides in a perfectly symmetrical fashion (also uniquely Lao). The whole image gives the

What's a Wat?

Technically speaking, a wat is a Buddhist compound where monks reside; without monks it isn't a wat. The word derives from the Pali-Sanskrit term *avasa* which means dwelling. Anywhere in Laos, a typical wat will contain the following structures: *uposatha* or *sim*, a chapel where monks are ordained; a *hǎw tài* (tripitaka library) where Buddhist scriptures are stored; *kuti* (monastic quarters); a *hǎw kawng* (drum tower); a *sǎaláa lóng thám* (open-air meeting place where monks and laity listen to *thám* (from the Sanskrit *dharma)* or Buddhist doctrine); and various *thâat* (stupas). The smaller stupas are *thâat kádùuk* (bone stupas), where the ashes of worshippers are interred; on *wán pha* (twice-monthly worship days), many people place lighted candles around the thâat kádùuk of their relatives.

Many wats also have a *hǎw phǐi khǔn wat* (spirit house), for the temple's reigning earth spirit – in spite of the fact that spirit worship is illegal in Laos today. Various other buildings may be added as needed for wat administration, but these are the basics. ■

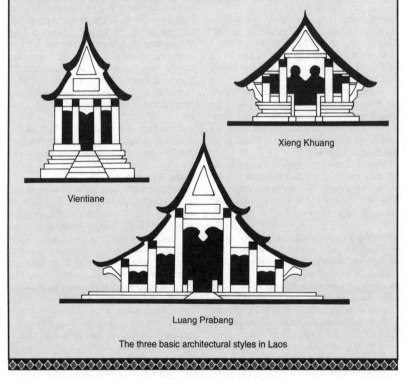

Xieng Khuang

Vientiane

Luang Prabang

The three basic architectural styles in Laos

distinct impression of a rocket in flight. Considering that the Lao custom at the end of the dry season is to fire bamboo rockets into the sky in a plea for rain, this may have been the sculptors' desired effect.

The other original Lao image type is the 'Contemplating the Bodhi Tree' Buddha. The Bodhi tree, or 'Tree of Enlightenment', refers to the large banyan tree that the historical Buddha purportedly was sitting beneath when he attained enlightenment in Bodhgaya, India, in the 6th century BC. In this image the Buddha is standing in much the same way as in the 'Calling for Rain' pose except that his hands are crossed at the wrists in front of his body.

The finest examples of Lao sculpture are found in Vientiane's Haw Pha Kaew and Wat Si Saket, and in Luang Prabang's National Museum.

Though uncommon overall, other styles of sculpture from Siam and Angkor can occasionally be seen in Laos.

Handicrafts

As already noted, the Lao are skillful carvers. This applies not only to sim porticoes and gold relief, but to everyday folk art. Wood and bone are the most popular carving mediums.

Among the Hmong and Mien hill tribes, silversmithing plays an important role in the maintenance of 'portable wealth' and inheritance. Silversmithing and goldsmithing is a traditional Lao art as well but in recent years has been in decline.

Mats and baskets woven of various kinds of straw and reed are also common and are becoming a small but important export to Thailand. Among the best baskets and mats are those woven by the Htin.

Weaving In traditional Lao society every woman knew how to weave, and it was one of the main qualities a man looked for in a spouse. In some areas of southern Laos, for example, Champasak Province, weaving styles have continued almost uninterrupted. But the weaving techniques of the north-east – often considered the most sophisticated of the Lao weaving styles – were almost completely lost due to conflicts along the Vietnamese border in the last two centuries. For this reason antique weavings – especially those from Thai tribal groups – are more highly valued today than modern ones. Fortunately during the last 10 years many styles have been revived, among them the highly regarded Lao Neua patterns of Sam Neua and Xieng Khuang – designs which probably originated in Yunnan's Sipsongpanna (Xishuangbanna) District in China and were

brought to Laos by the Thai Lü and Thai Neua.

Common motifs include *lái nàak* (S-shaped river dragons), *lái dàwk kūut* (ferns), *lái káw* (hooks), *sīi-hōh* (a mythical lion-elephant figure) and *lái nâam lāi* (flowing water).

Traditional wooden looms are in common use in lowland villages, with both cotton and silk as weaving mediums. Woven cloth is sewn into various kinds of clothing and can be used for decoration or in socio-religious ceremonies as well. The most common type of weaving is for the *phàa nung* (a long wraparound skirt worn by almost all Lao women). Synthetic dyes are replacing natural ones, but the resulting materials are always colourful. Gold or silver thread is frequently woven into the borders of fabrics, reminiscent of the *songket* fabric of Malaysia.

For information on shopping for Lao textiles, see Things to Buy in the next chapter and the colour aside facing page 81.

Music & Dance

As in other South-East Asian cultures, music in Laos can be divided into classical and folk traditions. The classical music of Laos is the least interesting, simply because it is so imitative of the classical traditions of Thailand and Cambodia. Lao classical music was originally developed as court music for royal ceremonies and classical dance-drama. The standard ensemble for this genre is called the *sep nyai* and consists of a set of tuned gongs called *khong wong*, a xylophone-like instrument called the *ranyat*, the *khui*, or bamboo flute, and the *pii*, a double-reed wind instrument similar to the oboe.

Nowadays, the only time you'll generally hear this type of music is during the occasional public performance of the *Pha Lak Pha Lam*, a dance-drama based on the Hindu epic *Ramayana*. The practice of classical Lao music and drama has been in decline for some time now – 40 years of intermittent war and revolution has simply made this kind of entertainment a low priority among most Lao.

Buddhist Wats in Vientiane

Top Left: A cement sculpture at Wat Xieng Khuan (Buddha Park)
Top Right: The interior walls of the cloister at Wat Si Saket
Bottom Left: Buddha sculptures on display around Wat Pha Kaew's terrace
Bottom Right: Buddha 'Calling for rain' at Wat Pha Kaew

JOE CUMMINGS

OLIVER HARGREAVE

JOE CUMMINGS

JOE CUMMINGS

Top Left: Novice monks in Luang Prabang
Top Right: Akha girl, Northern Laos
Bottom Left: Mien women, Luang Prabang Province
Bottom Right: Hmong women, Northern Laos

Not so with Lao folk music, which has always stayed close to the people. The principal instrument in the folk genre is the *khaen* (French spelling: *khene*), a wind instrument that is devised of a double row of bamboo-like reeds fitted into a hardwood soundbox. The rows can be as few as four or as many as eight. The khaen player blows (as with a harmonica, sound is produced whether the breath is moving in or out of the instrument) into the soundbox while covering or uncovering small holes in the reeds that determine the pitch for each. An adept player is able to produce a churning, calliope-like music that is quite danceable. The most popular folk dance is the *lam wong* (circle dance) in which couples dance circles around one another until there are three circles in all: a circle danced by the individual, the circle danced by the couple, and one danced by the whole crowd.

The khaen is often accompanied by the *saw* (sometimes written *so*), a bowed string instrument. In more elaborate ensembles the khui and khong wong may be added, as well as various hand drums. Khaen music can also incorporate a vocalist. Most Lao pop music is based on vocal khaen music. Melodies are almost always pentatonic, ie they feature five-note scales.

The Lao folk idiom also has its own theatre, based on the *māw lám (mō lám)* tradition. Māw lám is difficult to translate but means something like 'master, or priest, of dance'. Performances always feature a witty, topical combination of talking and singing that ranges across themes as diverse as politics and sex. Very colloquial, even bawdy language is employed; this is one art form that has always bypassed government censors, whether it's the French or the LPRP.

There are four basic types of māw lám. The first, *māw lám lūang* (great māw lám), involves an ensemble of performers in costume, on stage. *Māw lám khuu* (couple māw lám) features a man and woman who engage in flirtation and verbal repartee. *Māw lám chot* (juxtaposed māw lám) has two performers of the same gender who 'duel' by answering questions or finishing an incom-

plete story issued as a challenge. Finally, *māw lám diaw* (solo māw lám) involves only one performer. All types of māw lám are most commonly performed at temple fairs and on other festive occasions. You can also commonly hear māw lám khuu and māw lám diaw on Lao or north-eastern Thai radio stations.

Literature

Of all classical Lao literature, *Pha Lak Pha Lam*, the Lao version of India's epic *Ramayana*, is the most pervasive and influential in the culture. The Indian source first came to Laos with the Khmer roughly 900 years ago as stone reliefs which appeared on Wat Phu and other Angkor-period temples built in what is now central and southern Laos. Oral and written versions may also have been available; eventually, though, the Lao developed their own version of the epic, which differs greatly from the original and from Thailand's *Ramakian*.

Although the main theme remains the same – handsome and virtuous Rama (Pha Lam in Lao) loses his consort Sita (Sii-daa) to evil Ravana, the Lao have embroidered on the *Ramayana* by providing much more biographic detail on arch-villain Ravana and his wife Montho. Rama's brother Laksana (Pha Lak) also has a larger role, as suggested by the inclusion of his name in the Lao epic's title.

Various Thai tribes in Laos have their own renderings of the *Ramayana* story. In the Thai Lü version, for example, Rama is portrayed as an incarnation of the Buddha and Ravana is identified with Mara (Buddha's Satan-like tempter in canonical Buddhist mythology).

Also passed on from Indian tradition are the many *jatakas* or life-stories *(sáa-tók* in Lao) of the Buddha. Of the 547 jataka tales in the Pali *tripitaka* (Buddhist canon) – each one chronicling a different past life – most appear in Laos almost word-for-word as they were first written down in Sri Lanka. A group of 50 'extra' or apocryphal stories – based on Lao-Thai folk tales of the time – were added by Pali scholars in Luang Prabang 300 to 400 years ago. One of the most popular jatakas in Laos is a Pali original known as the Mahajati or Mahavessandara (Lao: *Mahaa-Vetsanthon*), the story of the Buddha's penultimate life. Interior murals in the sim or ordination chapel of many Lao wats typically depict this jataka and nine others: Temiya, Mahachanaka, Suwannasama, Nemiraja, Mahasotha, Bhuritat, Chantakumara, Nartha and Vithura.

SOCIETY & CONDUCT
Traditional Culture
Laos' complex ethnic stratification means that when one speaks of Lao culture, one is truly referring only to the lowland Lao or Lao Loum, who represent only about half the population. Lowland Lao culture predominates in the cities, towns and villages of the Mekong river valley, that is to say western Laos from Huay Xai to Pakse, but on the official level the customs practised in these areas are in large part taken to be the 'national culture' by the country's rulers.

A hand-painted propaganda billboard standing on a street corner near Wat Si Saket in Vientiane exemplifies this cultural mandate. It depicts a future Vientiane skyline marked by tall, modernistic buildings interspersed with Buddhist wats; in the foreground citizens wearing traditional Lao dress are dancing the lam wong, carrying Buddhist offerings and performing a *basi* ceremony. Hence the true Lao – according to official image propaganda – proudly bear the sartorial and artistic symbols of their culture, practise the majority religion and participate in important ceremonial acts that are deemed 'Lao'.

Dress In many ways the simplified billboard image mentioned above crystallises the perceived traditions of – and expectations for – the Lao people. A good Lao dons some portion of the traditional garb during ceremonies and celebrations – the men only a *phàa biang* or shoulder sash, the women a similar sash, tight-fitting blouse, and *phàa nung* or sarong. In everyday life a man dispenses entirely with traditional Lao clothing, dressing in the international shirt-and-trou-

sers style, as long as his clothing contributes to a neat, modest and clean appearance, and as long as his hair is kept neat and short.

Women, on the other hand, are expected to wear the phàa nung on a daily basis except when participating in sports or in a profession which requires a uniform. Other ethnicities living in urban Laos – particularly Chinese and Vietnamese women – forego the phàa nung as daily wear, but even they must don the Lao sarong when they visit a police or prefecture office; if they don't dress in the prescribed manner they risk having any civic requests denied by Lao bureaucrats – or perhaps won't be served at all.

Cultural Traits To a large degree 'Lao-ness' is defined by Buddhism, specifically Theravada Buddhism. More austere and inward-looking than its Mahayana counterparts in northern and eastern Asia, Theravada emphasises the cooling of the human passions and thus strong emotions are a taboo in Lao society (see the section on Religion below for more detail). *Kamma* (karma), more than devotion, prayer or hard work, is believed to determine one's lot in life, hence the Lao tend not to get too worked up over the future. This trait is often perceived by outsiders as a lack of ambition.

The cultural contrast between the Lao and the Vietnamese provides a good example of how the rugged Annamite Chain that separates Laos from Vietnam has also served as a cultural fault line dividing Indic and Sinitic – Theravada and Mahayana – zones of influence. Like their Chinese mentors, the Vietnamese are perceived in Asia as hard workers and aggressive businesspeople. The French coined a saying to highlight the differences among their Indochinese subjects: 'The Vietnamese plant rice, the Cambodians watch it grow and the Lao listen to it grow.' The Lao have their own proverb that says 'Lao and Viet, like cat and dog'.

Lao commonly express the notion that 'too much work is bad for your brain' and they often say they feel sorry for people who 'think too much'. Education in general isn't highly valued although this attitude is changing quickly with modernisation. Avoiding undue psychological stress, however, remains a cultural norm. From the typical Lao perspective unless an activity – whether work or play – contains an experiential element of *múan* ('fun'), it will probably lead to stress.

Hence the Lao are quite receptive to outside assistance and foreign investment, since it promotes a certain degree of economic development without demanding a corresponding increase in local productivity. The Lao government wants all the trappings of modern technology – the skyscrapers of the propaganda billboard – without having to give up any of the Lao traditions, among them the *múan* zeitgeist. The challenge for Laos in the future is to find a balance between cultural preservation and the development of new perceptions and attitudes that will lead the country toward a measure of self-sufficiency.

Etiquette

Visiting Temples The Lao are very devout Buddhists; upon visiting Lao Buddhist temples, you owe a measure of respect to the religion and to the people who so graciously allow you to enter their places of worship. Correct behaviour in temples entails several guidelines, the most important of which is to dress neatly and to take your shoes off when you enter religious buildings such as the sim. Shorts or sleeveless shirts are considered improper dress for both men and women; Lao citizens wearing either would be turned away by monastic authorities, but the Lao are often too polite to refuse entry to improperly clad foreigners.

Buddha images are sacred objects, so don't pose in front of them for pictures and definitely do not climb or sit upon them. When sitting in front of a Buddha image, do not point your feet towards the image. The Lao usually employ the 'mermaid pose' when facing an image, which keeps both feet pointed to the rear.

If you want to speak with a monk (the occasional monk can speak English or French), try to keep your head a bit lower than his. If he's sitting, you should sit, too (use the 'mermaid pose' again); if he's standing, you may have to bend down a bit to show proper respect. Women should never touch monks or hand them objects (place an object on a table or other surface in front of a monk instead).

A few of the larger wats in Vientiane charge small entry fees. In other temples, offering a small donation before leaving the compound is appropriate but not mandatory. Usually there are donation boxes near the entry of the sim or next to the central Buddha image at the rear. In rural wats, there may be no donation box available; in these, it's OK to leave money on the floor next to the central image or even by the doorway – no one is likely to steal it.

Social Gestures Traditionally, the Lao greet each other not with a handshake but with a prayer-like palms-together gesture known as a *nop* or *wài*. If someone nops you, you should nop back (unless it is a child). But nowadays the Western-style handshake is just as common and most Lao will offer the same to a foreigner.

The feet are the lowest part of the body (spiritually as well as physically) so don't point your feet at people (you shouldn't even point at objects with your feet). In the same context, the head is regarded as the highest part of the body, so don't touch Lao people on the head either.

When handing things to other people you should use both hands or your right hand only, never the left hand (reserved for toilet ablutions). Books and other written material are given a special status over other secular objects. Hence you shouldn't slide books or documents across a table or counter-top, and never place them on the floor – use a chair instead if table space isn't available.

Dress & Attitude Shorts – except knee-length walking shorts – sleeveless shirts, tank tops (singlets) and other beach-style attire are not considered appropriate dress in Laos for anything other than sporting events. Such dress is especially counter-productive if worn to government offices (eg when applying for a visa extension). The attitude of 'This is how I dress at home and no-one is going to stop me' gains nothing but disrespect from the Lao.

Sandals or slip-on shoes are OK for almost any but the most formal occasions. Short-sleeved shirts and blouses with capped sleeves likewise are quite acceptable in Laos.

When things go wrong, don't be quick to anger – it won't help matters, since losing one's temper means loss of face for everyone present. Remember that this is Asia, where keeping your cool is the paramount rule. Talking loudly is perceived as rude behaviour by cultured Lao, whatever the situation.

A smile and *sabai-di* (the Lao greeting) goes a long way toward calming the initial trepidation that locals may feel upon seeing a foreigner, whether in the city or the countryside.

Upcountry When travelling in minority villages, try to find out what the local customs and taboos are, either by asking someone or by observing local behaviour closely. Here are several other guidelines for minimising the negative impact on the local people.

- Many tribes fear photography, so you should always ask permission – through hand gestures if necessary – before pointing your camera at tribal people and/or their dwellings.
- Show respect for religious symbols and rituals. Avoid touching spirit houses, household altars, village totems and other religious symbols, as this often 'pollutes' them spiritually and may force the villagers to perform purification rituals after you have moved on. Keep your distance from ceremonies being performed unless you're asked to participate.
- Do not enter a village house without the permission or invitation of its inhabitants.
- Practise restraint in giving things to tribespeople or bartering with them. Food and medicine are not necessarily appropriate gifts if they result in altering traditional dietary and healing practices. The same goes for clothing. Tribespeople will abandon handwoven tunics for printed T-shirts if they are given a steady supply. If you want to give something to the people you encounter, the best thing is to make a donation to the village school or other community fund.

RELIGION
Theravada Buddhism
About 60% of the people of the LPDR are Theravada Buddhists. This proportion is mostly lowland Lao, along with a sprinkling of tribal Thais. Buddhism was apparently introduced to Luang Prabang (then Meuang Sawa) in the late 13th or early 14th centuries. The first monarch of Lan Xang, King Fa Ngum, was the first to declare Buddhism the state religion, which he did by accepting the Pha Bang Buddha image from his Khmer father-in-law. In 1356 AD, he built a wat in Meuang Sawa to house this famous image.

But Buddhism was fairly slow in spreading throughout Laos, even among the lowland peoples, who were reluctant to accept the faith instead of or even alongside *phii* (earth spirit) worship. King Setthathirat, who ruled Lan Xang from 1547 to 1571, attempted to make Vientiane a regional Buddhist centre, but it wasn't until the reign of King Sulinya Vongsa in the mid to late 17th century that Buddhism began to be taught in Lao schools. Since the 17th century, Laos has maintained a continuous Theravadin tradition.

Basically, the Theravada school of Buddhism is an earlier and, according to its followers, less corrupted form of Buddhism than the Mahayana schools found in east Asia or in the Himalayan lands. The Theravada (Teaching of the Elders) school is also called the 'Southern' school since it took the southern route from India, its place of origin, through South-East Asia (Myanmar, Thailand, Laos and Cambodia in this case), while the 'Northern' school proceeded north into Nepal, Tibet, China, Korea, Mongolia, Vietnam and Japan. Because the southern school tried to preserve or limit the Buddhist doctrines to only those canons codified in the early Buddhist era, the northern school gave Theravada Buddhism the name Hinayana (Lesser Vehicle). They considered themselves Mahayana (Great Vehicle) because they built upon the earlier teachings, 'expanding' the doctrine so as to respond more to the needs of lay people, or so it is claimed.

Theravada or Hinayana doctrine stresses the three principal aspects of existence: *dukkha* (suffering, unsatisfactoriness, disease), *anicca* (impermanence, transience of all things) and *anatta* (non-substantiality or non-essentiality of reality – no permanent 'soul'). Comprehension of anicca reveals that no experience, no state of mind, no physical object lasts. Trying to hold onto experience, states of mind, and objects that are constantly changing creates dukkha. Anatta is the understanding that no part of the changing world can we point to and say 'This is me' or 'This is God' or 'This is the soul'. These concepts, when 'discovered' by Siddhartha Gautama in the 6th century BC, were in direct contrast to the Hindu belief in an eternal, blissful, Self or *Paramatman*, hence Buddhism was originally a 'heresy' against India's Brahmanic religion.

Gautama, an Indian prince-turned-ascetic, subjected himself to many years of severe austerities to arrive at this vision of the world and was given the title Buddha, 'the Enlightened' or 'the Awakened'. Gautama Buddha spoke of four noble truths which had the power to liberate any human being who could realise them. These four noble truths are:

- The truth of dukkha – 'All forms of existence are subject to dukkha (suffering, unsatisfactoriness, disease, imperfectness)'.
- The truth of the cause of dukkha – 'Dukkha is caused by *tanha* (desire)'.
- The truth of the cessation of dukkha – 'Eliminate the cause of dukkha (ie desire) and dukkha will cease to arise'.
- The truth of the path – 'The eight-fold path is the way to eliminate desire/extinguish dukkha'.

The eight-fold path *(atthangika-magga)* consists of:

- right understanding
- right mindedness (or 'right thought')
- right speech
- right bodily conduct
- right livelihood
- right effort
- right attentiveness
- right concentration.

Temple motif from Luang Prabang

These eight limbs belong to three different 'pillars' of practice: morality or *sila* (3 to 5); concentration or *samadhi* (6 to 8); and wisdom or *pañña* (1 and 2).

The path is also called the Middle Way since ideally it avoids both extreme austerity as well as extreme sensuality. Some Buddhists believe the path is to be taken in successive stages, while others say the pillars are interdependent. Another key point is that the word 'right' can also be translated as 'complete' or 'full'.

The ultimate goal of Theravada Buddhism is *nibbana* (Sanskrit: *nirvana)*, which literally means the 'blowing-out' or 'extinction' of all causes of dukkha. Effectively it means an end to all corporeal existence – an end to that which is forever subject to suffering and which is conditioned from moment to moment by kamma (action). In reality, most Lao Buddhists aim for rebirth in a 'better' existence rather than the supramundane goal of *nibbana*, which is highly misunderstood by Asians as well as Westerners. Many Lao express the feeling that they are somehow unworthy of nibbana. By feeding monks, giving donations to temples and performing regular worship at the local wat they hope to improve their lot, acquiring enough 'merit' (Pali: *puña*; Lao: *bun*) to prevent or at least lessen the number of rebirths.

The making of merit *(hét bun)* is an important social as well as religious activity in Laos. The concept of reincarnation is almost universally accepted by Lao Buddhists, and to some extent even by non-Buddhists, and the Buddhist theory of kamma (Pali) or karma (Sanskrit) is well-expressed in the Lao proverb '*hét dịi, dâi dịi; hét sua, dâi sua*' – 'do good and receive good; do evil and receive evil'.

The *Trilatna*, or *Triratna* (Triple Gems), highly respected by Lao Buddhists, include the Buddha, the Dhamma (the teachings) and the Sangha (the Buddhist brotherhood). Each is visible in Lao towns, particularly in the Mekong Valley. The Buddha in his sculptural form is found on high shelves or altars in homes and shops as well as in temples. The Dhamma is chanted morning and evening in every wat. The Sangha is represented by the street presence of orange-robed monks, especially in the early morning hours when they perform their alms-rounds, in what has almost become a travel-guide cliche in motion.

Lao Buddhism has no particular 'Sabbath' or day of the week when Lao are supposed to make temple visits. Nor is there anything corresponding to a liturgy or mass over which a priest presides. Instead Lao Buddhists visit the wat whenever they feel like it, most often on *wán pha* (literally 'excellent days') which occur with every full and new moon, ie every 14 days. On such a visit typical activities include the offering of lotus buds, incense and candles at various altars and bone reliquaries around the wat compound, offering food to the temple Sangha (monks, nuns and lay residents – monks always eat first), meditating (individually or in groups), listening to monks chanting *suttas* or Buddhist discourse, and attending a *thêt* or dhamma talk by the abbot or other respected teacher. Visitors may also seek counsel from individual monks or nuns regarding new or ongoing life problems.

Monks & Nuns Socially, every Lao Buddhist male is expected to become a *khúu-bạa* (monk) for a short period in his life, optimally between the time he finishes school and starts a career or marries. Men or boys under 20 years of age may enter the Sangha as novices *(samanera* or *naen)* and this is not unusual since a family earns great merit when one of its sons takes robe and bowl. Traditionally the length of time spent in the wat is three months, during the Buddhist lent *(phansāa* or *watsa)* beginning in July, which coincides with the rainy season. However, nowadays men may spend as little as a week or 15 days to accrue merit as monks or novices.

A samanera adheres to 10 precepts or vows, which include the including the usual prohibitions against stealing, lying, killing, intoxication and sexual involvement, along with ones forbidding: eating after noon; listening to music or dancing; wearing

Most Lao men serve a short period as novices.

these a large percentage become scholars and teachers, while some specialise in healing and/or *sainyasat* (folk magic), although the latter is greatly discouraged by the current ruling party. There is no similar hermetic order for nuns, but women are welcome to reside in temples as *náang síi* (lay nuns), with shaved heads and white robes.

Náang síi only have to follow eight precepts. Because discipline for nuns is much less strenuous than it is for monks, they don't attain quite as high a social status as do monks. However, aside from the fact that they don't perform ceremonies on behalf of other lay persons, they engage in the same basic religious activities (meditation and dhamma study) as monks. The reality is that wats which draw sizeable contingents of eight-precept nuns are highly respected because women don't choose temples for reasons of clerical status – when more than a few reside at one temple it's because the teachings there are considered particularly strong.

jewellery, garlands or perfume; sleeping on high beds; and accepting money for personal use.

Monks must follow 227 vows or precepts as part of the monastic discipline. All things possessed by a monk must be offered by the lay community. Upon ordination a new monk is typically offered a set of three orange-yellow robes (lower, inner and outer), costing around 12,000 kip for standard grade cloth of cotton or dacron, a bit more for fancier grades. Other possessions he is permitted include a razor, cup, filter (for keeping insects out of drinking water), umbrella and alms bowl. The latter are usually plain black-lacquered steel bowls; monks carry them in shoulder slings to gather their daily food from householders in their monastery precincts.

In monasteries where discipline is lax, monks accumulate a great deal more than the prescribed requisites. Especially in outlying areas of Laos, eg Luang Nam Tha, monastic discipline has declined to the point where monks can be seen drinking liquor – in full view of the public eye – at religious festivals.

Many monks ordain for a lifetime. Of

Books about Buddhism If you want to learn more about Theravada Buddhism, recommended titles include:

Buddhism Explained by Phra Khantipalo, Trasvin Publications, 1991 (Chiang Mai)
What the Buddha Taught by Walpola Rahula, Motilal Banarsidass, 1971 (Delhi)
Buddhism in Transition by Donald K Swearer, Westminster Press, 1970 (Philadelphia)
Buddhism in the Modern World edited by Heinrich Dumoulin, Macmillan, 1976 (New York)
Buddhism, Imperialism, and War by Trevor Ling, D Reidel Publishing, 1980 (Dordrecht)
World Conqueror and World Renouncer by Stanley Tambiah, Cambridge University Press, 1976 (Cambridge)
Living Buddhist Masters by Jack Kornfield, Buddhist Publication Society, 1989 (Kandy)
The Central Conception of Buddhism by Th Stcherbatsky, Motilal Banarsidass, 1974 (Delhi)
Buddhist Dictionary by Mahathera Nyanatiloka, Island Hermitage Publications, 1950 (Dodanduwa)

Post-1975 Buddhism

During the 1964-73 war years, both sides sought to use Buddhism for their own propaganda purposes. In 1968 the LPF included as part of its platform a resolution:

To respect and preserve the Buddhist religion, the purity and freedom of public worship and preaching by monks, to maintain pagodas, to promote unity and mutual assistance between monks and lay followers of different Buddhist sects...

By the early '70s, the LPF was winning the propaganda war in the religious sphere, as more and more monks threw their support behind the communist cause.

But major changes were in store for the Sangha following the 1975 takeover. Initially, Buddhism was banned as a primary school subject and people were forbidden to make merit by feeding monks. Monks were also forced to till the land and raise animals in direct violation of their monastic vows.

Mass dissatisfaction among the faithful prompted the government to rescind their total ban on the feeding of monks in 1976. The giving of rice only was allowed but still the laity was not satisfied, since it was felt that not much merit was to be obtained from the mere offering of rice (which also meant that monks had to continue the cultivation of the soil). By the end of 1976, the LPDR government was not only allowing the traditional alms-giving, it was offering a daily ration of rice directly to the Sangha. In 1992 the government replaced the hammer-and-sickle emblem which crowned the Lao PDR national seal with a line drawing of Pha That Luang, the country's holiest Buddhist symbol.

The Department of Religious Affairs (DRA) controls the Sangha and ensures that the teaching of Buddhism is in accordance with Marxist principles. All monks now have to undergo political indoctrination as part of their monastic training. All canonical and extra-canonical Buddhist texts have been subject to 'editing' by the DRA, who make sure that everything contained therein is congruent with the development of socialism in Laos. Monks are also forbidden to promote phĭi worship, which has been officially banned in Laos along with sainyasat.

One of the more major changes in Lao Buddhism has been the abolition of the Thammayut sect. Formerly the Sangha in Laos was divided into two sects, the Mahanikai and the Thammayut (as in Thailand). The Thammayut is a minority sect that was begun by Thailand's King Mongkut and patterned after an early Mon form of monastic discipline which the King had practised as a *bhikkhu* (monk). Although the number of precepts or vows followed is the same for both sects, discipline for Thammayut monks has always been more strictly enforced than that of the Mahanikai sect. Thammayut monks are expected to attain proficiency in meditation as well as Buddhist scholarship or scripture-study; the Mahanikai monks typically 'specialise' in one or the other.

The Pathet Lao objected to the Thammayut sect because it was seen as a tool of the Thai monarchy (and hence US imperialism – even though the Thammayut were in Laos long before the Americans were in Thailand) for infiltrating Lao political culture. The LPRP not only banned the Thammayut sect but for a few years even banned all Buddhist literature written in the Thai language. This severely curtailed the availability of Buddhist literature in Laos, since Thailand has always been a major source of religious material – as it has for every other kind of written material. The Thammayut ban has also resulted in a much weaker emphasis on meditation *(vipassana)*, considered the spiritual heart of Buddhist practice in most Theravadin countries. Overall monastic discipline has become a great deal more lax as well.

In Laos nowadays there is only one official sect, the 'Lao Sangha' (Song Lao). Former Thammayut monks have either fled to Thailand or renounced their sectarian affiliation. Whether it is due to this exodus or because of the general strictness of policy, the total number of Buddhist monks in Laos declined between 1975 and 1988. Since the economic liberalisation of 1989 – which has made more donor support available to the temples – the number of monks has revived to pre-1975 levels. The ban on Thai Buddhist texts has been rescinded, and nowadays the government even allows Lao monks to study at Mahachulalongkorn Buddhist University at Wat Mahathat in Bangkok.

Spirit Cults

In spite of the fact that phĭi worship has been officially banned, it remains the dominant non-Buddhist belief system in the country. Even in Vientiane, Lao citizens openly perform the ceremony called *su khwăn* or *basi (baci* in the common French transliteration) in which the 32 guardian spirits known as *khwăn* are bound to the guest of honour by white strings tied around the wrists. Each of the 32 khwăn are thought to be guardians over different organs in a person's body.

Khwăn occasionally wander away from their owner, which isn't thought to be much of a problem except when that person is about to embark on a new project or on a journey away from home, or when they're very ill. Then it's best to perform the basi to ensure that all the khwăn are present and attached to the person's body.

Another obvious sign of the popular Lao devotion to phĭi can be witnessed in Vientiane at Wat Si Muang. The central image at the temple is not a Buddha figure but the *lák meuang* (city pillar), in which the guardian spirit for the city is believed to reside. Many local residents make daily offerings before the pillar.

Outside the Mekong river valley, the phĭi cult is particularly strong among the tribal Thai, especially the Black Thai (Thai Dam), who pay special attention to a class of phĭi called *ten*. The ten are earth spirits that preside not only over the plants and soil, but over entire districts as well. The Black Thai also believe in the 32 khwăn. Măw, who are specially trained in the propitiation and exorcism of spirits preside at important Black Thai festivals and ceremonies.

The Khamu tribes have a similar hierarchy of spirits they call *hrooi*. The most important hrooi are those associated with house and village guardianship. Ceremonies involving hrooi are closed to non-Khamu observers so little has been written about them. During the '60s, some Khamu participated in a 'cargo cult' that believed in the millennial arrival of a messiah figure who would bring them all the trappings of Western civilisation.

The Hmong-Mien tribes also practise

Basi Ceremony

A *măw pháwn* (wish priest) – usually an elder who has spent some time as a monk – presides over the ritual. Those participating in the basi sit on mats around a tiered *phakhuan* (centrepiece), which is decorated with flowers, folded banana leaves and branches with white cotton strings hanging down; pastries, eggs, bananas, liquor and money are placed surrounding the base of the phakhuan as offerings to the spirits in attendance.

After a few words of greeting, the măw pháwn chants in a mixture of Lao and Pali to convey blessings on the honoured guest while all in attendance hold their hands in a prayer-like, palms-together pose. For part of the chanting segment, everyone leans forward to touch the base of the phakhuan; if there are too many participants for everyone to reach the base, it's permissible to touch the elbow of someone who can reach it, thus forming a human chain.

Once the shaman has finished chanting, each person attending takes two of the white strings from the phakhuan and ties one around each wrist of the honoured guest(s) while whispering a short, well-wishing recitation. When all have performed this action, the guest is left with a stack of strings looped around each wrist and small cups of rice liquor are passed around, sometimes followed by an impromptu *lam wong* (circle dance). For the intended effect, the strings must be kept around the wrists for a minimum of three full days. Some Lao hold that the strings should be allowed to fall off naturally rather than cut off – this can take weeks!

Nowadays, the ceremony appears to have become more of a cheerful formality than a serious ritual, but few Lao would dare to undertake a long journey or initiate an important enterprise without participating. ∎

animism, along with ancestral worship. Some Hmong groups recognise a pre-eminent spirit that presides over all earth spirits; others do not. Some Hmong also follow a Christian version of the cargo cult in which they believe Jesus Christ will arrive in a jeep, dressed in combat fatigues. The Akha, Lisu and other Tibeto-Burman groups mix animism and ancestor cults, except for the Lahu, who add a supreme deity called Geusha.

Other Religions

A small number of Lao – mostly those of the remaining French-educated elite – are Christians. Various Christian missionary groups are trying to regain a foothold in Laos; the current Lao constitution, however, forbids religious proselytising or the distribution of religious materials. Foreigners caught distributing religious materials may be arrested and held incommunicado or expelled from the country.

Several Christian groups have tried to evade the law by proselytising in Laos under the guise of English-teaching or other aid work. The author ran into two French missionaries in Udomxai who were involved in the aid scam, pretending to seek a village that needed humanitarian aid help while actually choosing one based on its remoteness from central authority. This practice has made it somewhat more difficult for legitimate English teachers and small NGOs to obtain the proper permits to enter the country, as anyone from a group whose name isn't already known by the authorities to be legitimate is suspected of being a Christian front.

A very small number of Muslims live in Vientiane, mostly Arab and Indian merchants whose ancestry dates as far back as the 17th century. Vientiane also harbours a small Cham community, Cambodian Muslims who fled Pol Pot's Democratic Kampuchea in the '70s. The latter now have their own mosque in Vientiane. In northern Laos there are also pockets of Muslim Yunnanese, known among the Lao as *jʉ̀n háw*.

LANGUAGE
Language Milieu

The official language of the LPDR is Lao as spoken and written in Vientiane. As an official language, it has successfully become the lingua franca between all Lao and non-Lao ethnic groups in Laos. Of course, native Lao is spoken with differing tonal accents and with slightly differing vocabularies as you move from one part of the country to the next, especially in a north to south direction. But it is the Vientiane dialect that is most widely understood.

Modern Lao linguists recognise five basic dialects within the country: Vientiane Lao; northern Lao (spoken in Sainyabuli, Bokeo, Udomxai, Phongsali, Luang Nam Tha and Luang Prabang); north-eastern Lao (Xieng Khuang and Hua Phan), central Lao (Khammuan and Bolikhamsai); and southern Lao (Champasak, Salavan, Savannakhet, Attapeu and Sekong). Each of these can be further divided into subdialects; a distinction between the Lao spoken in the neighbouring provinces of Xieng Khuang and Hua Phan, for example, is readily apparent to those who know Lao well.

All dialects of Lao are members of the Thai half of the Thai-Kadai family of languages and are closely related to languages spoken in Thailand, northern Myanmar and pockets of China's Yunnan and Guangxi provinces. Standard Lao is indeed close enough to Standard Thai (as spoken in central Thailand) that, for native speakers, the two are mutually intelligible. In fact, virtually all speakers of Lao west of the Annamite Chain can easily understand spoken Thai, since the bulk of the television and radio they listen to is broadcast from Thailand. Among educated Lao, written Thai is also easily understood, in spite of the fact that the two scripts differ (to about the same degree that the Greek and Roman scripts differ). This is because many of the textbooks used at the college and university level in Laos are actually Thai texts.

Even closer to Standard Lao are Thailand's northern and north-eastern Thai dialects. North-eastern Thai (also called

Isan) is virtually 100% Lao in vocabulary and intonation; in fact there are more Lao speakers living in Thailand than in Laos. Hence if you are travelling to Laos after a spell in Thailand (especially the north-east), you should be able to put whatever you learned in Thailand to good use in Laos. (It doesn't work as well in the opposite direction; native Thais can't always understand Lao since they've had less exposure to it.)

Script

Prior to the consolidation of various Lao meuang in the 14th century, there was little demand for a written language. When a written language was deemed necessary by the Lan Xang monarchy, Lao scholars based their script on an early alphabet devised by the Thais (which in turn had been created by Khmer scholars who used south Indian scripts as models!). The alphabet used in Laos is closer to the original prototype; the original Thai script was later extensively revised (which is why Lao looks 'older' than Thai, even though it is newer as a written language).

Before 1975 at least four spelling systems were in use. Because modern printing never really got established in Laos (most advanced textbooks being in Thai, French, or Vietnamese before the Revolution), Lao spelling wasn't standardised until after the Pathet Lao takeover. The current system has been highly simplified by omitting all literally transcribed spellings from foreign loan words. Instead of transliterating the Sanskrit *nagara* (city) letter for letter, for example, the new script uses only the letters actually pronounced in Lao, eg, *nakhon*. Hence every letter written is pronounced, which means Lao script can be learned much more quickly than Thai or Khmer, both of which typically attempt to transcribe foreign borrowings letter for letter no matter what the actual pronunciation is.

Other scripts still in use include *láo thám* (dhamma Lao), used for writing Pali scriptures, and various Thai tribal scripts, the most popular and widespread being that of the Thai Neua (which has become standardised via Xishuangbanna, China).

The Lao script today consists of 30 consonants (but only 20 separate 'sounds') and 28 vowel and diphthong possibilities (15 separate 'symbols' in varying combinations). In addition to the consonant and vowel symbols are four tone marks, only two of which are commonly used to create the six different tones (in combination with all the other symbols). Written Lao proceeds from left to right, though vowel-signs may be written before, above, below, 'around' (before, above *and* below), *or* after consonants, depending on the sign. Although learning the alphabet is not difficult, the writing system itself is fairly complex, so unless you are planning a lengthy stay in Laos it should perhaps be foregone in favour of learning actually to speak the language. Names of provinces and towns are given in Lao script beside their respective headings, so that you can at least 'read' the names of destinations in a pinch, or point to them if necessary.

Tones

Basically, Lao is a monosyllabic, tonal language, like various dialects of Thai and Chinese. Borrowed words from Sanskrit, Pali, French and English often have two or more syllables, however. Many identical phonemes or vowel-consonant combinations are differentiated by tone only. Consequently, the word *sao*, for example, can mean 'girl', 'morning', 'pillar' or 'twenty' depending on the tone. For people from non-tonal language backgrounds, it can be very hard to learn at first. Even when we 'know' the correct tone, our tendency to denote emotion, emphasis and questions through tone modulation often interferes with uttering the correct tone. So the first rule in learning and using the tone system is to avoid overlaying your native intonation patterns onto the Lao.

Vientiane Lao has six tones (compared with five in Standard Thai, four in Mandarin and nine in Cantonese). Three of the tones are level (low, mid and high) while three follow pitch inclines (rising, high falling and low falling). All six variations in pitch are relative to the speaker's natural vocal range, so that one person's low tone is not necessarily the same pitch as another person's. Hence, keen pitch recognition is not a prerequisite for learning a tonal language like Lao. A relative distinction between pitch contours is all that is necessary, just as it is with all languages (English and other European languages use intonation, too, just in a different way).

On a visual curve the tones might look like this:

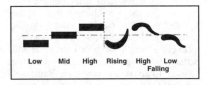

| Low | Mid | High | Rising | High Falling | Low |

- The low tone is produced at the relative bottom of your conversational tonal range – usually flat level (though not everyone pronounces it flat and level – some Vientiane natives add a slight rising tone to the end). Example: *di* (good).
- The mid tone is flat like the low tone, but spoken at the relative middle of the speaker's vocal range. No tone mark is used. Example: *het* (do).
- The high tone is flat again, this time at the relative top of your vocal range. Example: *heúa* (boat).
- The rising tone begins a bit below the mid tone and rises to just at or above the high tone. Example: *sãam* (three).
- The high falling tone begins at or above the high tone and falls to the mid level. Example: *sâo* (morning).
- The low falling tone begins at about the mid level and falls to the level of the low tone. Example: *khào* (rice).

Transliteration

The rendering of Lao words into Roman script is a major problem, since many of the Lao sounds, especially certain vowels, do not occur in English. The problem is compounded by the fact that because of Laos' colonial history, transcribed words most commonly seen in Laos are based on the old colonial French system of transliteration, which bears little relation to the way an English speaker would usually choose to write a Lao word.

A prime example is the capital of Laos, Vientiane. The Lao pronunciation, following a fairly logical English-Roman transliteration, would be Wieng Chan or Vieng Chan (some might hear it more as Wieng Jan). Since the French don't have a written consonant that corresponds to 'w', they chose to use a 'v' to represent all 'w' sounds, even though the 'v' sound in Lao is closer to an English 'w'. The same goes for 'ch' (or 'j'), which for the French was best rendered 'ti-'; hence Wieng Chan (which means Sandalwood City) comes out 'Vientiane' in the French transliteration. The 'e' is added so that the final 'n' sound isn't partially lost, as it is in French words ending with 'n'. This latter phenomenon also happens with words like *lâan* (million) as in Lan Xang, which most French speakers would write as 'Lane', a spelling that leads most English speakers to pronounce this word like thc 'lane' in 'Penny Lane' (which is way off base).

Many standard place names in Roman script use an 'x' for what in English is 's'. This 'x' stands for a Lao letter that historically was proinounced 'ch' but eventually became 's' in Laos. There is no difference in pronunciation of the two; pronounce all instances of 'x' as 's'.

Since there is no official method of transliterating the Lao language (the Lao government is incredibly inconsistent in this respect, though they tend to follow the old French methods), I am basically following the transcription system used in Lonely Planet's *Thailand* guide since the languages have virtually identical phonemes. Elsewhere in this guide, I've used the same system, except in instances where it differs greatly from common transliteration (eg, Vientiane vs Wieng Chan, Luang Prabang vs Luang Phabang).

The public and private sectors in Laos are gradually moving towards a more internationally recognisable system along the lines of the Royal Thai General Transcription (which is fairly readable across a large number of language types). This can also be problematic, however, as when an 'r' is used where an 'h' or 'l' is the actual sound, simply because the Lao symbols for these sounds look so much like the Thai 'r' (modern spoken Lao has no 'r' sound).

Recent government maps have finally started using the spelling 'Luang Phabang' rather than 'Luang Prabang'.

Vowels

◌ິ	i	as in 'it'
◌ີ	i	as in 'feet' or 'tea
ໄ◌ມ ໄ◌	a	as in 'pipe' or 'I'
◌າ	aa	long 'a' as in 'father'
◌ະ	a	half as long as 'a' above
ແ◌	ae	as in 'bat' or 'tab'
ແ◌ະ,ແ◌ອ	e	as in 'hen'
ເ◌	eh	like 'a' in 'hate'
ເ◌ົ,ເ◌	oe	as in 'rut' or 'hut' but more closed
◌ຸ	u	as in 'flute'
◌ູ	uu	as in 'food'
◌ື,◌ຶ	eu	as the 'i' in 'Sir'
ເ◌ົາ	ao	as in 'now' or 'cow'
◌ໍ	aw	as in 'jaw'
ໂ◌ະ,ໂ◌	o	as in 'phone'
ໂ◌	oh	as in 'toe'
ເ◌ຶອ	eua	diphthong of eu and a
◌ຽ◌,ເ◌ັຽ	ie	'i-a' as in the French rien
◌ົວ	ua	'u-a' as in 'tour'
◌ວຍ	uay	'u-a-i' (as in 'Dewey')
◌ິວ,◌ຶວ	iu	'i-u' (as in 'yew')
◌ຽວ	iaw	a triphthong of 'i-a-w' (as the 'io' in 'Rio')
ແ◌ວ	aew	'ae-w'
ເ◌ວ	ehw	'eh-w'
ເ◌ັວ	ew	like ehw, but shorter
ເ◌ີຍ	oei	'oe-i'

Consonants

ກ	k	as the 'k' in 'skin'; similar to 'g' in 'good', but unaspirated and unvoiced
ຂ,ຄ	kh	'k' as in 'kite'; aspirated
ງ	ng	as in 'sing' without the 'si'
ຈ	j	like second 't' in 'stature' or 'literature'; voiceless, unaspirated
ສ,ຊ	s/x	as in 'soap'
ຍ	ny	similar to the 'ni' in 'onion'; used as an initial consonant in Lao
ດ	d	as in 'dodo' or 'dig'
ຕ	t	as the 't' in 'forty'; unaspirated, unvoiced; similar to 'd'
ທ,ຖ	th	't' as in 'tea'; aspirated
ນນ ໝ	n	as in 'nun'
ບ	b	as in 'boy'
ປ	p	as the 'p' in 'stopper'; unvoiced and unaspirated; not like the 'p' in 'put'
ພນ ພ	ph	'p' as in 'put'; never as in 'phone'
ຝນ ຟ	f	as in 'fan'
ມນ ໝ	m	as in 'man'
ຢ	y	as in 'yo-yo'
ລນ ຫລ	l	as in 'lick'
ວ,ຫວ	w	as in 'wing'; often transliterated as 'v
ຮນ ຫ	h	as in 'home'

Greetings & Civiilties

Greetings/Hello.
sábąai-dįi ສະບາຍດີ

Glad to know you.
dįi-jai thii hûu ດີໃຈທີ່ຮູ້
káp jâo ກັບເຈົ້າ

Thank you.
khàwp jại ຂອບໃຈ

And you?
jâo dẹh? ເຈົ້າເດ້

Thank you very much.
khàwp jại lāi lāi ຂອບໃຈຫລາຍໆ

It's nothing. (Never mind/Don't bother.)
baw pẹn nyãng ບໍ່ເປັນຫຍັງ

Excuse me.
khãw thôht ຂໍໂທດ

Small Talk

Are you well?
sábąai-dįi baw? ສະບາຍດີບໍ່ ?

I'm fine.
sábąai-dįi ສະບາຍດີ

What is your name?
jâo seu nyang? ເຈົ້າຊື່ຫຍັງ ?

My name is ...
kháwy seu ... ຂ້ອຍຊື່ ...

Where do you come from?
jâo máa tae sai? ເຈົ້າມາແຕ່ໃສ ?

I come from ...
khǎwy máa tae ... ຂ້ອຍມາແຕ່ ...

How old are you?
jâo ạanyuu ják pịi? ເຈົ້າອາຍຸຈັກປີ ?

I'm ... years old.
khǎwy ạanyuu ... pịi ຂ້ອຍອາຍຸ ...ປີ

Are you married (yet)?
taeng-ngáan lâew ແຕ່ງງານແລ້ວ
lèu baw? ຫລືບໍ ?

Yes, I'm married.
taeng-ngáan lâew ແ ຕ່ງງານແລ້ວ

Not yet.
yáng baw taeng- ຍັງບໍ່ແຕ່ງ
ngáan ງານ

Language Difficulties

Can you speak
English?
jâo páak pháasaa ເຈົ້າປາກພາສາ
ạngkít dâi baw? ອັງກີດໄດ້ບໍ ?

Please speak slowly.
kálunaa wâo ກະລຸນາເວົ້າ
sâa-sâa ຊ້າໆ

Please repeat that.
kálunaa wâo mai ກະລຸນາເວົ້າໃໝ່
boeng dụu ບິ່ງດູ

(I) don't understand.
baw khào jại ບໍ່ເຂົ້າໃຈ

What?
nyāng? ຫຍັງ ?

Getting Around

I want to go to ...
khǎwy yàak pại ... ຂ້ອຍຢາກໄປ ...

Which street/road
is this?
bawn nîi thanon ບ່ອນນຸ້ນີທ
nyāng? ຢັງ ?

What time will
the (boat) leave?
(heúa) já àwk ják ເຮືອຈະອອກຈັກ
móhng? ໂມງ

bus station
sathǎanii lót ສະຖານລົດ
pájạm tháang ປະຈຳທາງ

bus stop
bawn jàwt lot ບ່ອນຈອດລ
pájạm tháang ປະຈຳທາງ

taxi stand
bawn jàwt lot ບ່ອນຈອດລົດແ
thaek-sîi ທກຊີ

I'd like a ticket.
khàwy yàak dâi pịi ຂ້ອຍຢາກໄດ້ປີ້

I'd like two tickets.
khàwy yàak dâi pịi ຂ້ອຍຢາກໄດ້ປີ້
sǎwng bại ສອງໃບ

How much per 'place'
(seat/deck/space, etc)?
bawn-la thao dại? ບ່ອນລະເທົ່າໃດ ?

Directions

Turn ... *lîaw ...* ລ້ຽວ ...
left *sâai* ຊ້າຍ
right *khwǎa* ຂວາ

Go straight ahead.
pại seu-seu ໄປຊື່

How far?
kại thao dại? ໄກເທົ່າໃດ ?

far/not far
kại/baw kại ໄກ / ບໍ່ໄກ

north *thit nēua* ທິດເໜືອ
south *thit tâi* ທິດໃຕ້
wes *thit tạawán* ທິດຕາເວັນ
tók ຕົກ
east *thit tạawán* ທິດຕາເວັນ
àwk ອອກ

Around Town

Can (I/we) change
money here?
pian ngóen yuu nîi ປ່ຽນເງິນຢູ່ນີ້
dâi baw? ໄດ້ບໍ ?

Where is the ... ?
... yùu sǎi? ...ຢູ່ໃສ ?

bank *thanáakháan* ທະນາຄານ
Buddhist *wat* ວັດ
temple
cemetery *baa sâa* ປ່າຊ້າ

cinema	*hóhng nãng*	ໂຮງໜັງ
monument	*ánu-sãa-walíi*	ອະນຸສາວະລີ
museum	*phiphithaphán*	ພິພິທະພັນ
park/garden	*sũan*	ສວນ
post office	*pại-sá-níi*	ໄປສະນີ
	(hóhng sãai)	(ໂຮງສາຍ)
stupa	*thâat*	ທາດ

Accommodation

Do you have a room?
  hàwng baw? — ຫ້ອງບໍ ?

How much per night?
  khéun-la thao dại? — ຄືນລະ ເທົ່າໃດ ?

Can (I/we) look at the room?
  khaw boeng hàwng dâi baw? — ຂໍເບິ່ງຫ້ອງ ໄດ້ບໍ ?

(I/we) will stay two nights.
  si phak sãwng khéun — ຊິພັກຢູ່ສອງ ຄືນ

hotel	*hóhng háem*	ໂຮງແຮມ
guesthouse	*hãw hap kháek*	ທີ່ຮັບແຂກ
air-con	*ạe yẹn*	ແອເຢັນ
bathroom	*hàwng nâam*	ຫ້ອງນ້ຳ
hot water	*nâam hâwn*	ນ້ຳຮອນ
room	*hàwng*	ຫ້ອງ
double room	*hàwng náwn tạang khuu*	ຫ້ອງນອນ ຕຽງຄູ່
single room	*hàwng náwn tạang diaw*	ຫ້ອງນອນ ຕຽງດຽວ

Shopping

How much?
  thao dại? — ເທົ່າໃດ ?

Can you bring the price down?
  lut láakháa dâi baw? — ຫຼຸດລາຄາໄດ້ບໍ ?

What is this made of?
  nîi het dûay nyãng? — ນີ້ເຮັດດ້ວຍຫຍັງ?

Health & Emergencies

Help!
  suay dae — ຊ່ອຍແດ່

Go away!
  pại dọe — ໄປເດີ

I am lost.
  khàwy lõng tháang — ຂ້ອຍຫຼົງທາງ

Call an ambulance!
  suay ôen lot hóhng mãw dae — ຊ່ອຍເອີ້ນລົດໂຮງໝໍ ໃຫແດ່

Call the police!
  suay ôen tam-lùat dae — ຊ່ອຍເອີ້ນຕຳຫຼວດ ແດ່

I need a doctor.
  khàwy tâwng-kạan mãw — ຂ້ອຍຕ້ອງການ ໝໍ

chemist/ pharmacy	*hâan khãai yạa*	ຮ້ານຂາຍ ຢາ
dentist	*mãw pụa khàew*	ໝໍປົວ ແຂວ
hospital	*hóhng mãw*	ໂຮງໝໍ

Days

today	*mêu nîi*	ມື້ນີ້
yesterday	*mêu wáan nîi*	ມື້ວານນີ້
tomorrow	*mêu eun*	ມື້ອື່ນ
Sunday	*wán ạathit*	ວັນອາທິດ
Monday	*wán jạn*	ວັນຈັນ
Tuesday	*wán ạngkháan*	ວັນອັງຄານ
Wednesday	*wán phut*	ວັນພຸດ
Thursday	*wán phahát*	ວັນພະຫັດ
Friday	*wán súk*	ວັນສຸກ
Saturday	*wán são*	ວັນເສົາ

Numbers

0	*sãun*	ສູນ
1	*neung*	ນຶ່ງ
2	*sãwng*	ສອງ
3	*sãam*	ສາມ
4	*sii*	ສີ່
5	*hàa*	ຫ້າ
6	*hók*	ຫົກ
7	*jét*	ເຈັດ
8	*pàet*	ແປດ
9	*kâo*	ເກົ້າ
10	*síp*	ສິບ
20	*sáo*	ຊາວ
30	*sãam-síp*	ສາມສິບ
100	*hâwy*	ຮ້ອຍ
200	*sãwng hâwy*	ສອງຮ້ອຍ
1000	*phán*	ພັນ

Books for Language Study

Lonely Planet publishes a pocket-sized *Lao phrasebook* which contains a complete discussion of Lao grammar and pronunciation along with several chapters organised by situation, eg Around Town, Accommodation, Food, Small Talk and Emergencies. English, Lao script and Roman transliteration accompanies all lists of words and phrases. It's available wherever Lonely Planet books are distributed, and is intermittently sold in Vientiane at Rain Tree Books and the Vientiane Department Store.

The *English-Lao, Lao-English Dictionary* by Russell Marcus (Charles Tuttle Co, Suido 1-chome, 1-6 Bunkyo-chu, Tokyo, Japan) is a handy book to have in Laos. Of course you won't be able to read the Lao-English section, but the English-Lao definitions are fairly extensive and the transliteration is more or less consistent. Transliterated Lao words are also accompanied by tone marks (the authors use numbers for the six tones), which are really necessary for any dictionary or phrasebook to be of real use.

The same company also publishes *Lao for Beginners: An Introduction to the Spoken and Written Language of Laos* by Tatsuo Hoshino and Russell Marcus. This 200-page primer is organised by situations (eg, 'Coming & Going', 'Touring Vientiane', 'Bargaining at the Market'), so the lessons are mostly quite relevant to everyday language use. The primer uses the same transliteration system as the dictionary described above, so the two go together nicely.

A more complete and newer dictionary is the 950-page *Modern English-Lao, Lao-English Dictionary* by Bounmy Soukbandith (contact PO Box 40021, San Diego, CA 92164, USA; or call ☎ (619) 464 3582 for ordering information).

For more serious students, little else is available. Probably the most complete text is the US Foreign Service Institute's *Lao Basic Course, Volumes 1 & 2* (Superintendent of Documents, Washington, DC 20402, USA, 1971). Volume 1 takes students step by step through the rudiments of pronunciation, grammar and writing. Volume 2 is a Lao reader (all written Lao with no translation) for advanced students. Both books are oriented toward pre-1975 Laos, with many references to the monarchy and so on.

Most of the above books can be purchased in Bangkok at Asia Books, Sukhumvit Rd Soi 15 (and several other locations).

Not much is available in Laos. In Vientiane's Phimphone Market you will find the 176-page *Learning Lao for Everybody* by Klaus Werner, a well-organised primer and phrasebook that's a bit costly at US$12 per copy. Since it's a translation of a German phrasebook, the English translations are off in places, though not really enough to hamper use. Another drawback for non-linguists is that transcriptions are made using the International Phonetic Alphabet, a very exact system which only those trained in IPA can read.

In Laos you can also pick up a copy of the little blue *English-Lao Dictionary* published by the State Printing Office and sold for 5000 kip. This pocket-sized tome contains over 10,000 entries; the Lao entries appear in Lao script only.

A draft copy of the *Lao Language Competencies for Peace Corps Volunteers in the LPDR* by Xamini de Abrew and Thong Khamphasinovanh was distributed in Vientiane in December 1991, just before the short-lived US Peace Corps experiment was shut down before it really got started. Only 30 copies were originally made, but a few photocopies are available here and there. You might also try inquiring from the USPC (CHPTO/PACEM, 1990 K St, Washington, DC 20026, USA). This text contains a good selection of structures and vocabulary but some tones are marked incorrectly and there are some minor vocabulary errors (eg, 'younger brother' is glossed as *nâwng são*, which actually means 'younger sister').

In Vientiane's government bookshops you can also purchase children's first-language primers, which aren't a bad way to start for those who will be staying a long time in Laos and want to master the written language.

For information on language courses, see

Lao Language Study under Courses in the Facts for the Visitor chapter.

If you plan to travel extensively in Lao Sung areas, Lonely Planet's *Thai Hill Tribes phrasebook* could be useful.

Other Languages

In the cities and towns of the Mekong river valley, French is intermittently understood. In spite of its colonial history, French remains the official second language of the government and many official documents are written in French as well as Lao. Shop signs sometimes appear in French (alongside Lao, as mandated by law), though signs in English are becoming more common these days. As in Vietnam, the former colonial language is increasingly viewed as irrelevant in a region that has adopted English as the medium of business and trade, and among young Lao students English is now much more popular than French. Among Lao over the age of 45, English is sometimes understood, but to a lesser extent than French.

Many Russian-trained Lao also speak Russian, though the language has drastically fallen from favour. The Russian Cultural Centre now offers more English courses than it does Russian, and the most popular event at the centre is an evening satellite TV programme of English-language shows. The occasional Lao who studied abroad in Cuba or Eastern Europe may be able to speak Spanish, Czech, Polish or Bulgarian.

But it pays to learn as much Lao as possible during your stay in the country, since speaking and understanding the language not only enhances verbal communication but garners a great deal of respect from the Lao you come into contact with.

Facts for the Visitor

PLANNING
When to Go
The best overall time for visiting most of Laos is between November and February – during these months it rains least and is not too hot. If you plan on focusing on the mountainous northern provinces, the early rainy season – say May to July – is not bad either, as temperatures are moderate at higher elevations.

Extensive road travel in remote areas like Attapeu, Phongsali and Sainyabuli may be impossible during the main rainy season, July to October, when roads are often inundated or washed out for weeks, even months at a time. River travel makes a good alternative during these months. If you intend to travel extensively by river November is the best overall month; flooding has usually subsided yet river levels are still high enough for maximum navigability throughout the country. Between January and June boat services on some rivers – or certain portions of some rivers – may be irregular due to low water levels.

Peak months for tourist arrivals are December through February and August, although peak season for Laos is a virtual vacuum compared to, say, Chiang Mai in Thailand or Ho Chi Minh City in Vietnam.

Maps
Good maps of Laos are difficult to find. Lonely Planet has a full-colour *Laos* travel atlas. It has 48 pages and includes topographic shading, a 1:1,000,000 scale and the most up-to-date road and place naming scheme for Laos so far published anywhere. Travellers might find the travel atlases to the adjacent countries of Vietnam and Thailand handy also.

The National Geographic Service (NGS; Kom Phaen Thii Haeng Saat in Lao or Service Géographique National in French) has produced a series of adequate maps of Laos and certain provincial capitals. A simple but relatively accurate and up-to-date 1:1,750,000 scale administrative map of the whole country (labelled in French only as *RDPL Carte Administrative*) was issued by the NGS in 1995 and is available at Raintree Bookstore, the State Book Shop, the Lane Xang Hotel and in some souvenir shops along Thanon Samsenthai. They can also be purchased direct from the National Geographical Service, which is located on a side street to the west of the Patuxai.

The most detailed maps of Laos available – based on Soviet satellite photography from 1981 – were updated for road schemes and place names by the NGS between 1983 and 1986. These topographic maps are labelled in English and French and are often seen on the walls of LPDR government offices. The National Geographic Service reprints many of these maps, and will usually sell them to foreigners in spite of the fact that most are marked *En Secret*.

Occasionally a gift shop in Vientiane will carry a couple of the large NGS 1:5,000,000 scale topo maps which cover the whole country on one sheet. There is also a set of five topo maps with a 1:1,000,000 scale, comparable to the LP Travel Atlas in overall detail though they're about 10 years out of date and each sheet measures 58 cm by 75 cm! More detailed are the 1986 vintage 1:500,000 scale topos, for which there are a total of 11. Only seven of these 11 are available from the NGS, who claim that the missing four are out of print. Other topo maps in the series decrease in scale to as low as 1:10,000, but anything below the 1:100,000 scale maps (for which it takes 176 to cover the whole country!) is overkill unless you're planning to drill an oil well. LP's *Laos* travel atlas or the more general NGS maps are really sufficient for most travel purposes.

The Lao National Tourist Authority (LNTA) now publishes tourist-oriented city maps of Vientiane, Luang Prabang, Tha

Khaek, Savannakhet and Pakse. These are reasonably accurate although not much beyond the larger hotels and government offices are marked on them; they may be purchased at Raintree Bookstore and the State Book Shop on Thanon Setthathirat in Vientiane, as well as at the NGS office. For all maps produced in Laos, including the city maps, the lowest prices are available through the National Geographic Service. Although this office is supposed to be open Monday to Friday 8 to 11.30 am and 2 to 4.30 pm, actual opening hours can be very erratic.

Map collectors or war historians may find American military maps from 1965 – now rather rare though they may still be available from the Defense Mapping Agency in the US – of some interest. These maps seem fairly accurate for topographic detail but they are woefully out of date with regard to road placement and village names. The same goes for the USA's highly touted Tactical Pilotage Charts, prepared specifically for air travel over Laos and virtually useless for modern ground navigation.

What to Bring
Pack light wash-and-wear, natural-fabric clothes, plus a sweater/pullover and a light jacket for chilling evenings and mornings during the height of the cool season (December/January).

Sunglasses are a must for most people and are difficult to find in Laos outside Vientiane. Slip-on shoes or sandals are highly recommended – they are cool to wear and easy to remove before entering a Lao home or temple. A small torch (flashlight) is a good idea, since power blackouts are common. A couple of other handy things are a compass and a fits-all sink plug.

Toothpaste, soap and most other toiletries can be purchased cheaply almost anywhere in Laos. Sunscreen, mosquito repellent, contraceptives and tampons are hard to find, however, so bring enough to last your trip. See the Health section for a list of recommended medical items to bring along.

One more item to bring is a tube of glue for pasting Lao postage stamps – which come without any adhesive backing – to letters and postcards. While all Lao post offices supply glue pots in their lobbies, carrying your own stamps and glue means you'll be able to use public mail boxes during non-business hours.

HIGHLIGHTS
Although Laos is a relatively small country, time and money constraints will compel most of us to decide – either in advance or as we go along – which parts we're going to see and which parts will have to be left out. Because of the lack of travel infrastructure it usually pays to be under-ambitious with one's travel plans. Don't try to see too much in too short an interval, you'll have to get used to waiting around for buses, boats and planes. In Laos none of these forms of transport keep the back-to-back schedules common to public transport modes in most other parts of Asia.

Most visitors begin their journey in Vientiane. Depending on how much time you have available, you might want to save your capital explorations until after you've seen other parts of the country. That way you'll be sure to have plenty of time upcountry in the 'real' Laos.

Historic Architecture & Museums
The former royal kingdoms of Luang Prabang, Vientiane and Champasak offer the most in terms of classic architecture, be it Buddhist temples from the 14th to 19th centuries or French colonial structures from the 19th to 20th centuries. Mysterious Wat Phu, a Khmer site in Champasak Province that may once have been the site of human sacrifices, dates back to the Chenla Kingdom (6th to 8th centuries) and Angkor period (9th to 13th centuries). The enigmatic Plain of Jars near Phonsavan also offers plenty of scope for speculation.

The Lao people are keen to restore older temples, villas and government offices around the country. Colonial architecture is most intact in Luang Prabang, Vientiane, Tha Khaek and Savannakhet. Owing to its rich selection of old temples and French provincial buildings, Luang Prabang was added to

Laos Provinces & Highlights

CHINA

Phongsali

PHONGSALI

VIETNAM

MYANMAR (BURMA)

LUANG NAM THA

Luang Nam Tha

BOKEO

Huay Xai

Muang Xai (Udomxai)

UDOMXAI

Sam Neua

LUANG PRABANG

HUA PHAN

Luang Prabang

XIENG KHUANG

Phonsavan

LUANG PRABANG
UNESCO-listed World Heritage city with 32 temples

PHONSAVAN
The mysterious Plain of Jars

Gulf of Tonkin

THAILAND

Sainyabuli

SAINYABULI

VIENTIANE

VIENTIANE PREFECTURE

Pakxan

BOLIKHAMSAI

SAISOMBUN SPECIAL ZONE

KHAMMUAN

Tha Khaek

SOUTH CHINA SEA

THAILAND

SAVANNAKHET

Savannakhet

VIENTIANE
Pha That Luang (sacred stupa) & Wat Ong Teu's huge bronze Buddha

BOLAVEN PLATEAU
Tribal villages & wildlife

SALAVAN

Salavan

SEKONG

Sekong (Lamam)

WAT PHU CHAMPASAK
Angkor-era ruins

CHAMPASAK

Pakse

ATTAPEU

Attapeu (Samakhi Xai)

DON KHONG
Irrawaddy dolphins and Mekong rapids

CAMBODIA

0   100   200 km

UNESCO's World Heritage List in 1995, joining such cultural and architectural treasures as the Taj Mahal and Angkor Wat.

Laos isn't a great museum destination yet, but historical museums worth seeing include Vientiane's Haw Pha Kaew and Luang Prabang's Royal Palace.

See the Arts section in the Facts about the Country chapter for more information on art styles and archaeological sites.

Handicrafts

Laos' ethnic diversity means a wide range of handicrafts is available for study or purchase throughout the country. Specialities include silverwork, woodcarving, tribal crafts, ceramics, rattan furniture and textiles, nearly all of which can be bought in Vientiane.

North-eastern Laos is famous for Sam Neua-style textiles, which feature rich brocade and dazzling colours. Original silk designs based on these styles are also produced at weaving centres in Vientiane. Simple Lao-style cotton fabrics are abundant in the south near Pakse and Don Khong, while Sekong and Attapeu feature their own styles of weaving unique to the Mon-Khmer tribes in the area.

Hilltribe crafts and jewellery are most abundantly available in Vientiane, though some very interesting work can also be found in Luang Prabang. With some luck, you'll also find good pieces in the heavily tribal provinces of Luang Nam Tha, Phongsali, Hua Phan, Bokeo, Salavan, Sekong and Attapeu. As yet there are few retail outlets in these latter places, so much depends on your initiative in turning up village sources on your own.

For more information on individual handicrafts, see Things to Buy at the end of this chapter.

Culture

Just soaking up the general cultural ambience is one of the main highlights of Laos travel, and is an activity which can be enjoyed almost anywhere in the country. You won't see much Lao culture if you spend most of your time sitting around in guest houses or hanging out in expat restaurants; fortunately these activities are for the most part restricted to Vientiane thus far, so simply leaving the capital will throw you into the real Laos.

For mainstream Lao culture your best venues are towns and villages sited on or near the Mekong river, traditional centres for the lowland Lao. Luang Prabang and the Si Phan Don regions in particular hold fast to older Lao customs. Vientiane and Savannakhet are marching ahead into a transitional mode between the traditional and the modern, though Savan shows far less foreign influence than Vientiane.

Those interested in Hmong-Mien and Thai tribal cultures will want to travel to the far northern provinces of Luang Nam Tha, Bokeo, Udomxai, Phongsali and Hua Phan. The interior of the south – especially Salavan, Sekong and Attapeu provinces – contains lesser known Mon-Khmer tribes, many of which are also encountered in the highlands of Vietnam.

At least once during your trip, try going to a small town well off the main tourist circuit, staying at a local guest house, and eating in Lao rice shops and noodle stands. It's not as easy as going with the crowd but you'll learn a lot about Laos.

Natural Environment

Laos boasts one of the least disturbed ecosystems in Asia due to its overall lack of development and low population density; but, for much the same reason, access to creatures in the wild is limited. With the creation in 1995 of 17 National Biodiversity Conservation Areas, the potential for wildlife observation and other ecotouristic pursuits has increased, but so far visitor facilities in these entities have yet to be developed. As with upcountry hilltribe visits, personal initiative in getting to the source is required. Nongovernmental organisations working in Laos, such as the Wildlife Conservation Society, may be able to offer some guidance to those with sincere interests. Tour agencies in Vientiane may also be able to help, especially if money's no object. Camping gear is a must, as virtually nothing along these lines is available in Laos.

Probably the two most rewarding areas for wilderness travel are the Nakai-Nam Theun NBCA on the Lao-Vietnamese border and the Khammuan Limestone NBCA east of Tha Khaek, both in Khammuan Province. The fauna in these areas – from rare birds to wild elephants – is abundant. For flora, parts of Luang Nam Tha and Hua Phan in the north and Attapeu and Champasak in the south offer plenty of primary monsoon forest.

The area around Si Phan Don – a complex of river islands found at the Mekong river's widest point – is of major interest for its riparian habitats and waterfalls. The southernmost reach of Si Phan Don also serves as a fragile home to the rare Irrawaddy dolphin (see the Si Phan Don section in the Southern Laos chapter for details).

SUGGESTED ITINERARIES

A tourist visa allows only 15 days travel in the country, although this term can be extended another 15 days fairly easily. Second extensions can be a little more difficult to obtain; see Visas further on for a rundown of regulations concerning visas and extensions. It bears re-emphasising that the sometimes unpredictable nature of travel in Laos – whether by road, river or air – means one can't count on sticking to a set itinerary, no matter how well planned.

If you only have a week to spend in Laos you can easily take in all the major sights in Vientiane and Luang Prabang, provided you fly between these two cities. A popular alternative is to enter the country at Huay Xai in Bokeo Province, opposite Chiang Khong, Thailand, and then to make the river run from Huay Xai to Luang Prabang, continuing south to Vientiane by plane. This saves having to backtrack from Luang Prabang to Vientiane.

With a full two weeks you can add side trips north of Vientiane to Vang Vieng and north-east to Xieng Khuang Province. If you want to see a bit of the south, substitute an excursion to the area between Pakse and the Cambodian border, taking in Champasak, Wat Phu and the Si Phan Don area. If Vietnam is next on your schedule, consider entering it by land via Savannakhet and Lao Bao.

A month's sojourn in Laos – which for tourists will require a visa extension – might begin in the north at Huay Xai and trace a loop through Luang Nam Tha around to Luang Prabang and Xieng Khuang, then on to Vientiane for a break from the rigours of Lao surface travel. From Vientiane one can move step by step down the Mekong Valley through the former colonial province capitals of Tha Khaek, Savannakhet and Salavan before heading east to remote Sekong and Attapeu provinces. From the latter you could jog back to the Mekong for a laid-back final few days in Si Phan Don before exiting the country at Chong Mek, Thailand, near Pakse.

The above suggested itineraries assume you want to see as much of the country as possible within a given interval. Another approach would be to spend more time in a few places rather than less time in many. Depending on your inclinations (see Highlights), you might decide to spend a full two weeks or even more just exploring the north. If you're into urban culture, a month spent in the towns and cities of the Mekong Valley could be very rewarding. Vientiane alone is such a pleasant Asian capital that many people find themselves lingering longer than expected.

TOURIST OFFICES

The government-sponsored Lao National Tourist Authority (LNTA) was established in Vientiane in the late 1980s as the sole travel agency and tour operator in the country. Following the privatisation of the travel business in the early '90s, its function as a travel agency has declined substantially although the office can still arrange tours and guides for travel around the country. Its private competitors (see Tours in the Getting Around chapter) do a much better job, however.

The LNTA's top officials organise endless meetings and seminars to discuss the future of tourism in Laos but in actual fact they wield very little power and as a governing body the office is ineffectual. The LNTA is also supposed to serve as a clearing house on Lao travel information but in this arena as well they are not able to offer much due to lack of funds and adequately trained personnel. I've noticed a slight increase in the amount of info available at the office over the last two years, but not enough to recommend it as a general information source.

To give an example of LNTA's lack of information and inability to communicate with outside provinces, LNTA officials assured me that the Vieng Xai caves in Hua Phan were open to all visitors and that no special permits were necessary for cave entry. Upon arrival in Vieng Xai a few days later the local Vieng Xai officials refused to let me even *look* at the outside of the caves and said a visit would require special permission from Vientiane.

The bottom line is that you're better off going just about anywhere else in Vientiane *but* the LNTA if you're seeking accurate, up-to-date information on travel in Laos. The LNTA do not supply information by mail and do not maintain any overseas offices. In a few provincial capitals you may find nominal LNTA offices staffed by lone individuals whose major function seems to be extorting money from tour groups visiting the province; the general lack of information at these local offices can be profound.

One of LNTA's main functions nowadays seems to be arranging Tourist Visa extensions; all applicants who visit the immigration department in Vientiane are now referred to the LNTA.

The head office (☎ /fax 212013) is on Thanon Lan Xang opposite the Centre du Langue Française.

VISAS & DOCUMENTS
Passport
Entry into Laos requires a passport valid for at least three months from the time of entry. If you anticipate your passport may expire while you're in Laos, you should obtain a new one before arrival or enquire from your government whether your embassy in Laos (if one exists – see the list of Embassies further on) can issue a new one after arrival.

Visas
Visas for foreigners who want to visit the LPDR are of the types given below. For all types of visas, the Lao Embassy requires that the official one-page visa application form be filled out in triplicate and submitted along with three passport photos and the appropriate fee. When applying from outside South-East Asia, you should allow at least two months for the visa process. This is because for all visas the embassies must await approval from authorities in Laos before they can issue them. In South-East Asia, the process is much faster – for no apparent reason, since in any case all the embassy has to do is phone or telex Vientiane for approval.

Tourist Visa Most travellers to Laos will be going on a Tourist Visa and in most countries you are required to apply for your visa through an authorised travel agency. There is no longer a requirement that you purchase a package tour for Laos in order to obtain a

visa, although some unscrupulous travel agencies may tell you this is still so.

The only way to find out whether you must go through a travel agency or not in any given country is to inquire at the local Lao embassy. In Yangon (Myanmar) and Phnom Penh (Cambodia) for example, you can pick up a Tourist Visa directly from the Lao embassy in just a day or two for US$12 to 15. In most other countries you will be directed to a local travel agency where the visa arrangements may cost up to five times this amount. In the latter case the agencies take care of all visa procedures, so you won't be getting directly involved with Lao embassies at all.

In Thailand you can easily arrange Lao visas through travel agencies in Bangkok, Chiang Mai, Nong Khai, Chiang Khong, Udon Thani and Ubon Ratchathani. Costs range from 1500 to 2700B depending on the agency and on the speed of visa delivery. Generally speaking the cheaper services take up to five business days to issue a visa, while the more expensive services usually provide one within 24 hours or less.

Major exceptions include Chiang Khong and Chiang Mai, where travel agencies can arrange visas in one to three days. Lao Aviation in Chiang Mai can arrange visas in conjunction with air tickets from Chiang Mai to Vientiane; the visa costs 1500B and is ready in three days. In Vietnam visas are available only from agencies in Hanoi and Ho Chi Minh City, at comparable cost. Occasionally one hears of a Vietnamese travel agency issuing a 'cheap' Lao visa for only US$25 or so.

A persistent rumour going round Vientiane says the government has been considering a change in regulations wherein a Tourist Visa could be granted upon arrival at Wattay Airport (variations on the rumour said the visas would be issued at any certified border crossing).

Visit, Non-Immigrant & Business Visas
The Visit Visa is good for up to 30 days and is the type usually issued to family or friends of foreigners who are working in Laos.

Expatriates in Laos must apply on their relative's or friend's behalf from within the country. The application fee for this visa is US$35. It is extendible for a second 30 days.

A person who has a short-term professional or volunteer assignment in Laos is generally issued a Non-Immigrant Visa that is good for 30 days and extendible for another 30 days. As with the Visit Visa, the application fee is US$35.

Journalists can apply for the Journalist Visa, which has the same restrictions and validity as the Non-Immigrant and Visit visas except that the applicant must also fill in a biographical form.

Business Visas, also good for 30 days, are relatively easy to obtain as long as you have a sponsoring agency in Laos. Many brokers in Vientiane (and a few in Thailand) can arrange such visas with one to two weeks advance notice. The visa fee itself costs 300B (US$12) at the Lao Embassy in Bangkok, though brokers charge a fee on top of that to cover the cost of paperwork and the expense of telexing the Lao Embassy in Bangkok. Business Visas can be extended from month to month indefinitely, although you will need a visa broker or travel agency to handle the extensions. After the first month's extension, the Business Visa can be converted to multiple-entry status, allowing you to leave and re-enter Laos as many times as you wish within the stated validity dates. Six-month Business Visas are also available.

While Non-Immigrant and Business Visas may be collected in one's home country, the Lao Embassy in Bangkok is a better place to pick them up since the staff are in daily contact with the appropriate ministries in Vientiane. Simply make sure that your sponsoring agency in Laos sends a confirmation telex or fax to the Bangkok embassy; if you can present the telex number or fax date to the embassy they'll be able to locate your telex/fax and issue your visa more quickly.

Transit Visa The Transit Visa is the easiest of all the visas to get but is the most restricted. It is intended for stopovers in Vientiane for people travelling between two other countries. It's common to ask for such a visa when travelling between Hanoi and Bangkok (either direction), for example. The visa is granted on the spot upon presentation of a confirmed ticket between the two places and a visa for the country of final destination. The maximum length of stay for the Transit Visa is 10 days, with no extension allowed. Some embassies and consulates abroad only offer five or seven days, in which case you may have to request the maximum 10 in advance. No travel outside Vientiane Province is permitted on this visa. The fee for this visa is usually US$10 to US$12.

Visa Extensions

Tourist Visas issued through a travel agency abroad usually come with notes scribbled alongside them that limit the Tourist Visa holder to applying through a specified travel agent in Vientiane for visa extensions. If you obtained your Tourist Visa directly from a Lao embassy abroad, you should theoretically be able to extend your visa at any immigration office in Laos. In actual practice only a few offices – usually the more remote ones – will grant extensions. As of this writing, the Luang Prabang immigration office was no longer granting Tourist Visa extensions; in Luang Nam Tha, Attapeu and several other of the more remote areas extensions were readily available. In some of these areas an extension is available even if your visa was arranged by a travel agency.

The cost of an extension is highly variable depending on the level of corruption at the particular agency or immigration office with which you're dealing. In most cases the procedure is worked out so that the extracted fees are split between the travel agencies and the government officials involved. In Vientiane the immigration office was referring all applicants to the LNTA office on Thanon Lan Xang, where an extension could be arranged with an hour's worth of paperwork and a cost of US$3 a day. Some travel agencies were charging US$4 to US$5 per day. In the provinces the immigration offices usually charge US$1 a day although some asked for more. Many travellers have reported being able to negotiate the extension fee downwards.

A second or even third extension of up to 15 days is possible from most sources though some immigration offices upcountry have been known to balk at the idea. In such cases you can usually arrange to pay a small 'fine' to smooth things along. In this manner you could extend a Tourist Visa almost indefinitely though it usually comes down to a question of how much you can afford to continue spending. If you anticipate needing to stay more than a month in Laos, you should investigate the possibility of obtaining a Non-Immigrant Visa or a Business Visa.

Visit Visas, Non-Immigrant Visas, Journalist Visas and Business Visas must be extended through the sponsoring person or organisation. In these cases the extension fee is also highly variable; for consulting agencies the fee may be comparable to the fees charged for Tourist Visa extensions, though for long-term visitors – those staying more than a month – the fees are usually more reasonable.

The Transit Visa cannot be extended under any circumstances.

Overstaying Your Visa If you overstay your visa, you will have to pay a fine at the immigration checkpoint upon departure from Laos. The standard fine at the moment is US$5 for each day you've stayed beyond the visa's expiry date. Obviously if your sponsoring agency is asking US$5 per day for a visa extension, you may as well overstay and pay the equal fine upon exit, saving yourself the paperwork and hassle of dealing with an extension. Before attempting this, however, be sure to check with immigration as to the latest regulations regarding overstays; penalties could increase at any time.

Photocopies

It's a good idea to keep photocopies of all vital documents – passport data page, credit card numbers, airline tickets, travellers' cheque serial numbers and so on – in a separate place from the originals. In case you lose the originals, replacement will be much easier to arrange if you can provide issuing agencies with copies. You might consider leaving extra copies of these documents with someone at home or in a safe place in Vientiane.

Travel Restrictions

For nearly 20 years following the 1975 revolution, the Lao government required travel permits *(bai anuyâat dọen tháang* in Lao or *laissez passer* in French) for all travel outside Vientiane Prefecture. Both foreigners and Lao citizens were required to carry them. In March 1994 the permit system was abolished and foreigners are now theoretically free to travel throughout most of the country without any special permission other than a valid passport containing a valid visa.

When the Lao government made the announcement they said a few places might still be off limits to foreigners, but so far they still haven't announced where these places are! Repeated enquiries to the LNTA have yielded no guidelines, and no-one else in Vientiane seems willing to risk a definitive answer on this topic either. The only way to find out for sure is to try going yourself or to ask other travellers who have been around the country.

Recent travel experience suggest that local permits may still be required in areas where there's considerable undetonated ordnance (eg the Ho Chi Minh Trail) and in 'sensitive' areas like Sainyabuli (insurgents, opium), Hua Phan (re-education camps, the Pathet Lao caves) and most of all in the new Saisombun Special Zone – what used to be eastern Vientiane Province at the borders of Luang Prabang, Xieng Khuang and Bolikhamsai provinces. The latter area is militarily insecure and is plagued by attacks on vehicles passing through; for more see the Dangers & Annoyances section.

Some of the more 'remote' provinces like Sekong, Attapeu and Hua Phan are still run like independent fiefdoms by the local police, and in these areas travellers may occasionally come across officials who bar

Tourism Policy in Laos

Many Lao National Tourist Authority officials (supported by local and international package tour companies) would most prefer to see tourism in Laos become a sort of private club to which only wealthy tourists can gain membership. They hold the perspective that a policy of unrestricted individual entry into Laos would result in 'cultural pollution'. They also claim that the country will derive maximum economic benefit from restricted, preferably package, tourism.

Although officials seem genuinely more concerned about dignity and security than tourist dollars, the intention to screen tourists using monetary criteria seems a bit misguided to anyone who has followed world tourism trends. For one thing it tends to narrow the visiting segment to people whose socio-economic status is probably least sympathetic to the Lao political system. From the perspective of the dedicated traveller, the exclusive approach tends to insulate tourists from the people and culture of Laos. Travellers who have seen the country since the retraction of the travel permit system in 1994 say that the Lao they meet along the way are practically unanimous in their preference for the individual (as opposed to the package) tourist. This is not to say that package tourism is bad per se – they're great for busy people with more money than time – it's just that if it's the *only* form of leisure travel allowed it tends to undermine the very premise of tourism as an economic development tool.

When travellers move through the country on their own, the average Lao peasant or small tradesperson derives more of a monetary benefit than when pre-arranged package tours hurry through with hired guides and prepaid accommodation, meals and transport. This has been substantiated repeatedly in empirical studies carried out by researchers in the field of world tourism. Such research clearly demonstrates a significant difference in the economic and sociocultural impact between 'institutionalised, conventional, mass tourism' and 'noninstitutionalised, low-budget, modern youth tourism'. Even when the gross foreign exchange effect per destination of a youth/budget tourist is lower than that of a conventional mass tourist, primary domestic and primary national income effect tends to be equal or higher because of lower leakages from the local and national economy.

Big-spending tourists bring in a lot of money but they also demand more imported goods, which reduces local income and has greater cultural impact. Rather than using money to screen visitors the Lao tourism sector might attempt – through an appropriate public relations campaign – to screen for attitude and behaviour, and to develop infrastructure and attractions that lure people who are sensitive to cultural differences and respect local traditions. By limiting visitors to those from high socio-economic levels or on package tours the government may unwittingly be promoting the rise of large-scale, low-return tourism.

As to the question of cultural integrity, it would seem that the parading of wealthy tourists through such a comparatively undeveloped country creates more of an obvious sociocultural disparity than allowing individuals of varying economic backgrounds the chance to interact with the people on a more natural basis. On the other hand, such one-to-one contact could lead to subversive' thinking, in the perception of the Lao government, so perhaps freedom of thought is the real issue here. Current research in world tourism suggests that the presence of an expatriate elite (something Laos has plenty of in the form of UN, NGO and diplomatic staff) typically has more of a sociocultural impact than all other types of non-military foreign presence.

At any rate Lao officials seem to be more aware – or more conscientious – than the Thais or the Vietnamese about the trade-offs between the quality of life and the income you get from marketing culture and the natural environment. The current policy – whatever its ultimate effect – shows they're at least somewhat concerned with developing a sustainable tourism market rather than letting millions of visitors in to 'use up' the attractions. ■

---

entry. In such cases it's best simply to obey the orders of the police and head in the opposite direction; it's no use arguing with people who have the power to incarcerate you indefinitely without trial.

Checkpoints The Lao government still has one major way of keeping track of your whereabouts. Each time you enter and leave a province – whether by land, air or water – you must stop at a customs or police office and get *jâeng khào* and *jâeng àwk* ('inform enter' and 'inform leave') rubber stamps on your departure card or on a slip of blank paper provided by the checkpoint officials. The police usually collect a charge for this service, anywhere from 100 to 1500 kip per chop.

If you do much interprovincial travel in Laos, the little paper slips fill up quickly with red and black visa stamps. Failing to get stamped in or out seems to be a fairly minor offence in most places. The main risk is being sent back to a place you've already been; for example, if you've just spent all day on a truck from Muang Xai (capital of Udomxai) to Pakbeng – an official exit point for boat travel from Udomxai to Luang Prabang or Bokeo – being sent back to Muang Xai would be a major inconvenience.

Every airport in the country has a desk or booth where officials check arriving and departing passengers in and out of the province, so if you're flying it's easy to comply with regulations. For road and river travel there are very few controls in most places and local officials don't seem to care whether you're stamped in or not. In fact it can be very difficult to locate anyone who will give you the necessary chops. A major exception is Luang Prabang where there has recently been an all-out effort to 'capture' as many unstamped visitors as possible in order to collect a 3000 kip penalty. See the Luang Prabang section for details on how the police try to entrap visitors.

It's worth keeping abreast of the general trends regarding interprovincial stamps. As with visa extensions, it's an area that remains very fluid. The future will most likely be determined by local officials who scheme to collect as much money as possible through chop fees and penalties.

Onward Tickets
Unlike many countries, Laos makes no effort to ensure you possess onward flight tickets upon entry to the country. Most visitors arrive by land or river.

Travel Insurance
As when travelling anywhere in the world a good travel insurance policy is a wise idea. Travel insurance is a way to regain your money if your flights are cancelled, for example. Read the small print in any policy to see if hazardous activities are covered or if certain countries are not covered by the policy. Laos is generally considered a high-risk area.

If you undergo medical treatment in Laos or Thailand, be sure to collect all receipts and copies of the medical report, in English if possible, for your insurance company.

Driving Licence & Vehicle Insurance
An international driving permit is necessary for any visitor who intends to drive a motorised vehicle while in Laos. Anyone staying beyond 30 days is supposed to obtain a Lao driving licence issued by Vientiane municipality's Vehicle Control Office, situated at the corner of Thanons Setthathirat and Sakarin. Upon presentation of a valid driving licence from your home country or a valid international driving permit, plus the filling out of some papers and payment of fees, the Lao licence will be issued automatically. If you don't already possess a valid driving licence or permit you'll have to take a written driving test; these are available in English, French, Lao and Chinese. A temporary three-month licence will be followed by a permanent one which is valid indefinitely.

Third-party insurance is required for all vehicles, including motorcycles. Only one company in Laos is authorised to sell such insurance: Assurances Generales du Laos (☎ 215903, fax 215904), That Dam Place, Vientiane. Other documents which should be carried with the vehicle include road tax papers and a current registration sticker, both issued twice yearly. These may be kept up to date through the Vehicle Control Office. For hired vehicles, all of these documents should be supplied by the owner.

Marriage Permits
No matter what type of visa they hold, foreign residents must have the approval of both the Ministry of Interior and Ministry of Foreign Affairs before they can legally marry a Lao citizen. Without such approval any foreigner who marries (or cohabits with) a Lao citizen is subject to arrest and confiscation of passport. Of late marriage permits have been very difficult to obtain.

EMBASSIES
Lao Embassies Abroad

If you're obtaining your visa through a travel agency, you won't deal directly with any Lao embassies, since the agencies handle all visa arrangements. To apply for a visa on your own, you can try one of these embassies or consulates:

Australia
> 1 Dalman Crescent, O'Malley, Canberra, ACT 2606 (☎ (06) 286-4535)

Cambodia
> 1517 Thanon Keomani, Phnom Penh (☎ 26441)

China
> 11 E 4th St, Sanlitun, Chao Yang, Beijing (☎ 5321224)
> Consulate: N 23 Haigeng Rd, Rm 501, Kunming (☎ 4141678)

Germany
> Amlessing 6, 5330 Koenigswinter 1, Bonn (☎ 23925)

France
> 74 Av Raymond Poincare, 75116 Paris (☎ 45 53 02 98)

India
> Friends Colony East, New Delhi 110065 (☎ 634013)

Japan
> 3-21, 3-Chome, Nishi Azabu, Minato-ku, Tokyo (☎ 5411-2291)

Malaysia
> Jalan Bellamy, 50460 Kuala Lumpur (☎ 2483895)

Mongolia
> 27 Stalin Ave, 2nd Floor, Apartment 10-11, Ulan Baatar (☎ 26440)

Myanmar
> A1 Diplomatic Headquarters, Tawwin (Fraser) Rd, Yangon

Russian Federation
> Ul Katchalova 18, Moscow 121069 (☎ 2031454)

Sweden
> Nornsgatan 82-B, 1 TR, 11721 Stockholm

Thailand
> 520, 502/1-2 Soi Ramkhamhaeng 39, Bang Kapi, Bangkok (☎ 5396667)

USA
> 2222 S St NW, Washington, DC 20006 (☎ 6670058)

Vietnam
> 22 Tran Binh Trong, Hanoi (☎ 52271)
> Consulate: 181 Hai Ba Trung, District 3, Ho Chi Minh City (☎ 299272)

Foreign Embassies in Laos

Seventy-five nations have diplomatic relations with Laos, of which around 25 maintain embassies and consulates in Vientiane (many of the remainder, for example Canada and UK, are served by their embassies in Bangkok, Hanoi or Beijing). The addresses and telephone numbers of the principal consular offices are listed below and several of the more important ones (embassies that Lonely Planet readers are likely to visit) are indicated on the Vientiane map.

Australia
> Thanon Phonxai Noi (☎ 413610, 413805)

Cambodia
> Thanon Saphan Thong Neua (☎ 314952)

China
> Thanon Wat Nak Yai (☎ 315103)

France
> Thanon Setthathirat (☎ 215528, 215259)

Germany
> Thanon Sok Pa Luang 26 (☎ 312111, 312110)

India
> Thanon That Luang (☎ 413802)

Indonesia
> Thanon Phon Kheng (☎ 413910)

Japan
> Thanon Sisangvon (☎ 212623, 414002)

Malaysia
> Thanon That Luang (☎ 414205)

Mongolia
> Thanon Tha Deua Km 2 (☎ 315220)

Myanmar (Burma)
> Thanon Sok Pa Luang (☎ 314910)

North Korea
> Wat Nak, Muang Sisattanak (☎ 315261)

Russia
> Tha Palonxai (☎ 312219)

Sweden
> Thanon Sok Pa Luang (☎ 315018, 315000)

Thailand
> Thanon Phon Kheng (☎ 214582, 214585)

USA
> Thanon That Dam (Bartholomie) (☎ 212580, 212581)

Vietnam
> Thanon That Luang (☎ 413400, 413409)

CUSTOMS

Customs inspections at ports of entry are very lax as long as you're not bringing in more than a moderate amount of luggage. You're not supposed to enter the country with more than 500 cigarettes or one litre of distilled spirits. All the usual prohibitions on drugs, weapons and pornography apply, otherwise you can bring in just about anything you want, including unlimited amounts of Lao and foreign currency.

Border officials didn't start handing out customs declaration forms until 1993 – and typically no one bothers to check them when you leave the country.

MONEY
Costs
Except for the high rates travel agencies charge to arrange visas, Laos is a relatively inexpensive country to visit by most standards.

Six years ago hotel rates in Vientiane were among the highest in South-East Asia relative to the quality of rooms and service available but in the last few years a number of less expensive places to stay in the cities have become available, with rates starting at around US$5 a night. Outside Vientiane basic local hotels and guest houses typically charge 1000 to 2000 kip per bed, nicer places 5000 to 8000 kip. Tourist hotels range from around US$25 a night to a high of US$65 or so.

The average meal in a Lao restaurant costs less than US$2 per person. A cup of coffee costs about US$0.21, a huge bowl of *fõe* (rice noodles) around US$0.53 upcountry or US$0.75 in Vientiane, and a litre of draught beer just US$0.70.

Bus transport averages around US$0.12 to US$0.28 per km depending on road conditions; the worse the road, the more expensive the ride. Flying cuts into your budget but over long hauls saves time and thus hotel and food costs. Sample fares: Vientiane to Luang Prabang US$46, Luang Prabang to Xieng Khuang US$31, Vientiane to Pakse US$95.

Estimating a per diem cost for Laos is difficult since it depends on how much you try to see, whether you travel by road, river or air and whether you choose to stay in hotels with air-conditioning and hot water. In Vientiane or Luang Prabang you can squeeze by for about US$10 a day if you stay in the cheaper guest houses and eat local food; in remote areas where everything's less expensive you can whittle this figure down to

around US$6 to 8 a day. Budgets for those who need air-con, hot water and *falang* (foreign) food leap to around US$25 per day minimum if you economise, as much as US$60 for top-end hotels and food. Of course you can spend even more if you stay in the best suites in the best hotels and eat at the most expensive restaurants in town, although such a scenario exists only in Vientiane, Luang Prabang and Pakse for the moment.

Currency
The official national currency in the LPDR is the kip. Although only kip is legally negotiable in everyday transactions, in reality the people of Laos use three currencies for commerce: kip, Thai baht and US dollars. In larger towns such as Vientiane, Luang Prabang, Pakse and Savannakhet, baht and US dollars are readily acceptable at most business establishments, including hotels, restaurants and shops.

In smaller towns and villages kip or baht may be preferred. The rule of thumb is that for everyday small purchases, prices are quoted in kip. More expensive goods and services (eg, long-distance boat hire) may be quoted in baht, while just about anything costing US$100 or more (eg, tours, long-term car rental) is usually quoted in US dollars. This is largely due to the relative portability of each currency (see the following Changing Money section).

In spite of the supposed illegality of foreign currency usage, a three-tier currency system remains firmly in place. In keeping with the local system, prices in this guidebook may be given in kip, baht or US dollars depending on how they were quoted at the source.

Kip notes come in denominations of one, five, 10, 20, 50, 100, 500 and 1000 kip. Notes smaller than 50 kip are rarely seen, however. Kip *aat* (coins) were once available but are being withdrawn from circulation since anything below one kip is virtually worthless.

Laos has no restrictions on the amount of money you exchange upon entry.

Changing Money

Relative to most currencies, the kip has held fairly steady since 1990, even increasing in value against the dollar a bit between 1990 and 1993. During late 1994 an overheated economy led to a surplus of hard currency, which resulted in a deflation of around 200 kip per dollar. At the moment the bank rate per dollar purchased is 923 kip, with parallel market rates reaching as high as 950 kip. Though no one can say for sure, financial observers predict the kip will hit the 1000 mark over the next year or so. Some comparative rates are:

Country	Currency		kip
Australia	A$1	=	677
Canada	C$1	=	653
Germany	DM1	=	648
France	FFr1	=	180
Hong Kong	HK$1	=	81.16
Japan	¥	=	9
Switzerland	SFr	=	795
Thailand	B1	=	36.9
UK	UK£1	=	1420
USA	US$1	=	925

With some exceptions the best exchange rates are available at banks rather than moneychangers. At banks, travellers' cheques receive a slightly better exchange rate than cash. Banks in Vientiane can change UK pounds, German marks, Canadian, US and Australian dollars, French francs, Thai baht and Japanese yen. Outside of Vientiane most provincial banks will accept only US dollars or baht.

In 1995 the best overall exchange rate was that offered at the Banque pour le Commerce Extérieur Lao (BCEL; Thanaakhaan Kaan Khaa Daang Pathet Lao in Lao, or Lao Foreign Trade Bank in English). The LFTB takes a 0.09% commission on dollar-to-kip and baht-to-kip changes, or 0.04% commission in the reverse direction. By contrast, foreign banks may take up to a US$2 commission on each US$100 changed.

Licensed moneychangers also maintain booths around Vientiane (including the Talaat Sao or Morning Market) and at some border crossings. Without exception their rates and commissions are not as good as the exchange at LFTB or other banks; their only advantage is being open longer hours.

Outside of Vientiane and Luang Prabang it can be difficult to change travellers' cheques; even at Wattay Airport the moneychanger is sometimes short of kip (be sure to ask whether they can cover your cheque(s) before signing). Hence visitors are advised to carry plenty of cash outside Vientiane. If you plan to carry baht and US dollars along for large purchases (as is the custom), be sure to arrange your cash stash in these currencies before you leave the capital. Even in Luang Prabang, the most touristed town in Laos after Vientiane, it is impossible to get anything but kip at the bank.

Parallel Market Rates Officially the kip is a free-floating currency but in reality higher rates than those offered by licensed banks are usually available from retail shops and non-licensed, freelance moneychangers in Vientiane. Typically these rates run about 20 to 25 kip more per dollar – with no commission – for crisp US$100 or B1000 notes. This represents a gain over the official rate of about 2700 kip per each US$100 changed – the price of a meal and a beer at most Lao restaurants.

The row of unofficial moneychangers seen inside Vientiane's Morning Market (Talaat Sao) a few years ago are now gone, but near the market you will find a few clumps of moneychangers sitting on wooden stools beneath umbrellas. These generally offer the best overall rates for baht or US dollars. Once you've established an exchange rate with these moneychangers (beforehand you should have a thorough knowledge of the current bank rates), be sure to count your kip *before* handing over your dollars or baht. This way if there's any dispute or misunderstanding as to the count or the rate you can always back out of the deal. So far the sleight-of-hand short-changing scams practised in some other countries don't seem to be a problem in Laos, but you should change with caution

Cash Strategies

As part of the 'baht bloc' (along with Thailand, Vietnam, Cambodia and Myanmar), Laos relies most heavily on the Thai baht for the domestic cash economy. An estimated one-third of all cash circulating in Vientiane, in fact, bears the portrait of the Thai king. This proportion has increased slightly following the recent issuance of the 1000 baht note, which takes the place of 37,000 kip. Five 1000 baht notes – about US$200 worth- – are quite a bit easier to carry around than 185 1000-kip notes, clumped in bundles of ten by the bank!

Hence if you plan on making major transactions (eg, over US$40 each) you can save luggage space by carrying most of your cash in baht, along with smaller amounts of kip and dollars. A workable plan would be to carry half your cash in baht and a quarter each in kip and US dollars. But if you plan to make only small purchases (under US$40 per transaction) and you won't be travelling more than a few days, carry kip.

Toward the end of a lengthy trip it's best to spend all your kip and put aside some baht for your return to Thailand. Once you cross the Mekong no one – except perhaps other travellers on their way into Laos – will want your kip.

Credit Cards

Many hotels, upscale restaurants and gift shops in Vientiane accept Visa and MasterCard credit cards. A few also accept American Express; the national representative for Amex is Diethelm Travel Laos.

BCEL on Thanon Pangkham offers cash advances/withdrawals on MasterCard credit/debit cards for a 2% transaction fee if you take kip, 2.3% to get baht or 3% for US dollars. For Visa the BCEL adds a further half percent to the foregoing rates. Thai banks in Vientiane, eg Thai Farmer's Bank, Siam Commercial Bank and Bangkok Bank, tend to collect up to US$5 per Visa or MasterCard exchange transaction as a 'communication charge' for this service. Depending on the amount you're planning to exchange, you should be able to make a saving with one or other of these bank schemes.

Outside of Vientiane credit cards are virtually useless. At the time of writing Luang Prabang's Phu Vao Hotel and Pakse's Champa Residence were the only upcountry hotels which would accept Visa for room and restaurant charges.

Banking

Foreign residents of Laos are permitted to open US dollar, baht or kip accounts at several banks in Vientiane, including branches of six Thai banks. Unfortunately, if you already have an account at a Thailand-based branch of one of the latter banks, you won't be permitted to withdraw any money in Laos; you must open a new account. As of 1995 typical savings account interest rates were 3% for US dollars, 5% for baht and 12% for kip.

Most banks in Laos are open from 8.30 to 4 pm Monday to Friday.

A number of expatriates living in Vientiane maintain accounts at Thai banks across the river in Nong Khai because interest charges are higher (eg, 6 to 8% for baht) and because more services – such as wire transfers – are available. Once a month or so they simply tuk-tuk down to Tha Deua, hop a ferry to Nong Khai and take care of any financial chores. To do this, of course, you must have a multiple-entry visa.

Tipping

Tipping is not customary in Laos except in upscale Vientiane restaurants where 10% of the bill is appreciated – but only if a service charge hasn't already been added to the bill.

Bargaining

Good bargaining, which takes practice, is one way to cut costs. Anything bought in a market should be bargained for; in some shops prices are fixed while in others bargaining is expected (the only way to find out is to try).

In general the Lao are gentle and very scrupulous in their bargaining practices. A fair price is usually arrived at quickly with little attempt to gouge the buyer (some tour operators are an exception to this rule).

Remember there's a fine line between bargaining and niggling – getting hot under the collar over 100 kip (about US$0.14) makes both seller and buyer lose face.

Transportation between cities and within them is very reasonable; again, bargaining (when hiring a vehicle) can save you a lot of kip. See the Getting Around chapter later in this book for more information.

POST & COMMUNICATIONS
Postal Rates

Postage from Laos is reasonable in price, although most people who plan to send parcels overseas wait until they return to Thailand since the Thai postal service is more reliable.

Lao stamps are printed in Cuba and Vietnam – most come without glue so you must use your own or take advantage of glue pots provided at every post office. Sample letter rates (in kip):

Weight (g)	Thailand	Australia	Europe	USA
up to 10	200	275	285	330
10 to 20	210	330	350	430
20 to 30	490	690	720	850

Parcels weighing under 300g start at 3000 kip for a parcel to Europe, up to 8000 kip for a one kg parcel to America.

Sending & Receiving Mail

Outgoing mail is fairly reliable and inexpensive. The safe arrival of incoming mail is less certain, especially for packages. Express Mail Service (EMS) or *páisánii duan phisèht* is available to 28 countries and is considered more reliable than regular mail. When posting any package – even small padded mailers – you must leave the package open for inspection by a postal officer. Incoming parcels must also be opened for inspection; there is a charge of around 800 kip for this mandatory 'service'.

The GPO in Vientiane has a poste restante service – be sure that those who write to you use the full name of the country, 'Lao People's Democratic Republic' or at least 'Lao PDR'.

The GPO is open Monday to Friday 8 am to 5 pm, Saturday 8 am to 4 pm and Sunday until noon. If you're moving to Vientiane note that there's no home mail delivery service. Post office boxes are available for rent; box areas are open Monday to Saturday 8 am to 6 pm.

Throughout the country you can recognise post offices by the colour scheme: mustard yellow with white trim.

Telephone

Telephone service in Laos, both domestic and international, is on-again, off-again at best. In the towns and cities of the Mekong Valley service has improved substantially in the last couple of years and International Direct Dialling (IDD) finally became available for businesses and private residences in Vientiane in 1993. With the arrival of satellite telecommunications via IntelSat and AsiaSat, you can now dial 155 countries from Vientiane.

The best place to make international calls is the Public Telephone Office on Thanon Setthathirat in Vientiane, which is open daily 7.30 am to 10 pm. Service at this office has greatly improved over the last couple of years; when I visited Vientiane in 1989, the office was still using an ancient, wooden French manual switchboard.

Today the operators still cannot place collect calls or reverse phone charges – you must pay for the call in cash kip when it is completed. All calls are operator-assisted.

In provincial capitals, international telephone service is usually available at the main post office although some cities are now establishing separate telephone offices. When a separate phone office exists, hours typically run from 7.30 am to 9.30 pm or 8 am to 10 pm.

Direct-dialled domestic long distance calls cost 150 to 250 kip per minute, while operator-assisted calls cost 450 to 750 kip for the first three minutes plus 150 to 250 kip for each additional minute.

International calls are also charged on a

Mekong River

The 12th longest river in world – 10th largest in terms of volume – the Mekong is also one of the world's most untamed waterways. Before the completion of the Thai-Lao Friendship Bridge at the end of 1993, not a single span crossed its entire South-East Asian length, and it is still undammed (though not for long). Except in Vietnam's Mekong Delta, there are no large cities or industrial zones located anywhere along its banks.

For long the main artery of travel within Laos, especially by ferry and speedboat, the Mekong is now increasingly giving way to the all-weather roads that run north and south of Vientiane (though the ferry is still considered safer because of bandit activity south of Luang Prabang). However it will continue to remain an important medium of transport for many years to come.

Marco Polo was probably the first European to cross the Mekong, which he accomplished in the 13th century. In the 16th century a group of Portuguese emissaries forded the river at Vientiane, and in the following century the Dutch merchant Gerard van Wuystoff arrived by boat. The Treaty of Bangkok, signed by the French and Siamese on 30 October 1893, officially designated the river as the border between Siam and Indochina.

Now that peace has come to Laos, its hydroelectric and navigation potential will undoubtedly be tapped; a half-dozen hydroelectric facilities and dams are planned, and there is talk of blasting the upper Mekong (north of Luang Prabang) to make it navigable year-round. The river's hydroelectric potential alone is equivalent to the entire petroleum production of Indonesia. Pa Mong, a new 210-m dam planned north of Vientiane, will flood at least 609 sq km and result in 43,000 relocations. Upstream, the Chinese government plans to build 23 dams along the Mekong and its tributaries over the next 30 years, much to the chagrin of the countries further down. ■

JOE CUMMINGS

Above: Monks repairing a boat on the Mekong

Below: Sunset over the Mekong in Vientiane

GLENN BEANLAND

Lao Weaving

JOE CUMMINGS

A ltogether Laos is said to have some 16 basic weaving styles divided among four basic regions. In north-eastern Laos (especially Hua Phan's Sam Neua and Xieng Khuang's Muang Phuan) the Thai Neua, Phuan, Thai Lü, Thai Daeng, Thai Dam and Phu Thai mainly produce weft brocade *(yìap kǫ)* using raw silk, cotton yarn and natural dyes, sometimes mixed with mat-mìi techniques. Large diamond patterns are common. In central Laos, typical weavings include indigo-dyed cotton mat-mìi and minimal weft brocade *(jók* and *khit)*, along with techniques borrowed from all over the country (brought by migrants to Vientiane – many of whom fled war zones). Gold and silver brocade is typical of traditional Luang Prabang patterns, along with intricate patterns *(lái* and imported Thai Lü designs). Northerners generally use frame looms: the waist, body and *thin sin* (bottom border) of a phàa nung or sarong are often sewn together from separately woven pieces.

Southern weavers, who tend to use footlooms, practise Laos' most continuous textile traditions in terms of styles and patterns, some of which haven't changed for a century or more. One-piece phàa nung are more common than those sewn from separate pieces. Southern Laos is known for the best silk weaving and for intricate mat-mìi designs that include Khmer-influenced temple and elephant motifs. Synthetic as well as natural dyes are commonly used. In Sekong and Attapeu, borders often contain cryptic-looking symbols; the recent introduction of simple helicopter and airplane motifs suggests the beginnings of a possible post-war cargo cult among the Lao Theung.

Along with the rebirth of Lao weaving has come a renewed interest in natural dyes. Natural sources for Lao dyes include ebony (both seeds and wood), tamarind (seeds and wood), red lacquer extracted from the *Coccus lacca* (an insect that bores into certain trees), turmeric (from a root) and indigo. Among tribal Thai weavers, indigo recipes are often the most closely guarded dye secrets. To make indigo dye, a weaver soaks the *Indigofera tinctoria* plant in water for several days, then adds lime to activate the colour. Once the dye is active, the weaver works it into a thick paste (which can be thinned later for dyeing) along with an idiosyncratic mix of ingredients (eg, lime peels, tamarind, salt) to obtain the correct Ph balance, texture and hue. This basic palette of five natural colours – black, orange, red, yellow and blue – can be combined to create an endless variety of new colours. ■

JOE CUMMINGS

Top Left: Distinctive geometric designs are a feature of Lao weaving.

Right: Traditional weaving process in Vientiane

per-minute basis, with a minimum charge of three minutes. Sample rates per minute:

Country	kip
Australia	1000
Canada	2600
France	2300
Germany	2600
Hong Kong	2000
India	3000
Thailand	520
USA	3000

Country, Access & Area Codes Until recently most cities in Laos could only be reached through a Vientiane operator. Nowadays it's possible to direct-dial to and from many places in Laos using IDD phone technology.

The country code for calling Lao PDR is 856. For long distance numbers within the country, dial 0 first, then the area code and number. For international calls dial 00 first, then the country code, area code and number.

Fax, Telex & Telegraph
At the Public Telephone Office in Vientiane fax/telex/telegraph services are available daily from 7.30 am to 9.30 pm.

In provincial capitals fax, telex and telegraph services are handled at the GPO or at the separate telephone office, where such exists.

BOOKS
Books on Laos can be difficult to find. The government bookshops in Vientiane carry mostly Lao and Vietnamese books. One private bookshop in Vientiane, Raintree Bookstore, stocks new and used titles that include a number of titles on Laos.

Overseas, the libraries of universities with Asian Studies departments or faculties often carry some of the following English-language books. If you read French, you'll find others as well. Until recently very few books on Laos in any language had been published since the 1975 Revolution. Now that Laos is 'open', newer books are beginning to trickle onto the shelves of bookstores in Bangkok and Singapore; a few even manage to find their way to Europe, Australia, the USA and Canada.

Guidebooks
What you hold in your hand is the only modern guide devoted to Laos available in English.

The classic two-volume *Guide Madrolle* guide to Indochina, last updated in 1939, is worth reading in the original French (if you can find it). The volume that includes Laos is entitled *Indochine du Nord* (Société d'Éditions Géographiques, Maritimes et Coloniales, Paris, 1939). Of course, many of the place names have changed several times since 1939 (and some places were bombed

Laos Area Codes

Town	Area code	Town	Area code
Attapeu	31 (61)*	Sekong	38 (31)*
Huay Xai	84	Tha Khaek	52
Luang Nam Tha	86	Udomxai	81 (71)*
Luang Prabang	71	Vang Vieng	21
Pakse	31	Vientiane	21
Pakxan	54	Xieng Khuang (Phonsavan)	61 (71)*
Phongsali	88		
Sainyabuli	74		
Salavan	38 (31)*	*Numbers in parentheses are temporary area codes being used in 1995; it is not known when the permanent codes will go into effect.	
Sam Neua	64 (71)*		
Savannakhet	41		

out of existence), but for guidebook buffs it's a must-read.

An English version of the *Guide Madrolle* was also issued in 1939 (entitled *Indochina*) by the same publisher, but the two volumes were condensed into one so it's not nearly as complete as the French.

Culture

The large-format, coffee-table-style *The Mekong* by John Hoskins (Post Publishing, Bangkok, 1991) contains a wealth of photographs of Mekong river life as well as a compendium of fact and lore about the great river.

Visitors interested in Lao weaving should have a look at Patricia Cheesman's *Lao Textiles: Ancient Symbols – Living Art* (White Lotus, Bangkok, 1988), which offers a thorough and well-illustrated explanation of the various weaving styles and techniques – old and new – found in Laos.

Atlas des ethnies et des sous-ethnies du Laos, written by Laurent Chazee, published in 1995 and sold in Bangkok and Vientiane, is based on ethnographic research accomplished between 1988 and 1994. This colour-illustrated book comes with a map tucked into a pocket in the back cover which diagrams the locations of 119 ethnic groups in Laos.

History

History of Laos by Maha Sila Viravong (Paragon Book Reprint Corp, New York, 1964) is a fairly complete early (pre-War of Resistance) history written by a Thai. *A New History of Laos* by ML Manich Jumsai (Chalermnit Books, Bangkok, 1971) is basically a slight expansion and update of Viravong's work.

Historical Dictionary of Laos by Martin Stuart-Fox and Mary Kooyman (The Scarecrow Press, New York & London, 1992) contains a very detailed chronology of Laos dating from 500,000 BC through 1991. The dictionary-style organisation alphabetically lists key terms, personalities and events in Lao history and supplies lots of near-trivia

about the country you won't find anywhere else.

Notes on Lao History, a thin, self-published work by Lao author Somphavan Inthavong, attempts to present Lao history from a provocative 'new' point of view but distorts the statements of earlier researchers by taking substantial chunks of Austro-Thai history out of context in support of Lao nationalism. The author's conclusions contain a decidedly anti-Thai bent.

Laos: War & Revolution by Nina Adams & Alfred McCoy (Harper Colophon Books, New York, 1970) was commissioned by the Committee of Concerned Asian Scholars. This book represents the basic Western academic left-wing view of pre-1975 Laos, a perspective that now seems out of date in the context of current developments in the country.

The Ravens: Pilots of the Secret War of Laos by Christopher Robbins (Bantam Press, New York, 1988) is a very impressive piece of research on the US-directed secret war, with plenty of historical context as well as tactical specifics. Robbins' earlier *Air America: The Story of the CIA's Secret Airlines* (Putnam, New York, 1979), which focuses on the infamous guns & drugs airline, was turned into an American comedy film starring Mel Gibson. In the more recent and wider-focused *Back Fire* (Simon & Schuster, 1996), author Roger Warner sifts through declassified US government material and interviews key figures to uncover more on the CIA's secret war in Laos.

Tragic Mountains: The Hmong, the Americans and the Secret Wars for Laos, 1942-1992 written by former Laos foreign correspondent Jane Hamilton-Merritt (University of Indiana Press, Bloomington, 1992), follows the Hmong struggle for freedom, from WW II, when the Hmong sided with the French against the Japanese, through their '50s battles with the Viet Minh to the '60s to '70s war with the Pathet Lao and North Vietnamese armies.

Readers interested in the politics, economics and history of opium in Laos should seek out Alfred W McCoy's classic *The Pol-*

itics of Heroin in Southeast Asia (Harper & Row, New York, 1972) and Dr Joseph Westermeyer's *Poppies, Pipes, and People: Opium and Its Use in Laos* (University of California Press, Berkeley, 1982). The former details the CIA-Mafia-Nationalist Chinese involvement in the worldwide opium and heroin trade in the '60s and '70s, while the latter is a detailed study of opium production and addiction in Laos through 1975.

Politics & Society

A collection of academic essays called *Contemporary Laos: Studies in the Politics & Society of the Lao People's Democratic Republic* edited by Martin Stuart-Fox (University of Queensland Press, St Lucia & London, 1982) includes detailed discussions of the history and workings of the Lao People's Party, minority politics, Buddhism since the 1975 Revolution, Lao-Thai and Lao-Vietnamese relations and Lao refugees. Some essays are quite well researched while others seem somewhat removed from 1980s Lao reality.

Laos: Politics, Economics, & Society by the same author (Pinter Publishers, New York & London, or Lynne Riemer Publishers, Boulder, Colorado, 1983) is a good overview of Laos during the early years of the Revolution, with some details on the post-1979 economic reforms. Arthur J Dommen's *Laos: Keystone of Indochina* (Westview Press, Boulder & London, 1985) updates the LPDR's political history a bit but sheds little new light on the subject overall.

Lao Peasants Under Socialism by Grant Evans (Yale University Press, New Haven, 1990) presents a severe socio-economic analysis of Lao communism backed by thorough empirical research. Evans concludes that the Lao rulership has failed in attempting to move the country out of feudalism toward anything resembling socialism.

Laos: Beyond the Revolution (ed Joseph Zasloff & Leonard Unger, St Martin's Press, New York, 1991) presents a collection of thoughtful essays on political and economic history through 1989. *Indochina's Refugees:*

Oral Histories from Laos, Cambodia and Vietnam by Joanna C Scott (McFarland & Co, Jefferson, NC 1989) contains several personal stories describing events that prompted 10% of the population to leave after 1975. One essay, 'Laos – Land of the Seminar Camps', provides sobering accounts of the PL's re-education camps.

General

Laos: A Country Study (US Government Printing Office, 1971) is one of American University's Area Handbook Series, researched and written by the Foreign Area Studies Department. Probably the most comprehensive book available in English about pre-1975 Lao society, politics, history and economics, it's also remarkably objective considering it was commissioned by the US Army. You can sense the authors holding back, though, when recounting the events of the early '60s leading to US involvement in Laos.

Laos' State Printing Enterprise publishes a large and poorly done pictorial guide called *Laos* (also available in Spanish, French, Russian and Lao) that is available at the Lane Xang Hotel gift shop and at the State Book Shop west of Namphu Square.

NEWSPAPERS & MAGAZINES

The new *Vientiane Times*, launched the day before the opening of the Thai-Lao Friendship Bridge in April 1994, is a weekly English-language newspaper produced by the Ministry of Information & Culture. For the most part it's a business-oriented paper, with occasional articles on Lao culture and a short but useful list of ongoing cultural events and social activities in the capital. Since all the staff are government employees, the paper is careful not to print anything critical of the government or anyone in the government. Despite self-censorship it is still the best single source of news on Laos available anywhere.

Until recently the only English-language periodical legally published in Laos was the skimpy, typewritten *Lao PDR News Bulletin*. Produced by Khao San Pathet Lao (or KPL, the government news service and successor to the pre-Revolutionary Agence Lao Presse), it's basically a list of announcements regarding the latest international trade agreements, National Assembly meetings and new government policies.

The national Lao-language newspaper is *Pasason* (The People), a somewhat propagandising government mouthpiece. *Wiangchan Mai* (New Vientiane) is a Vientiane daily with similar content. Other Lao-language newspapers include the *Khao Thulakit* (Business News) published by Lao National Chamber of Commerce and *Sieng Khaen Lao* (Sound of the Lao Khaen), a new cultural organ for the Lao Writers' Association committed to literary endeavours and the maintenance of Lao language standards.

The government controls all distribution of the *Bangkok Post* and it is legally available only by subscription. Day-old issues of the *Post* can be purchased at Phimphone Minimart in Vientiane but the paper is rarely seen elsewhere in Laos except in government offices! Raintree Bookstore in Vientiane carries *Time, Asiaweek, Far Eastern Economic Review* and a few other news periodicals – but not the *Bangkok Post*.

Foreign embassies and consulates are a good source of reading material in Vientiane. The Australian, French, UK and US posts all welcome visitors to their respective lounges, where dated newspapers and magazines are available for perusal.

RADIO

The LPDR has one radio station, Lao National Radio. English-language news is broadcast twice daily on LNR but most expats prefer the English-language news available from the usual short-wave radio programming. With a short-wave radio you can easily pick up BBC, VOA, Radio Australia, Stockholm Radio, Radio Manila, Radio France International and others with transmitters in South-East Asia.

TELEVISION

Lao National Television sponsors two TV channels – 3 and 9 – which can only be received in the Mekong river valley and are only broadcast from 7 to 11 pm daily. Typical fare includes Lao-dubbed episodes of ALF and Roadrunner cartoons. Most Lao watch Thai television, which can be received anywhere in the Mekong river valley. Thailand's channels 5 and 9 telecast a variety of English-language programmes.

Satellite TV setups can pick up transmissions from Palapa C1, AsiaSat 1 & 2, Thaicom 1A & 2, PAS 2 & 4 and Apstar 1, including satellite channels such as CNN International (Turner Broadcasting), BBC World Service, STAR TV, and various private and public broadcast channels from India, Thailand, Japan, Hong Kong and Myanmar. No licence or special permit is necessary for the purchase and use of a satellite TV dish.

Most hotel sat-TV hookups are set to receive a minimal number of channels, usually around four or five – sometimes only one, which changes from hour to hour according to the whims of the staff.

FILM & PHOTOGRAPHY

Film is reasonably priced in Laos (Vientiane, Luang Prabang, Savannakhet, Pakse) but the selection is generally limited to Fuji, Konica or Kodak colour print films in ASA 100 or 200. A few of the better-stocked photo shops in Vientiane and Luang Prabang carry slide films, typically Ektachrome Elite 50 or 100 and/or Fujichrome Sensia 100. Print film generally costs around 2500 to 4000 kip per roll, slide films 6000 to 8000 kip. For B&W film or other slide films, you'd best stock up in Bangkok, where film is relatively cheap, before you come to Laos. A fair selection of film is available in Thailand's Nong Khai and Udon Thani as well.

Most of the shops that sell and process film in Vientiane can be found along Thanon Samsenthai and along Thanon Khun Bulom. Processing is limited to negative and E-6 positive films. For Kodachrome you're better off waiting to process your film back home or in Bangkok or Singapore.

As in other tropical countries, the best times of day for photography are early to mid-morning and late afternoon. A polarising filter would be helpful for cutting glare and improving contrast, especially when photographing temple ruins or shooting over water. If you'll be in Laos during the rainy season (June to October), pack some silica gel with your camera to prevent mould growing on the inside of your lenses.

Restrictions

In rural areas people are often not used to having their photos taken, so be sure to smile and ask permission before snapping away. In tribal areas *always* ask permission before photographing people or religious totems; photography of people is taboo among several of the tribes. Use discretion when photographing villagers anywhere in the country as a camera can be a very intimidating instrument.

Lao officials are sensitive about photography of airports and military installations; when in doubt refrain.

Airport Security

So far only Vientiane airport uses X-ray machines to view luggage, so employ the usual protective procedures (lead-lined bags, hand inspection) if you're flying in or out of Vientiane and are concerned about X-ray damage to film.

TIME

Laos, like Thailand, is seven hours ahead of GMT/UTC. Thus noon in Vientiane is 10 pm the previous day in San Francisco, 1 am in New York, 5 am in London, 1 pm in Perth and 3 pm in Sydney.

ELECTRICITY

The LPDR uses 220-volt AC circuitry; power outlets most commonly feature two-prong round or flat sockets. Bring adapters and transformers as necessary for any appliances you're carrying. Adapters for common European plugs are available at shops in Vientiane.

Blackouts are common during the rainy season, so it's a good idea to bring a torch (flashlight).

WEIGHTS & MEASURES

The international metric system is the official system for weights and measures in the LPDR. Shops, markets and highway signs for the most part conform to the system. In rural areas distances are occasionally quoted in *meun*; one meun is equivalent to 12 km. Gold and silver are sometimes weighed in *bàht*; one *bàht* is 15 grams.

HEALTH

It is very important that you take adequate medical precautions before coming to Laos as the availability of decent emergency medical services is practically nil. Most foreigners who experience any serious health problems must be evacuated to Thailand.

Pre-Departure Preparations

Medical Kit For basic first aid, I recommend carrying the following:

- Large self-adhesive bandages and band-aids to help protect ordinary cuts or wounds from infection
- Butterfly closures for cuts that won't close on their own
- Antibacterial ointment and powder to treat or prevent infection of wounds
- Immodium or Lomotil to mitigate the symptoms of diarrhoea
- Antibiotic eye ointment for all-too-common eye infections
- Scissors, tweezers and a thermometer
- Aspirin/acetaminophen/paracetamol for headaches, fever
- Rehydration mixture for treatment of severe diarrhoea
- Insect repellent, sun block, suntan lotion and lip balm

The best book I've seen on health maintenance in Asia is Dirk Schroeder's *Staying Healthy in Asia, Africa, and Latin America* (Moon Publications, 1994). In fact, you might want to make this handy little book part of your first aid kit as it clearly describes symptoms and recommended treatment for illnesses common in Laos (and elsewhere in Asia).

When seriously ill or injured, you should

seek medical attention from a qualified doctor, clinic or hospital if at all possible; employ self-treatment only as a last resort.

Health Preparations Make sure you're healthy before you start travelling, and if you are embarking on a long trip make sure your teeth are OK. If you wear glasses bring a spare pair and your prescription. Losing your glasses can be a real problem, although in Vientiane or just across the Thai border in Nong Khai you can get new spectacles made up quickly, cheaply and competently.

If you require a particular medication, take an adequate supply as it may not be available locally. Take the prescription, with the generic rather than the brand name, which may be unavailable, as it will make getting replacements easier. It's a wise idea to have the prescription with you to show that you legally use the medication; it's surprising how often over-the-counter drugs from one place are illegal without a prescription or even banned in another.

Immunisations There are no health requirements for Laos in terms of required vaccinations unless you are coming from an infected area. A tetanus booster would be a good idea in case you injure yourself while travelling. You should also check if vaccinations are required by any countries you are going to after visiting Laos. A Japanese encephalitis vaccination is a good idea for those who think they may be at moderate or high risk while in Laos (see the Japanese encephalitis section for more information). Your doctor may also recommend booster shots against measles or polio.

Plan ahead for getting your vaccinations since some of them require an initial shot followed by a booster, while some vaccinations should not be given together. The World Health Organisation also recommends that travellers take malaria tablets (see Malaria in this section).

Basic Rules
Care in what you eat and drink is the most important health rule; stomach upsets are the most likely travel health problem, but the majority of these upsets will be relatively minor. Don't become paranoid – trying the local food is part of the experience of travel, after all.

The number one rule is *don't drink tap water*. If you don't know for certain that water is safe always assume the worst. Reputable brands of bottled water or soft drinks are generally fine, although in some places refilled bottles are not unknown. Take care with fruit juice, particularly if water may have been added. Tea or coffee should also be OK since the water should be boiled.

Salads and fruit should be washed with purified water or peeled where possible. Ice cream is usually OK if it is a reputable brand name, but beware of ice cream from street vendors and ice cream that has melted and been refrozen. Thoroughly cooked food is safest, but not if it has been left to cool or if it has been reheated. Take great care with shellfish or fish and avoid undercooked meat.

If a place looks clean and well run and the vendor also looks clean and healthy then the food is probably safe. In general, places that are packed with travellers or locals will be fine, while empty restaurants are questionable.

Nutrition If you're travelling hard and fast and therefore missing meals, or if you simply lose your appetite, you can soon start to lose weight and place your health at risk.

Make sure your diet is well balanced. Eggs, tofu, beans, lentils and nuts are all safe ways to get protein. Fruit you can peel (bananas, oranges or mandarins, for example) are safe and a good source of vitamins. Try to eat plenty of grains (rice) and bread. Remember that although food is generally safer if it is cooked well, overcooked food loses much of its nutritional value. If the food is insufficient it's a good idea to take vitamin and iron pills.

Make sure you drink enough; don't rely on feeling thirsty to indicate when you should drink. Not needing to urinate or very dark yellow urine is a danger sign. Always carry a water bottle with you on long trips. Excessive sweating can lead to loss of salt and therefore muscle cramping. Salt tablets are not a good idea as a preventative but in places where salt is not used much, adding additional salt to food can help.

Food & Water As with any Asian country, care should be taken in consuming food or drink. As mentioned above, don't drink tap water. Lao soft drinks are safe to drink, as is the weak Chinese tea served in most restaurants. Ice is produced from purified water under hygienic conditions and is therefore theoretically safe. During transit to the local restaurant, however, conditions are not so hygienic (you may see blocks of ice being dragged along the street). The rule of thumb is that if it's chipped ice, it probably came from an ice block (which may not have been handled well) but if it's ice cubes or 'tubes', it was delivered from the ice factory in sealed plastic.

In rural areas, villagers mostly drink collected rainwater. Most travellers can drink this without problems, but some people can't tolerate it. It is best to buy fruit that you can peel and slice yourself (cheaper, too), but most fare at food stalls is reasonably safe.

Water Purification Boiling is the only absolutely reliable way to purify water. In general, bringing water to a brisk boil will make it safe to drink.

Simple filtering will not remove all dangerous organisms, so if you cannot boil water it should be treated chemically. Chlorine tablets (puritabs, steritabs or other brand names) will kill many, but not all pathogens. Iodine is very effective in purifying water and is available in tablet form (such as Potable Aqua), but follow the directions carefully and remember that too much iodine can be harmful.

If you can't find tablets, tincture of iodine (2%) can be used. Two drops of tincture of iodine per litre or quart of clear water is the recommended dosage, and the water should then be left to stand for 30 minutes. Iodine loses its effectiveness if exposed to air or

damp so keep it in a tightly sealed container. Flavoured powder will disguise the taste of treated water and is a good idea if you are travelling with children.

In most towns in Laos bottled water is cheap and readily available. In other places in the country hotels almost always provide thermoses full of purified water with the rooms; in the north it's usually hot water (a Chinese/Vietnamese influence) while in the south it's usually cool.

General Health Normal body temperature is 98.6°F or 37°C, more than 2°C higher is a 'high' fever. A normal adult pulse rate is 60 to 80 beats per minute (children 80 to 100, babies 100 to 140). You should know how to take a temperature and a pulse rate. As a general rule the pulse increases about 20 beats per minute for each °C rise in fever.

Respiration rate (breathing) is also an indicator of illness. Count the number of breaths per minute: between 12 and 20 is normal for adults and older children (up to 30 for younger children, 40 for babies). People with a high fever or serious respiratory illness (like pneumonia) breathe more quickly than normal. More than 40 shallow breaths a minute usually means pneumonia.

Many health problems can be avoided by taking care of yourself. Wash your hands frequently; it's quite easy to contaminate your own food. Clean your teeth with purified water rather than straight from the tap. Avoid climatic extremes, keep out of the sun when it's hot. Avoid potential diseases by dressing sensibly. You can get worm infections through bare feet. You can avoid insect bites by covering bare skin when insects are around, by screening windows or beds or by using insect repellents.

Medical Problems & Treatment

Potential medical problems can be broken down into several areas. First there are the climatic and geographical considerations – problems caused by extremes of temperature, altitude or motion. Then there are diseases and illnesses caused by unsanitary conditions, insect bites or stings, animal or human contact. Simple cuts, bites or scratches can also cause problems.

Self diagnosis and treatment can be risky; wherever possible seek qualified help. An embassy or consulate can usually advise a good place to go. So can five-star hotels, although they often recommend doctors with five-star prices. This is when that medical insurance really becomes useful! In some places standards of medical attention are so low that for some ailments the best advice is to get on a plane and go somewhere else.

Environmental Hazards

Sunburn In the tropics you can get sunburnt surprisingly quickly even through cloud. Use a sunscreen and take extra care to cover parts of your body which don't normally see sun – your feet for example. A hat provides added protection and use zinc cream or some other barrier cream for your nose and lips. Calamine lotion is good for mild sunburn.

Prickly Heat Prickly heat is an itchy rash caused by excessive perspiration trapped under the skin. It usually strikes people who have just arrived in a hot climate whose pores have not yet opened sufficiently to cope with greater sweating. Keeping cool by bathing often, using a mild talcum powder, or even by resorting to air-con may help until you acclimatise. One of the best nonprescription medicated powders in Laos is a Thai brand called Prickly Heat Powder.

Heat Exhaustion Dehydration or salt deficiency can cause heat exhaustion. Take time to acclimatise to high temperatures and make sure you get sufficient liquids. Salt deficiency is characterised by fatigue, lethargy, headaches, giddiness and muscle cramps and in this case salt tablets may help. Vomiting or diarrhoea can deplete your liquid and salt levels. Anhydrotic heat exhaustion, caused by an inability to sweat, is quite rare and unlike the other forms of heat exhaustion is likely to strike people who have been in a hot climate for some time, rather than newcomers.

Heat Stroke This serious, sometimes fatal, condition can occur if the body's heat regulating mechanism breaks down and the body temperature rises to dangerous levels. Long, continuous periods of exposure to high temperatures can leave you vulnerable to heat stroke and you should avoid excessive alcohol or strenuous activity when you first arrive in a hot climate.

The symptoms are feeling unwell, not sweating very much or at all and high body temperature (39 to 41°C). Where sweating has ceased the skin becomes flushed and red. Severe, throbbing headaches and lack of coordination will also occur and the sufferer may be confused or aggressive. Eventually the victim will become delirious or convulse. Hospitalisation is essential, but meanwhile get the victim out of the sun, remove clothing and cover them with a wet sheet or towel, and then fan them continually.

Fungal Infections Hot-weather fungal infections are most likely to occur on the scalp, between the toes or fingers (athlete's foot), in the groin (jock itch or crotch rot) and as ringworm on the body. You get ringworm (which is a fungal infection, not a worm) from infected animals or by walking on damp areas, like shower floors.

To prevent fungal infections, wear loose, comfortable clothes, avoid artificial fibres, wash frequently and dry carefully. If you do get an infection, wash the infected area daily with a disinfectant or medicated soap and water, and rinse and dry well. Apply an antifungal powder like the widely available Tinaderm. Try to expose the infected area to air or sunlight as much as possible and wash all towels and underwear in hot water and change them often. Public or hotel laundries often wash everything in cold water with very little soap – washing your own underwear will go a long way toward preventing yeast and fungal problems in the crotch area.

Motion Sickness Eating only lightly before and during a trip will reduce the chances of motion sickness. If you are prone to motion sickness, try to find a place that minimises disturbance – near the wing on aircraft, close to midships on boats, near the centre on buses. Fresh air usually helps; reading or cigarette smoke doesn't. Commercial antimotion-sickness preparations, which can cause drowsiness, have to be taken before the trip commences; when you're feeling sick it's too late. Ginger and peppermint (including mint-flavoured sweets) are natural preventatives.

Diseases of Insanitation

Diarrhoea Traveller's diarrhoea, which can be caused by water, food or climate, may strike some visitors who stay for any length of time outside Vientiane, but usually subsides within a few days. A few rushed toilet trips with no other symptoms is not indicative of a serious problem. Moderate diarrhoea, involving half-a-dozen loose movements in a day, is more of a nuisance.

Dehydration is the main danger with any diarrhoea, particularly for children, so fluid replenishment is the number one treatment. Weak black tea with a little sugar, flat soft drinks diluted with water or soda water are all good. With severe diarrhoea a rehydrating solution is necessary to replace minerals and salts. You should stick to a bland diet (rice or noodle soups are good) and cut out all alcohol and caffeine as you recover.

Lomotil or Immodium can be used to bring relief from the symptoms of diarrhoea, although they do not actually cure them. Only use these drugs if absolutely necessary: if you *must* travel for example. For children under 12, Lomotil and Immodium are not recommended. Do not use these drugs if you have a high fever or are severely dehydrated. Antibiotics may be useful in treating severe diarrhoea, eg if you have watery diarrhoea with fever and lethargy, or persistent diarrhoea not improving after 48 hours.

The recommended drugs (adults only) would be either norfloxacin 400 mg twice daily for three days or ciprofloxacin 500 mg twice daily for three days. The drug bismuth subsalicylate has also been used successfully. The dosage for adults is two tablets or 30ml and for children it is one tablet or 10ml. This dose can be repeated every 30 minutes

to one hour, with no more than eight doses in a 24-hour period. The drug of choice in children would be co-trimoxazole (Bactrim, Septrin, Resprim) with dosage dependent on weight. A five-day course is given. Ampicillin has been recommended in the past and may still be an alternative. Three days treatment should be sufficient and an improvement should occur within 24 hours.

Watery diarrhoea with blood and mucus (gut-paralysing drugs like Immodium or Lomotil should be avoided in this situation) may indicate amoebic dysentery, which can be serious if left untreated – in this case you should see a doctor.

Giardiasis This intestinal parasite is present in contaminated water and the symptoms are stomach cramps, nausea, bloated stomach, watery, foul-smelling diarrhoea and frequent gas. Giardiasis can appear several weeks after you have been exposed to the parasite. The symptoms may disappear for a few days and then return; this can go on for several weeks. Metronidazole, known as Flagyl, is the recommended drug, but should only be taken under medical supervision – antibiotics are no use. The affliction is relatively rare in Laos.

Dysentery This serious illness is caused by contaminated food or water and is characterised by severe diarrhoea, often with blood or mucus in the stool. There are two kinds of dysentery. Bacillary dysentery is characterised by a high fever and rapid development; headache, vomiting and stomach pains are also symptoms. It generally does not last longer than a week, but it is highly contagious.

Amoebic dysentery is more gradual in developing, with fever or vomiting less likely, but is a more serious illness. It is not a self-limiting disease but will persist until treated and can recur and cause long term damage.

A stool test is necessary with dysentery, but if no medical care is available ciprofloxacin is the prescribed treatment for bacillary dysentery, metronidazole (Flagyl) for amoebic dysentery.

Cholera Cholera vaccination is not required by the World Health Organisation (WHO) as a condition of entry into any country, as the vaccine is not very effective. Outbreaks of cholera are generally widely reported so you can avoid afflicted areas. The disease is characterised by a sudden onset of acute diarrhoea with 'rice water' stools, vomiting, muscular cramps and extreme weakness. If you contract cholera you need medical help, but treat for dehydration (which can be extreme) and, if there is an appreciable delay in getting to hospital, begin taking tetracycline. This drug should not be given to young children or pregnant women and it should not be used past its expiration date.

Viral Gastroenteritis This is not caused by bacteria but, as the name suggests, a virus and is characterised by stomach cramps, diarrhoea, sometimes vomiting, sometimes a slight fever. All you can do is rest and drink lots of fluids.

Hepatitis Hepatitis A is the most common form of this disease and is spread by contaminated food or water. The symptoms are fever, chills, headache, fatigue, feelings of weakness and aches and pains, followed by loss of appetite, nausea, vomiting, abdominal pain, dark urine, light coloured faeces, jaundiced skin and the whites of the eyes may turn yellow. In some case you may feel unwell, tired, have no appetite, experience aches and pains and the jaundiced effect. You should seek medical advice, but in general there is not much you can do apart from rest, drink lots of fluids, eat lightly and avoid fatty foods. People who have had hepatitis must forego alcohol for six months after the illness, as hepatitis attacks the liver and it needs that amount of time to recover. A preventive injection of immune serum globulin (called gamma globulin) also provides immunity for a limited time. Havrix is a more effective vaccine, where you develop antibodies which give lasting immunity.

Hepatitis B, which used to be called serum hepatitis, is spread through contact with infected bodily fluids, for example through sexual contact or unsterilised needles, via small breaks in the skin and in blood transfusions. Avoid having your ears pierced, tattoos done or injections given where you have doubts about the sanitary conditions. The symptoms of type B are much the same as type A except they are more severe and may lead to irreparable liver damage or even liver cancer. Although there is no treatment for hepatitis B, an effective prophylactic vaccine is readily available in most countries. The immunisation schedule requires two injections at least a month apart followed by a third dose five months after the second, then boosters every three to five years. The initial injection can be given over as short a period as 28 days if more rapid protection is required. Persons who should receive a hepatitis B vaccination include anyone who anticipates contact with blood or other bodily secretions in Laos – either as health care workers or through sexual contact with the local population – as well as anyone who will be staying in the country more than six months. This vaccine is available in Bangkok and Singapore.

Hepatitis Non-A Non B This is a blanket term formerly used for several different strains of hepatitis, which have now been separately identified. Hepatitis C is similar to B but is less common. Hepatitis D (the 'delta particle') is also similar to B and always occurs in concert with it. Hepatitis E, however, is similar to A and is spread in the same manner, by water or food contamination.

Tests are available for these strands (except Hepatitis E) but are very expensive. Travellers shouldn't be too paranoid about this apparent proliferation of hepatitis strains; they are fairly rare (so far) and following the same precautions as for A and B should be all that's necessary to avoid them.

Typhoid Typhoid fever is another gut infection that travels the faecal-oral route, ie contaminated water and food are responsible. Vaccination against typhoid is only 60 to 80% effective and it is one of the most dangerous infections, so medical help must be sought.

The early symptoms are like so many others: you may feel like you have a bad cold or flu on the way, with a headache, sore throat and fever which rises a little each day until it is around 40°C or more. The pulse is often slow for the amount of fever present and gets slower as the fever rises, unlike a normal fever where the pulse increases. There may also be vomiting, diarrhoea or constipation.

In the second week the high fever and slow pulse continue and a few pink spots may appear on the body, along with trembling, delirium, weakness, weight loss and dehydration. If there are no further complications, the fever and symptoms will slowly go during the third week. However you must get medical help before this as common complications are pneumonia (acute infection of the lungs) or peritonitis (burst appendix), and typhoid is very infectious.

The victim's fever should be treated by keeping them cool and dehydration should also be watched for. Ciproflaxin is the recommended antibiotic. If not available, chloramphenicol can be used, but may be associated with side effects.

Worms These parasites are most common in rural, tropical areas. They can be present on unwashed vegetables or in undercooked meat and you can pick them up through your skin by walking in bare feet. Infestations may not show up for some time, and although they are generally not serious, if left untreated they can cause severe health problems. If you think you might have contracted them sometime during your travels, it's not a bad idea to have a stool test when you get home. A stool test is necessary to pinpoint the problem and medication is often available over the counter.

Schistosomiasis Also known as bilharzia or 'blood flukes', this disease is caused by tiny flatworms that burrow their way through the skin and enter the bloodstream. Humans contract the worms when swimming or bathing in contaminated fresh water (the flukes can't survive in salt water). The worm enters through the skin, and the first symptom may be a tingling and sometimes a light rash around the area where it entered. Weeks later, when the worm is busy producing eggs, a high fever may develop. A general feeling of being unwell may be the first symptom; once the disease is established abdominal pain and blood in the urine are other signs. The infection often causes no symptoms until the disease is well established (several months to years after exposure) and damage to internal organs irreversible.

The overall risk for this disease is quite low, but highest in the southern reaches of the Mekong river – avoid swimming or bathing in this area. If submersion is for some reasons unavoidable, vigorous towel-drying reduces the risk of penetration. If schistosomiasis symptoms appear, consult a physician; the usual treatment is a regimen of praziquantel (often sold as Biltricide).

Opisthorchiasis One additional health warning specific to Laos is to be on guard against 'liver flukes' or opisthorchiasis. These are tiny worms that are occasionally present in freshwater fish in Laos. The main risk comes from eating raw or undercooked fish. Travellers should in particular avoid eating uncooked *pąa dàek* (an unpasteurised fermented fish used as an accompaniment for many Lao foods) when travelling in rural Laos. The pąa dàek in Vientiane and Luang Prabang is said to be safe (or safer) simply because it's usually made from noninfected fish, while the risk is greatest in the south.

Pathologists consider the overall risk of contracting liver flukes in Laos to be low. In neighbouring north-eastern Thailand – where liver flukes are endemic – the Thai government is running a full-scale campaign to convince Lao-Thais not to consume the stuff.

In rural areas pa dàek is often carried around in bamboo tubes – slung over the shoulders of farmers. Since it's considered a great delicacy, it's often offered to guests – this is one case where you have to weigh carefully the possible health consequences against the risk of offending your hosts. I've eaten quite a bit of it without ill effect but I might just be lucky.

A much less common way to contract liver flukes is by swimming in rivers. According to a Czech parasitologist who spent several months researching opisthorchiasis in Laos, the only known area where the flukes might be contracted by swimming in contaminated waters is in the Mekong river around Khong island in southern Laos. Here again I've thrown caution to the wind and survived (actually I had no choice when the boat I was cruising down the Mekong in became stuck on some rocks just north of Khong island, an incident in which all the passengers had to get out of the boat and into the Mekong – chest deep – to extricate the vessel).

The intensity of symptoms depends very much on how many of the flukes get into your body. At low levels, there are virtually no symptoms at all; at higher levels, an overall fatigue, low-grade fever and swollen or tender liver (or general abdominal pain) are the usual symptoms, along with worms or worm eggs in the faeces.

Persons suspected of having liver flukes should have a stool sample analysed by a competent doctor or clinic in Vientiane or Bangkok. The best medication is 25 mg per kg body weight of praziquantel (often sold as Biltricide) three times daily after meals for two days.

Tetanus This potentially fatal disease is found in undeveloped tropical areas and is difficult to treat but is preventable with immunisation. Tetanus occurs when a wound becomes infected by a germ which lives in the faeces of animals, so clean all cuts, punctures or animal bites. Tetanus is known as lockjaw and the first symptom may be discomfort in swallowing, stiffening of the jaw and neck, then painful convulsions of the jaw and whole body.

Rabies Rabies is caused by a bite or scratch from an infected animal. Dogs are a noted carrier. Any bite, scratch or even lick from a mammal should be cleaned immediately and thoroughly. Scrub with soap and running water, then clean with an alcohol solution. If there is any possibility that the animal is infected, medical help should be sought immediately. Even if the animal is not rabid, all bites should be treated seriously as they can become infected or can result in tetanus. A rabies vaccination is now available and should be considered if you are in a high-risk category, for example, cave explorers (who might get bat bites), people working with animals, children, cyclists and those who will be more than two days away from medical attention.

Sexually Transmitted Diseases Sexual contact with an infected sexual partner spreads these diseases and while abstinence is the only 100% preventative, use of a latex condom is also effective. In Laos the most common STD is gonorrhoea, followed by non-specific urethritis (NSU). Typical symptoms for both gonorrhoea and NSU are discharges or pain when urinating. Symptoms may be less marked or not observed at all in women. Syphilis is less common; initial symptoms include sores in the genital area, followed by rash and flu-like symptoms. The symptoms of syphilis eventually disappear completely but the disease continues and can cause severe problems in later years. Treatment of gonorrhoea, NSU and syphilis is by antibiotics.

Two STDs reported in Laos for which no cure is available are herpes simplex and the human immuno-deficiency virus (HIV). The latter leads to Acquired Immune Deficiency Syndrome (AIDS) or AIDS-Related Complex (ARC), both of which are fatal diseases. The incubation period (time before an infection registers in laboratory tests) is up to three years.

HIV can also be spread through infected blood transfusions or by dirty needles – vaccinations, acupuncture and tattooing can potentially be as dangerous as intravenous drug use if the equipment is not clean. In Laos HIV is most commonly spread through intravenous drug use. As of late 1995 the

Ministry of Public Health had officially recorded 59 HIV-positive cases, along with 10 AIDS deaths. Since Laos has a relatively low doctor-to-citizen ratio and most people never visit a hospital or trained physician – even when deathly ill – most probably the actual numbers of infected individuals is significantly higher.

The use of condoms greatly decreases but does not eliminate the risk of STD infection. The Lao phrase for 'condom' is *thõng anáamái*. Latex condoms are more effective than animal-membrane condoms in preventing disease transmission. Condoms can be purchased at most *khãi yạa* (pharmacies). It is worth bringing your own condoms from home. Lao condoms may be of lesser quality and insufficient size for some.

The medical blood supply in Laos cannot be considered fully screened for HIV; if you need a transfusion the nearest safe supply is in neighboring Thailand where adequate screening procedures are followed.

Insect-Borne Diseases

Malaria This serious disease is spread by mosquito bites. Resistance to anti-malarials is on the increase all over Asia, and most malaria in Laos is chloroquine resistant.

Before leaving home, it is wise to get in contact with an infectious diseases hospital or other relevant government health body in your country to find out the latest information regarding malarial prophylactics. Armed with this information, consult a doctor (preferably one with experience in travel medicine). Factors such as your length of stay and the areas you plan to visit are relevant in prescribing antimalarials. All commonly prescribed malarial suppressants have the potential to cause side effects.

For all practical purposes, Laos is considered completely chloroquine and fansidar resistant. Mefloquine and doxycycline (100mg/day) are the most commonly recommended prophylactics for Laos, though there is some mefloquine resistance. Doxycycline will prevent some forms of bacilliary dysentery.

Halofantrine (as well as mefloquine) can be used for presumptive treatment of fever

in a person who may have malaria but is, for some reason, unable to obtain a diagnostic blood test. It is not available in many countries but is in Thailand (HalFan). It is associated with (rare) life-threatening side-effects and so should be avoided by some people. Its use should be discussed with a doctor.

The highest risk area in Laos seems to be the lower Mekong river valley south of Vientiane and in the area around Luang Nam Tha near the Chinese border. Malaria research in Laos has been very sparse so far, so exactly which areas are the riskiest is not a cut-and-dried issue.

As well as using a prophylactic antimalarial medication, if appropriate, you should take a few other simple precautions that can greatly reduce your chances of contracting any kind of malaria. First of all, apply a good mosquito repellent to skin and clothes whenever and wherever mosquitoes are about. The best repellents are those which contain DEET (N, N-diethyl-metatoluamide). A concentration of 15-20% DEET has been shown to provide excellent protection without running the risk of toxic effects from absorption of the chemical through the skin. Repellents containing more than 20% DEET have the advantage of needing to be applied less frequently but are associated with toxic effects, especially in children.

For those with an allergy or aversion to synthetic repellents, citronella makes a good substitute but its repellent effect lasts only about 30 minutes, so it needs to be applied frequently. Mosquito coils do an excellent job of repelling mosquitoes in your room and are readily available in larger towns. Day mosquitoes do not usually carry malaria, so it is mainly in the night that you have to worry – peak biting hours are a few hours after dusk and a few hours before dawn.

According to the US and Australian embassies in Vientiane, there is virtually no risk of malaria in urban areas. Since malaria-carrying mosquitoes *(Anopheles)* generally only bite from early evening to early morning, you should sleep under a mosquito net (if possible) when in rural areas, even if you see only a few mosquitoes. The Australian Clinic in Vientiane sells light travel mosquito nets impregnated with permethrin for US$20 each. If you are outside during the biting hours, use an insect repellent. Even in a malarial area, not every mosquito is carrying the parasite responsible for the disease. Hence, the most important thing is to prevent as many of the critters from biting you as possible, to lessen the odds that you will be 'injected' by one carrying the parasite.

Once the parasites are in your bloodstream, they are carried to your liver where they reproduce. Days, weeks, or even months later (some experts say it can take as long as a year in certain cases), the parasites will enter the bloodstream again from the liver and this is when the symptoms first occur. Symptoms generally begin with chills and headache, followed by a high fever that lasts several hours. This may be accompanied by nausea, diarrhoea and more intense headaches. After a period of sweating the fever may subside and other symptoms go into remission. Of course, a severe flu attack could produce similar symptoms. That is why if you do develop a high fever and think you may have been exposed to the disease, it is imperative you get a blood check for malaria. Virtually any clinic or hospital in Thailand can administer this simple test.

Early treatment is usually successful in ridding the victim of the disease for good. If untreated or improperly treated, the symptoms will keep returning in cycles as the parasites move from liver to bloodstream and back. In the case of *falciparum*, the disease can be fatal if left untreated.

Like many other tropical diseases, malaria is frequently mis-diagnosed in Western countries. If you should develop the symptoms after a return to your home country, be sure to seek medical attention immediately and inform your doctor that you may have been exposed to malaria.

Dengue Fever In some areas of Laos there is a risk of contracting dengue fever via mosquito transmission. This time it's a day variety *(Aedes)* you have to worry about.

Dengue is found in urban as well as rural areas, especially in areas of human habitation (often indoors) where there is standing water. A yearly outbreak occurs in Vientiane during the early rainy season, so take special care from May to July.

Unlike malaria, dengue fever is caused by a virus and there is no chemical prophylactic or vaccination against it. In Laos there are four strains (serotypes) of dengue and once you've had one you usually develop an immunity specific to that strain. The symptoms come on suddenly and include high fever, severe headache and heavy joint and muscle pain (hence its older name 'breakbone fever'), followed a few days later by a rash that spreads from the torso to the arms, legs and face. Various risk factors such as age, immunity and viral strain may mitigate these symptoms so that they are less severe or last only a few days. Even when the basic symptoms are short-lived, it can take several weeks to fully recover from the resultant weakness.

In rare cases dengue may develop into a more severe condition known as dengue haemorrhagic fever (DHF), which is fatal. DHF is most common among Asian children under 15 who are undergoing a second dengue infection, so the risk for DHF for most international travellers is very low.

Although the latest estimate says you have only a one in 10,000 chance of contracting dengue when bitten by the *Aedes* mosquito (ie only 1 in 10,000 *Aedes* mosquitoes is infectious), I have personally known several travellers (including myself) who have come down with the disease over the years. By contrast I've only ever met one *falang* (foreigner) who contracted malaria in Laos or Thailand. Probably the fact that more people are outdoors in the daytime means exposure is greater. The best way to prevent dengue, as with malaria, is to take care not to be bitten by mosquitoes.

The only treatment for dengue is bed rest, constant rehydration and acetaminophen (Tylenol, Panadol) every four hours. Avoid aspirin, which increases the risk of haemorrhaging. Hospital supervision is necessary in extreme cases.

Japanese Encephalitis A few years ago this viral disease was practically unheard of. Although long endemic to tropical Asia (as well as China, Korea, Japan and eastern Russia), there are regular rainy season epidemics in northern Thailand and Vietnam. A night-biting mosquito *(Culex)* is the carrier for JE and the risk is said to be greatest in rural zones near areas where pigs are raised or rice is grown, since pigs and certain wild birds, whose habitat may include rice fields, serve as reservoirs for the virus.

Persons who may be at risk of contracting JE in Laos are those who will be spending long periods of time in rural areas during the rainy season. If you belong to this group, you may want to get a JE vaccination. The vaccination course consists of three injections given over 30 days. The vaccine has been associated with serious allergic reactions so the decision to have it should be balanced against the risk of contracting the illness. Check with the government health service in your home country before you leave to see if it's available; if not, arrange to be vaccinated in Bangkok, Hong Kong or Singapore, where the vaccine is easy to find.

A booster is recommended every two years after the initial course of three injections. The symptoms of JE are sudden fever, chills and headache, followed by vomiting and delirium, a strong aversion to bright light, and sore joints and muscles. Advanced cases may result in convulsions and coma. Estimates of the fatality rate for JE range from 20 to 60%, depending on the country in which it's diagnosed.

As with other mosquito-borne diseases, the best way to prevent JE (outside of the vaccine) is to avoid being bitten.

Cuts, Bites & Stings

Cuts & Scratches In hot, humid climates like that of Laos throughout much of the year, even small wounds can become infected easily. Always keep cuts and scrapes scrupulously clean, especially those on the lower extremities. If a small wound does become infected, clean it regularly with a good antiseptic (eg povidone-iodine). If it's serious, you may have to take a course of antibiotic medication. If the infection is on the legs or feet, lie down as much as possible until the infection subsides.

Snake Bite To minimise your chances of being bitten always wear boots, socks and long trousers when walking through undergrowth where snakes may be present. Don't put your hands into holes and crevices and be careful when collecting firewood.

Snake bites do not cause instantaneous death and anti-venenes are usually available. Keep the victim calm and still, wrap the bitten limb tightly, as you would for a sprained ankle, and then attach a splint to immobilise it. Then seek medical help, if possible with the dead snake for identification. Don't attempt to catch the snake if there is any remote possibility of being bitten again. Tourniquets and sucking out the poison are now comprehensively discredited.

Bedbugs & Lice Bedbugs live in various places, particularly dirty mattresses and bedding. Spots of blood on bedclothes or on the wall around the bed can be read as a suggestion to find another hotel. Bedbugs leave itchy bites in neat rows. Calamine lotion may help.

Lice cause itching and discomfort and make themselves at home in your hair (head lice), your clothing (body lice) or in your pubic hair (crabs). They get to you by direct contact with infected people or through the sharing of combs, clothing and the like. Powder or shampoo treatment will kill the lice, and infected clothing should then be washed in very hot water.

Leeches & Ticks Leeches may be present in damp monsoon forest conditions and attach themselves to your skin to suck your blood. Hikers often get them on their legs or in their boots. Salt or a lighted cigarette end will make them fall off. Do not pull them off as the bite is then more likely to become infected.

The best way to prevent leeches from

attaching themselves to you is to apply insect repellent to your boots and lower trouser legs. You should always check your body if you have been walking through a potentially tick-infested area as ticks can cause skin infections and other more serious diseases. If a tick is found attached, press down around the tick's head with tweezers, grab the head and gently pull upwards. Avoid pulling the rear of the body as this may squeeze the tick's gut contents through the attached mouth parts into the skin, increasing the risk of infection and disease. Smearing chemicals on the tick will not make it let go and is not recommended.

Women's Health

Gynaecological Problems Poor diet, lowered resistance due to the use of antibiotics for stomach upsets and even contraceptive pills can lead to vaginal infections when travelling in hot climates. Keeping the genital area clean, wearing cotton underwear and skirts or loose-fitting trousers will help to prevent infections.

Yeast infections, characterised by a rash, itch and discharge can be treated with a vinegar or even lemon juice douche or with yogurt. Nystatin, miconazole or clotrimazole suppositories are the usual medical prescription. Trichomonas and gardnerella are more serious infections with a smelly discharge and sometimes a burning sensation when urinating. Sexual partners must also be treated and if a vinegar-water douche is not effective medical attention should be sought. Flagyl is the prescribed drug.

Pregnancy Most miscarriages occur during the first three months of pregnancy so this is the most risky time to travel. The last three months should also be spent within reasonable distance of good medical care as quite serious problems can develop at this time. Pregnant women should avoid all unnecessary medication, but vaccinations and malarial prophylactics should still be taken where possible. Additional care should be taken to prevent illness and particular attention should be paid to diet and nutrition.

Medical Emergencies

Laos has no facilities for major medical emergencies; the state-run hospitals are among the worst in South-East Asia in terms of hygiene, staff training, equipment and the availability of medicines. Expatriate foreigners generally make use of the Australian embassy clinic (see the Vientiane chapter for its location), which will treat visitors with relatively minor health problems.

For any serious or chronic conditions, you're better off crossing the river to Thailand. If a medical problem can wait till you're in Bangkok, all the better, since excellent hospitals are available there (eg, the Seventh Day Adventist Hospital, 430 Phitsanulok Rd).

For medical emergencies that can't wait till Bangkok and which can't be treated at one of the embassy clinics, you can arrange to have ambulances summoned from nearby Udon Thani or Khon Kaen in Thailand. Wattana Private Hospital (☎ (042) 241031/3) in Udon Thani is the closest; Lao Westcoast Helicopter (☎ 512023, fax 512055) at Hangar 703, Wattay Airport, will fly emergency patients to Udon for around US$200. Si Nakharin Hospital (☎ (043) 237602/6) is farther away in Khon Kaen but is supposed to be the best medical facility in northeastern Thailand. From either of these hospitals, patients can be transferred to Bangkok as necessary.

TOILETS & SHOWERS

In Laos, as in many other Asian countries, the 'squat toilet' is the norm except in hotels and guest houses geared toward tourists and international business travellers. Instead of trying to approximate a chair or stool like a modern sit-down toilet, a traditional Asian toilet sits more or less flush with the surface of the floor, with two footpads on either side of the porcelain abyss. For persons who have never used a squat toilet it takes a bit of getting used to. If you find yourself feeling awkward the first couple of times you use one, you can console yourself with the knowledge that, according to those who study such matters, people who use squat toilets are much less likely to develop hemorrhoids than people who use sit toilets.

Next to the typical squat toilet is a bucket or cement reservoir filled with water. A plastic bowl usually floats on the water's surface or sits nearby. This water supply has a two-fold function; toilet-goers scoop water from the reservoir with the plastic bowl and use it to clean the nether regions while still squatting over the toilet. Since there is usually no mechanical flushing device attached to a squat toilet, a few extra scoops must be poured into the toilet basin to flush waste into the septic system. More rustic toilets in rural areas may simply consist of a few planks over a hole in the ground.

Even in places where sit-down toilets are installed, the plumbing may not be designed to take toilet paper. In such cases there will be the usual washing bucket nearby or there will be a waste basket where you're supposed to place used toilet paper.

Public toilets are uncommon outside hotel lobbies and airports. While on the road between towns and villages, it is perfectly acceptable to go behind a tree or bush or even to use the roadside when nature calls.

Bathing

Most hotels and guest houses in the country do not have hot water, though places in the larger cities will usually offer small electric shower heaters in their more expensive rooms. Very few boiler-style water heaters are available.

The vast majority of rural Lao bathe in rivers or streams. Those living in towns or cities may have washrooms where a large jar or cement trough is filled with water for bathing purposes. A plastic or metal bowl is used to sluice water from the jar or trough over the body. Even in homes where showers are installed, heated water is uncommon. Most Lao bathe at least twice a day.

If ever you find yourself bathing in a public place you should wear a *phàa salóng* or *phàa sìn* (cotton wraparounds for men and women respectively); nude bathing is not the norm.

WOMEN TRAVELLERS

Everyday incidents of sexual harassment are much less common in Laos than in virtually any other Asian country. Lonely Planet, in fact, has had no reports of any such incidents among visitors to Laos so far. In general all visitors to Laos are treated with the utmost respect and courtesy.

Comparisons with Thailand are inevitable, and the two are rather similar with regard to women's social status. One major difference between the two countries is that prostitution is much less common in Laos, where it is a very serious criminal offence. While a Thai woman who wants to preserve a 'proper' image usually won't associate with foreign males for fear of being perceived as a prostitute, in Laos this is not the case (although a Lao woman generally isn't seen alone with any male in public unless married). But Lao women drink beer and *lào-láo* (rice liquor), something 'proper' Thai females rarely do (even in Bangkok).

Hence a foreign woman seen drinking in a cafe or restaurant isn't usually perceived as 'loose' or available as she might be in Thailand. This in turn means that there are generally fewer problems with uninvited male solicitations.

What *is* often perceived as improper or disrespectful behaviour by foreign females is the wearing of clothes that bare the thighs, shoulders or breasts. Long trousers and walking shorts (for men too), as well as skirts, are acceptable attire; tank tops, sleeveless blouses and short skirts or shorts are not.

GAY & LESBIAN TRAVELLERS

Lao culture is very tolerant of homosexuality although there is not as prominent a gay/lesbian scene as in neighbouring Thailand. Public displays of affection – whether heterosexual or homosexual – are frowned upon.

DISABLED TRAVELLERS

With its lack of paved roads or footpaths (sidewalks) – even when present the latter are often uneven – Laos presents many physical obstacles for the mobility-impaired.

Rarely do public buildings feature ramps or other access points for wheelchairs, nor do any hotels consistently make efforts to provide handicapped access. Hence you're pretty much left to your own resources. Public transport is particularly crowded and difficult, even for the fully ambulatory.

For wheelchair travellers, any trip to Laos will require a good deal of advance planning. Fortunately a growing network of information sources can put you in touch with those who may have wheeled through Laos before. There is no better source of information than someone who's done it.

Three international organisations which act as clearing houses for information on world travel for the mobility-impaired are: Mobility International USA (☎ (503) 343-1284), PO Box 10767, Eugene, OR 97440, USA; Access Foundation (☎ (516) 887-5798), PO Box 356, Malverne, NY 11565, USA; and Society for the Advancement of Travel for the Handicapped (SATH) (☎ (718) 858-5483), 26 Court St, Brooklyn, NY 11242, USA.

Abilities magazine (☎ (416) 766-9188, fax 762-8716), PO Box 527, Station P, Toronto, ON, Canada M5S 2T1, carries a new column called 'Accessible Planet' which offers tips on foreign travel for people with disabilities. One story described how two French wheelchair travellers trekked around northern Thailand, an experience which would be very comparable to much travel in Laos. The book *Exotic Destinations for Wheelchair Travelers* by Ed Hansen and Bruce Gordon (Full Data Ltd, San Francisco) contains useful information on South-East Asia (including Thailand), though nothing specific to Laos.

If you're passing through Bangkok – as most people who visit Laos do – you might try contacting Disabled Peoples International, Council of Disabled People of Thailand (☎ (02) 255-1718, fax 252-3676) at 78/2 Tivanond Rd, Pak Kret, Nonthaburi 11120 and Handicapped International at 87/2 Soi 15 Sukhumvit Rd, Bangkok 10110.

TRAVEL WITH CHILDREN

Like many places in South-East Asia, travelling with children in Laos can be a lot of fun

as long as you come well prepared with the right attitudes, physical requirements and the usual parental patience. Lonely Planet's *Travel with Children* by Maureen Wheeler et al contains useful advice on how to cope with kids on the road and what to bring along to make things go more smoothly, with special attention paid to travel in developing countries.

The Lao love children and in many instances will shower attention on your offspring, who will find ready playmates among their Lao counterparts and temporary nanny service at practically every stop.

For the most part parents needn't worry too much about health concerns though it pays to lay down a few ground rules – such as regular hand-washing – to head off potential medical problems. All the usual health precautions apply (see the Health section earlier for details); children should especially be warned not to play with animals encountered along the way since rabies is very common in Laos.

DANGERS & ANNOYANCES
Road Travel

Until 1994 it was difficult to get permission to travel by road in Laos simply because the Lao government was terrified of losing tourists to natural and not-so-natural mishaps, thus tarnishing the country's international image. The natural risks are obvious – road conditions and vehicle maintenance outside the Mekong river valley are quite substandard and if you were to become involved in a serious injury accident it might take days to reach a hospital.

Since the repeal of the travel permit requirement you can now travel almost anywhere in the country by road – that is, where you can find a road. The risk of breakdowns and accidents is as great as ever but the increased frequency and availability of interprovincial public transport over the last two years mean there's a slightly better chance of reaching assistance more quickly than before.

With a couple of exceptions most areas of the country are secure in the military sense.

Every year several buses and trucks are attacked on Route 13 between Vientiane and Luang Prabang near Kasi; how many Lao have been killed in these attacks is not known since the government never allows the national press to report on them. Perhaps 10 to 15 people a year are killed by small-arms fire or mortar attacks in the Kasi area; in late 1995 two French travellers on a public bus from Luang Prabang to Kasi were wounded in such an attack.

Official reports assign the blame to 'bandits' but antigovernment rebels – most likely Hmong remnants from General Vang Pao's disbanded army – may be responsible. Route 13 has been upgraded and paved as far as Kasi, and the remaining portion between Kasi and Luang Prabang is due to be finished in the next couple of years. Once this happens, the Lao army will probably be able to secure this area. Until the area is declared safe, you travel this road at your own risk; we recommend flying or going by boat along the Mekong instead, until the attacks in this area have entirely subsided for at least a year. Ask around in Vientiane or Luang Prabang to get the latest story.

Another section of road where there were frequent ambushes between 1993 and 1995 was the western portion of Route 7 in Xieng Khuang Province, between the road's westernmost terminus at Route 13 and its crossing over the Nam Ngum river near Muang Sui (east of Phonsavan). An Australian engineer was killed in this area in early 1995 and several Lao have also died in attacks. At the moment military checkpoints along this section of Route 7 turn back anyone travelling without military escort.

South of the aforementioned road is Saisombun Special Zone, a new administrative district which is definitely *not* safe as of this writing. Carved out of eastern Vientiane, south-western Xieng Khuang and north-western Bolikhamsai provinces in 1994, this 7105 sq km district (larger than the province of Bokeo) is considered a 'troubled' area. Four UN Drug Control Programme staff – all Lao – died in an attack in this zone in 1994 and there have been some vicious attacks on

local buses as well. The Lao government created the new zone with the intent of clearing up the guerrilla/bandit problem in the area and have stationed two military battalions here to accomplish the task. The capital of this new zone is Long Tieng (Long Chen), formerly a CIA/USAF/Hmong army base during the Indochinese War; the town has been renamed Saisombun.

Route 6 north from Pakxan through Saisombun Special Zone to just south of Muang Khun (Xieng Khuang Province) continues to be plagued with security problems. North of Muang Khun, all the way to Sam Neua in Hua Phan Province, this road is relatively safe.

Another area in the north where attacks have occurred in the past – but not recently – is along the road between Luang Nam Tha and Huay Xai, especially in the vicinity of Vieng Phukha, a former Hmong guerrilla stronghold. As of 1995 this road is reportedly secure and many people have traversed it without any problem. A Thai company is currently upgrading this road all the way from Huay Xai to the Chinese border.

In 1992 bandits attacked a couple of buses and robbed the passengers on Route 13 north-west of Pakxan, around 50 km south-east of Vientiane. Since that time nothing else has occurred along this section of road and it is considered safe.

While it might seem ironic that the former Liberated Zones are still the most insecure parts of Laos even though the war ended in 1974, the fact is that most of the Lao territory outside the Mekong river valley was never secure. Even at the height of the Lan Xang Kingdom and later French colonial rule, the highland peoples retained a high degree of independence. The rugged mountains and upland valleys make as good a hiding place for anti-LPRP organisations and other unruly sorts today as for the PL during the war.

UXO

In the eastern portions of the country toward the Vietnamese border – particularly in the provinces of Hua Phan, Xieng Khuang, Sekong and Attapeu (although 10 provinces are affected to at least some degree) – there are large areas contaminated by unexploded ordnance (UXO) left behind by nearly a hundred years of warfare. The numerical majority of UXO found today was left behind by ground battles and includes French, Chinese, American, Soviet and Vietnamese materials, among them mortar shells, munitions, white phosphorus canisters, land mines and cluster bombs. Cluster bombs (known as *bombi* to the Lao) pose by far the greatest potential danger to people living or travelling through these areas and account for most of the estimated 60 to 80 casualties per year. Most of those injured or killed are Lao citizens, an estimated 40% of whom are children.

Statistically speaking, the UXO risk for the average foreign visitor is quite low, but travellers should exercise caution when considering off-road wilderness travel in the aforementioned provinces. Never touch an object on the ground that may be UXO, no matter how old, crusty and defunct it may appear.

Theft

On the whole, the Lao are trustworthy people and theft is not much of a problem. Still, it's best if you keep your hotel room locked when you're out and while sleeping at night. If you ride a crowded bus, watch your luggage and don't keep money in your trouser pockets.

Queues

The Lao follow the usual South-East Asian method of queuing for services, which is to say they don't form a line at all but simply push en masse toward the point of distribution, whether it's ticket counters, post office windows or bus doors. It won't help to get angry and shout 'I was here first!' since first-come, first-serve simply isn't the way things are done here. Learn to play the game the Lao way, by pushing your money, passport, letters or whatever to the front of the crowd as best you can. Eventually you'll get through.

Paranoid Officials

Some of the more remote corners of eastern Laos, eg Hua Phan and Attapeu provinces, are renowned for the suspicious attitude of the local officials toward foreign visitors. In part this can be explained by the simple reality that some places see very few foreigners. It may also be due to the fact there are still PL hardliners running the show in these areas who haven't yet cottoned to the political liberalisation taking place elsewhere in the country.

In such police fiefdoms the typical scenario begins to unfold when you try and comply with the requirement that you check in with provincial immigration. Sometimes a particularly intransigent official will spend a half hour – up to an hour in some cases, as unbelievable as it may seem – thumbing through your passport, examining every single visa it contains two or three times over. Occasionally they may want to hold onto your passport for safekeeping, to make sure you don't leave town for parts unknown without their knowledge.

In such instances the best thing to do is to stay patient and wait it out, as eventually you'll be sent on your way. Trying to speed things up by bribing officials isn't a good practice since it only contributes to further corruption and will almost certainly result in future requests for bribes from every other foreigner who happens along.

If your papers aren't in order – in particular if your visa has expired – you could be in for a small hassle. Although in most places in Laos the penalty for overstaying your visa is a simple fine of 3000 to 5000 kip per day, in the eyes of a hardliner you might be perceived as some sort of provocateur. Again it pays to remain patient and to comply with all requests for further explanation or documentation. Usually the worst that can happen is that you'll be sent back in the direction whence you came. On rare occasions you may be subject to a couple days of questioning during which your passport is held at the police station and you're confined to town.

Incidents involving excessive suspicion such as described above are quite rare overall. As more foreigners travel to the far-flung corners of the country they should become even less frequent.

BUSINESS HOURS

Government offices are generally open from 8 to 11.30 am or noon and 2 to 5 pm. Shops and private businesses open and close a bit later and either stay open during lunch or close for just an hour.

HOLIDAYS & FESTIVALS

The traditional Lao calendar, like the calendars of China, Vietnam, Cambodia and Thailand, is a solar-lunar mix. The year itself is reckoned by solar phases, while the months are divided according to lunar phases (unlike the Western calendar in which months as well as years are reckoned by the sun). The Buddhist Era (BE) calendar usually figures year one as 543 BC, which means that you must subtract 543 from the Lao calendar year to arrive at the Christian calendar familiar in the West (eg, 1997 AD is 2540 BE according to the Lao Buddhist calendar). An earlier Lao system – seen in some archaeological inscriptions – follows a scheme in which year one is 638 BC (eg, 1997 AD = 2635 BE).

Festivals in Laos are mostly linked to agricultural seasons or historical Buddhist holidays. The general word for festival in Lao is *bun* (or *boun*). See the table on the following pages for festival dates.

ACTIVITIES
Cycling

The overall lack of vehicular traffic makes cycling an attractive proposition in Laos although this advantage is somewhat offset by the general absence of roads in the first place. For any serious out-of-town cycling you're better off bringing your own bike, one that's geared to very rough road conditions.

In terms of road gradient and availability of food and accommodation, the easiest long-distance ride in the country is along Route 13 from Vientiane south to the Cambodian border. In the dry season this road becomes very dusty, and trucks – though

nowhere near as overwhelming as in Vietnam or Thailand – can be a bit of a nuisance. Other cycling routes of potential interest – all of them currently unpaved and rough but due to be upgraded over the next decade – include: Luang Prabang to Muang Khua; Huay Xai to Luang Nam Tha; Pakse to Attapeu; and Sam Neua to Phonsavan. The latter two routes are quite remote and require that you be prepared to camp if necessary along the way.

For obvious routes to avoid, see the Dangers & Annoyances section earlier.

Hiking & Trekking

Laos' mountainous, well-forested geography makes it a potentially ideal destination for people who like to walk in the outdoors. All 13 provinces have plenty of hiking possibilities, although the generally cautious nature of the authorities means that overnight trips that involve camping or staying overnight in villages are viewed with suspicion. So far not a single travel agency in Laos has been granted permission to lead overnight treks in any of the tribal areas, though several have tried to arrange such itineraries.

Day hiking is another story and you're free to walk in the mountains and forests almost anywhere in the country except the Saisombun Special Zone. See the Dangers & Annoyances section for more information on this new military-controlled district and for warnings on areas of eastern Laos contaminated by unexploded ordnance.

Provinces in Laos with the highest potential for relatively safe wilderness walking include Bokeo, Luang Nam Tha, Luang Prabang, Vientiane, Khammuan and Champasak. In particular the 17 newly designated National Biodiversity Conversation Areas (NBCAs) should yield rewarding territory for exploration (see the Ecology & Environment section in the previous chapter).

Except at the occasional waterfall near towns or cities, recreation areas with public facilities are nonexistent in Laos.

Boating

The rivers and streams of Laos provide

potential venues for all sorts of recreational boating, particularly rafting, canoeing and kayaking. No modern equipment exists, however, so it's strictly bring-your-own. Nor are there any regular bamboo-raft trips as in Thailand, though the country is prime territory for such.

As with bicycles, you shouldn't have any special customs difficulties in bringing your own small boat to Laos. Because of the difficulties of overland transport, however, the smaller and lighter your craft is, the more choices you'll have for places to paddle.

For trained paddlers almost any of the major waterways draining from the western slopes of the Annamite chain toward the Mekong river valley could be interesting. In the north, the Nam Ou, Nam Tha, Nam Khan, Nam Ngum and of course the Mekong river are navigable year-round by self-propelled craft. In central and southern Laos the Nam Theun, Se Don, Se Set and Se Kong as well as the Mekong are safe bets. The upstream areas of all these rivers can be accessed by road, so drop-offs and pick-ups are limited only by the availability of public or private vehicle travel.

Between Vientiane and Tha Khaek,

Lao Festivals

April

Pĭi Mai The lunar new year begins in mid-April and practically the entire country comes to a halt and celebrates. Houses are cleaned, people put on new clothes and Buddha images are washed with lustral water. In the wats, offerings of fruit and flowers are made at various altars and votive mounds of sand or stone are fashioned in the courtyards. Later the citizens take to the streets and douse one another with water, which is an appropriate activity as April is usually the hottest month of the year. This festival is particularly picturesque in Luang Prabang, where it includes elephant processions. The 15th, 16th, and 17th of April are official public holidays.

May

International Labour Day (1st) This honours workers all over the world. In Vientiane there are parades, but elsewhere not much happens. Public holiday.

Visakha Bu-saa (Visakha Puja, Full Moon) This falls on the 15th day of the 6th lunar month, which is considered the day of the Buddha's birth, enlightenment and *parinibbana* (passing away). Activities are centred around the wat, with much chanting, sermonising and, at night, beautiful candlelit processions.

Bun Bang Fai (Rocket Festival) This is a pre-Buddhist rain ceremony that is now celebrated alongside Visakha Puja in Laos and north-eastern Thailand. This can be one of the wildest festivals in the country, with plenty of music and dance (especially the irreverent *măw lám*

performances), processions and general merrymaking, culminating in the firing of bamboo rockets into the sky. In some places male participants blacken their bodies with lamp soot, while women wear sunglasses and carry carved wooden phalli to imitate men. The firing of the rockets is supposed to prompt the heavens to initiate the rainy season and bring much-needed water to the rice fields.

July

Khao Phansaa (also *Khao Watsa*, Full Moon) This is the beginning of the traditional three-month 'rains retreat', during which Buddhist monks are expected to station themselves in a single monastery. At other times of year they are allowed to travel from wat to wat or simply to wander in the countryside, but during the rainy season they forego the wandering so as not to damage fields of rice or other crops. This is also the traditional time of year for men to enter the monkhood temporarily, hence many ordinations take place.

August/September

Haw Khao Padap Din (Full Moon) This is a sombre festival in which the living pay respect to the dead. Many cremations take place – bones being exhumed for the purpose – during this time, and gifts are presented to the Sangha so that monks will chant on behalf of the deceased.

October/November

Awk Phansaa (Awk Watsa, Full Moon) This celebrates the end of the three-month rains retreat. Monks are allowed to leave the monasteries to several tributaries which feed into the Mekong are smaller and less known than the aforementioned but very scenic since they run through karst topography. In particular the Nam Xan, Nam Kading and Nam Hin Bun seem to be wide, relatively clean rivers. You're somewhat limited in choice by the availability of roads to take you upstream for drop-off; see the Southern Laos chapter for more details on which areas are accessible.

Between Champasak and the Cambodian border, the area of the Mekong known as Si Phan Don (Four Thousand islands) is easily accessible and provides superior paddling

possibilities among verdant islands and rapids.

There's one big caveat lurking behind the attainment of what could surely be described as paddler heaven: the legalities of floating down Lao waterways are a bit hard to discern. Local people don't need permits of any kind to launch self-propelled craft on any stream or river; technically foreigners aren't subject to any special regulations either as long as they're not transporting commercial cargo or fee-paying passengers. But should you travel this way on your own you ought to be prepared to face the occa-

---

travel and are presented with robes, alms-bowls and other requisites of the renunciative life. On the eve of Awk Phansaa many people fashion small banana-leaf boats carrying candles, incense and other offerings, and float them in rivers, a custom known as *lãi hũa fái*, similar to Loy Krathong in Thailand.

A second festival held in association with Awk Phansaa is *Bun Nam* (Water Festival). Boat races *(suang héua)* are commonly held in towns located on rivers, such as Vientiane, Luang Prabang and Savannakhet; in smaller towns these races are often postponed until National Day (2 Dec) so that residents aren't saddled with two costly festivals in two months.

November

That Luang Festival (Full Moon) This takes place at Pha That Luang in Vientiane. Hundreds of monks assemble to receive alms and floral votives early in the morning on the first day of the festival. There is a colourful procession between Pha That Luang and Wat Si Muang. The celebration lasts a week and includes fireworks and music, culminating in a candlelit circumambulation *(wien thien)* of That Luang. For more information on this major festival, see the Vientiane chapter.

December

Lao National Day (2nd) This celebrates the 1975 victory of the proletariat over the monarchy with parades, speeches etc. Lao national and communist hammer-and-sickle flags are flown all over the country. Celebration is mandatory, hence many poorer communities

postpone some of the traditional Awk Phansaa activities – usually practised roughly a month earlier – until National Day, thus saving themselves considerable expense (much to the detraction of Awk Phansaa). Public holiday.

December/January

Bun Pha Wet This is a temple-centred festival in which the *jataka* or birth-tale of Prince Vessantara, the Buddha's penultimate life, is recited. This is also a favoured time (second to Khao Phansaa) for Lao males to be ordained into the monkhood. The scheduling of Bun Pha Wet is staggered so that it is held on different days in different villages. This is so that relatives and friends living in different villages can invite one another to their respective celebrations.

February

Magha Puja (Makkha Bu-saa, Full Moon) This commemorates a speech given by the Buddha to 1250 enlightened monks who came to hear him without prior summons. In the talk, the Buddha laid down the first monastic regulations and predicted his own death. Chanting and offerings mark the festival, culminating in the candlelit circumambulation of wats throughout the country (celebrated most fervently in Vientiane and at the Khmer ruins of Wat Phu, near Champasak).

Vietnamese Tet & Chinese New Year This is celebrated in Vientiane, Pakse and Savannakhet with parties, deafening nonstop fireworks and visits to Vietnamese and Chinese temples. Chinese and Vietnamese-run businesses usually close for three days.

sional suspicious official along the way, simply because you're doing something that's out of the ordinary. Main navigational thoroughfares such as the Mekong and Nam Ou have riverbank checkpoints placed at or near provincial borders where you'll need to have your papers stamped.

Should you want to navigate in the local Lao way, small new or used wooden canoes can be purchased for US$50 to 120 without a motor; add US$35 to 50 for motorised canoes. Small Japanese outboard motors of 5.5 to 11 hp can be bought in any of the larger cities along the Mekong river. These sorts of boats are suitable only for well-navigated waterways as their weight and bulk prohibits portage around shallows or rapids.

COURSES
Language Study
Short-term courses in spoken and written Lao are available at the following study centres in Vientiane:

Centre de Langue Française
    Thanon Lane Xang (☎ 215764)
Lao-American Language Center
    152 Thanon Sisangvon, Ban Naxay (☎ 414321, fax 413760)
Mittaphap School
    Km 3 Tha Deua (☎ 313452)
Saysettha Language Centre
    Thanon Nong Bon, Ban Phonxai (☎ 414480)
Vientiane University College
    Thanon That Luang, opposite the Ministry of Foreign Affairs (☎ 414873, fax 414346)

Mrs Kesone Sayasane at Burapha Development Consultants (☎ 216708, fax 212981), 14 Thanon Fa Ngum, will tutor the Lao language privately or arrange custom-designed group courses. Mrs Kesone was a member of the short-lived Peace Corps Laos training staff and has worked with South-East Asian summer language courses given yearly at major university Asian studies departments in America.

Meditation Study
If you can speak Lao or Thai, or can arrange an interpreter, you may be able to study *vipassana* (insight meditation) with Ajaan Sali, the abbot of Wat Sok Pa Luang in south-east Vientiane. See the Vientiane chapter for more detail.

WORK
With Laos' expanding economy and the quickening influx of aid organisations and foreign companies, the number of jobs available to foreigners increases slightly each year although one can't count on finding employment immediately. By far the greatest number of available positions – as they occur – will be found in the nation's capital.

Possibilities include teaching English privately or at one of the several language centres in Vientiane, which is currently paying around US$10 an hour. Certificates or degrees in English teaching aren't absolutely necessary though they increase your chances of hire considerably.

If you possess a technical background or international volunteer experience, you might be able to find work with a UN-related programme or a nongovernmental organisation involved with foreign aid or technical assistance to Laos. For positions such as these, your best bet is to visit the Vientiane offices of each organisation and enquire about personnel needs and vacancies.

Liste du corps diplomatique et consulaire à Vientiane, published in French only by the Ministry of Foreign Affairs, contains the addresses of the main UN organisations working in Laos. Another booklet entitled *Non-Governmental Organisations in Laos* lists contact information as well as programme descriptions for 40 NGOs registered in Laos. Either publication can be purchased at Raintree Bookstore or the Lane Xang Hotel in Vientiane.

International companies hire locally on the rare occasion. A list of such companies in Laos is available from the Ministry of Foreign Affairs.

Once you have a sponsoring employer, a visa valid for working and residing in Laos is relatively easy to obtain. The most time-consuming part of the process is receiving ministry approval in Vientiane; depending on the sponsoring organisation and type of work, permission from more than one ministry may be necessary. If your sponsor takes care of all the paperwork in Laos, however, this should culminate in an order to a Lao embassy abroad to issue you the appropriate visa in a day or two.

ACCOMMODATION

Laos does not have a great number or variety of hotels but, unlike in China or Myanmar, foreigners aren't restricted to certain hotels, except in the rare instance where a provincial guest house is reserved for government officials. Tourist hotels are typically priced in US dollars, while guest houses and less expensive business hotels (common in Huay Xai, Luang Prabang, Savannakhet and Pakse) are priced in baht or kip.

It is almost always cheaper to pay in the requested currency rather than let the hotel or guest house convert the price into another currency. If the price is quoted in kip, you'll do best to pay in kip; if priced in dollars, pay in dollars. If you ask to pay a dollar-quoted tariff in kip (or vice versa), you'll lose out to the hotel's mandated lower exchange rate. Room rates in this book are given in the currency medium quoted by the particular establishment.

Outside the Mekong river valley, most provincial capitals have only two or three basic hotels or guest houses although the number and quality of places to stay seems to be increasing every year. Hotel rooms in Vientiane, Luang Prabang, Savannakhet and Pakse offer private bathrooms and fans as standard features for around US$10 to 15 a night. Higher cost rooms have air-con, and sometimes hot water, for US$15 to 25. Hot water is hardly a necessity in lowland Laos (where it is most likely to be available), but would be nice in the mountains (where it's almost never available).

Small business hotels in Luang Prabang, Muang Xai, Savannakhet and Pakse cost around US$5 to 8 per night for simple double rooms. Vientiane has a few guest houses now with rooms costing as low as US$5 or US$6 a night with shared toilet and bathing facilities. In the more farflung areas of the country rustic guest houses with shared facilities cost only 1000 to 3000 kip (about US$1 to US$3) per night per person. Though oriented toward local guests, these guest houses generally welcome foreigners.

Large hotels oriented toward the Asian business and leisure traveller or the occasional Western tour group are beginning to multiply in the larger cities. At these, tariffs of US$25 to 60 are common for rooms with air-con, hot water, TV and mini-refrigerator. The LPDR government has plans to build more hotels of this nature over the next decade using foreign (mostly Thai, Singaporean and Taiwanese) capital. The only Western chain that has so far entered the hotel market in Laos is Accor Australia Pacific, which recently took over The Belvedere in Vientiane for their Novotel chain.

FOOD

Lao cuisine is very similar to Thai cuisine in many ways. Like Thai food, almost all dishes are cooked with fresh ingredients, including *phák* (vegetables), *pǫa* (fish), *kai* (chicken), *pét* (duck), *mūu* (pork) and *sìn ngúa* (beef) or *sìn khwái* (water buffalo).

Because of Laos' distance from the sea, freshwater fish is more commonly used than saltwater fish or shellfish. In rural areas wild rather than domestic animals – especially deer, wild pig, squirrels, civets, monitor lizards, junglefowls/pheasants, dhole (wild dog), rats and birds – provide most of the meat in local diets, though the eating of endangered species causes much consternation among international wildlife conservation agencies. In part this practice is due to the expense involved in animal husbandry, in part due to the everyday Lao cultural preference for the taste of wild game. In rural villages, domesticated animals such as pigs, chickens, ducks, and cattle are reserved for ceremonial occasions.

Lime juice, lemon grass and fresh coriander leaf are added to give the food its characteristic tang. To salt the food, various fermented fish concoctions are used, most commonly *nâam pǫa*, which is a thin sauce of fermented anchovies (usually imported from Thailand), and p̩aa dàek, a coarser, native Lao preparation that includes chunks of fermented freshwater fish, rice husks and rice 'dust'. Nâam p̩aa dàek is the sauce poured from p̩aa dàek. (See the Health section earlier in this chapter for warnings on eating p̩aa dàek.)

Other common seasonings include the khaa (galingale root), màak phét (hot chillies), màak thua d̩ɪn (ground peanuts – more often a condiment), nâam màak khāam (tamarind juice), kh̩ɪng (ginger) and nâam màak phâo or nâam kát (coconut milk). Chillies are sometimes served on the side in hot pepper sauces called jaew. In Luang Prabang, nāng khwái hàeng (dried water-buffalo skin) is a quite popular ingredient in local dishes.

One of the most common Lao dishes is làap, which is a Lao-style salad of minced meat, fowl or fish tossed with lime juice, garlic, khào khūa (roast, powdered sticky rice), green onions, mint leaves and chillies. It can be very hot or rather mild, depending on the cook. Meats mixed into làap are sometimes raw (díp) rather than cooked (súk). Làap is typically served with a large plate of lettuce, mint and steamed leaves of various sorts. Using your fingers you wrap a little làap in the lettuce and herbs and eat it accompanied with balls of sticky rice which you roll by hand.

Another dish you will often come across is t̩am màak hung (more commonly known as t̩am sòm in Vientiane), a spicy, tangy salad made by pounding shredded green papaya, lime juice, chillies, garlic, p̩aa dàek, nàam phàk-kàat (a paste of boiled, fermented lettuce leaves) and various other ingredients together in a large mortar. This is favourite market and street vendor food – customers typically inspect the array of possible t̩am màak hung ingredients the vendor has spread out on a table next to the mortar, then order a custom mix. For something different, ask the pounder to throw in a few màak kàwk, a sour, olive-shaped fruit. Sàep lāi (very delicious)!

Many Lao dishes are quite spicy because of the Lao penchant for màak phét. But the Lao also eat a lot of Chinese and Vietnamese food which is generally, but not always, less spicy. Fõe (rice noodle soup) is quite popular as a snack or even for breakfast, and is almost always served with a plate of fresh lettuce, mint, coriander, mung-bean sprouts, lime wedges and sometimes basil for adding to the soup as desired. In some places – especially in the south – people mix their own fõe sauce of lime, crushed fresh chili, káp and sugar at the table using a little saucer provided for that purpose.

Khào pûn, flour noodles topped with a sweet/spicy nâam kát (coconut sauce), is another popular noodle dish. These noodles are also eaten cold with various Vietnamese foods popular in urban Laos, particularly nāem neúang (barbecued pork meatballs) and yáw (spring rolls).

Rice is the foundation for all Lao meals (as opposed to snacks), as elsewhere in South-East Asia. In general, the Lao eat khào nīaw ('sticky' or glutinous rice), although khào jâo (ordinary white rice) is also common in urban areas. Sticky rice is served in lidded baskets called típ khào and eaten with the hands: the general practice is to grab a small fistful of rice from the típ khào, then roll it into a rough ball which is used to dip into the various dishes. At the end of the meal it's considered bad luck not to replace the lid on top of the típ khào.

Khào jâo, on the other hand, is eaten with a fork and spoon. The fork is only used to prod food onto the spoon, which is the main utensil for eating this type of rice. Mâi thuu (chopsticks) are only used for eating fõe or other Chinese noodle dishes.

Where to Eat

Many restaurants or foodstalls, especially outside Vientiane, do not have menus, so it is worthwhile memorising a standard 'repertoire' of dishes. Those restaurants that do offer written menus don't always have an English version (in fact, it's rare when they do). Most provinces have their own local specialities in addition to the standards and you might try asking for aahāan phi-sét (special food), allowing the proprietors to choose for you. In remote areas of the north and south, choices can be rather limited.

The most economical places to eat and the most dependable are *hàan fõe* (noodle-shops) and night markets. Most towns and villages have at least one night market and several *hàan fõe*. The next step up is the Lao-style cafe or *hàan kheûang deum* (drink shop) or *hàan kịn deum* (eat-drink shop), where a slightly more varied selection of dishes is usually served. Most expensive is the *hàan aahãan* (food shop), where the menu is usually posted on the wall or on a blackboard (in Lao).

Many *hàan aahãan* serve mostly Chinese or Vietnamese food. The ones that serve real Lao food can usually be distinguished by a large pan of water on a stool – or a modern lavatory – somewhere near the entrance for washing the hands before eating (since Lao food is traditionally eaten with the hands).

What to Eat

Except for the 'rice plates' and noodle dishes, Lao meals are usually ordered 'family style', which is to say that two or more people order together, sharing different dishes. Tradition-ally, the party orders one of each kind of dish, for example, one chicken, one fish, one soup etc. A few extras may be ordered for a large party. One dish is generally large enough for two people. If you come to eat at a Lao restau-rant alone and order one of these 'entrees', you had better be hungry or know enough Lao to order a small portion. Eating alone is some-thing the Lao generally consider unusual; but then as a falang you're an exception anyway. In Chinese or Thai restaurants a cheaper alter-native is to order dishes *làat khào* (over rice).

In Vientiane, Savannakhet and Luang Prabang, French bread is a popular break-fast food. Sometimes it's eaten plain with *kạa-féh nóm hâwn* (hot milk coffee), some-times it's eaten with *khai* (eggs) or in a baguette sandwich that contains Lao-style pat, and vegetables. When they're fresh, Lao baguettes are superb. Croissants and other French-style pastries are also available in the bakeries of Vientiane.

A list of standard dishes follows. Below the English is a transliterated pronunciation of the Lao names using the system outlined in the Language section, along with the Lao script so you can point to the name if neces-sary.

Appetisers ('Drinking Food')

Lao have a categtory of dishes called *káp kâem*, which are meant to be eaten on picnics or while consuming alcoholic beverages.

fried peanuts *thua jẹun*	ກົ່ວຈືນ
fried potatoes *mán falang jẹun*	ມັນຝະຫຼັ່ງຈືນ
shrimp chips *khào kiap kûng*	ເຂົ້າຂຽບກຸ້ງ
fried spring rolls *yáw jẹun*	ຍໍຈືນ
fresh spring rolls *yáw díp*	ຍໍດິບ
toasted pork *pîng mũu*	ປີ້ງໝູ
grilled chicken *pîng kai*	ປີ້ງໄກ່
spicy green papaya salad *tạm-sòm/tạm màak-hung*	ຕຳໝາກຫຸ່ງ

Soups

mild soup with vegetables & pork *kạeng jèut*	ແກງຈືດ
mild soup with vegetables, pork & bean curd *kạeng jèut tâo-hûu*	ແກງຈືດເຕົ້າຫູ້
soup with chicken, *khaa* & coconut *tôm khaa kai*	ຕົ້ມຂ່າໄກ່
fish & lemon grass soup with mushrooms *tôm yám pạa*	ຕົ້ມຍຳປາ
whole-rice soup *khào pìak*	ເຂົ້າປຽກປາ

Eggs

hard-boiled egg
khai tôm ຕົ້ມໄຂ່

fried egg
khai dạo ໄຂ່ດາວ

plain omelette
khai jẹun ຈືນໄຂ່

scrambled eggs
khai khùa ໄຂ່ຂົ້ວ

Bread & Pastries

plain bread (usually
French-style)
khào jii ເຂົ້າຈີ່

croissants
kwaa-song ກົວຊອງ

Chinese doughnuts
(Mandarin: *doujiang*)
pá-kô or ປະກ້ອງໂກ້ະ or
khanōm khuu ເຂົ້າໜົມຄູ

butter
bọe ເບີ

French bread with butter
khào jii bọe ເຂົ້າຈີ່ເບີ

Rice Dishes

fried rice
khào phát/khào khùa ເຂົ້າຜັດ

steamed white rice
khào nung ເຂົ້າໜຶ້ງ

sticky rice
khào nīaw ເຂົ້າໜຽວ

curry over rice
khào làat keng ເຂົ້າລາດແກງ

Noodles

flat rice-noodle soup with
vegetables & meat
fõe ເຝີ

flat rice-noodle soup
without broth
fõe hàeng ເຝີແຫ້ງ

flat rice noodles with gravy
làat nàa ລາດໜ້າ

yellow wheat noodles in
broth, with vegetables & meat
mii nâam ໝີ່ນ້ຳ

yellow wheat noodles
without broth
mii hàeng ໝີ່ແຫ້ງ

fried noodles with soy sauce
phát sáyûu ຜັດສະອິ້ວ

white flour noodles, served
with sweet-spicy sauce
khào pûn ເຂົ້າປຸ້ນ

Fish

crisp-fried fish
jẹun pạa ຈືນປາ

fried prawns
jẹun kûng ຈືນກຸ້ງ

grilled prawns
pîng kûng ປິ້ງກຸ້ງ

steamed fish
nèung pạa ໜຶ້ງປາ

grilled fish
pîng pạa ປິ້ງປາ

catfish
pạa dúk ປາດຸກ

eel
ian ອຽນ

giant Mekong catfish
pạa béuk ປາບຶກ

sheatfish
pạa sa-ngũa ປາສະຫງົ້ວ

carp
pạa pàak ປາປາກ

serpent fish
pạa khaw ປາຄໍ

freshwater sting ray
pạa fãa lái ປາຝາໄລ

Sweets

custard
sāngkha-nyāa ສັງຂະຫຍາ

egg custard
màw kạeng ເຂົ້າໜົມໝໍ້ແກງ

banana in coconut milk
nâam wāan màak kûay ນ້ຳຫວານໝາກກ້ວຍ

sticky rice in coconut
cream
   khào nīaw dǫeng ເຂົ້າໜຽວແດງ

sticky rice in coconut
cream & ripe mango
   khào nīaw màak muang ເຂົ້າໜຽວໝາກມ່ວງ

sticky rice cakes
   khào nóm ເຂົ້າໜົມ

sticky rice in coconut
milk cooked in bamboo
   khào lāam ເຂົ້າຫລາມ

Fruit
mandarin orange
   màak kîang ໝາກກ້ຽງ

watermelon
   màak móh ໝາກໂມ

mangosteen
   màak máng-khut ໝາກມັງຄຸດ

rambutan
   màak ngaw ໝາກເງາະ

rose-apple
   màak kǫang ໝາກກຽງ

banana
   màak kûay ໝາກກ້ວຍ

pineapple
   màak nat ໝາກນັດ

mango
   màak muang ໝາກມ່ວງ

durian
   màak thu-lían ທຸລຽນ

longan
   màak yám yái ໝາກຍ່ຳໄຍ

papaya
   màak hung ໝາກຫຸງ

custard-apple
   màak khìap ໝາກຂຽບ

lime or lemon
   màak náo ໝາກນາວ

guava
   màak sīi-dǫa ໝາກສີດາ

betel nut
   màak ໝາກ

jackfruit
   màak mîi ໝາກມີ້

Useful Food Sentences
I eat only vegetarian food.
   Khàwy kịn tae phàk
   thao-nân. ຂ້ອຍກິນແຕ່ຜັກ

(I) don't like it hot & spicy.
   Baw mak phét. ບໍ່ມັກເຜັດ

(I) like it hot & spicy.
   Mak phét. ມັກເຜັດ

What do you have that's
special?
   Míi nyãng pẹn
   phi-sēt? ມີຫຍັງພິເສດ

I didn't order this.
   Án-nîi khàwy
   baw dâi sang. ຂ້ອຍບໍ່ໄດ້ສັ່ງແນວນີ້

Do you have ...?
   Míi ... baw? ມີ...ບໍ່?

Durian
The durian is held in high esteem by the Lao
and throughout South-East Asia, but most
Westerners dislike this fruit. There are several
varieties, so keep trying until you find the
variety that you find out of this world! ■

DRINKS
Nonalcoholic Drinks
Water Water purified for drinking purposes
is simply called *nâam deum* (drinking
water), whether boiled or filtered. *All* water
offered to customers in restaurants or hotels

will be purified, so one needn't fret about the safety of taking a sip (for more information on water safety, see the Health section earlier in this chapter). In restaurants you can ask for *nâam pao* (plain water, which is always either boiled or taken from a purified source) served by the glass at no charge, or order by the bottle. A bottle of carbonated or soda water costs about the same as a bottle of plain purified water but the bottles are smaller.

Coffee Good coffee, both arabica and robusta, is grown in the Bolaven plateau area of southern Laos. Bolaven Coffee Plantation, a joint Russian/Lao company and the country's 17th biggest company, produces around 6000 tonnes per year, while smaller enterprises add another 4000 tonnes. Ninety percent of the beans produced are exported; the largest export share – about 14% – goes to France and another 10% is consumed in Vietnam, despite the fact that Lao coffee costs more per tonne than any other coffee in the world.

The Lao tend to brew coffee without adding ground tamarind seed as in Thailand. Traditionally, Lao coffee is roasted by wholesalers, ground by vendors and filtered just before serving. On the other hand the typical Lao restaurant – especially those in hotels, guest houses and other tourist-oriented establishments – serves instant coffee with packets of artificial non-dairy creamer on the side. Sometimes restaurants or vendors with the proper accoutrements for making traditional filtered coffee keep a supply of Nescafé just for falangs. To get real Lao coffee ask for *kaa-féh thõng* (literally, 'bag coffee'), which refers to the traditional method of preparing a cup of coffee by filtering hot water through a bag-shaped cloth filter. Another term used occasionally is *kaa-féh tôm* (boiled coffee).

The usual brewed coffee is served mixed with sugar and sweetened condensed milk – if you don't want either be sure to specify *kaa-féh dam* (black coffee) followed with *baw sai nâam-tan* (without sugar). Coffee is often served in a glass instead of a ceramic cup – to pick up a glass of hot coffee, grasp it along the top rim.

In central and southern Laos coffee is almost always served with a chaser of hot *nâam sáa* (weak Chinese tea), while in the north it's typically served with a glass of plain hot water.

Tea Both Indian-style (black) and Chinese-style (green or semi-cured) teas are commonly served in Laos. The latter predominates in Chinese restaurants and is also the usual ingredient in *nâam sáa*, the weak, often lukewarm, tea traditionally served in restaurants for free. The aluminium teapots commonly seen on tables in Chinese and Vietnamese restaurants are filled with nâam saa; ask for a plain *jàwk pao* (glass) and you can drink as much as you'd like at no charge. For iced nâam sáa ask for a glass of ice (which usually costs 25 kip) and pour your own; for stronger fresh Chinese tea, request *sáa jin*.

Black tea, both imported and locally grown, is usually available in the same restaurants or foodstalls that serve real coffee. An order of *sáa hâwn* (hot tea) almost always results in a cup (or glass) of black tea with sugar and condensed milk. As with coffee you must specify beforehand if you want black tea without milk and/or sugar.

drinking water *nâam deum*	ບໍ່ດື່ມ
boiled water *nâam tôm*	ບໍ່ຕົ້ມ
ice *nâam kâwn*	ບໍ່ກອນ
weak Chinese tea *nâam sáa*	ບໍ່ຊາ
hot water *nâam hâwn*	ບໍ່ຮອນ
cold water *nâam yén*	ບໍ່ເຢັນ
hot Lao tea with sugar *sáa dam hâwn*	ຊາຮອນ

hot Lao tea with milk & sugar
  sáa nóm hâwn ຊານົມຮ້ອນ

iced Lao tea with milk & sugar
  sáa nóm yén ຊານົມເຢັນ

iced Lao tea with sugar only
  sáa dạm yén ຊາທວານເຢັນ

no sugar (command)
  baw sai nâm-tạan ບໍ່ໃສ່ນ້ຳຕານ

hot Lao coffee with milk & sugar
  kạa-féh nóm hâwn ກາເຟນົມຮ້ອນ

iced Lao coffee with milk & sugar
  kạa-féh nóm yén ກາເຟນົມເຢັນ

hot Lao coffee with sugar, no milk
  kạa-féh dạm ກາເຟດຳ

iced Lao coffee with sugar, no milk
  kạa-féh oh lîang ໂອລຽງ

hot Nescafe with milk & sugar
  net nóm ເນສນົມ

hot Nescafe with sugar, no milk
  net dạm ເນສດຳ

Ovaltine
  oh-wantin ໂອວັນຕິນ

orange juice (or orange soda)
  nâam máak kîang ນ້ຳໝາກກຽງ

plain milk
  nâam nóm ນ້ຳນົມ

yoghurt
  nóm sòm ນົມສົ້ມ

beer
  bɩa ເບັຍ

rice whiskey
  lào láo ເຫຼົ້າລາວ

soda water
  nâam sōh-dạa ນ້ຳໂສດາ

Alcohol

Beer The recently privatised Lao Brewery Co, located on the outskirts of Vientiane, was first established in 1973 by the government and is now the 13th largest company in Laos. LBC is currently a joint venture which is 49% government-owned, and 51% a joint holding between two Thai companies, neither of which are involved with beer production in Thailand. Production is now 21 million litres per year, up from three million in 1973.

LBC's main product is the very drinkable Bia Lao, the romanised name for which was recently converted from the French 'BiSre Larue' to English 'Beerlao' (sometimes spelt 'Beer Lao'). A draught version (*bɩa sòt* or 'fresh beer') is available only in beer bars in Vientiane and like all Beerlao contains 5% alcohol. The price is standard at about 650 to 700 kip per litre.

Beerlao also comes in glass bottles for a standard 450 to 500 kip per 330 ml bottle or 800 to 1000 kip for the larger 660 ml bottle (prices can run much higher in tourist hotels or restaurants). Look for the tiger's head on the label. A 330 ml canned Beerlao is also now available.

Imported Tiger beer from Singapore is available in 330 ml cans, which cost as much as a 660 ml bottle of Beerlao but tastes only half as good. From Australia comes Swan and the occasional Foster's.

In the northern provinces bordering China, various Chinese brands of beer are available – these generally cost about 40% less than Lao beer (but are about 80% less drinkable!).

Distilled Spirits Rice whisky or *lào láo* (Lao liquor) is a popular drink among lowland Lao. The best kinds of *lào láo* come from Phongsali and Don Khong, the northern and southern extremes of the country, but are available virtually everywhere, at around 600 kip per 750 ml bottle. Strictly speaking, *lào láo* is not legal but no one seems to care. The government distils its own brand, Sticky Rice, which costs around 900 kip for a bottle.

Lào láo is usually drunk neat, with a plain water chaser. In a Lao home the pouring and drinking of *lào láo* at evening mealtime takes on ritual characteristics. Usually toward the end of the meal, but occasionally beforehand, the hosts bring out a bottle of the stuff to treat their guests. The usual procedure is for the host to pour one jigger of *lào láo* onto the floor or a used dinner plate first, to appease the house spirits. The host then pours another jigger and downs it in one gulp. Jiggers for each guest are poured in turn; guests must take at least one offered drink or risk offending the house spirits.

Three brands of lower-alcohol sticky rice liquor similar in taste to Thailand's famous 'Mekong whisky' are also available as Phan Thong (the label reads Chevreuil d'Or in French), Sing Thong (Gold Tiger) and Mae Khong – each costing around 1500 kip for a 750 ml bottle. These are best taken over ice with a splash of soda and a squeeze of lime, though some prefer to mix them with Coke (imported from Thailand) or Pepsi (made in Laos).

In rural provinces, a weaker version of lào láo known as *lào hái* (jar liquor) is fermented by households or villages. Lào hái is usually drunk from a communal jar using straws. It's not always safe to drink, however, since unboiled water is often added to it during and after the fermentation process.

Tourist hotel bars in the larger cities carry the standard variety of liquors.

Wine In Vientiane decent French and Italian wines are abundantly available at restaurants and in shops specialising in imported foods. You will also find a limited selection in Luang Prabang, Savannakhet and Pakse. Luang Prabang is famous for a type of light rice wine called *khào kam*, a red-tinted, somewhat sweet beverage made from sticky rice. It can be quite tasty when properly prepared and stored, rather mouldy-tasting if not.

ENTERTAINMENT
Music & Dancing

For most of non-urban Laos local entertainment involves sitting around with friends over a few jiggers of lào láo, telling jokes or recounting the events of the day, and singing *phéng phêun múang* (local Lao folk songs).

Religious and seasonal festivals are an important venue for Lao folk and pop music performances – see Holidays & Festivals earlier in this chapter for details.

Almost every provincial capital has a couple of dance halls – called 'discos' by the Lao in spite of the fact that they usually host live bands nightly and play no recorded music. Food as well as beverages are always available at Lao dance halls, though most people drink rather than eat. The music is mostly Lao, though in the north and northeast you'll also hear Chinese and Vietnamese songs mixed into the night's repertoire. Dance styles in any given place vary from the traditional *lám wóng* to American country-style line dancing to wiggle-your-hips-and-dangle-your-fingertips pop styles – all in one night. You'll even see a foxtrot now and then.

In Vientiane foreign embassies (particularly the French and US) sponsor occasional pop, rock or classical concerts.

Cinema & Video

The arrival of video in Laos has completely killed off local cinema save for one surviving cinema house in Vientiane. Video shops in the larger cities rent pirated versions of all the latest Chinese, Thai and Western videos.

See the Vientiane Entertainment section for information on other film venues found only in the capital.

SPECTATOR SPORTS

Football (soccer) and other stadium sports can occasionally be seen at the National Stadium in Vientiane. Admission fees are inexpensive. Elsewhere in the country inter-provincial games take place on fields or stadiums built in each provincial capital. Laos participated in the 1995 SEA Games in Chiang Mai, Thailand, where the national team took several bronze medals in running and boxing events.

Boxing

Many Lao living in the western part of the country are glued to their TV sets during the Sunday afternoon *muay thai* (Thai kickboxing) matches telecast from Bangkok's Ratchadamnoen Stadium. Though very popular, kickboxing is not nearly as developed a sport in Laos as in Thailand and is mostly confined to amateur fights at upcountry festivals. It's not uncommon for the better Lao pugilists to drift across the Mekong to compete in Thai boxing rings, where there's more money to be made.

As in muay thai, in the Lao version of kickboxing all surfaces of the body are considered fair targets and any part of the body except the head may be used to strike an opponent. Common blows include high kicks to the neck, elbow thrusts to the face and head, knee hooks to the ribs and low crescent kicks to the calf. A contestant may even grasp an opponent's head between his hands and pull it down to meet an upward knee thrust. Punching is considered the weakest of all blows and kicking merely a way to 'soften up' one's opponent; knee and elbow strikes are decisive in most matches.

International boxing *(múay sāakǫn)* is gaining popularity in Laos and is encouraged by the government in spite of the obvious Lao preference for the bang-up South-East Asian version. At local festival programmes, an eight-match lineup might include three matches in the international style and five in the Lao-Thai style.

Kataw

Kátâw, a game in which a woven rattan – or sometimes plastic – ball about 12 cm in diameter is kicked around, is almost as popular in Laos as in neighbouring Thailand and Malaysia. It was originally introduced to the SEA Games by Thailand but the Malays seem to win most international championships.

The traditional way to play kataw is for players to stand in a circle (the size of the circle depends on the number of players) and simply try to keep the ball airborne by kicking it soccer-style. Points are scored for style, difficulty and variety of kicking manoeuvres.

A popular variation on kataw – and the one used in local or international competitions – is played with a volleyball net, using all the same rules as in volleyball except that only the feet and head are permitted to touch the ball. It's amazing to see the players perform aerial pirouettes, spiking the ball over the net with their feet.

THINGS TO BUY

Shopping in Laos continues to improve. Many of the handicrafts and arts available in Laos are easily obtainable in Thailand too, but some items – as noted below – are unique to Laos. Hill-tribe crafts can be less expensive in Laos, but only if you bargain.

Like elsewhere in South-East Asia, bargaining is a local tradition (originally introduced to the area by early Arab and Indian traders). Although most shops nowadays have fixed prices, fabric, carvings and jewellery are usually subject to bargaining.

Warning – there is a *total* ban on the export of antiques and Buddha images from Laos, though the enforcement of this ban appears to be very slack.

Fabric (Textiles)

Silk and cotton fabrics are woven in many different styles according to the geographic provenance and ethnicity of the weavers. Although Lao textiles share certain similarities with other South-East Asian textiles, Lao weaving techniques are unique unto themselves in both loom design and weaving styles, generating fabrics that are very recognisably Lao.

Generally speaking, the fabrics of the north feature a mix of solid colours with complex geometric patterns – stripes, diamonds, zig-zags, animal and plant shapes – usually in the form of a *phàa nung* (a women's wraparound skirt). Sometimes gold or silver thread is woven in along the borders. Another form the cloth takes is the *phàa bìang*, a narrow Lao-Thai shawl that men and women wear singly or in pairs over the shoulders during weddings and festivals.

Southern weaving styles are often marked by the *mat-míi* technique, which involves 'tie-dying' the threads before weaving. The result is a soft, spotted pattern similar to Indonesian *ikat*. Mat-míi cloth can be used for different types of clothing or for wall-hangings. Among Lao Theung and Khmer communities in the south is a mat-míi weaving tradition that features pictographic story lines, sometimes with a few Khmer

Textiles feature designs and styles that are recognisably Lao.

words, numerals or other non-representational symbols woven into the pattern.

Among the Hmong and Mien tribes, square pieces of cloth are embroidered and quilted to produce strikingly colourful fabrics in apparently abstract patterns that contain ritual meanings. In Hmong these are called *pa ndau* (flower cloth). Some larger quilts feature scenes that represent village life, including both animal and human figures.

Many tribes among both the Lao Sung and Lao Theung groups produce woven shoulder bags in the Austro-Thai and Tibetan traditions, like those seen all across the mountains of South and South-East Asia. In Laos, they're called *nyaam*. The Musoe (Lahu) make a particularly strong and good-looking bag.

The best place to buy fabric is in the weaving villages themselves, where you can watch how it's made and get 'wholesale' prices. Failing this, you can find a pretty good selection as well as reasonable prices at open markets in provincial towns, including Vientiane's Talaat Sao. The most expensive places to buy fabric are in tailor shops and handicraft stores.

Carvings

The Lao produce well-crafted carvings in wood, bone and stone. Subjects can be everything from Hindu or Buddhist mythology to themes from everyday life. Opium pipes seem to be plentiful in Laos and some-times have intricately carved bone or bamboo shafts, along with engraved ceramic bowls.

To shop for carvings, look in antique or handicraft stores. Don't buy anything made from ivory; quite apart from the elephant slaughter caused by the ivory trade, most Western governments will confiscate any ivory items found in your luggage upon your return home.

Jewellery

Gold and silver jewellery are good buys in Laos, although you must search hard for well-made pieces. Some of the best silverwork is done by the hill tribes. Gems are also sometimes available, but you can get better prices in Thailand.

Most provincial towns have a couple of shops that specialise in jewellery. You can also find jewellery in antique and handicraft shops.

Antiques

Vientiane, Luang Prabang and Savannakhet each have a sprinkling of antique shops. Anything that looks old could be up for sale in these shops, including Asian pottery (especially Ming dynasty porcelain), old jewellery, clothes, carved wood, musical instruments, coins and bronze statuettes. Because of the government's lax enforcement of the ban on the export of antiques, due to an overall lack of funds and personnel, you might be tempted to buy these objects.

However, bear in mind not only that it is illegal to take them out of the country but that if you do so you would be robbing the country of its precious and limited heritage.

Getting There & Away

AIR

Vientiane is the only legal port of disembarkation in Laos for foreign air passengers. At the moment, Vientiane has regularly scheduled international air links only with Bangkok, Chiang Mai, Hanoi, Ho Chi Minh City (Saigon), Phnom Penh, Kunming (China), Yangon (Myanmar) and Singapore.

Lao Aviation has plans to add Hong Kong, Jinghong (China), Kuala Lumpur and Taipei to its international routes over the next couple of years. The company uses a Boeing 737 leased from an American company for all international flights except those to Chiang Mai, for which it employs a French ATR-72.

To/From Bangkok

Flights to Vientiane leave from Bangkok International Airport daily, a service that alternates between Thai Airways International (THAI) and Lao Aviation depending on the day of the week.

Lao Aviation flights tend to be overbooked because the company is connected to two different computer reservation systems which apparently don't reconcile their flight lists. (Lao Aviation officials at Bangkok International Airport are also quick to take bribes when a 'VIP' needs a seat, so that people holding confirmed tickets may be bumped.) During the research trip for this edition, it took nearly an hour of argument to get Lao Aviation to accept my confirmed Bangkok-Vientiane ticket even though I was the first passenger in line at check-in. THAI often fills up as well because it has more cachet among international business travellers. The solution is to book early, preferably with THAI so that you can be sure your ticket will be honoured at check-in. Flights departing on Saturday and Sunday are usually less in demand than weekday flights.

The flight takes about an hour to reach Wattay Airport on the outskirts of Vientiane. The fare is the same for both airlines – US$100 one way in economy, US$120 business. Weekend fare specials as low as US$75 are sometimes available on THAI. Both Lao Aviation (international only) and THAI will accept major credit cards for ticket purchases. Either airline can issue tickets for the other on this route. The smaller discount agencies that sell cheap international tickets can't get a better fare than THAI or Lao Aviation themselves. Some agencies add a surcharge over and above the listed ticket price.

Some people save money by flying from Bangkok to Udon Thani in Thailand first, then carrying on by road to Nong Khai and over the new Friendship Bridge to Vientiane. Udon Thani is 55 km south of Nong Khai and a Bangkok-Udon air ticket aboard THAI costs US$52. Thai Airways operates an express van direct from Udon airport to Nong Khai for 100B per person or you can take a local bus for 15B; count on around 35 minutes for the former, a bit over an hour for the latter.

To/From Chiang Mai

Lao Aviation flies to and from Chiang Mai every Thursday and Sunday. The one hour flight costs US$70 each way. In Chiang Mai the Lao Aviation office can arrange Tourist Visas (1500B) in conjunction with air tickets (see Lao Aviation Offices Abroad, below).

To/From Hanoi

Direct flights between Hanoi and Vientiane leave four times weekly aboard Vietnam Airlines, twice weekly with Lao Aviation. Flights take approximately an hour and cost US$70 to 90 one-way.

To/From Ho Chi Minh City (Saigon)

Lao Aviation flies between Ho Chi Minh City (Saigon) and Vientiane every Friday for US$155 one way; the flight takes about three hours. Vietnam Airlines also fields four Vientiane-bound flights weekly to/from Ho Chi Minh City via Hanoi for the same fare. Either airline can issue tickets for the other.

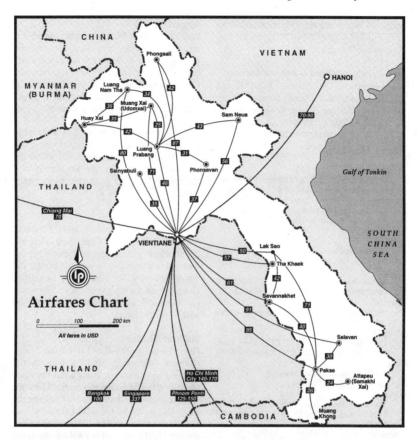

Airfares Chart

All fares in USD

To/From Kunming

Lao Aviation flies between Kunming and Vientiane every Sunday, while China Southern Airlines does the job every Thursday. Both airlines usually charge US$100 one way but special fares as low as US$88 are occasionally available. Flights take 80 minutes. Lao Aviation and CSA can issue tickets for either airline on this route.

To/From Phnom Penh

Lao Aviation flies between Phnom Penh and Vientiane on Friday. The flight takes about 1½ hours and costs US$125 one way. Royal Air du Cambodge also flies from Phnom Penh to Vientiane once a week for the same fare. Either airline can issue tickets for the other.

To/From Singapore

Silk Air flies between Singapore and Vientiane twice weekly for US$337 each way.

To/From Yangon

Lao Aviation flies from Vientiane to Yangon and back every Thursday. The flight usually costs US$150 one way (specials as low as US$128 are occasionally available) and takes 1¾ hours each way. Myanmar Airways International acts as the sales agent for Lao Aviation in Yangon.

Lao Aviation Offices & Agents Abroad

Lao Aviation (☎ 212058, 212051, fax 212056) has its main headquarters in Vientiane; see Getting There & Away in the Vientiane section for details.

Following are the international offices and agents for Lao Aviation:

Australia
  Orbitours, Suite 17, 7th fl, Dymocks Bldg, 428 George St, Sydney, NSW (☎ (02) 9674-2758)
Cambodia
  Lao Aviation, 58B Sihanouk Ave (☎ /fax 2653)
  Royal Air du Cambodge, 62 Tou Samuth St, Phnom Penh (☎ (21) 25887)
Canada
  Skyplan Business Development, 200-35 Mctavish Pl NE, Calgary, Alberta (☎ (403) 250 1605)
France
  Air Cambodge Laos Vietnam, 100 Blvd de Belleville 75020, Paris (☎ 43.66.76.33, fax 43.66.91.88)
Germany
  Muller & Partner, Friedrichstrasse, Berlin (☎ (30) 282 3262, fax 282 3686)
Hong Kong
  China Travel Air Service, 5/F CTS House, 78-83 Connaught Rd, Central (☎ 853 3468, fax 544 6174)
Italy
  Vivtours, Via a Volta 10, Milan (☎ (2) 657 0441, fax 657 1943)
Japan
  Transindo Japan, Mita Sanshin Bldg 2-7-16, Mita Minto-Ku, Tokyo (☎ 3453 3391, fax 3454 3350)
Thailand
  Lao Aviation, 491/17 Silom Plaza, Silom Rd, Bangkok (☎ 236-9822)
  Lao Aviation, 240 Prapokklao Rd, Chiang Mai (☎ (053) 418258, 211044)
Vietnam
  Vietnam Veterans Tourism Services, 41 Quang Trung St, Hanoi (☎ (844) 266538)
  Minh Chau Tourism & Trading Ltd, 39/3 Tran Nhat Duat, Dist 1, Ho Chi Minh City (☎ (848) 442807, fax 442723)
  Vietnam Airlines, 25 Trang Thi St, Hanoi (☎ (844) 53842)
  Vietnam Airlines, 116 Blvd Hue, Ho Chi Minh City (☎ (848) 292118
USA
  Lao-American, 338 South Hancock Ave, South Elgin, IL 60177 (☎ (708) 742 2159, fax 742 4320)

Airport Arrival

Plane arrivals at Wattay Airport are generally rather casual events. Customs and immigration procedures are much less cumbersome than in most other countries. Carry-on bags are not usually inspected if that's all you've brought; checked baggage, when claimed at the baggage counter, sometimes is.

The government bank has a foreign exchange counter in the terminal but if you have Thai baht and US dollars – which are just as acceptable as kip in Vientiane – there's no need to rush out and change money.

LAND

Laos shares land borders with Thailand, Myanmar, Cambodia, China and Vietnam, all of which permit overland crossings for locals living on either side of the border but not necessarily for foreigners. Legalities change from month to month so it's worth checking with a Lao embassy or consulate abroad for the latest.

To/From Thailand

Nong Khai The Thai-Lao Friendship Bridge (Saphan Mittaphap Thai-Lao) spans the Mekong river between Nong Khai Province (specifically Hat Jommani) on the Thai side and Vientiane Province (Tha Na Leng) on the Lao side and is the main land crossing into Laos at the moment. The 1240m Australian-financed bridge opened in 1994 amidst much hoopla about how it would improve transport and communications between the two countries. It is only the second bridge ever to have been erected anywhere along the Mekong's entire length (the first is in China).

In spite of its two 3.5-metre-wide traffic lanes, two 1.5-metre footpaths and space for a railway line down the centre the bridge has done little to fulfil its design potential. Shuttle buses ferry passengers back and forth across the bridge from designated terminals nearby for 10B per person; there are departures every 20 minutes from 8 am to 5.30 pm. You must arrange your own transport to the bridge bus terminal from Nong Khai. The bus stops at Thai immigration control on the bridge, where you pay 10B to have your passport stamped with an exit visa. Passengers then re-board the bus and after crossing the bridge stop at Lao immigrations and customs, where you will pay a fee of 20B to have your passport stamped (40B between 12 and 2 pm and on weekends).

From the bridge it's 80B by jumbo or 100B by car taxi to Vientiane, about 20 km away. You can also catch a No 14 bus into town for 200 kip; fifteen buses a day (6.30 am to 5 pm) pass the bridge area on their way from Tha Deua (the old ferry pier) to Vientiane's Morning Market.

The Lao government has made it very difficult for foreign-registered vehicles to obtain permission to cross the bridge even for temporary visits, hence so far there are no private transport services across the Friendship Bridge other than the shuttle. In December 1995 the Ministry of Communication & Transport in Laos finally issued approval for a 24-seat 'VIP' (sleeper) bus service between Bangkok and Vientiane. These are scheduled to cost 550B with two departures daily from either end. At the outset the bus will be available to Lao and Thai nationals only but foreigners may be permitted to board once a testing period has passed; enquire at Bangkok's Northern Bus Terminal. An air-conditioned government bus from the same Bangkok terminal to Nong Khai – open to all nationalities – costs 263B and takes around 11 hours. Non-aircon buses are also available for a mere 150B but these take a couple of hours longer to reach Nong Khai.

Chong Mek Since April 1993 a land crossing from Chong Mek in Thailand's Ubon Ratchathani Province to Champasak has been open for use by foreign visitors. One no longer needs a specially endorsed visa to use this crossing – any visa will do.

To get to Chong Mek from Ubon, take a bus first to Phibun Mangsahan (12B), then switch to a Phibun-Chong Mek *songthaew* (14B). At Chong Mek you simply walk across the border (Lao Immigration and

Customs are open 8 am to noon and 1 to 4.30 pm) and proceed from Ban Mai Sing Amphon – the village on the Lao side of the border – to Pakse. It is about an hour from the border via bus/taxi and ferry. See under Pakse in the Champasak Province section in the Southern Laos chapter for details on transport to Pakse.

Chiang Khong In early 1996 a Thai company began constructing a second bridge over the Mekong river, this time between Chiang Khong and Huay Xai. This bridge will connect with a 250 km surfaced road running north-east to the Chinese border via Bokeo and Luang Nam Tha provinces. From Huay Xai the only way to head south to Luang Prabang or Vientiane – at the moment – is via long-distance river ferry, speedboat or airplane. For details see the Getting There & Away sections for each of these destinations.

Train to Nong Khai & Ubon Express trains from Bangkok's Hualamphong Railway Station run daily to Nong Khai (11 hours) and Ubon Ratchathani (10 hours). Both lines offer sleeping accommodation on overnight trains, a very convenient way to get an early morning start across the border while saving money on a hotel room. Basic one-way fares are 215B (Nong Khai) and 200B (Ubon) 2nd class or 450B (Nong Khai) and 416B (Ubon) 1st class respectively, not including surcharges for express service (30B) or sleeping berths.

On Time Travel (☎ 313003), attached to Vientiane Motors on Thanon Setthathirat in Vientiane, can book Thai railway tickets for a nominal surcharge over the normal fare.

To/From Vietnam
Border officials at Lao Bao, a small town on the Lao-Vietnamese border near Sepon (directly east from Savannakhet) will permit visitors holding valid Laos visas to enter the country overland from Vietnam. It's important to reach the border early in the morning since there's only one bus a day to Savannakhet. Otherwise your best bet is to

arrange transport to Sepon and spend the night there. In the reverse direction – from Laos to Vietnam – you'll also need a visa from a Vietnamese embassy or consulate in Laos. For more information see the Savannakhet Getting There & Away section in the Southern Laos chapter.

Two other border crossings between Laos and Vietnam – at Sob Hun in Phongsali Province (to/from Dien Bien Phu) and at Kaew Neua in Bolikhamsai Province (to/from Vinh) are open only to Lao and Vietnamese citizens at the moment.

To/From China

From Mengla district in southern Yunnan Province in China it is legal to enter Laos via Boten, Luang Nam Tha Province, if you possess a valid Lao visa. From Boten there are morning and afternoon buses onward to the provincial capitals of Luang Nam Tha and Udomxai, three and four hours away respectively.

The Lao Consulate in Kunming, China, issues both seven-day transit and 15-day tourist visas. These cost US$28 and US$50 respectively and take three to five days to process. You must bring *four* photos and already have a visa from a third country (such as Thailand) stamped in your passport. Most travellers from Kunming go via Jinghong to Mengla and thence to the border at Mohan. As the bus journey from Jinghong will take the better part of the day, you will probably have to overnight at Mengla. You can't currently get into Mengla County without a Lao visa.

A second China-Laos crossing from the same area of Yunnan may be possible via Bun Neua district in Phongsali Province. Lao and Chinese citizens regularly use this crossing as a short cut from north-western Laos, traversing a narrow section of Yunnan Province that juts down between the Lao provinces of Luang Nam Tha and Phongsali. Although it's an official border crossing for Chinese and Lao citizens only, in 1995 we met some Japanese visitors who managed to cross at Bun Neua with advance written permission from a Lao consulate in China.

To/From Cambodia

Lao and Cambodian citizens are permitted to cross back and forth at Voen Kham, Champasak Province. Rumours say this crossing will be open to foreigners as soon as the new ADB – financed highway from Pakse to Voen Kham is finished.

Other Countries

Rumours persist that foreigners will soon be allowed to cross the border between Champasak Province in Laos and Stung Treng Province in Cambodia. Apparently some foreigners have actually managed to accomplish this crossing – most likely with the palms-up cooperation of the local border police – but according to Lao officials in Vientiane it's not yet kosher for everyday travel.

We've had similar reports – balanced by denials from the Lao government – regarding entry from Myanmar at the Lao town of Xieng Kok, on the Mekong river in Luang Nam Tha Province. Travellers who want to attempt either crossing will increase their chances of success if they arrive at the border with a valid visa.

RIVER
Thailand

Since the opening of the Friendship Bridge, the Tha Deua ferry in Nong Khai has been closed to non-Thai, non-Lao citizens. However it is still legal for non-Thai foreigners to cross the Mekong river by ferry from Thailand into Laos at the following points: Nakhon Phanom (opposite Tha Khaek), Chiang Khong (opposite Huay Xai) and Mukdahan (opposite Savannakhet). One no longer needs special permission attached to one's visa for any of these crossings. Regular Lao tourist visas can be obtained from travel agencies in each of these towns if you haven't already got one. When the bridge under construction between Chiang Khong and Huay Xai is completed, passenger ferry service at this crossing will probably be discontinued.

Thais are permitted to cross at all of the above checkpoints plus at least a half-dozen others from Thailand's Loei and Nong Khai provinces, including Pak Chom, Chiang Khan, Beung Kan, Ban Pak Huay, Ban Nong Pheu and Ban Khok Phai. For the most part these checkpoints are only good for day crossings (Thai and Lao only). In the future one or more of these may become available for entry by foreign visitors as well, particularly those crossings along the Sainyabuli Province border.

A third Mekong bridge is tentatively planned to span the river at either Tha Khaek or Savannakhet. When it is built, the ferry service for foreigners will probably be discontinued at that particular crossing.

LEAVING LAOS
By Air

As with entry, Vientiane's Wattay International Airport is the only official exit point for international flights. Unlike domestic flights, international flights out of Vientiane generally leave on time.

The international terminal has a large aircon snack bar upstairs near the waiting room.

The international departure tax is US$5, which can be paid in kip, baht or dollars.

By Land & River

Officially, as of December 1995, you are allowed to exit Laos overland or over the Mekong via Huay Xai, Bokeo Province (opposite Chiang Khong, Thailand); Tha Na Leng, Vientiane Province (opposite Hat Jommani, near Nong Khai); Tha Khaek,

Khammuan Province (opposite Nakhon Phanom); Savannakhet (opposite Mukdahan) and Pakse/Ban Mai Sing Amphon, Champasak Province (opposite Chong Mek).

With a valid Vietnamese visa, you are also allowed to exit Laos via Sepon (entering Vietnam at Lao Bao). With a visa for China, you can exit via Boten, Luang Nam Tha Province. No special permission is needed to use these exit points.

WARNING

The information in this chapter is particularly vulnerable to change: prices for international travel are volatile, routes are introduced and cancelled, schedules change, special deals come and go, and rules and visa requirements are amended. Airlines and governments seem to take a perverse pleasure in making price structures and regulations as complicated as possible. You should check directly with the airline or a travel agent to make sure you understand how a fare (and ticket you may buy) works. In addition, the travel industry is highly competitive and there are many lurks and perks.

The upshot of this is that you should get opinions, quotes and advice from as many airlines and travel agents as possible before you part with your hard-earned cash. The details given in this chapter should be regarded as pointers and are not a substitute for your own careful, up-to-date research.

Getting Around

AIR

Lao Aviation handles all domestic flights in Laos with Vientiane as the main hub – all flights originate and terminate at Wattay International Airport with the exception of one plane kept in Pakse for certain southern routes. Following the 1994 abolition of the interprovincial travel permit system, you can now book Lao Aviation tickets yourself, without any sponsoring agency or special permit.

At the moment Lao Aviation does not accept credit cards for domestic ticket purchases – all payments must be made in cash. Prices are quoted in dollars but you can pay in kip. Depending on the current exchange rate, it may be cheaper to pay in kip, especially if, as in late 1995, the kip prices hadn't yet caught up with the devaluation of the national currency. At that time a ticket to Luang Nam Tha could be bought for either US$80 or 62,500 kip; Lao currency bought at the parallel market rate of 950 amounted to just US$65 so that if you paid in kip you saved yourself US$15. Rates will be quoted in dollars throughout this book since most likely the kip prices will soon be raised to match current exchange rates. Dollar prices should remain fairly steady, with slight increases probable.

Since January 1995 Lao Aviation has been 60% owned by China's Yunnan Airlines, which has a 20-year management contract with the Lao government. The main aircraft used for Lao Aviation's domestic flights are the 15-passenger Chinese Y-12 and the 50-passenger Chinese Y-7, both copies of Russian Antonov aircraft with upgraded features. When the company is short of Chinese planes, an old Antonov 24 may be pulled from retirement and used instead. In 1995 the entire domestic fleet amounted to eight aircraft (three Y-12s, three Y-7s, one AN-24 and one 25-person ME-8 helicopter). All seem to be fully operational and it isn't as difficult to book seats as it was two years ago when only three of the eight were functioning regularly.

Safety records for Lao Aviation aren't made public. At the moment Lao Aviation pilots must rely on visual flying techniques. When heavy cloud cover is present they are forced to circle the area searching for a hole through which to descend; if none is found within the time allotted by fuel capacity, the pilots either return to the original departure point or land at another airport in the same region. After a short wait and refuelling on the ground, they give it another go! A Y-12 crashed into a cloud-obscured mountain near Phonsavan in December 1993, killing all aboard, so this method obviously has its shortcomings. We've heard a rumour that radar equipment is being installed at some airports, starting with tricky landing sites such as those at Attapeu and Sam Neua; according to this rumour instrument landings will eventually become the norm throughout the country.

All departure and arrival times given throughout this guide are *scheduled* flight times. In everyday practice, flights are often delayed an hour or two due to weather conditions in the mountains – which includes all destinations except Vientiane, Savannakhet and Pakse.

Luang Prabang airport is undergoing improvement and expansion so it will be able to field larger planes. Wattay International Airport itself reportedly will be expanded with Singaporean assistance. There has also been talk of allowing a Thai company – possibly Bangkok Airways – to supplement domestic flight schedules in Laos.

Fares & Taxes

Air fares for Lao citizens are subsidised at less than half what a foreigner must pay. Children ages five to 12 are charged half the adult fare, infants pay only 10%. See the Airfares chart for regular adult fares.

The departure tax for domestic flights is 300 kip. Passengers must also pay immigration officers at each domestic airport 100 kip for the privilege of checking in or out of the province each time they arrive or depart by air.

Offices

The offices of Lao Aviation are in Vientiane; see under Getting There and Away in the Vientiane section for details.

Helicopter

Lao Westcoast Helicopter Co (☎ 512023; overseas fax (856) 512055), Hangar 703, Wattay Airport, charters five-passenger French AS 350B Squirrel copters with expatriate pilots for aerial surveys, photography or passenger transport to just about anywhere in Laos (subject to government permission obtained by the passengers). The usual rate is US$1050 per airborne hour. A 13-passenger Bell 212 may be added to the fleet by the beginning of 1994.

ROAD

The road system in Laos remains very undeveloped. Although the French installed full highway systems in Vietnam and Cambodia, they only built one road of significance in Laos, Route Coloniale 13 along the lower Mekong river, plus the less impressive Routes Coloniales 7 and 9 through two Annamite mountain passes. As of 1966 Laos had the lowest highway density in the world – calculated at 0.1 roads per sq km.

Later contributors to the current road system have been the Chinese and North Vietnamese, who constructed a number of all-weather roads in northern Laos (all of them within the former liberated zone) in the '60s and early '70s. In return for their labour, the Chinese were allowed to cut and export as much timber as they liked. Most of these roads radiate out from Udomxai and Xieng Khuang, often only as far as provincial borders. From Phonsavan (the capital of Xieng Khuang Province), for example, the road is in fair condition until it reaches the Hua Phan Province border, then it's lousy as far as Sam Neua, then good again all the way to the Vietnamese border.

As of 1995 Laos had 13,971 km of classified roads, most of which can charitably be termed 'in a deteriorated condition'. An estimated 25% are tarred; 34% are graded and sometimes covered with gravel; the remaining 41% are ungraded dirt tracks. The roads around Vientiane Prefecture, as far out as Vang Vieng, are surfaced and adequate for just about any type of vehicle. Elsewhere in the country, unsurfaced roads are the rule. Since Laos is 70% mountains, even relatively short road trips involve incredibly long intervals (eg, a typical 200 km upcountry trip takes around 10 to 18 hours to accomplish).

A number of international aid projects promise to upgrade the current system and build new roads by the end of the decade. The Swedish government, with support from the Asian Development Bank (ADB), has completed the regrading and paving of Route 13 between Vientiane and Kasi and a South Korean company is currently working on the Kasi-Luang Prabang section. From Luang Prabang the road will continue to Pak Mong in northern Luang Prabang Province, where it will connect with the Chinese-built Xieng Khuang-Udomxai highway. Another Swedish project expects to finish the Vientiane-Savannakhet portion of Route 13 by late 1996. The Pakse-Salavan road has already been upgraded and is now one of the best roads in the country. The national target is to completely seal Route 13 from Luang Prabang to the Cambodian border by 1998, followed by three sealed east-west thoroughfares along Routes 1, 9 and 18.

The Thais have offered to assist in the construction of roads that would link Thailand with Vietnam via Savannakhet (targeted for Danang), Tha Khaek (for Vinh) and Pakse (for Saigon). A 1998 completion date has been set for these projects. Thailand, Myanmar, China and Laos also agreed in May 1993 to develop road links in the area bordering the upper reaches of the Mekong river, thus linking Thailand's Chiang Rai Province with Xishuangbanna (Yunnan) in south China via Laos' Bokeo and Luang Nam Tha provinces. As of early 1996 a Thai company had graded about a third of 220 km

Route 3, which stretches from Huay Xai to Boten; a mid-1997 completion was predicted.

Buses & Trucks

The availability of interprovincial public transport has increased markedly since the last edition of this book. It is now possible to travel to at least parts of every province in Laos by some form of public road conveyance. Regular buses – mostly Japanese or Korean-made – ply Route 13 between Vientiane and Pakse an average of two or three times daily. Other routes in the south, eg Pakse to Sekong, typically use large flat-bed trucks mounted with a heavy wooden carriage containing seats in bus-like rows.

In the north, Russian, Chinese, Vietnamese or Japanese trucks are often converted into passenger carriers by adding two long benches in the back. These passenger trucks are called *thaek-sii* (taxi) or in some areas *sāwng-thâew*, which means 'two rows' in reference to the two facing benches in the back.

Because of road conditions, intercity bus service is for the most part limited to a few satellite towns around provincial capitals. On roads where there is no regular public transport, eg the southern route from Pakse to Attapeu, cargo trucks will sometimes carry passengers. As each of the major highway projects is completed, public transport options will continue to multiply and the frequency of bus departures will increase.

Around Vientiane, buses can be crowded and dilapidated but very cheap (less than 700 kip per 100 km). Where the roads are surfaced, they're a very acceptable way to get from one point to another.

If you're waiting by the side of the road for a ride, it helps to know whether approaching vehicles are likely to take on passengers. You can identify proprietorship by looking at the licence tags – black tags with yellow letters mean the vehicle is licensed to carry paying passengers; yellow means it's a privately owned vehicle; red is military-owned (not likely to pick up passengers); blue is civil service, UN or NGO; and white tags belong to embassies or international organisations (who will sometimes pick up foreign passengers). White tags with red lettering mean the vehicle has right-hand drive!

Vehicle Hire

Small Japanese pickups can be chartered between towns or provinces. Because Lao roadways generate a high degree of wear and tear on these vehicles, hire charges run as high as US$100 a day. In Vientiane you can hire a 4WD vehicle – and driver – for upcountry trips for US$150 to 160 a day; prices are kept high by the tendency for UN organisations to shell out up to US$300 a day for the same vehicles. Long-term 4WD rentals of around US$65 per day are possible. One of the more reliable places to hire vehicles and drivers is Asia Vehicle Rental (☎ 217493), at 8/3 Thanon Lan Xang, in Vientiane.

TRAIN

Not yet – but a Thai-Lao joint venture is currently studying the feasibility of constructing a 1400 km railway through Laos, including 210 km of tunnels, using a British consortium as contractor. If such a railway becomes a reality, it will connect with the Thai railhead in Nong Khai (in turn linked to rail lines through Malaysia and Singapore) as well as rail networks in China and Vietnam.

RIVER

Rivers are traditionally the true highways and byways of Laos, the main thoroughfares being the Mekong, Nam Ou, Nam Khan, Nam Tha, Nam Ngum and Se Kong. The Mekong is the longest and most important water route and is navigable year-round between Luang Prabang in the north and Savannakhet in the south.

With the increase in road travel, passenger services are declining year by year. In the south, for example, only a few long-distance ferry services still operate – all of them below Pakse – and these will probably fall by the wayside once Route 13 is sealed all the way to the Cambodian border.

River Ferries

For long distances, large diesel river ferries designed for cargo transport are used. Some of these boats have two decks, one over the other, with sleeping areas and on-board foodstalls. Others have only one deck and stop only occasionally for food. For overnight trips, it's a good idea to ascertain whether food will be available on board; if not, be sure to bring food along.

Ferry facilities are quite basic; passengers sit, eat and sleep on wooden decks. The toilet – when one exists – is an enclosed hole in the deck. Women are expected to ride inside and to the back of the boat; men are permitted to sit on the front and top decks. The fare for a typical 24 hour river ferry trip is 5000 to 6000 kip; a three or four day trip (say upriver from Vientiane to Luang Prabang) is about 12,000 kip. Fares do not include food – if food is available.

For boats leaving out of Luang Prabang in any direction, the boat mafia asks an extra 50% for foreigners. This means that even though the upriver trip from Vientiane to Luang Prabang takes longer, you pay the normal Lao price of 12,000 kip, while in the faster downriver direction you will probably be charged 18,000 kip.

River Taxis

For shorter river trips, for example, from Luang Prabang to the Pak Ou caves, it's usually best to hire a river taxi since the large river ferries only ply their routes once a day at most, sometimes only a couple of times a week. The *héua hãng nyáo* (long-tail boats) with engines gimbal-mounted on the stern are the most typical, though for a really short trip, say crossing a river, a *héua phái* (rowboat) can be hired. The héua hãng nyáo are not as cheap to hire as you might think – figure on around 3000 kip an hour for a boat with an eight to 10 person capacity. Larger boats that carry up to 20 passengers are sometimes available for around 6000 kip per hour.

Along the upper Mekong river between Huay Xai and Vientiane, and on the Nam Ou between Luang Prabang and Hat Sa (Phong-sali), Thai-built *héua wái* (speedboats) – shallow, five-metre-long skiffs with 40 hp Toyota outboard engines – are common. These are able to cover a distance in six hours that might take a river ferry two days or more. They're not cheap – charters cost about US$20 per hour – but some ply regular routes so that the cost can be shared among several passengers.

LOCAL TRANSPORT
Car & Motorcycle

Visitors with valid International Driving Permits are permitted to drive cars in Laos, though a car and driver can be hired for less than the cost of a rental car in most towns (see under Taxi further on in this section for information on car-and-driver hire, or under Vehicle Hire earlier for 4WD rental).

The number of vehicles in the country – including all cars, trucks, buses, jeeps and motorcycles – totals less than 150,000; there are nearly four times as many motorcycles as cars. In spite of this, bringing your own motorised vehicle into the country – whether a car, truck or motorcycle – is wellnigh impossible unless you work for a company or other organisation doing business in Laos (even then it's a major bureaucratic headache). It's much easier to either buy or rent a vehicle in Laos rather than import one.

Small motorbikes – under 150cc – can be rented from some motorbike dealers in Vientiane as well as in Luang Prabang and Savannakhet. The going rate is US$8 to 10 a day. A new Honda Dream II 100cc motorbike (assembled in Laos) costs 1.4 million kip (US$1475).

Petrol costs around 265 kip per litre at stations in the Mekong river valley, up to 300 or 400 kip in remote provinces.

Siam Bike Travel (fax (053) 495987) in Chiang Mai, Thailand, arranges two-week, 1500 km overland motorbike trips through Laos from Thailand to China and back.

Road Rules

Watch carefully for vehicles making left turns from a side road. Lao drivers typically turn into the left lane before moving over to the right – a potentially dangerous situation if you're not ready for it. Rather than stop and wait for traffic to pass, motorists usually merge with oncoming traffic without bothering to look to the rear, reasoning that any big or fast-moving vehicle approaching from behind will sound a horn.

Like many places in Asia, every two-lane road has an invisible third lane in the middle that all drivers feel free to use at any time. Passing on hills and curves is common – as long as you've got the proper Buddhist altar on the dashboard, what could happen?

Taxi

Each of the four largest towns – Vientiane, Luang Prabang, Savannakhet and Pakse – has a handful of car taxis that are used by foreign businesspeople and the occasional tourist. The only place you'll find these are at the airports (arrival times only) and in front of the larger hotels. Until rather recently the cars were mostly of Eastern European or Russian origin, with the occasional older US car turning up, but nowadays Japanese cars are more common. Taxis like these can be hired by the trip, by the hour or by the day. Typical all-day hires within a town or city cost US$20 to US$40 depending on the vehicle and your negotiating powers. By the trip, you shouldn't pay more than US$0.50 per km.

Three-wheeled motorcycle taxis are common in these same towns as well as in some smaller ones. This type of vehicle can be called *thaek-sii* (taxi) or *sãam-lâw* (samlor or three-wheels). The larger ones made in Thailand are called *jamboh* (jumbo) and can hold four to six passengers. In Vientiane they are also sometimes called *túk-túk* as in Thailand (although in Laos this usually refers to a slightly larger vehicle than the jumbo), while in the south (Pakse, Savannakhet) they may be called *Sakai-làep* (Skylab) because of the perceived resemblance to a space capsule! Fares generally cost about 200 kip per km (you must bargain to get the correct rate). They can go anywhere a regular taxi can go, but aren't usually hired for distances greater than 20 km or so.

Pedicab

The bicycle *samlor*, once the mainstay of local transport for hire throughout urban Laos, has nearly become extinct. These used to be commonly called *cyclo (sii-khlo)* following the French, but this term is being used less frequently than samlor nowadays. If you can find a samlor, fares cost about the same as motorcycle taxis but are generally used only for distances less than two km or so. Bargaining is sometimes necessary to get the correct fare, though the aging pedicab drivers seem to be more honest than the motorcycle taxi drivers.

Bicycle

Bicycles are a popular form of transport throughout urban Laos and can be hired in Vientiane, Luang Prabang, Savannakhet and Don Khong for around 1000 to 1500 kip per day – some hotels and guest houses even loan them out for free. These Thai or Chinese-made street bikes come in varying degrees of rideability; you can buy a new one on your own for US$70 to 90. The Chinese bikes tend to be sturdier, the Thai bikes more comfortable. Low-quality Chinese or Taiwan-made mountain bikes are also available for US$90 to 140.

Lao customs doesn't object to visitors bringing their own bicycles into the country for personal transport. If you plan to do any extensive interprovincial cycling, consider taking along the following items:

- pump
- tyre patch kit
- bike wrench
- chainbreaker
- spoke wrench
- spare spokes
- allen wrenches as necessary
- toothbrush (for cleaning bike parts)
- chain oil
- brake pads
- booting material for tyres
- spare seat & stem bolts
- light raingear
- hammock, space blanket, portable mosquito net

ORGANISED TOURS

All tours in Laos are handled by agencies authorised by the Lao National Tourism Authority (LNTA). Such authorisation isn't easy to obtain as the LNTA requires that each agency maintain a US$50,000 bond, two minivans and telex, fax, and phone numbers.

In 1995 there were around 25 agencies operating in Vientiane, some of which maintain branches in other cities such as Luang Prabang, Pakse and Phonsavan. For the most part, each agency has a standard set of packages, ranging from two nights in Vientiane only to 14 days in Vientiane, Luang Prabang, the Plain of Jars (Xieng Khuang), Savannakhet, Salavan and Champasak. Some agencies advertise tours which they can't actually deliver, while better ones can go almost anywhere and can create custom itineraries.

Standard prices vary little from company to company; the main difference is linked to the number of people signing up for a package. Per-person rates drop – typically around US$50 to 100 per person – for each person added to the group. Costs for one person travelling solo can be as much as US$200 or more per day, while four to six persons travelling together can arrange packages for under US$50 per person per day. If you don't mind travelling with other people, ask if you can join a group already scheduled to depart – some agencies will allow this while others try to keep the groups as small as possible in order to collect the most loot.

It is also possible to bargain in some cases. Several readers have written to describe how they shopped around from agency to agency and were able to get at least a few tour operators to lower their asking rates.

If you book a tour outside Laos, you must deal with an authorised agent of one of the Lao agencies. This means additional cost to you, as the tour operators have to pay a base fee to the agencies in Laos.

The costs can vary widely from agency to agency, but in general it's a bit cheaper to book upcountry tours in Vientiane rather than outside the country. In some cases the difference in price between tours booked in Vientiane and those booked in the outer provinces represents yet another layer of markups. One Vientiane agency, for example, charged US$287 for a Xieng Khuang add-on operated by a local Xieng Khuang party that only charges US$60 for the same services if booked locally.

In general, tours arranged by the Vientiane agencies are not bad value as far as package tours go. Except for the obvious inconvenience of having to put up with a group (although sometimes the group is as small as two to four people) and follow a guide around, the tours are generally well planned and genuinely informative. Guides are usually flexible when it comes to the itinerary, adding or deleting bits (within obvious time, distance and cost limits) according to your needs.

At each destination, the agencies arrange all accommodation (double occupancy) and a tour guide. In more expensive packages in-country transport and meals are included. Prices for packages without meals are much lower, and eating out on your own is often more fun than eating pre-arranged hotel meals anyway.

Meals, where they are included, are plentiful if a bit on the bland side, but you can sometimes request local specialities. Or simply inform your guide that you want to eat real Lao food during the tour, not the ersatz version usually offered to Westerners.

Unlike early China tours in which visitors were herded from factory to agricultural collective, Laos itineraries do not try to present visitors with a proletarian paradise – political rhetoric is in fact relatively absent from guide commentary.

Vientiane Tour Operators

The following are some reputable tour operators in Vientiane:

Aerocontact Asia
　　29 Thanon Wat Xieng Nhun (☎ 216409, fax 414346)
Diethelm Travel Laos
　　Namphu Square, Thanon Setthathirat, PO Box 2657 (☎ 215920, fax 217151).
Inter-Lao Tourisme
　　Cnr of Thanons Pangkham and Setthathirat (☎ 214832, fax 216306).

Lane Xang Travel & Tour
   Thanon Pangkham, PO Box 4452 (☎ 215804, fax 215777)
Lao Travel Service
   8/3 Thanon Lan Xang, PO Box 2553 (☎ 216603, fax 216150)

SODETOUR (Societé de Development Touristique)
   16 Thanon Fa Ngum, PO Box 70 (☎ 216314, fax 216313)
That Luang Tour
   28 Thanon Kamkhong, PO Box 3619 (☎ 215809, fax 215346)

Vientiane Province

VIENTIANE ວຽງຈັນ
History

Vientiane is three entities: province (population around 528,000), prefecture (260,000) and city (133,000). Located on a bend in the Mekong river, it was originally one of the early Lao river-valley fiefdoms or *meuang* that were consolidated around the time Europe was leaving the Dark Ages. The Lao that settled here chose the area because the surrounding alluvial plains are so incredibly fertile. Early on, the Vientiane meuang prospered and enjoyed a fragile sovereignty.

At various times over the 10 or so centuries of its history, however, Vientiane lost its standing as an independent kingdom and was controlled by the Burmese, Siamese, Vietnamese and Khmers. When the kingdom of Lan Xang (Million Elephants) was established in the 14th century by the Khmer-supported conqueror Fa Ngum, it was originally centred in Meuang Sawa (Luang Prabang), but by the early 16th century the capital had been moved to Vientiane. When Laos became a French protectorate in the late 19th and early 20th centuries, Vientiane was named the capital city and has remained so under communist rule today.

The name translates as Sandalwood City and is actually pronounced Wieng Chan (Wieng means City or Place with Walls in Lao; 'Chan' is the Lao pronunciation of the Sanskrit 'Chandana'). The French gave the city its common romanised spelling. It is one of three classic Indochinese cities (including Saigon/Ho Chi Minh City and Phnom Penh) that most strongly conjures up images of exotic Eurasian settings. For the most part, Vientiane lives up to these images, with its intriguing mix of Lao, Thai, Chinese, Vietnamese, French, US and Soviet influences. Of the three capitals, Vientiane is by far the most laid-back in atmosphere.

Although Vientiane is the largest city in the country, it's still small enough to get to

HIGHLIGHTS

- Pha That Luang, the national symbol of Laos, and one of its most sacred sites
- Wat Si Saket, one of the oldest and most interesting wats in Vientiane
- Wat Ong Teu, with its huge bronze Buddha
- Buddha Park (Xieng Khuan), a riverside collection of whimsical Hindu-Buddhist sculptures
- Vang Vieng, surrounded by karst formations and limestone caves

know easily. Parts of town are really quite attractive, particularly in the older section of town along the Mekong river. Tree-lined boulevards and old temples impart an atmosphere of timelessness, in spite of passing traffic (which is growing year by year but is never very heavy) and new construction here and there.

Orientation

The city curves along the Mekong river following a bent north-west to south-east axis, with the central district of Chanthabuli at the central bend. Most of the government offices, hotels, restaurants and historic temples are in Muang Chanthabuli, near the

◇◇◇◇◇◇◇◇◇◇◇◇◇◇◇◇◇◇◇◇◇◇◇◇

Vientiane's Monarchs
During approximately the last century and a
half of the Lan Xang Kingdom's history (1548-
1707), the royal seat was situated in Vientiane.
In 1707 Lan Xang split into the separate kingdoms of Vientiane, Luang Prabang and
Champasak. The kingdom of Vientiane was
ruled by the following monarchs:

Sai Ong Hue	1707-35
Ong Long	1735-60
Ong Boun	1760-78
interregnum	1778-82
Nan	1782-92
In	1792-1805
Chao Anou (Anouvong)	1805-28

◇◇◇◇◇◇◇◇◇◇◇◇◇◇◇◇◇◇◇◇◇◇◇◇

river. A few old French colonial buildings
and Vietnamese-Chinese shophouses
remain alongside newer structures built
according to the Social Realist school of
architecture.

In this district new blue-and-white street
signs in Lao and English have made life
easier for foreigners, though outside
Chanthabuli the street signs are mostly
written in Lao script only, and occasionally
in French. The English and French desig-
nations for street names varies (eg, route,
rue, road and avenue) but the Lao script
always reads *thanŏn*, which means the same
as all the French and English variations.
Therefore, when asking directions it's
always best to avoid possible confusion and
just use the Lao word thanŏn.

The main streets in the downtown district
are Thanon Samsenthai, which is the pre-
eminent shopping area; Thanon Setthathirat
(pronounced Setthathilat since there is no 'r'
sound in modern Lao), where several of the
most famous temples are located; and
Thanon Fa Ngum, which runs along the river
and is lined with eucalyptus, pipal and teak
trees. Branching off northward, out of
Muang Chanthabuli and into Muang
Saisettha, is Thanon Lan Xang, Vientiane's
widest street.

The main portion of Thanon Lan Xang is

a divided boulevard that leads from the pres-
idential palace past Talaat Sao (the Morning
Market) to the Patuxai or Victory Gate. After
the Patuxai, it splits into two roads, Thanon
Phon Kheng and Thanon That Luang.
Thanon Phon Kheng leads to the Unknown
Soldiers Memorial, the Lao People's Army
Museum and the Thai Embassy. Thanon
That Luang leads to Pha That Luang.

To the north-east of Muang Chanthabuli is
Muang Saisettha, where Pha That Luang and
several embassies are located. This is also a
residential area of newer French and US-
style mansions inhabited by European and
Asian expatriates who work for aid programmes or multinational companies.

To the south-east of central Vientiane is
the mostly local residential meuang of
Sisattanak and to the west is the similarly
residential Muang Sikhottabong.

The meuangs of Vientiane are broken up
into *bâan*, which are neighbourhoods or villages associated with local wats. Wattay
Airport, for example, is in Ban Wattai, a
village in the southern part of Muang
Sikhottabong centred around Wat Tai.

Maps & Guides The *Vientiane Tourist Map*,
published by the LNTA in 1993, is a fairly
usable street map of the city featuring major
sites and the mostly unlabelled locations of
many hotels and public services. It's available at the National Geographic Service,
Raintree Bookstore, Phimphone Market and
several retail shops in the city.

The three pages of fold-out maps at the
back of the Women International Group's
Vientiane Guide are more detailed and
feature a useful index. This helpful book,
revised annually, contains over 190 pages of
practical information on what to see and do
in Vientiane. It's oriented toward the newly
arrived expatriate who is setting up house in
Vientiane, so not all of the information (eg,
hiring domestic staff, electrical repair) is
useful for travellers who are just passing
through. The guide costs US$12 and can be
purchased at Raintree Bookstore, Phimphone Market, Lane Xang Hotel and various
shops around the city.

Information

Tourist Office The Lao National Tourism Authority (LNTA) – also known as the Lao National Tourism Company or the National Lao Tourist Authority – has a new office on Thanon Lan Xang between Talaat Sao and the Patuxai monument. This office (☎ /fax 212013) is little more than a thinly disguised travel agency, and one that is not very competitive with the private agencies in town in terms of price or service. As an information source on where to go, or even on official tourism policy, it is nearly worthless (see the Tourist Offices entry in the Facts for the Visitor chapter) and you're better off relying on this guidebook or on tourist information material that is available from various souvenir shops downtown.

The LNTA office is supposed to be open Monday to Friday 8 am to 5 pm, but as in other government offices you'll rarely find anyone around between 11.30 am and 2.30 pm.

Money La Banque pour le Commerce Extérieur Lao (BCEL; The Lao Foreign Trade Bank) at Thanons Pangkham and Fa Ngum, near Lao Aviation and the Lane Xang Hotel, has the best foreign exchange rate of any bank in Vientiane. It's open from 8.30 am to 4.30 pm Monday to Friday, and until 11 am Saturday. Both BCEL and Thai Farmers Bank (80/4 Thanon Lane Xang) can issue cash advances/debits for Visa and MasterCard.

Other banks well equipped to handle foreign exchange include:

Bangkok Bank
    28/13-15 Thanon Hatsady (Thanon Talaat Sao)
Joint Development Bank
    31-33 Thanon Lan Xang
Siam Commercial Bank
    602/4-5 Thanon Nong Bon, north-east of Talaat Sao
Thai Military Bank
    69 Thanon Khun Bulom

Licensed moneychanging booths can also be found in Talaat Sao and in a few other locations around town. The one opposite the Asian Pavilion Hotel on Thanon Samsenthai accepts Visa, travellers' cheques and cash – for a sizeable commission. You can also change on the 'parallel market' at various shops in town for no commission or from the unofficial moneychangers hanging out on Thanon Lan Xang near Talaat Sao. The latter usually offer the best rates in Vientiane but it helps to be on your toes as far as knowing what the going rates are; count your money carefully. See Banking in the Money section of the Facts for the Visitor chapter for details on exchange restrictions, bank accounts and credit/debit card cash advances.

Post The Post, Telephone & Telegraph office (PTT) is on the corner of Thanons Lan Xang and Khu Vieng, across the road from Talaat Sao. Business hours are from 8 am to 5 pm Monday to Friday, till 4 pm Saturday and until noon Sunday.

Telephone & Fax The PTT office is only for calls within Laos. Overseas calls and fax transmissions can be arranged at the Public Telephone Office on Thanon Setthathirat. It's open daily 7.30 am to 10 pm. Fax services are available in a separate room in the same building from 7.30 am to 9.30 pm; to transmit a fax costs 400 kip plus the phone toll. Faxes can also be received here for a reasonable charge of 200 kip per page.

Local calls can be made from any hotel lobby – usually there is no charge. The area code for Vientiane is 21.

Couriers International courier services in Vientiane include DHL Worldwide Express (☎ 216830, fax 214869), 52 Thanon Nokeo Kumman;, TNT Express Worldwide (☎ /fax 214361), Thanon Lan Xang; and Lao Inter Airborne Express (☎ 212993, 212996), 72-1 Namphu Square.

Travel Agencies See the Organised Tours section in the Getting Around chapter for a list of authorised tour operators in Vientiane.

Bookshops Vientiane does not offer much in the way of books in English. Located near

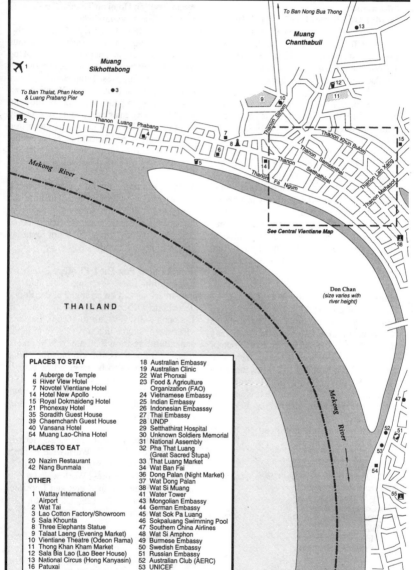

PLACES TO STAY

4 Auberge de Temple
6 River View Hotel
7 Novotel Vientiane Hotel
14 Hotel New Apollo
15 Royal Dokmaideng Hotel
21 Phonexay Hotel
35 Soradith Guest House
39 Chaemchanh Guest House
40 Vansana Hotel
54 Muang Lao-China Hotel

PLACES TO EAT

20 Nazim Restaurant
42 Nang Bunmala

OTHER

1 Wattay International
  Airport
2 Wat Tai
3 Lao Cotton Factory/Showroom
5 Sala Khounta
8 Three Elephants Statue
9 Talaat Laeng (Evening Market)
10 Vientiane Theatre (Odeon Rama)
11 Thong Khan Kham Market
12 Sala Bia Lao (Lao Beer House)
13 National Circus (Hong Kanyasin)
16 Patuxai
17 State Geographic Service

18 Australian Embassy
19 Australian Clinic
22 Wat Phonxai
23 Food & Agriculture
   Organization (FAO)
24 Vietnamese Embassy
25 Indian Embassy
26 Indonesian Embasssy
27 Thai Embassy
28 UNDP
29 Setthathirat Hospital
30 Unknown Soldiers Memorial
31 National Assembly
32 Pha That Luang
   (Great Sacred Stupa)
33 That Luang Market
34 Wat Ban Fai
36 Dong Palan (Night Market)
37 Wat Dong Palan
38 Wat Si Muang
41 Water Tower
43 Mongolian Embassy
44 German Embassy
45 Wat Sok Pa Luang
46 Sokpaluang Swimming Pool
47 Southern China Airlines
48 Wat Si Amphon
49 Burmese Embassy
50 Swedish Embassy
51 Russian Embassy
52 Australian Club (AERC)
53 UNICEF
55 Wat Ammon

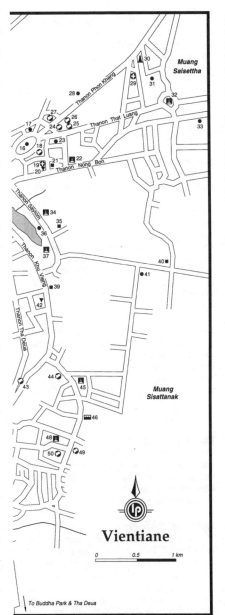

Muang
Saisettha

Thanon Phon Kheng

Thanon That Luang

Thanon Nong Bon

Thanon Setkham

Thanon Khu Vieng

Thanon Tha Deua

Muang
Sisattanak

Vientiane

0   0.5   1 km

To Buddha Park & Tha Deua

the fountain on Thanon Pangkham (next to the THAI office), Raintree Bookstore (☎ 217260) stocks a selection of mostly used paperbacks, magazines and other periodicals; most reading materials are in English, though the shop also maintains smaller inventories of French and German material. Hours are Monday to Saturday 8.30 am to 5 pm.

The nearby State Book Shop on the northeast corner of Thanons Setthathirat and Manthatulat near Namphu Square carries books and magazines in Lao and English, along with posters, political comic books and a few Lao handicrafts. It's open Monday to Saturday 8 to 11.30 am and 2 to 4.30 pm.

The gift shop at the Lane Xang Hotel has a few books in English for sale, and rather expensive maps of Vientiane and Laos. Phimphone Market and Phimphone Minimart, on opposite sides of Thanon Samsenthai near the Hotel Ekalath Metropole, also carry a few English and French-language materials.

Cultural Centres The Centre de Langue Française (☎ 215764), on Thanon Lan Xang directly opposite the LNTA office, offers French and Lao language classes, weekly French films and a small French library (open Monday to Saturday).

The Russian Cultural Centre (☎ 212030) at the corner of Thanons Luang Prabang and Khun Bulom offers similar services oriented toward Russian language and culture.

Laundry Most hotels and guest houses offer laundry services (a few even include it with room charges). Several laundry and dry cleaning shops can be found in Vientiane's Chinatown area, especially along Thanon Heng Boun and Thanon Samsenthai just east of Thanon Chao Anou. Typical laundry rates run about 300 to 500 kip per piece, and one-day service is usually available if you drop off your clothes in the morning.

Medical Services Medical facilities in Vientiane are quite limited. The two state hospitals, Setthathirat and Mahasot, operate on levels of skill and hygiene quite below that available next door in Thailand. Mahasot Hospital operates a Diplomatic Clinic 'especially for foreigners' that is open 24 hours, but the reality is that very few foreigners use this clinic.

The Australian Embassy in Vientiane maintains a clinic that can treat minor problems. The Australian Clinic (☎ 413603; after hours ☎ 312343) is open Monday to Friday from 8.30 am to noon and 2 to 5 pm, except Wednesday when it closes at 12.30 pm. The clinic is staffed by registered nurses but isn't equipped to handle major medical emergencies. Treatment fees are substantial.

The 150-bed Hôpital de l'amitié (☎ /fax 413663) is a new centre for trauma and orthopedics operated by the Association Médicale Franco Asiatique (AMFA) and located at the site of the old Soviet Hospital north of the city on the road to Tha Ngon. For emergencies you're supposed to be able to call ☎ 413306 for a radio-dispatched ambulance, but early tests of this procedure have found it lacking in verisimilitude. At night the hospital is closed and locked, with no staff on duty.

If a medical problem can wait till you're in Bangkok, all the better, since excellent hospitals are available there. For medical emergencies that can't wait till Bangkok and which can't be treated at the embassy clinic, you can arrange to have ambulances summoned from nearby Udon Thani or Khon Kaen in Thailand or use the services of Lao Westcoast Helicopter. See the Health section in the Facts for the Visitor chapter for names and addresses.

Vientiane's better pharmacies are found along Thanon Nong Bon near Talaat Sao. Pharmacie Kamsath (☎ 212940) and Pharmacie Sengthong Osoth (☎ 213732), both on Thanon Nong Bon in this vicinity, have a greater selection of pharmaceuticals than most other pharmacies in the city, and the stock is typically larger and fresher then elsewhere as well.

Emergency The six districts within Vientiane each have a police station, but you're unlikely ever to have contact with them unless you're involved in an accident. In an emergency, you could contact police at the police kiosk on Thanon Setthathirat.

The following three-digit emergency phone numbers are supposed to bring help immediately:

Fire	190
Police	191
Ambulance	195

Dangers & Annoyances Vientiane has an unofficial curfew that's applied to all parts of the city outside downtown. Anyone out after midnight or so may be hassled by military types. These incidents seem to be most common in the north-eastern and north-western edges of town; in the typical scenario a foreigner or group of foreigners is stopped by two or three armed men – often not wearing any type of uniform – and firmly escorted back to their homes or hotels with no explanation. This kind of occurrence happens to foreign residents as well as to visiting foreigners. Repeated enquiries on the part of the author have failed to discover the reason for these incidents, though the most obvious guess would be that these are security guards acting to 'protect' you from unsavoury elements that might be out and about. If you stick to well-trafficked areas after midnight you're not likely to have such an encounter.

Pha That Luang ພະທາດຫຼວງ
The Pha That Luang, Laos' most important and imposing monument, is located at the end of Thanon That Luang. For a full description of Pha That Luang and its history see the section starting on page 144.

Wat Si Saket ວັດສີສະເກດ
This temple sits more or less opposite the Presidential Palace at the north-eastern corner of Thanons Lan Xang and Setthathirat. Built in 1818 by King Anouvong (Chao Anou), it is the oldest temple still standing in Vientiane today – all the others were either built after Wat Si Saket or were

rebuilt after destruction by the Siamese in 1828. King Anouvong, more or less a vassal of the Siamese state, had Wat Si Saket constructed in the early Bangkok style. This is probably why the Siamese spared this wat from destruction when they quashed Anouvong's rebellion against Siamese rule.

In spite of the Siamese architectural influence, Wat Si Saket has several unique features. The interior walls of the cloister are riddled with small niches that contain over 2000 silver and ceramic Buddha images. Over 300 seated and standing Buddhas of varying sizes and materials (wood, stone, silver and bronze) rest on long shelves below the niches, most sculpted or cast in the characteristic Lao style (see the Arts section in the Facts About the Country chapter for details on Lao religious sculpture). Most of the images are from 16th to 19th-century Vientiane but a few hail from 15th to 16th-century Luang Prabang. A slightly damaged Khmer-style Naga Buddha – in which the Buddha is seated on a coiled cobra deity whose multi-headed hood shelters the image – is also on display; it was brought from a Khmer site at nearby Hat Sai Fong. Along the western side of the cloister is a pile of broken and half-melted Buddhas from the 1828 Siamese-Lao war.

The *sim* is surrounded by a colonnaded terrace in the Bangkok style and topped by a five-tiered roof. The interior walls bear hundreds of Buddha niches similar to those in the cloister, as well as beautiful – but decaying – *jataka* murals depicting the Buddha's life story. Portions of the Bangkok-style painted murals are unrestored 1820s originals, some parts are a 1913 restoration. UNESCO announced it would fund a restoration of the murals in 1991 but so far the murals are still fading.

The flowered ceiling was inspired by Siamese temples in Ayuthaya, which were in turn inspired by floral designs in the royal palace at Versailles. At the rear interior of the sim is an altar with several Buddha images, bringing the total number of Buddhas at Wat Si Saket to 6840! The standing Buddha to the left on the upper altar is said to have been cast to the same physical proportions as King Anouvong. The large gilt wood candlestand in front of the altar is an original, carved in 1819.

On the outside veranda at the rear of the sim is a five-metre-long wooden trough carved to resemble a naga or snake deity. This is the *láang song nâam pha* (image-watering rail), which is used during Bun Pi Mai (Lao New Year) to pour water over Buddha images for ritual cleansing.

To the far left of the entrance to the cloister, facing Thanon Lan Xang, is a raised *haw tai* (tripitaka library) with a Burmese-style roof. The scriptures that were once contained here are now in Bangkok. Only one of the four doors is original: the other three restored in 1913.

The hours and admission fee at Wat Si Saket are the same as for Pha That Luang. A Lao guide who speaks French and English is usually on hand to describe the temple and answer questions. There is no charge for the services of the guide.

Haw Pha Kaew ຫໍພະແກ້ວ

Just down Thanon Setthathirat, about 100m from Wat Si Saket, is the former royal temple of the Lao monarchy, Haw Pha Kaew. It has been converted to a museum and is no longer a regular place of worship.

According to the Lao, the temple was originally built in 1565 by command of King Setthathirat. Setthathirat had been a ruler of the nearby Lanna Kingdom in northern Thailand while his father King Phothisarat reigned over Lan Xang. After his father died, he inherited the Lan Xang throne and moved the capital of Lan Xang to Vientiane. From Lanna he brought with him the so-called Emerald Buddha (Pha Kaew in Lao, which means Jewel Buddha Image – the image is actually made of a type of jade). Wat Pha Kaew was built to house this image and to serve as the King's personal place of worship. Following a skirmish with the Lao in 1779, the Siamese took the Emerald Buddha and installed it in Bangkok's own Wat Phra Kaew (Phra is the Thai word for Buddha image; Pha is Lao). Later during the

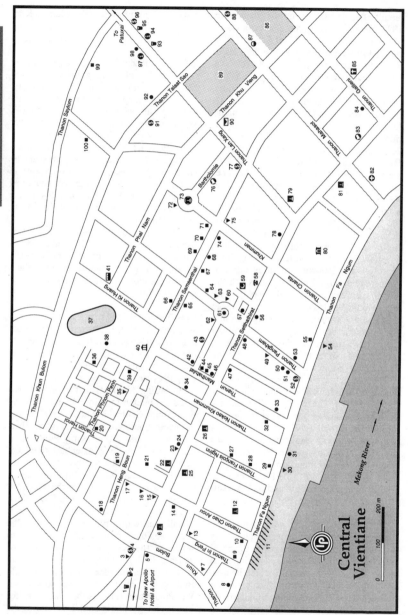

Central
Vientiane

Mekong River

0   100   200 m

PLACES TO STAY

9 Phomthip Guest House
10 Inter Hotel
14 Saysana Hotel
19 Anou Hotel
20 Vannasinh Guest House
21 Lani I Guest House
27 Lao International Guest House
28 Tai-Pan Hotel
29 Mixai Guest House
32 Samsenthai Hotel
36 Syri Guest House
39 Santisouk Guest House & Restaurant
44 Phantavong Guest House
45 MC&I Guest House
55 Lane Xang Hotel
64 Pangkham Guest House
65 Settha Guest House
66 Lao Hotel Plaza (under construction)
67 Lao Paris Hotel
69 Hua Guo Guest House
70 Asian Pavilion Hotel
71 Hotel Ekalath Metropole/ Phimphone Market
99 Lani II Guest House
100 Saylomyen Guest House

PLACES TO EAT

3 Phikun Restaurant
7 Nang Kham Bang
11 Night Vendors
13 Restaurant Le Vendôme
15 Nai Xieng Chai Yene
16 Sweet Home & Liang Xiang Bakeries
17 Le Chanthy (Nang Janti)
23 Le Bayou
30 Mixay Café
35 Thai Food (Phikun) Restaurant
49 Le Souriya
54 Sukiyaki Bar & Restaurant/ Lao Restaurant
60 Namphu & L'Opera Restaurants
62 Scandinavian Bakery/ Restaurant Le Provençal
63 The Taj Restaurant
72 Soukvimane Lao Food
75 Kua Lao

OTHER

1 Win West Pub (Bane Saysana)
2 Shell Station
4 Thai Military Bank
5 Russian Cultural Centre
6 Wat In Paeng
8 SODETOUR
12 Wat Chan
18 Maningron Supermarket
22 Wat Hai Sok
24 Lane Xang Travel
25 Wat Ong Teu
26 Wat Mixai
31 Haw Kang
33 The Art of Silk
34 Lao Textiles
37 National Stadium
38 Tennis Club de Vientiane
40 Lao Revolutionary Museum
41 National Pool
42 IMF
43 Bank of Lao PDR
46 State Book Shop
47 Lao Air Booking
48 Inter-Lao Tourisme
50 Raintree Bookstore
51 Thai International (THAI)
52 La Banque pour le Commerce Extèrieur Lao (Lao Foreign Trade Bank)
53 Lao Aviation
56 National Library
57 Diethelm Travel
58 Public Telephone Office
59 Mosque
61 Fountain Circle
68 Souvenir & Handicraft Shops
73 That Dam ('Black Stupa')
74 Phimphone Minimart
76 US Embassy
77 Siam Commercial Bank
78 Ministry of Foreign Affairs
79 Wat Si Saket
80 Presidential Palace (Haw Kham)
81 Haw Pha Kaew
82 Mahasot Hospital
83 French Embassy
84 Le Club France
85 Catholic Church
86 Khua Din Market
87 Bus Terminal
88 Siam Commercial Bank
89 Talaat Sao (Morning Market)
90 Post, Telephone & Telegraph office (PTT)
91 Bangkok Bank
92 Immigration Office
93 Crêperie-Pub Belle Ile
94 Lao National Tourism Authority
95 Nightclub Vienglatry
96 Thai Farmer's Bank
97 Tourist Authority of Thailand
98 Centre de Langue Française

VIENTIANE PROVINCE

Siamese-Lao war of 1828, Vientiane's Wat Pha Kaew was razed.

Between 1936 and 1942, the temple was rebuilt, supposedly following the exact same original plan. Herein lies the problem in dating the original temple. If the currently standing structure was restored in the original style, it doesn't seem likely that the original could have been built in the mid-16th century, as it doesn't resemble any known structure in Siam, Laos, Myanmar or Cambodia from that period. In fact it looks very much like a 19th century Bangkok-style sim. On the other hand, if the restoration's architects chose to use the more common 19th century style (as exemplified by Wat Si Saket) because they really didn't have the original plans, then it's possible the original was constructed in 1565 as claimed (if it wasn't, it casts the whole Emerald Buddha story into doubt).

At any rate, today's Haw Pha Kaew (Hall of the Jewel Buddha Image) is not very impressive except in size. The rococo ornamentation that runs up and down every door, window and base looks unfinished. But some of the best examples of Buddhist sculpture found in Laos are kept here, so it's worth visiting for that reason alone. A dozen or so prominent sculptures are displayed along the surrounding terrace. These include a 6th to 9th century Dvaravati-style stone Buddha; several bronze standing and sitting Lao-style Buddhas – including the 'Calling for Rain' (standing with hands at his sides), 'Offering Protection' (palms stretched out in front) and 'Contemplating the Tree of Enlightenment' (hands crossed at the wrist in front) poses; and a collection of inscribed Lao and Mon stelae. Most of the Lao bronzes are missing their *usnisa* or flame finial.

Inside the sim are royal requisites such as a gilded throne, more Buddhist sculpture (mostly smaller pieces, including a wooden copy of the Pha Bang, the original of which is stored in Luang Prabang), some Khmer stelae, various wooden carvings (door panels, candlestands, lintels), palm-leaf manuscripts and bronze frog drums. A bronze 'Calling-for-Rain' Buddha, tall and lithe, is particularly beautiful; also unique is a 17th century Vientiane-style bronze Buddha in the 'European pose', ie with the legs hanging down as if seated on a chair or bench.

A stone Khmer Buddha, a marble Mandalay Buddha and several other figures stand at the front altar. Visiting Thais worship here and, although the place is no longer used as a wat, they lay offerings of money on a small platform atop the wooden naga image (from Xieng Khua) after worship.

The sim is surrounded by a nicely landscaped garden. At the back of the building is a large reconstructed stone jar from Xieng Khuang's Plain of Jars.

Haw Pha Kaew is open Tuesday to Sunday 8 to 11.30 am and 2 to 4.30 pm and is closed Monday and public holidays. A French and English-speaking guide is occasionally available. When rains are unusually heavy, the grounds of Wat Pha Kaew become flooded and the entrance may be closed until the water level goes down.

Wat Ong Teu Mahawihan
ວັດອົງຕື້ມະຫາວິຫານ

Called Wat Ong Teu (Temple of the Heavy Buddha) for short, this temple is one of the most important in all of Laos. It was originally built in the mid 16th century by King Setthathirat and as such is a contemporary of Pha That Luang, but like every temple in Vientiane except Wat Si Saket, it was destroyed in later wars with the Siamese, then rebuilt in the 19th and 20th centuries. The Hawng Sangkhalat (Deputy Patriarch) of the Lao monastic order resides at Wat Ong Teu and presides over the Buddhist Institute, a school for monks who come from all over the country to study *dhamma* in the capital.

The temple's namesake is a large 16th-century bronze Buddha of several tons that sits in the rear of the sim, flanked by two standing Buddhas. This sim is also deservedly famous for the wooden facade over the front terrace, a masterpiece of Lao carving.

Wat Ong Teu is on a shady stretch of Thanon Setthathirat between Thanons Chao Anou and Nokeo Kumman.

Wat Hai Sok ວັດຫາຍໂສກ

Across Thanon Setthathirat from Way Ong Teu is the less acclaimed Wat Hai Sok, which recently underwent restoration. It's worth a quick look because of the impressive five-tiered roof (nine if you count the lower terrace roofs).

Wat Mixai ວັດມີໄຊ

Wat Mixai is in the next block east from Wat Ong Teu and Wat Hai Sok along the same street. The sim is in the Bangkok style, with a veranda that goes all the way round. The heavy gates, flanked by two *nyak* (guardian giants), are also Bangkok style. An elementary school shares the compound.

Wat In Paeng ວັດອິນແປງ

A rough translation of this monastery's name is Assembled by Indra, a tribute to the artistry displayed in the sim's stucco relief. Over the front veranda gable hangs an impressive wood and mosaic facade. The temple occupies the next block west of Wat Ong Teu.

Wat Chanthabuli (Wat Chan)
ວັດຈັນທະບຸລີ

This one's on Thanon Fa Ngum near the river, a block south of Wat Ong Teu. The carved wooden panels on the rebuilt sim are typically Lao and well executed. Inside the sim is a large bronze seated Buddha from the original temple that stood at this site (the Buddha was never moved). In the courtyard are the remains of a stupa that once had standing Buddha images in the 'Calling for Rain' pose on all four sides; one image remains.

Wat Si Muang ວັດສີເມືອງ

These temple grounds – the most heavily worshipped in all of Vientiane – are the site of the *lák meuang* (city pillar/phallus) and are thus considered the home of the guardian spirit of Vientiane. Legend has it that the spot was selected in 1563 as the site for a new wat by a group of sages when King Setthathirat moved his capital to Vientiane. Once the spot was chosen, a large hole was dug to receive the heavy stone pillar (probably taken from an ancient Khmer site nearby), which was suspended over the hole with ropes. Drums and gongs were sounded to summon the townspeople to the area and everyone waited for a volunteer to jump in the hole as a sacrifice to the spirit. A pregnant girl finally leapt in and the ropes were released, thus establishing the town guardianship.

The sim (destroyed in 1828 and later rebuilt in 1915) was constructed around the lák múang, which forms the centre of the altar. The stone pillar is wrapped in sacred cloth, and in front of it is a carved wooden stele with a seated Buddha in relief. The stele is wrapped in blinking red and green lights.

Several other Buddha images surround the pillar. One worth noting is kept on a cushion a little to the left and in front of the altar. The rather crude, partially damaged stone Buddha survived the 1828 destruction in one of the original thâat on the wat grounds. The locals believe this image has the power to grant wishes or answer troubling questions – the practice is to lift the image off the pillow three times (alternatively two sets of three) while mentally phrasing a question or request. If your request is granted, you're supposed to return to Wat Si Muang later with an offering of bananas, young coconuts, flowers, incense and candles (usually two of each). This is why so many platters of fruit, flowers and incense are sitting around the sim!

Behind the sim is a crumbling laterite *jedi* (stupa), probably of Khmer origin. Devotees deposit broken deity images and broken pottery around the jedi's base in the belief that the spirits of the jedi will 'heal' the bad luck created by the breaking of these items. In front of the sim is a little public park with an unlabelled statue of King Sisavang Vong (1904-1959) – the identifying plaque was removed after the 1975 Revolution. In his hand the king holds a palm-leaf manuscript representing the country's first legal code.

Wat Si Muang is located at a three-way intersection where Thanon Setthathirat and Thanon Samsenthai converge to become Thanon Tha Deua.

Wat Sok Pa Luang ວັດໂສກປ່າຫຼວງ

Wat Mahaphutthawongsa Pa Luang Pa Yai is the full name for this *wat paa* (forest temple) in south Vientiane's Sisattanak district. It's famous for its rustic herbal saunas, which are usually administered by eight-precept nuns who reside at the temple. Some preparation is involved, so it's wise to make arrangements in advance. After the relaxing sauna, you can take herbal tea while cooling off; expert massage is also available. For optimum medicinal results you're not supposed to wash away your accumulated perspiration for two or three hours afterwards. Apparently, this allows the herbs to soak into your pores. Nearby Wat Si Amphon also does herbal saunas (see the Getting There & Away section below). Neither temple charges fees for saunas, but you should leave a donation of at least 1000 kip per person.

Wat Sok Pa Luang is also known for its course of instruction in *vipassana*, a type of Buddhist meditation that involves careful mind-body analysis. The abbot and teacher is Ajaan Sali Kantasilo, who was born in Yasothon, Thailand, in 1932. Ajaan Sali (Chali in Thai) came to Laos in 1953 at the request of monks and laity in Vientiane who wanted to study vipassana. He accepts foreign students but only speaks Lao and Thai, so interested people will have to arrange for an interpreter if they don't speak either of these languages. Before 1975 he had many Western students; since then he's taught only Lao followers and a small trickle of interested Westerners, primarily Russians.

Getting There & Away Taxi, jumbo and tuk-tuk drivers all know how to get to Wat Sok Pa Luang. If you're travelling by car or bicycle, take Thanon Khu Vieng south past Talaat Sao for about 2.5 km until you come to a fairly major road on the left (this is Thanon Sok Pa Luang, but it's unmarked). Turn left here; the entrance to the wat is about half a km on the left. The temple buildings are back in the woods so all you can see from the road is the tall, ornamented gate.

Wat Si Amphon is farther south off Thanon Si Amphon. A few hundred metres past Thanon Sok Pa Luang, turn right on Thanon Si Amphon; Wat Si Amphon is on the left.

That Dam ທາດດຳ
The so-called 'Black Stupa' or That Dam is on Thanon Bartholomie, between the Hotel Ekalath Metropole and the US Embassy. Local mythology says the stupa is the abode of a dormant seven-headed dragon that came to life during the 1828 Siamese-Lao war and protected local citizens. The stupa appears to date from the Lanna or early Lan Xang period and is very similar to stupas in Chiang Saen, Thailand. Until recently That Dam was overgrown with weeds sprouting through cracks in its brick-and-stucco structure; a 1995 renovation sealed the cracks but it still looks old and atmospheric.

Xieng Khuan ຊຽງຄວນ
Often called 'Buddha Park' (Suan Phut), this collection of Buddhist (and Hindu) sculpture in a meadow by the side of the Mekong river lies 24 km south of the town centre off Thanon Tha Deua.

The park was designed and built in 1958 by Luang Pu (Venerable Grandfather) Bunleua Sulilat, a yogi-priest-shaman who merged Hindu and Buddhist philosophy, mythology and iconography into a cryptic whole. He developed a very large following in Laos and north-eastern Thailand, and moved to Thailand around the time of the 1975 Revolution. In 1978, he established the similarly inspired Wat Khaek in Nong Khai, Thailand, where he now resides. Originally, Bunleua is supposed to have studied under a Hindu *rishi* in Vietnam. According to legend he was walking in the mountains when he fell through a sinkhole and landed in the rishi's lap! He remained in the cave, called Kaew Ku (Jewel Grotto), for several years.

The cement sculptures at Xieng Khuan (Spirit City) are bizarre but compelling in their naive confidence. They includes statues of Shiva, Vishnu, Arjuna, Buddha and every other Hindu or Buddhist deity imaginable, as well as a few secular figures, all supposedly cast by unskilled artists under Luang Pu's direction. The style of the figures is remarkably uniform. Children will enjoy cavorting around some of the more fantastic shapes, such as the deity with octopus-like tentacles.

There is only one building on the grounds, a large pumpkin-shaped cement monument with three levels joined by interior spiral stairways. It's said that the three levels represent hell, earth and heaven. The rooms inside are filled with small sculptures and are designed so that you can either enter them for viewing or merely look in through windows from an outer hallway at each level. The last spiral stairway leads onto the top of the structure, from where you can view the huge sculptures outside.

A few food vendors in the park offer fresh young coconuts, soft drinks, beer, *pîng kai* (grilled chicken) and *tạm màak-hung* (spicy green papaya salad).

Since Luang Pu abandoned the site, the municipality has turned it into a public park. It's open daily from 8 am to 5 pm; entry is 300 kip.

Getting There & Away To reach Buddha Park by bus, take bus No 14 or 49, which leaves Talaat Sao terminal every 40 minutes or so throughout the day for 200 kip per person. Alternatively, a chartered jumbo costs around 3000 kip one way, 6000 kip return. Or hop a share jumbo (300 kip) as far as the ferry pier at Tha Deua and then walk or take a samlor the final four km to the park. You could also pedal a rented bicycle here fairly easily – assuming you don't find 24 km a daunting distance – as the road is relatively flat all the way.

Patuxai ປະຕູໄຊ
The Patuxai, a large monument reminiscent of the Arc de Triomphe in Paris, is known by a variety of names. The official Lao name, Patuxai, is in fact roughly equivalent to Arch (*pátu*, also translated as door or gate) of Triumph (*xái*, from the Sanskrit *jaya* or victory). Ironically, though begun in the early '60s it was completed in 1969 with US-purchased cement that was supposed to have been used for the construction of a new airport. Hence local residents sometimes refer to it as 'the vertical runway'.

Since its purpose was to commemorate the Lao who had died in pre-Revolutionary wars, current Lao maps typically label it 'Old Monument' (Ancien Monument in French, or Anusawali Kao in Lao) in contrast to the newer Unknown Soldiers Memorial. Many expats redundantly call it the Anusawali Monument (*anusawali* means monument in Lao). Old French guidebooks sometimes call

it the Monument aux Morts (Monument to the Dead).

Whatever you call it, this huge arch at the end of Thanon Lan Xang is within walking distance of the town centre and is worth a quick visit if the weather's agreeable. From a distance, it looks very much like its French source of inspiration. Up close, however, the Lao design starts to come out. The bas-relief on the sides and the temple-like ornamentation along the top and cornices are typically Lao. A stairway leads to the top levels of the monument, where for a 200 kip fee you can look out over the city. The stairs are open daily from 8 am to 5 pm.

Lao Revolutionary Museum
ພິພິທະພັນກອງປະຕິວັດລາວ
The Lao Revolutionary Museum (Phiphitta-phan Patiwat Lao) is housed in a well-worn classical mansion on Thanon Samsenthai. Originally built in 1925 as the French governor's residence, in post-independence Laos the building was used as a royal residence, a state guest house and as various ministerial offices before assuming its museum function in 1985. For the most part, the museum contains a collection of artefacts and photos from the Pathet Lao's lengthy struggle for power. Many of the displays consist of historic weaponry; some labels are in English as well as Lao.

The rooms near the entrance feature small cultural and geographical exhibits, as if these were incidental to the Revolution rather than vice versa. The more interesting items include several Khmer sandstone sculptures of Hindu deities and a display of traditional Lao musical instruments.

Inner rooms are dedicated to the 1893-1945 French colonial period, the 1945-54 struggle for independence, the 1954-63 resistance to American imperialism, the 1964-69 provisional government and the 1975 communist victory. Labels often employ the 'running dog'-style vocabulary commonly used by Asian communists; a picture of a road crew tamping earth during the French era is labelled 'barbarous slavery'.

No mention is made of the thousands of

Vietnamese troops who occupied eastern Laos during the war, although in one room a bust of Ho Chi Minh stands next to one of Lenin. An interesting diorama of the PL caves at Vieng Xai is labelled in Lao only. One of the more curious items on display is a chest expander, enshrined in a glass cabinet, used by Kaysone 'in the gymnastic session during the elaboration of the plan to seize power'.

Posted hours (which are not scrupulously followed) for the museum are from 8 to 11.30 am and 2 to 4.30 pm weekdays; entry is 200 kip.

Unknown Soldiers Memorial
ພີ່ພິຫະພັນທະຫານຫານຫາບເສິກລີກລັບ

This white thâat-like structure was built to commemorate the Pathet Lao who died during the 1964-73 War of Resistance. It's north of Pha That Luang off Thanon Phon Kheng.

Kaysone Phomvihane Memorial & Museum
ອະນຸສາວະລີແລະພີ່ພິຫະພັນໄກສອນພົມວິຫານ

Opened in late 1995 to celebrate the late president's 75th birthday, this new facility serves as a tribute to Indochina's most pragmatic communist leader. It's worth visiting only if you have an interest in the history of the Lao communist revolution. A bronze bust of Kaysone, fashioned by a North Korean sculptor, stands in the central entrance hall, around which the various exhibiting rooms are arranged. The first room displays pictures of Laos' most important cultural and historic sites. Another contains a mockup of his childhood home in Ban Na Seng, Savannakhet Province, while another exhibit evokes Kaysone's youth and includes a school desk from the French school he attended at Ban Tai, surmounted by family pictures.

Further exhibits of historic photography and minor artefacts chronicle the founding of the Lao Issara and the Indochinese communist Party. A model of a portion of 'Kaysone Cave' in Hua Phan Province contains a revolver, binoculars, radio and other personal effects; given the difficulties inherent in receiving permission to view the real cave in Vieng Xai, this may be your only chance to see what it looks like. This is followed by minor exhibits covering events in the '50s and '60s, ending with a summary of the 1975 Revolution and subsequent nation-building.

The museum-memorial is located off Route 13 south near Km 6 in the military compound where Kaysone lived up until his death. If you're coming by private transport, turn left about 300m before the new Children's Home; follow the road about 300m and turn left again just before the gate to the army post. Follow this road for 800m; you'll round a curve to the right and then see the museum (signed 'Area of Memorial Museum of Former President Kaysone Phomvihane') on your right. It's open daily, except Monday and holidays, from 8 to 11 am and 2 to 4.30 pm; admission is 200 kip.

National Ethnic Cultural Park
ສວນວັດທະນະທັມແຫ່ງຊາດ

This new facility on the Mekong river at Km 18, Thanon Tha Deua, has yet to live up to its name. So far the only attractions are a small zoo containing monkeys, bears and birds, a children's playground, statues of dinosaurs, a few souvenir shops and a long-distance view of the Thai-Lao Friendship Bridge. Lao-style buildings under construction will ostensibly contain exhibits having to do with Lao culture. Kids would probably like this place in spite of its obvious shortcomings for most adults. It's open daily 9 am to 5 pm, 500 kip entry.

Dong Dok University
ມະຫາວິຫະຍາລັຍດົງໂດກ,

Travellers who'd like to meet Lao university students might want to visit Dong Dok University. It's about nine km north of the city off the road to Tha Ngon (Route 10). Students at the university's Foreign Language Institute are usually delighted to meet someone who speaks the language that they're studying (Vietnamese, French, Japanese and English are common languages of study).

Language Courses

See Courses in the Facts for the Visitor chapter for details on Vientiane language schools which teach Lao.

Swimming Pools

There are now several places in Vientiane where you can work on your strokes or simply take a cooling dip. Sokpaluang Swimming Pool on Thanon Sok Pa Luang in south-eastern Vientiane offers a large pool with marked swimming lanes, a shallow kids' pool, snack bar with Lao and *falang* food, lockers and changing rooms for the reasonable rate of 1000 kip per person per day. It's open daily 9 am to 8 pm.

Near the south-east corner of the National Stadium is a public pool that costs only 300 kip a day but cleanliness is not always up to par; most of the girls who swim here wear their street clothes rather than bathing suits (at Sokpaluang bathing suits are compulsory).

The simple, clean pool at the Royal Dokmaideng Hotel on Thanon Lan Xang is open to the public for 2000 kip per day.

The kidney-shaped swimming pool (and pool bar) at the Lane Xang Hotel may be used by non-guests for a steep US$4 per day.

See also Recreation Clubs, under Entertainment, in this chapter for information on the pool at the Australian Embassy Recreation Club (AERC).

Tennis, Squash & Golf

The Vientiane Tennis Club, next to the National Stadium off Thanon Samsenthai, has three decent illuminated courts available to members only. Foreigners may apply but memberships are limited.

The Australian Club maintains a squash court which is open to AERC members only. See Recreation Clubs under Entertainment for more detail.

The new Santisuk Lane Xang Golf Club at Km 14, Thanon Tha Deua, offers a 2800 yard, nine hole course, par 35. It's open to the public and green fees are reasonable.

The Vientiane Golf Club (☎ 130261) at Km 6, Route 13 south, is a members-only club with a fair nine hole course, clubhouse and pro shop.

Yoga & Exercise

L'Eden Health Centre (☎ 213528), off Thanon Setthathirat a little east of Mahasot Hospital, offers yoga classes each Wednesday from 5.15 to 6.45 pm along with daily dance aerobics and toning classes Monday through Saturday between 2 and 9 pm.

The AERC also holds aerobics classes for members.

Hash House Harriers

This is one expat organisation that doesn't charge a membership fee. The Vientiane Hash has a blackboard at the Australian Club (see the Entertainment section) which announces the changing location of the weekly hash run, which is held Mondays at 5.30 pm (5 pm December to February). Postings may also be seen at The Fountain and at Phimphone Market. To participate in the four to five km race, you contribute US$5, which pays for the beer, soft drinks and food at the end of the run. Newcomers are usually coerced into downing quite a lot of Beerlao.

Festivals

If you happen to be in Vientiane in early November, don't miss the That Luang Festival (Bun That Luang), Laos' largest temple fair. Along with all the religious fervour comes a trade show and a number of carnival games. The festivities begin with a *wíen thíen* (circumambulation) around Wat Si Muang, followed by a procession to Pha That Luang, which is illuminated all night for a week or so. The festival climaxes on the morning of the full moon with the *tàak bàat* ceremony, in which several thousand monks from around the country receive food alms from Lao Buddhist laypeople. That evening there's a final *wíen thíen* around Pha That Luang in which devotees carry *paasàat*, miniature temples (often mistranslated as 'castles' in the English press) made from banana stems and decorated with flowers and other offerings. Fireworks cap off the evening and everyone makes merit or makes merry till dawn.

PHA THAT LUANG

Pha That Luang (Great Sacred Reliquary, or Great Stupa) is the most important national monument in Laos, a symbol of both the Buddhist religion and Lao sovereignty. Its full official name, Pha Jedi Lokajulamani, means World-Precious Sacred Stupa, and it appears on the national seal. Legend has it that Ashokan missionaries from India erected a *thâat* or reliquary stupa here to enclose a breastbone of the Buddha as early as the 3rd century BC, but there is no evidence to confirm this. However, excavations suggest that a Khmer monastery may have been built near here between the 11th and 13th centuries AD.

When King Setthathirat moved the Lan Xang capital from Luang Prabang to Vientiane in the mid-16th century, he ordered the construction of That Luang in its current form, on the site of the Khmer temple. Construction began in 1566 AD and in succeeding years four wats were built around the stupa, one on each side. Only two remain today, Wat That Luang Neua to the north and Wat That Luang Tai to the south. Wat That Luang Neua is the monastic residence of the Supreme Patriarch (Pha Sangkhalat) of Lao Buddhism. The main building, in its present form, is a reconstruction from the early years of this century.

The monument looks almost like a missile cluster from a distance. Surrounding it is a high-walled cloister with tiny windows. (This was added by King Anouvong in the early 19th century as a defence against invaders.) Even more aggressive-looking than the thick walls are the pointed stupas themselves, which are built in three levels . From a closer perspective, however, the Great Stupa opens up and looks much more like a religious monument.

The Great Stupa is designed to be mounted by the faithful, so there are walkways around each level, with stairways between. Each level of the monument has different architectural features in which Buddhist doctrine is encoded; visitors are supposed to contemplate the meaning of these features as they walk round. The first level is a square base measuring 68 by 69m that supports 323 *sima* (ordination stones). There are also four arched *haw wái* (prayer-gates), one on each side, with short stairways leading up to and beyond them to the second level. The second level is 48 by 48m and is surrounded by 120 lotus petals. There are 288 simas on this level, as well as 30 small stupas symbolising the 30 Buddhist perfections *(pálamíi sãam-síp thàat)*, beginning with alms-giving and ending with equanimity. These stupas at one time contained smaller gold stupas and gold leaves, but these were taken by Chinese bandits while That Luang was abandoned in the 19th century.

Arched gates again lead to the next level, which is 30m along each side. The tall central stupa, which has a brick core that has been stuccoed over, is supported here by a bowl-shaped base reminiscent of India's first Buddhist stupa at Sanchi. At the top of this mound the superstructure, surrounded by lotus petals, begins.

The curvilinear, four-sided spire resembles an elongated lotus bud and is said to symbolise the growth of a lotus from a seed in a muddy lake bottom to a bloom over the lake's surface, a metaphor for human advancement from ignorance to enlightenment in Buddhism. The stupa is crowned by a

Pha That Luang as seen by Louis Delaporte in 1867

Pha That Luang

In 1641, Gerard van Wuystoff, an envoy of the Dutch East Indies Company, visited Vientiane and was received by King Sulinya Vongsa at That Luang in an apparently magnificent ceremony. The Lan Xang Kingdom was at the peak of its historical glory and van Wuystoff wrote that he was deeply impressed by the 'enormous pyramid, the top of which was covered with gold leaf weighing about a thousand pounds'(454 kg).

Unfortunately, the glory of Lan Xang and That Luang was only to last another 60 years or so. The stupa and the temples were damaged considerably during the 18th and 19th centuries by invading Burmese and Siamese armies. During a Siamese invasion in 1828, Vientiane was ransacked and depopulated to such an extent that That Luang remained abandoned until it was badly restored under French rule in 1900.

Thirty-three years earlier, a French explorer named Louis Delaporte had stumbled on the overgrown That Luang and had made detailed sketches of the monument. Between 1931 and 1935, a French university department reconstructed That Luang according to Delaporte's sketches. Or so say the French. The Lao today claim it was they who carried out the reconstruction, because they didn't like the way the French botched the job in 1900. Either way, the building has survived to become the archetypal symbol of the Lao nation. ■

JOE CUMMINGS

JOE CUMMINGS

Top Right: Monks strolling at Pha That Luang

Left: The That Luang Festival, which occurs in November

Bathing in the glow of late afternoon, Pha That Luang's four-sided spire is said to symbolise the growth of a lotus.

JOE CUMMINGS

stylised banana flower and parasol; the entire thâat was regilded in 1995 to celebrate the LPDR's 20th anniversary. From ground to pinnacle, That Luang measures 45m tall.

The encircling cloister (85m on each side) contains various Buddha images. Both classic Lao sculpture and Khmer figures are displayed on either side of the front entrance (inside). Worshippers sometimes stick balls of rice to the walls (especially during the That Luang Festival) to pay respects to the spirit of King Setthathirat.

Pha That Luang is about four km north-east of the centre of Vientiane at the end of Thanon That Luang. Facing the compound is a statue of King Setthathirat.

A small booklet on the temple's history costs 200 kip at the entrance. A well-illustrated, 56-page book (in French) called *Le That Luang de Vientiane*, has a history and description of the monument, and is available at the *Vientiane Times* office on Thanon Pangkham and at the State Book Shop for 5800 kip.

Pha That Luang is the site of a major festival in early November; see the Festivals section later in this chapter.

Pha That Luang is open to visitors from Tuesday to Sunday from 8 to 11.30 am and 2 to 4.30 pm, closed Monday and public holidays. Admission is 200 kip per person. ■

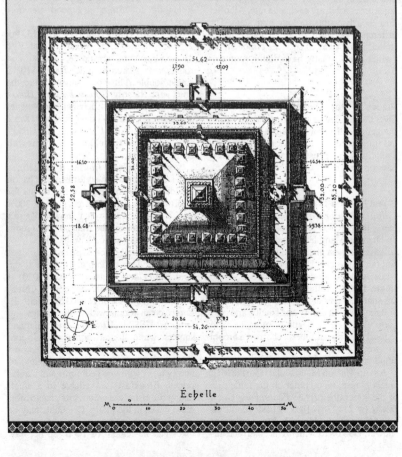

Échelle

Places to Stay

Vientiane has a choice of over 50 hotels and guest houses to accommodate all tourists, travellers, businesspeople, spies and other visitors who come to town.

Many hotels and guest houses in Vientiane quote US dollar or Thai baht rates and some of the more expensive require payment in US currency despite the recent ban on all currencies other than kip. At less expensive places you can usually pay with any of the three currencies, though if the rate is established in dollars or baht and you want to pay in kip you'll be at the mercy of the management's sometimes arbitrary exchange rate. All offer 5 to 20% discounts for long-term stays. The difference between a 'guest house' and a 'hotel' is the array of services provided; the former don't usually have dining rooms or bars.

Places to Stay – bottom end

Over the last couple of years the selection of budget-priced accommodation in Vientiane has broadened considerably, making the city a relatively inexpensive place to spend a few days or weeks.

Guest Houses The multi-storey *Ministry of Culture & Information Guest House* (formerly the SECP Guest House), at the corner of Thanons Manthatulat and Setthathirat, is still the cheapest place in town. Large, three-bed fan rooms cost US$3 per person a night, while two-bed air-con rooms are US$8/10 single/double. Toilet and shower facilities are shared. Rates are payable in kip, baht or dollars. It's a bit dreary and smelly, and isn't particularly clean – guests often have to request a change of sheets or borrow a broom to sweep out their own rooms. There's a small coffeeshop next door.

Just up Thanon Manthatulat from the MCI Guest House, on a corner on the same side of the street, the private *Phantavong Guest House* (☎ 214738) offers 12 basic rooms for US$5/8 single/double with shared toilet and shower, US$10/15 with private bath and air-

con. An attached outdoor dining area offers cheap meals (at about half the price of the cafe next door to the MCI Guest House.

Another government ministry-run place, the *Agriculture & Forestry (A&F) Guest House* (☎ 216890), on Thanon Hatsady opposite the immigration office, has mouldy three, five and seven-bed rooms for US$2 per person – it's only for the desperate.

Santisouk Guest House (☎ 215303), above the Restaurant Santisouk on Thanon Nokeo Kumman, has plain but clean rooms with wooden floors, high ceilings and shared bath for US$10 to 12 depending on the size. The restaurant downstairs is a good breakfast spot.

The *Mixai Guest House* (☎ 216213, fax 215445), opposite the Mixai Cafe at 30/1 Thanon Fa Ngum, has simple, clean, air-con rooms with shared facilities for US$10/12 single/double. A little out from the centre, the quiet and friendly *Senesouk Guest House* (☎ 215567, fax 217449), behind the Novotel Vientiane off Thanon Luang Prabang (Km 2 Ban Khounta), costs US$8 with fan, US$12 air-con for small to medium-size rooms with shared facilities.

Saylomyen Guest House (☎ 214246), a two-storey shophouse-style place on Thanon Saylom, has eight simple, clean rooms for 200B with fan and cold-water shower, 300B with air-con and hot-water shower. There's some street noise in the front so take a room towards the back if you have a choice.

A new, centrally located place that bridges the gap between bottom and middle is the *Vannasinh Guest House* (☎ /fax 222020) at 51 Thanon Phnom Penh at the edge of Chinatown (a block north of Thanon Samsenthai). Large, clean rooms with high ceilings and fans cost US$8 to 10 with shared toilet and shower, while similar rooms with air-con, private toilet and hot-water shower cost US$15 to 20. There are also a couple of family units with two bedrooms and similar prices. Breakfast is available in a small dining room and the proprietors plan to offer more meals in the future. Discounts may be negotiated for long-term stays and decent bikes can be rented for 1000 kip per day.

Proprietors Somphone and Mayulee speak very good French and English.

A half block north of the fountain square, at 72/6 Thanon Pangkham, a narrow four-storey building houses the new *Pangkham Guest House* (☎ 217053). Small rooms with fan and attached toilet and hot-water shower cost US$10 while similar rooms with air-con cost US$15. Slightly larger rooms are available for US$20. Rooms at the back are quieter than those which face Thanon Pangkham. The manager speaks good English.

Downtown toward the river, the *Lao International Guest House* (☎ 216571) on Thanon Francois Nginn, north of the Tai-Pan Hotel, offers 11 rooms with varying prices. A room with fan and shared bath on the rather unimpressive 2nd floor costs US$8, while ones with attached bath on the same floor are US$10. Up on the better-decorated 3rd floor, smaller air-con rooms with hot-water showers go for US$16; add TV and fridge for a total of US$20. A restaurant on the ground floor serves Lao, Chinese and European food at medium-high prices.

Three blocks west, tucked away on parallel Thanon In Paeng, is the similarly varied but better-designed *Phornthip Guest House* (☎ 217239). Spacious, clean, basic rooms with bath and fan cost US$7/12 single/double, while air-con rooms go for US$12/16.

Hotels *Hotel Ekalath Metropole* (☎ 213420) on the corner of Thanons Samsenthai and Chantha Khumman has undergone at least three incarnations, starting with the pre-1975 Imperial Hotel. The latest version is basically a middle-price hotel, but a semi-attached annex contains cheap, plain fan rooms for US$6 to 8 single and US$10 double with fan and shared cold-water shower, or US$12 single and US$14 double with fan and attached cold shower (but shared toilet).

Inter Hotel (☎ 215137) at the corner of Thanons Chao Anou and Fa Ngum is near the river. Rates here are US$12 to 16 single/double, depending on the size of the room; all rooms come with air-con. Larger

two-room units with hot-water showers cost US$20. Formerly the Lao Chaleune Hotel, this hotel is well located and often full, although the rooms are nothing special. One definite drawback is the hotel's bar/disco, which when active causes the whole building to shake.

Samsenthai Hotel at 15 Thanon Manthatulat near the river has gone downhill considerably over the last year or so and is not very clean any more – but at least the rates have dropped to match the standards. Rooms with fan and shared bath now go for US$6 single/double, while for US$12/15 you can get air-con and a private cold-water shower. The dimly-lit, cavernous lobby is off-putting.

Hotel Phonexay on Thanon Saylom near Wat Phonxai is a large, dilapidated hotel that serves as a holding place for South Asians – Indians, Pakistanis, Bangladeshis – waiting for visas to Thailand. Large rooms cost around US$5 to 10 a night but are hardly worth it (unless you want to practise your Bengali or Punjabi) considering the better deals downtown.

Places to Stay – middle
Guest Houses Vientiane has an abundance of mid-range guest houses catering to incoming or temporary NGO staffers and long-term visitors who prefer the family-like atmosphere such places provide over the typical hotel ambience. Discounts for long-term stays are usually available.

One of the more centrally located places of this type is *Lani I Guest House* (☎ 216103, fax 215639) at 281 Thanon Setthathirat, near Wat Hai Sok. Large, comfortable air-con rooms in an old house cost US$25 to 30 single and US$30 to 35 double. There is a pleasant terrace dining area attached. A second branch, *Lani II* at 268 Thanon Saylom (☎ 213022, fax 216095), is also located well off the street in a large house – if anything it's quieter than Lani I. Large, nicely decorated rooms start at US$15/20 single/double with air-con, fan and a lavatory in the room, with toilet and hot-water shower down the hall. Add private toilet, hot-water shower and fridge for US$25/30, or get a larger room for US$30/35. At either place bicycles are loaned to guests at no charge. The Lani I is often full; write to Lani Guest Houses, PO Box 58, Vientiane, for reservations.

Another well-located place is the friendly *Syri Guest House* (☎ 212682, fax 217251) in a large house in the old Chao Anou residential quarter. Spacious air-con rooms are US$17 single/double with shared hot-water bath, US$20/20/25 single/double/triple with private hot-water bath. With a little negotiating you should be able to knock US$5 off these rates as the place is beginning to show its age. On the upper floor is a terrace sitting area that overlooks the street.

Down Thanon Samsenthai in an easterly direction, just opposite the new Lao Hotel Plaza, the Chinese-owned *Settha Guest House* (☎ 213241) is ensconced in a modern four-storey building set back off the road directly opposite Lao Hotel Plaza. Air-con suites with hot water and separate sitting rooms cost US$20 for one bedroom, US$30 for two, but it's a bit sterile overall. On the ground floor is the banquet-style Hong Kong Restaurant, serving Chinese food of course.

Villa That Luang (also called That Luang Guest House; ☎ 413370) is on Thanon That Luang, not far from Pha That Luang. It's clean, and the staff seem eager to please. Large, air-con rooms are US$25 to 30, including daily laundry service.

French-owned *Auberge de Temple* (☎ 214844), at 184/1 Thanon Sikhotabang, is a large house 20m off Thanon Luang Prabang opposite the Blue Star nightclub. The inn's eight rooms are tastefully decorated with furniture of the owner's design. There are two air-con rooms with one large bed each and shared bath for US$10, another two rooms with two beds and shared bath for US$18 and four double rooms with attached bath for US$20. Breakfast is served in a small dining room downstairs. Rooms with windows facing Thanon Luang Prabang catch some street noise, so choose a room at the back if you prefer quiet.

East and south of the centre of town in leafy residential areas near the canal and Wat Sok Pa Luang are a number of other mid-priced guest houses. In this area it can be hard to find taxis or jumbos into town at night, though it's within easy pedalling distance if you have a bike. The quiet and friendly *Chaemchanh Guest House* (☎ 312700) at 73 Thanon Khu Vieng (actually 50m north of Thanon Khu Vieng) offers large rooms with air-con and hot water for US$20; room sizes tend to vary widely, so it pays to look first. More spacious apartments complete with kitchenette, sitting room and bedroom are also available for US$33. The beautiful garden surrounding the house is an attractive addition (the proprietors offer plants for sale).

The brick-and-tile *Thiengthong Guest House* (☎ 313782, fax 312125), off Thanon Sok Pa Luang in Ban Wat Nak, has air-con rooms with hot water for US$20 single/double, including breakfast and laundry. A small restaurant on the premises serves Lao and European food.

The quiet *Soradith Guest House* (☎ /fax 413651), at 150 Ban Dong Palan Thong (near Talaat Dong Palan), offers 15 well-appointed, immaculate rooms in a converted modern family home for US$25 a night single/double, or US$35 for a larger room, all with air-con, hot water, fridge and TV. A relatively pricey restaurant serving European food is attached.

Wonderland Guest House (☎ 314682), 200m north of Thanon Khu Vieng in Ban Phonsavan Tai, Si Sattanak, has 10 clean rooms furnished with rattan in a two-storey brick building, all with hot-water shower and air-con, for US$15 to 25. Half the rooms have small balconies. There's a restaurant downstairs and a 2nd-floor veranda with a sitting area.

Situated in the north-west part of town near the Talaat Noi and Talaat Thong Khan Kham markets, *Sisavad Guest House* (☎ 212719, fax 212719) at 99/12 Ban Sisawat Neua offers modern bungalows with large, clean air-con rooms for US$20 single/double. All rooms have private hot-water showers, and there's a pool on the premises.

Hotels *Asian Pavilion Hotel* (☎ 213430, fax 213432), Thanon Samsenthai, is a good mid-priced choice with a bit of history behind it. In its pre-Revolutionary incarnation, this was the Hotel Constellation (immortalised in John Le Carré's novel *The Honourable Schoolboy*). The original owner, a former Royal Lao Army colonel who had been trained in the USA, was sent to a re-education camp from 1975 until 1988; he reopened the hotel under the name of the Vieng Vilay Hotel in 1989. After a 1991 renovation the hotel changed names yet again. 'Standard' (read 'old') rooms in the back of the hotel are a reasonable US$24 and include fan, air-con, telephone and private hot-water bath, while more modern and slightly larger 'superior' rooms with TV are US$38. If you stay two days or more the rates drop to US$22 and US$35. Rooms are relatively well kept and the staff is helpful and efficient, which is why a lot of medium-budget businesspeople stay here. It's also relatively quiet since there is no disco. Visa credit cards are accepted for room charges.

On the opposite side of the Thanon Samsenthai, a bit further west toward Thanon Pangkham, stands the newly re-named *Lao-Paris Hotel* (☎ 216382, fax 222229). It's a modern building where single/double rooms with air-con, fridge and private hot-water bath cost US$25, or US$35 with TV. The management, who share ownership with the Pangkham Guest House around the corner, seem efficient and friendly. Downstairs is a Lao-Thai restaurant.

Saysana Hotel (☎ 213580), Thanon Chao Anou, has recently closed for yet another renovation and the new rates weren't yet available. From the looks of the new design, the finished hotel will probably cost somewhere in the neighbourhood of US$35 to 45 a night.

The Vietnamese-run *Hotel Ekalath Metropole* (☎ 213420) at Thanons Samsenthai and Chantha Khumman has large but decaying air-con rooms for US$22/28

single/double, which includes a complimentary breakfast in the hotel dining room. Try to get a room away from the disco if you seek quiet. Visa is accepted for these rooms (but not for the guest house rooms mentioned in Places to Stay – bottom end). All in all there are better deals available in the mid-range guest houses.

Anou Hotel (☎ 213630, fax 213635) at the corner of Thanon Heng Boun and Thanon Chao Anou has smallish rooms for US$18 single, US$30 double, all with air-con, hot water, operator-assisted phone and mini-fridge. A lot of the cheaper tour packagers in Bangkok use this hotel.

Vientiane Hotel (☎ 212928) is at Thanon Setthathirat, just before it becomes Thanon Luang Prabang. Fan rooms are US$15, air-con doubles are US$20 and air-con doubles with hot water are US$25. Rooms here are not good value by local standards; again some low-end tour packagers use this hotel.

North-east of the town centre on Thanon Nahaidio (a bit north of the Patuxai monument) is *Le Parasol Blanc Hotel* (☎ 216091), where modern air-con rooms around a pool and garden cost US$33 single/double. A restaurant/piano bar serves Swiss-Italian cuisine. Confirmed reservations at this hotel sometimes aren't honoured; be sure to have a backup plan in case you're refused a room for the night.

Similar, but a bit more out of the way on Thanon Phon Than north-east of Wat Sok Pa Luang, the quiet, well-run *Vansana Hotel* (☎ 413171) has large, clean rooms with fan, air-con and phones for US$33 single, US$44 double. Facilities include a library with English, French and Russian books, a pool and a dining room. Visa is accepted. Jumbos and samlors seem to be very scarce in this area, so the Vansana is best used by visitors who have their own transport.

Muang Lao-China Hotel (☎ 312380) Thanon Tha Deua, Km 4, is a bit out of town, on the way to the Tha Deua ferry, and is on the Mekong river (near the Australian Club). Large, clean, all air-con rooms go for US$25 to 40. There's a cafe downstairs. The management at this place has changed several times over the past few years so room rates and conditions are more variable than usual.

Places to Stay – top end

Vientiane's original luxury hotel, the *Lane Xang Hotel* (☎ 214102, fax 214108) faces the Mekong on Thanon Fa Ngum, around the corner from Lao Aviation, THAI and BCEL. This four-storey wonder was until very recently the LPDR's classiest digs and the hotel of choice for visiting high-rollers. Until 1994 it was also Vientiane's largest single source of foreign currency.

The 109 clean and spacious rooms at the Lane Xang have a socialist-era feel – some rooms still feature Russian air-conditioners, fridges and hot-water heaters. Bathrooms are huge. The hotel now has a lift along with a restaurant, swimming pool, putting green, two badminton courts, gift shop, and a fitness centre out the back with sauna and exercise equipment. Rooms are now US$47/61 single/double, two-room suites US$74; all rates include breakfast. Another renovation is soon due after which rates are expected to rise substantially. Major credit cards are accepted.

Also next to the river but quieter and more secluded is the Thai-owned, 32-room *River View Hotel* (☎ 216224, fax 216232) at the corner of Thanons Sithan Neua and Fa Ngum. Spacious, clean rooms cost US$40/40/44 single/double/triple with air-con, hot water and TV, or US$50 to 60 for a suite with fridge and river views. Visa is accepted.

Currently Vientiane's best top-end value is the very clean and sedate *Tai-Pan Hotel* (☎ 216906, fax 216223, or in Bangkok (02) 269-9888, fax 259-7908) at 2-12 Thanon François Nginn, a half block from the river. All rooms in this modern four-storey hotel feature individual terraces, TV with satellite and video, fridge, IDD phone and polished wooden floors for US$54/68 single/double including American breakfast, free airport pickup, tax and service. There is a US$5 discount off all rates for long-term stays.

Vientiane's largest international-class hotel is the four-storey *Novotel Vientiane* (☎ 213570, fax 213572), a 233-room estab-

lishment at Km 2 on Thanon Luang Prabang (just west of the western end of Thanon Samsenthai near the three-headed elephant statue). Built by Singaporeans as The Belvedere a few years ago, the newly acquired Novotel boasts an airport reservation desk and free airport shuttle, 24 hour business centre, restaurant serving imported food, a pool, *pétanque* and tennis courts. All rooms come with IDD telephone, central air-con, minibar and coffeemaker. Rates are US$90/100 standard, US$120 junior suite, US$140 executive suite; lower corporate rates are sometimes dispensed.

Another newcomer in the high-class category is the huge and imposing *Royal Dokmaideng Hotel* (☎ 214455, fax 214454), on Thanon Lan Xang near the Patuxai monument. This five-storey hotel features lots of wood and marble in the public areas; large rooms with all the modern conveniences cost US$80/90/120 single/double/triple, not including tax and service. Facilities and services include a pool, herbal sauna-massage centre, Chinese nightclub, lobby bar, business centre and KTV lounge.

The *New Apollo Hotel* (☎ 213244, fax 214462) at 69A Thanon Luang Prabang (formerly the Apollo Hotel and before that the Santiphap Hotel) has reopened following two years of renovations. Rather ordinary rooms, by international standards, come with air-con, hot water, TV and fridge and cost US$69/79 single/double. Larger rooms go for US$80/89. In 1995 discounted rates of around US$40 to 50 were available, which is more in line with what this hotel should cost. The hotel's hostess-style nightclub makes it popular with Thai, Japanese and Chinese business travellers. A bit of hotel trivia: in its first life as the Santiphap Hotel, this was the first building in Vientiane to contain a lift (elevator).

Two new top-end hotels currently under construction include the *Lao Hotel Plaza*, a huge multi-storey complex – said to be a joint Lao/Australian venture – on Thanon Samsenthai near the Revolutionary Museum, and the *Douang Deuane Hotel* (☎ 222300) on Thanon Nokeo Kumman toward the river. Lao Hotel Plaza, managed by Thailand's Felix Hotels & Resorts, will contain 163 rooms, a fitness centre, restaurants, a nightclub and a business centre. The Douang Deuane expects to offer rates and and facilities similar to those at the Tai-Pan Hotel.

Places to Eat

Vientiane is a good town for food, with a wide variety of cafes, street vendors, beer gardens and restaurants offering everything from rice noodles to filet mignon.

Breakfast Most of the hotels in Vientiane offer set 'American' breakfasts (two eggs, toast and ham or bacon) for around 1000 to 3000 kip. Or you could get out on the streets and eat where the locals do. One popular breakfast is khào jɨi pá-têh, a split French baguette stuffed with Lao-style pâté (which is more like English or American luncheon meat than French pâté) and various dressings. Vendors who sell these breakfast sandwiches also sell plain baguettes (khào jɨi) – there are several regular bread vendors around town, but especially on Thanon Heng Boun between Thanons Chao Anou and Khun Bulom.

Down at the north-west corner of Thanons Pangkham and Samsenthai, a no-name *coffee shop* serves very good kàa-féh nóm hâwn (Lao-style milk coffee) and khào jɨi khai dạo (two fried eggs with sliced baguette). You can also eat Chinese doughnuts (pá-kôh or khào-nõm khuu) or plain French bread with coffee.

Another good spot for breakfast is the *Restaurant Santisouk* (also known by its pre-Revolutionary name, *Café La Pagode)* on Thanon Nokeo Kumman, near the Lao Revolutionary Museum. The menu includes a variety of Western breakfasts (including marvellous potato omelettes) as well as pastry plates and good coffee; prices are very reasonable.

Bakeries *Scandinavian Bakery* (☎ 215199), on the Fountain Circle, sells fresh bread, pies, cakes, croissants, sandwiches and ice cream; there are a few tables inside and outside the bakery if you want to eat in. It's open Monday through Saturday 7 am to 7 pm, Sunday 9 am to 7 pm.

Two side-by-side cafes on Thanon Chao Anou, *Liang Xiang Bakery House* and *Sweet Home Bakery*, sell decent croissants and other pastries – at about half the price of the fare at the Scandinavian Bakery – from around 7 am till 9 pm; each has a couple of tables out the front where you can eat with a view of street life, as well as a row of inside tables. Breakfasts of khào jɨi khai dạo and other egg dishes are also available at each. The Sweet Home has ice cream sundaes.

Noodles, Chinese & Vietnamese Noodles of all kinds are very popular in Vientiane, especially along Thanons Heng Boun, Chao Anou and Khun Bulom, which outline the unofficial Chinatown. In the noodle department the basic choice is *fõe*, a rice noodle that's popular throughout mainland South-East Asia (known as *kwethio* or *kuaythiaw* in Thailand, Malaysia and Singapore), *mii*, the traditional Chinese egg noodle and *khào pũn*, very thin wheat noodles with a spicy Lao sauce. Fõe and mii can be ordered as soup (eg, *fõe nâam*), dry-mixed in a bowl (eg,*fõe hàeng)* or fried (eg,*fõe khùa*), among other variations.

Haan Khai Mii (no English or transliterated sign), a few doors east of the Asian Pavilion Hotel, has inexpensive, tasty rice and wheat noodles as well as a selection of one-plate rice dishes and a small Chinese buffet.

The very clean, air-con *Guangdong Restaurant*, on Thanon Chao Anou near the two bakeries, offers a few varieties of dim sum (100 kip each), fresh mii, and a 70-item menu of various Chinese specialities in the 1200 to 2400 kip range. Over on Thanon Heng Boun east of Chao Anou, the government-run *Dao Vieng, Vientiane 2* and *Vieng Ni Nhom* are dark, cavernous Chinese spots with so-so menus and a lack of clientele, always a bad sign. In the same stretch the *Dam Lou Restaurant*, however, is very popular for noodles and for its small Chinese buffet.

One of my favourite kinds of Lao-Vietnamese noodle dishes is khào pìak sên, a bowl of toothy, round rice noodles served in chicken broth with strips of chicken. The best place in downtown Vientiane to sample khào pìak sên is a couple of sidewalk vendors on the east side of Thanon Pangkham about midway between Thanon Samsenthai and the Fountain Circle amidst a row of tailor shops. One vendor commands an area next to Adam Tailleur, the other next to Saigon Tailor. The scissors standing in the chopsticks jar are used to cut khào-nõm khuu into bite-sized pieces to be added to the soup, along with dollops of fresh crushed ginger, chilli jam and a possible medley of other condiments found on each table.

Chanthy (Le Janti) Cuisine Vietnamienne, a small shop on Thanon Chao Anou, one door south of the corner of Thanons Chao Anou and Heng Boun, makes very good Lao-style khào pũn with a choice of three toppings – it's probably the best place downtown to try this dish. Janti also offers Vietnamese nãem neũang (barbecued pork meatballs) and yáw (spring rolls), usually sold in 'sets' *(sut)* with cold khào pũn, fresh lettuce leaves, mint, basil, various dipping sauces, sliced starfruit and sliced green plantain.

Right around the corner on Thanon Heng Boun west of Thanon Chao Anou are two more popular Chinese-Vietnamese places with similar fare – *Nang Suli* (also known as *Lao Chaloen*, or to local expats, 'Green Hole in the Wall') and, next door, *Vieng Sawan* (no English signs for either). Both specialise in nãem neũang and yáw; the Vieng Sawan is the better of the two. You can also order sìn jụm, thinly sliced pieces of raw beef which customers boil in small cauldrons of coconut water placed on the table and eat with dipping sauces.

Several óp pét (roast duck) restaurants can be found along the east side of Thanon Khun Bulom toward the river, while farther north on the west side of this same street are four fõe places in a row. This is the best area in town for fõe, especially at night when it's very busy.

For all-round quality, one of the better – and more expensive – Chinese-Vietnamese places in Vientiane is the casual but clean *Restaurant Ha-wai*, around the corner from the Anou Hotel on Thanon Chao Anou. The lengthy menu features Vietnamese, Cantonese and a few Lao dishes; almost everything is made from scratch, so it takes a while to get served.

Moving still further upscale, the *Ban Haysok Restaurant* (☎ 215417), opposite the Anou Hotel at 34 Thanon Heng Boun, is a glassed-in air-con place with good if somewhat pricey southern Chinese food.

Lao For authentic, low-priced Lao meals, Vientiane's night markets and street vendors are your overall best source. Most extensive is the *Dong Palan night market*, off Thanon Ban Fai (marked Thanon Dong Palan on some maps), at the back of the Nong Chan ponds near the Lan Thong Cinema. Vendors sell all the Lao standards, including làap and pĩng kai.

In the central, downtown area, the best pĩng kai vendors are found in a spot opposite Maningom Supermarket near the corner of Thanons Khun Bulom and Heng Boun from around 5.30 pm till around 8 or 9 pm. A set of tables behind the vendors allows you to eat the fare on the premises, though most people do take-aways. Towards the northern end of Thanon Chao Anou, on the right-hand side before it crosses Thanon Khun Bulom, a slightly smaller group of vendors also offer slightly less expensive pĩng kai, along with tạm (spicey mortar-pounded salads) made with shredded green papaya or green beans, all for take-away only. If tạm màak hung (spicy green papaya salad) is a particular favourite, seek out the famous stall belonging to *Thim Manivong*, in front of Wat Phoxai at Km 4, Thanon Tha Deua. Thim reputedly makes the best tạm màak hung in Vientiane.

A small, open-air *night market* of sorts convenes along the high levee beside the Mekong river; look for a string of well-spaced bamboo tables and chairs which begins just west of the Inter Hotel and extends to very near the Mixay Cafe. Some of the vendors here offer cold beer and soft drinks only, others prepare pîng kai, tạm màak hung or nãem (minced sausage mixed with rice, herbs and roasted chillies with a plate of greens on the side). This is a peaceful spot to watch Mekong sunsets or full moons (some of the vendors stay open late) while enjoying cheap snacks.

If you're looking to eat pîng kai with a roof over your head, the clean, popular and inexpensive *Nang Bunmala* (no Roman-script sign) on Thanon Khu Vieng is your best choice. The chickens cooked here are much plumper than the Lao norm and roasted to perfection. Also available are pîng kai, pîng pét (grilled duck), tam màak tàeng (spicy cucumber salad, sticky rice and draught beer. It's open daily 11 am to 10 pm.

The famous *Mixay Cafe* (Haan Kin Deum Mixai, ☎ 216213) is a wooden building that's open on three sides and overlooks the Mekong river near the intersection of Thanons Fa Ngum and Nokeo Kumman. The menu is not very extensive, but the làap (the English menu reads 'lard') is very tasty and can be ordered with chicken, pork, beef or fish. Also good are tạm màak hung and tôm yám (lemongrass soup). The Mixai also serves cold draught beer in plastic pitchers for 750 kip a litre (half a pitcher). This is a great spot to watch the sun set over the Mekong river, with the Thai town of Si Chiengmai visible on the other side, and if you sit here long enough someone you've met in your travels is likely to come along. The proprietors play an interesting selection of music on their tape system, from Lao folk to US rockabilly. A few expats still refer to the Mixai as 'the Russian cafe' because it was one of the few nightspots Russian expats could afford in the days when Soviet aid was part of the national budget.

Serious Lao food connoisseurs should seek out *Soukvimane Lao Food* (☎ 214441), an enclosed restaurant at the end of an alley next to That Dam off Thanon That Dam. The menu is now in Lao and English though very little English or French are spoken. Among the house specialities (which vary from day to day) are kạeng pạa khai mot (fish soup with ant larvae) and làap pạa (spicy minced fish salad).

On the opposite side of That Dam *Sala Luang Prabang* serves a number of Luang Prabang dishes as well as Thai and southern Lao food under palm-thatched shelters. The medium-priced menu includes tasty ûa naw mâi (stuffed bamboo shoots) and mok pàa fàwk (coconut fish patties. It's open Monday through Saturday for lunch and dinner.

Another very good place for traditional Lao dishes is the friendly and inexpensive *Nang Kham Bang*, at 97 Khun Bulom St in a little house not far from the river. This one also has a bilingual menu; specialities include stuffed frogs (kóp yat sài), roast quail (thàwt nok), roast fish (pîng pạa), pickled lettuce (sòm pákàat), beef or chicken làap and yám sìn ngúa. It's open daily for dinner.

Compared to the foregoing, *Kua Lao* (☎ 215777) at the corner of Thanons Samsenthai and Chanta Kumman seems tame and pricey though the food is quite OK. Housed in a large, renovated French colonial mansion, the menu actually consists of a mix of Lao and Thai standards, which makes it popular among Thai tourists. It's open daily for lunch and dinner.

Even more touristy is the grandiose *Lao Residence* (Tamnak Lao) on Thanon That Luang, north-east of the Patuxai monument on the way to Pha That Luang. The menu here is more Thai than Lao, but neither genre is prepared authentically as the chefs seem bent on creating bland dishes oriented toward their mostly package-tour clientele.

European There are several commendable French, French-Lao and Italian restaurants in Vientiane, and the number continues to grow year by year as Laos becomes the darling of the aid-and-development set. Most are quite expensive by local standards but good value compared to continental cuisine just about anywhere else in the world.

One that is particularly good value is *Restaurant Santisouk* (formerly called *Café La Pagode*; ☎ 215303) on Thanon Nokeo

Kumman, near the Lao Revolutionary Museum. Although the bland, slightly tatty decor does nothing to engage the senses – the clientele is mostly Lao – the cuisine is of the simple 'French grill' type and quite tasty. A filling plate of steak or filet mignon – served on a sizzling platter – or filleted fish or roast chicken with roast potatoes and veggies costs less than 3500 kip. Breakfasts are also very good. It's open daily 7 am to 10 pm.

Le Bistrot Snack Bar (☎ 215972), opposite the Tai-Pan Hotel on Thanon François Nginn, is owned by an older Lao couple who spent most of their lives in Paris. The fare includes good, relatively inexpensive French dishes such as poulet provençal and boeuf bourguignon (both of which come with vegetables and potatoes or rice), along with a spicey salade chinoise made with bean-thread noodles and chicken, and a variety of couscous meals offered with chicken, mutton or merguez (spicey Moroccan lamb sausage). Don't let the sometimes empty dining room put you off – for some reason this place hasn't caught on yet (perhaps because service is a tad slow for the technocratic set) but it's good value.

Popular with techies, diplomats, UN staff, and other expats on large salaries is the intimate *Restaurant-Bar Namphu* (☎ 216248) on the Fountain Circle off Thanon Pangkham. The food and service are generally impeccable and the menu includes a number of German and Lao dishes as well as French – the popular blue-cheese hamburger adds an American touch; there's also a well-stocked bar. Prices average 9000 kip per entrée, or roughly one-tenth Laos' annual per-capita income. It's open daily from 10.30 am to 3 pm and 6.30 pm to 11.30 pm.

Relatively new on the scene is the *Restaurant Le Provençal* (☎ 217251), also on the Fountain Circle and nicely decorated in brick and wood. Complimentary appetisers start things off; there's a good French wine list and fully stocked bar. The cuisine tends toward the more rustic southern French style with dishes such as salade nicoise and poulet moutarde, along with various daily specials. Prices are lower than at the Namphu. It's

open Monday to Saturday for lunch and dinner.

Further down Thanon Pangkham near Lao Aviation is *Le Souriya* (☎ 215887), a similarly well-appointed, somewhat pricey place with a shorter menu of well-prepared French dishes.

The cozy, French-owned *Le Vendôme* (☎ 216402) is tucked away in an old house on a small street behind Wat In Paeng. The restaurant has a pleasant candle-lit, bamboo-curtained outdoor seating area plus an air-con indoor section. The menu offers a selection of salads, French and Lao food; though baked in a wood-fired oven the pizza is mediocre. Prices are moderate; it's open Monday to Friday for lunch and dinner, Saturday and Sunday for dinner only.

Le Bayou Bar Brasserie on Thanon Setthathirat, diagonally opposite Wat Ong Teu, is a simple but charming spot with a choice of seating in the air-con dining room or narrow beer garden alongside. Prices are very reasonable – among the lowest of any European restaurant outside the Santisouk and Le Bistrot – and the fare includes draught beer, breakfasts, pasta, pizza, sandwiches, fondue and brochettes. The various salads and fruit shakes are especially good.

Restaurant Sourichanh (☎ 222235), a little west of Le Bayou on Thanon Setthathirat and next door to the Samlo Pub, is a friendly, pleasant air-con restaurant with Lao (mostly Luang Prabang-style), Thai and French food. Prices are reasonable.

Thirty-year veteran *Arawan Restaurant* (☎ 215373) at 478-480 Thanon Samsenthai is the longest-running European eatery in Vientiane and specialises in French grill, choucroute maison, coq au vin, boeuf bourguignon and other French standards, as well as French wines and cheeses. An attached *charcuterie* supplies the town with cured meats, cheese, pâtés, wines and other hallmarks of French civilisation. The Arawan is closed on Sunday.

Over on Thanon Lan Xang near the Vienglatry Lao dance hall is the Lao and French-owned *Belle Ile Crêperie-Pub* (☎ 214942). Patronised mostly downstairs as a late-night bar destination, the Belle Ile has an upstairs dining room serving an array of French crêpes. It's open Tuesday through Sunday 11 am to midnight.

Vientiane now has two Italian restaurants, both of high standard. Opposite the Restaurant-Bar Namphu on the Fountain Circle is the older and very popular *L'Opera Italian Restaurant* (☎ 215099), a branch of a restaurant of the same name in Bangkok. The mostly Italian menu includes pizzas (served with fresh ground chilli and oregano on the side), pasta, antipasti, seafood, salads, plus a selection of Italian coffees and wines. Big spenders are sometimes offered complimentary liqueurs. An attached gelato bar offers take-away gelato. Quality is consistent, prices medium high.

The newer *Lo Stivale* (☎ 215561) at 44/2 Thanon Setthathirat takes the prize for best pizza and gnocchi in town. An array of other pasta dishes, soups, salads, coffees and tasty desserts are also available. Prices are a bit higher than the norm for Vientiane, even for European food.

Also new on the scene, *Europe Restaurant*, attached to Soradith Guest House (☎ /fax 413651) at 150 Ban Dong Palan Thong (near Talaat Dong Palan), offers the most elegant atmosphere of any restaurant in Vientiane. The changing menu represents nearly the full range of Swiss cuisine, mixing German, French and Italian influences. Prices are similar to those at the Restaurant-Bar Namphu.

Beer Gardens Vientiane abounds in casual outdoor places built of bamboo and thatch where patrons while away the hours drinking Lao beer and eating traditional snacks or *káp kâem*.

Three or four tiny places right on the river can be found in the vicinity of the River View Hotel, the most distinguished of which is *Sala Khounta* about 120m upstream from the hotel. Also known as the 'Sunset Bar' among those who can't remember the name, it's basically a small bamboo platform over the Mekong, decorated with orchids, planters, fishtraps and basketry. Beerlao is the main

attraction, but the friendly and enterprising proprietors also offer an array of Lao and Vietnamese snacks that vary from week to week or season to season. One of the occasional specialities here is delicious yám màak klûay, a tangy and spicy salad made by pounding green bananas (including the skins), chillies, màak khẽua (pea eggplants), fish sauce, garlic and lime together in a mortar. Savoury yáw jẹun (fried Vietnamese spring rolls) – sliced into sections and served with khào pûn, lettuce, mint, coriander and steamed mango leaves – sell out fast here. The Sala Khounta usually closes after sunset, though it may stay open longer in hot weather.

A bit downriver on the same side of the road and south of the River View Hotel, *Sala Mahien* has a similar ambience with the addition of recorded traditional Lao music; the owner is a musician from Luang Prabang.

Right in the centre of town is the *Namphou Garden*, a set of tables and chairs encircling the renovated fountain (now lit with coloured lights) where you can get Lao, European and Indian food, beer and cocktails till around 11 pm. When the weather's hot, this place becomes packed with patrons seeking the cooling effects of the large fountain.

South-east of town on Thanon Tha Deua at Km 12, near the Lao Government Brewery, is the thatched-roof *Salakham Beer Garden* where you can drink inexpensive Lao draught beer (bia sót, literally fresh beer – and it doesn't get any fresher than this) and eat Lao snacks.

Thai With all the Thais visiting Vientiane for business and pleasure these days, Thai restaurants are becoming more common. On Thanon Samsenthai just past the Lao Revolutionary Museum is the *Phikun* (English sign reads 'Thai Food'), which has all the Thai standards, including tôm yam kûng (prawn and lemon grass soup) and kài phàt bai kaphrao (chicken fried in holy basil). Curries are good here – something you don't see much of in Lao cuisine. A second branch of the Phikun on Thanon Luang Prabang, near the Thai Military Bank just west of Thanon Khun Bulom, is now open. It's open daily from 11 am to 9 pm.

A smaller place with a Thai buffet, *Aahaan Thai* (no English sign), is found on Thanon Khun Bulom near the intersection with Thanon Samsenthai.

Indian *The Taj* (☎ 212890) on Thanon Pangkham opposite Nakhonluang Bank (just north of the fountain) has an extensive menu of well-prepared North Indian dishes, including tandoor, curries, vegetarian plates and many Indian breads. Service is good and the place is very clean, though à la carte prices are a bit high by Vientiane standards. The Taj also has a sizeable daily lunch buffet for 3800 kip and set evening dinners for 3700 to 4500 kip. It's open daily from 11 am to 2.30 pm and 6 to 10.30 pm.

Cheaper Indian food can be found at *Nazim Restaurant* (☎ 413671) on Thanon Phonexay near the Aussie embassy and opposite the Phonexay Hotel. The extensive menu includes mostly North Indian dishes along with a few South Indian items such as masala dosa and idli. An outdoor area in front of the restaurant looks closed, but carry on into the enclosed dining room. It's open for lunch and dinner daily.

The *Namphou Garden* at the Fountain Circle serves a few Indian dishes, most notably a variety of stuffed naan.

Other The *Vientiane Department Store* (part of Talaat Sao) has a small but excellent food centre with an extensive variety of Thai and Lao dishes for 500 to 1200 kip.

Just for Fun, a tiny shop on Thanon Pangkham near Raintree Bookstore, offers vegetarian food and homemade desserts; it's open Monday to Saturday 9 am to 10 pm. For fresh fruit shakes – solo or mixed – one of the best and least expensive places is *Nai Xiang Chai Yene* on Thanon Chao Anou, just a few shops down from the Liang Xiang and Sweet Home bakeries towards the river and next door to the Guangdong Restaurant.

Sakura Japanese Restaurant (☎ 212274),

at Soi 3 Khounta Thong (off Thanon Luang Prabang near the Novotel Vientiane), serves good Japanese cuisine, including sushi and teishokus.

Tha Ngone, in Ban Udomphon at Km 21 on Route 10 north of town, is a fish farm where you catch 'em and they cook 'em; you pay by the kg. Or if you don't want to drop hook and line, you can order pîng paa (roast fish), tam màak-hung or the house speciality, phán khào pún (fish sausage with khao pun). This is a popular local picnic spot on weekends.

Mini-Markets For the largest selection of fresh groceries and the best prices, you should stick to the open-air Lao markets (see the Things to Buy section in this chapter). But if there's something 'Western' you're yearning for, an increasing number of mini-markets catering to the foreign community have opened during the last three years.

Among the most popular is the *Phimphone Market* on the corner of Thanons Samsenthai and Chantha Khumman, attached to the Hotel Ekalath Metropole. Phimphone carries an expensive selection of biscuits, canned and frozen foods as well as toiletries and day-old editions of the *Bangkok Post*. The original but smaller *Phimphone Minimart* across the street at 94/6 Thanon Samsenthai is still open. Both are open daily from 7.30 am to 10 pm.

Maningom Supermarket (☎ 216050), at the corner of Thanons Heng Boun and Khun Bulom, carries butter, milk, cheese, yoghurt, breakfast cereals, biscuits, canned foods and imported chocolate; it's open daily 7.30 am to 9.30 pm. *Foodland*, on Thanon Chao Anou just south of Thanon Heng Boun, stocks a similar selection of refrigerated, frozen and canned foodstuffs.

Attached to the *Arawan Restaurant* is a grocery shop with pâtés, cured meats, wines and cheeses from France, plus Lao coffee dark-roasted in the French style. *Simuang Minimart* (☎ 214295), at 51 Thanon Samsenthai near the statue of King Sisavang Vong at Wat Si Muang, stocks a very good selection of imported foods, wines and spirits; credit cards are accepted.

The *Vientiane Department Store* at Talaat Sao contains a food section with Asian foods imported from Thailand and Singapore.

Entertainment

Vientiane is no longer the illicit pleasure palace it was when Paul Theroux described it in his 1975 *The Great Railway Bazaar* as a city where 'The brothels are cleaner than the hotels, marijuana is cheaper than pipe tobacco and opium easier to find than a cold glass of beer'. Nowadays brothels are strictly prohibited, Talaat Sao's marijuana stands have been removed from prominent display and cold beer has definitely replaced opium as the nightly drug of choice. Most of the city's bars, restaurants and discos in fact close by midnight.

Dancing Vientiane has at least six 'discos', though the term is rather a misnomer (it's what the Lao call these places), because often the music is live. Although younger Lao tend to predominate, there is usually a mix of generations and the bands or disc jockeys play everything from electrified Lao folk (for *lam wong* dancing) to Western pop. By law all entertainment places are supposed to close by 11.30 pm.

Still the most popular place in town is the large *Nightclub Vienglatry* on Thanon Lan Xang, a bit north of Talaat Sao on the same side of the street. Basically a dance floor surrounded on three sides by padded sofas and tables, the Vienglatry features live Lao bands nightly and also serves food and liquor (but no Beerlao, only Carlsberg); by 10.30 pm the cavernous room is packed. It closes between 11.30 and midnight.

Between Vienglatry and Talaat Sao is the much smaller *Belle Ile*, a local favourite with expats as well as a sprinkling of Lao. Although primarily a bar (with an upstairs crêperie), a small dance floor toward the back often fills up late at night with people grooving to the proprietors' eclectic selection of older Western pop. The Belle Ile occasionally manages to stay open well past legal closing time.

Other Lao nightclubs with live bands, whirling lights and dark sitting areas include the *Nokkeo Latry*, *Blue Star* and *Marina*, all out on Thanon Luang Prabang past the Novotel Vientiane between Kms 2 and 5.

Hotel Clubs The *Anou Hotel*, *Saysana Hotel*, *Ekalath Metropole* and *Inter Hotel* each have nightly discos which are a bit smaller in scale than the Nightclub Vienglatry; the Anou Cabaret has been the most popular and is about to reopen after many months of renovation. Big, flashy Hong Kong-style nightclubs can be found in the *New Apollo Hotel* and the *Royal Dokmaidaeng Hotel*.

Bars Outside of the hotels, Vientiane doesn't have many bars. Until two or three years ago the ones that did exist seemed semi-clandestine, perhaps semi-legal, but today several operate more or less within the full extent of Lao law. All serve beer, along with a colonial history of other alcoholic beverages – French champagne, Johnny Walker and Stolichnaya – and the newer arrivals carry a great deal more, including various liqueurs.

Samlo Pub, next door to Restaurant Sourichanh on Thanon Samsenthai (opposite Wat In Paeng), is a small, well-stocked bar that's popular with visitors and expats alike. Draught Beerlao is available on tap.

Other watering holes worth checking out include the tiny but well-serviced bar at *Restaurant-Bar Namphu*. On hot nights *Namphou Garden*, the collection of outdoor tables around the fountain, is also quite popular.

If you're looking for something with more of a local flavour, and less expensive than the expat bars, your best bet is one of the many bịa sót (draught beer) bars around town. These are usually nondescript rooms filled with wooden tables at the bottom of a shophouse – look for plastic jugs of beer on the tables. One of the better deals is *Bia Sot Si Meuang* at the south-eastern end of Thanon Samsenthai near Wat Si Muang. Operated by a couple of off-duty Lao Aviation flight attendants, Bia Sot Si Meuang offers draught Beerlao at a mere 650 kip per litre, along with the bottled stuff for 800 kip per large bottle.

Sala Bia Lao (Lao Beer House), on Thong Kham Square near Talaat Thong Khan Kham, is a hipper beer bar decorated with Lao folk and old-West motifs; live Lao and Thai pop is featured from 5 pm to 1 am nightly. *Bane Saysana*, also known as the *Win-West Pub*, follows the Thai model in providing an ersatz old-West atmosphere; it's near the Shell station at the intersection of Thanons Luang Prabang, Setthathirat and Khun Bulom.

Cinema & Video Lao cinema houses have all but died out in the video shop tidal wave of recent years. A lone survivor, the *Odeon Rama* (also known as *Vientiane Theatre*, ☎ 214613) near Talaat Thong Khan Kham in Ban Nong Duang, maintains a regular schedule of Thai, Chinese and Western movies, all of which are dubbed in Lao by a live team of dubbers using three microphones. The manager, a recently returned Lao-American, is determined to keep cinema alive in Laos against almost overwhelming odds. All films shown here must be approved by government censors, who require that even Thai films receive Lao dubbing – despite the fact that virtually everyone living in Vientiane can understand Thai! One showing per night may be screened with the original soundtrack. Once in a while the theatre runs a new foreign – usually American – film.

The *Centre de Langue Française* (☎ 215764) on Thanon Lan Xang screens French films (subtitled in English) each Thursday at 7.15 pm. Admission is 700 kip and the screenings are open to the general public. Film titles for the following week are usually listed in the weekly *Vientiane Times* or you can call the centre for information.

The *Australian Club* and Centre de Langue Française each have video rental libraries – but you need your own VCR to see them! There are various private video shops around town that hire Thai and English-language videos for 500 to 800 kip per night.

National Circus The old Russian Circus established by the Soviets, now known as

Hong Kanyasin or the National Circus, continues to present performances of the Lao national circus troupe from time to time. Look for announcements in the *Vientiane Times*. The venue also occasionally hosts pop and classical musical performances sponsored by the French Embassy; such musical events are usually announced widely well in advance.

Recreation Clubs The *Australian Embassy Recreation Club* (AERC; ☎ 314921), or the *Australian Club* for short, is out of town on the way to the Thailand ferry pier at Thanon Tha Deua, Km 3. The club has a brilliant pool, right next to the Mekong river, and at sunset many expats (mostly non-Australian!) gather here for an impromptu social hour. On Fridays from 6 to 7 pm there is an official Happy Hour at the snack bar. There are also squash courts, a ping-pong table, billiards and darts. Memberships are usually purchased by the year, but shorter-term memberships can be arranged. Or find someone who's a member and go along as their guest. The Club is open from 10 am to 10 pm, though members may use the pool beginning at 7 am.

The *Centre de Langue Française* on Thanon Lan Xang maintains a French library with over 20,000 books and also some videos.

The *Library Club* is in the garden of the Australian Residence in a building called 'the Stockade', which is off Thanon Nehru near the Australian Embassy. It's open to members on Tuesday and Thursday from 1 to 6 pm and on Saturday from 9 am to 1 pm. An annual membership is US$10 (plus a refundable US$10 deposit).

An *International Chess Club* meets every Thursday evening at 7.30 pm at the Russian Cultural Centre at the corner of Thanons Khun Bulom and Luang Prabang.

Things to Buy

Just about anything made in Laos is available for purchase in Vientiane, including hilltribe crafts, jewellery, traditional textiles and carvings. The main shopping areas are Talaat

Sao (including shops along Thanon Talaat Sao), along the east ends of Thanon Samsenthai (near the Asian Pavilion and Ekalath Hotels) and Thanon Setthathirat, and on Thanon Pangkham.

Textiles & Clothing Talaat Sao (the Morning Market, though it runs all day) is a good place to look for fabrics; the stalls with modern styles of fabric are run by Indians and Pakistanis while traditional Lao-style textiles are sold by Lao vendors. Many carry antique as well as modern fabrics, plus utilitarian items such as shoulder bags (some artfully constructed around squares of antique fabric), cushions and pillows. Lao Antique Textiles (☎ 212381) in stall A2-4 has a good selection, though her competitors in the market continue to improve. Mrs Chanthone Thattanakham, the proprietor of Lao Antique Textiles, also maintains a textile gallery in her home at 72/08 Thanon Tha Deua (near Km 2) in Ban Suanmon.

Lao Textiles (☎ 212123) on Thanon Nokeo Kumman (look for an old two-storey French-Lao house) sells high-end contemporary, original-design fabrics inspired by older Lao weaving patterns, motifs and techniques. The woman behind the original designs, American Carol Cassidy, employs Lao weavers who use modified Swedish looms to produce wider pieces of fabric. Her textiles mix tapestry, brocade, *ikat*, and weft ikat techniques, applied only to silk fabrics and completely hand-dyed with natural dyes. Items available for purchase include scarves, shawls, wall-hangings and home-furnishing accessories. Prices are what you might expect from a weaving house that has exhibited in galleries and museums in major cities around the world. It's open Monday to Friday, 8 to noon and 2 to 5 pm, Saturday 8 am to noon, or by appointment.

Supported by the Lao Women's Union, UNICEF and SIDA, The Art of Silk (☎ 214308), opposite the Samsenthai Hotel on Thanon Manthatulat, carries a selection of silk and cotton weavings in traditional and modern designs.

To see Lao weaving in action, seek out the weaving district of Ban Nong Bua Thong, north-east of the town centre in Muang Chanthabuli. About 20 families (many originally from Sam Neua) live and work here, including a couple of households who sell textiles directly to the public and welcome visitors who want to observe the weaving process. The Nanthavongduangsy family (☎ 217341) is the most equipped for visitors; their large, white, two-storey house is in the centre of the neighbourhood.

The Lao Women's Pilot Textile Project, a UNDP-sponsored programme, has a shop called Lao Cotton (☎ 215840) on Thanon Setthathirat that's open from 9 am to 5 pm Monday to Saturday. It specialises in handwoven Lao cotton products, both modern and traditional designs, including shirts, dresses, handbags, place mats, table linen, napkins etc. Simple short-sleeved men's shirts are a great buy. The Project's main office and workshop is in Ban Khunta, off Thanon Luang Prabang around 2.5 km west of the town centre. Another branch can be found at the new Regent Shopping Centre on Thanon Luang Prabang, near the Novotel Vientiane.

Lao Vilai Fashion (☎ 216716) at 107/3 Thanon Samsenthai (behind the Anou Hotel) specialises in contemporary women's clothing made with handwoven Lao cotton. Yani (☎ 212918), in the Mixay Arcade on Thanon Setthathirat, is a small shop owned by a French Vietnamese dress designer with Paris fashion school experience; some of the women's clothing designs here are very becoming, with an eye towards ethnic chic, Lao-style.

Tailors & Cobblers The tailor shops along Thanon Pangkham also sell fabric and can design and cut clothes to fit. Queen's Beauty Tailor at No 21 has a good reputation and fair prices but is slow (two to three weeks). Mai Tailleur at No 65/1 and Nova Tailleur around the corner at 64 Samsenthai can cut and sew a pattern in a week.

Teng Liang Ki at 51 Pangkham makes inexpensive men's leather shoes and also does shoe and luggage repair. There are also a few cobblers at Talaat Thong Khan Kham and along Thanon Khu Vieng near Talaat Sao.

Handicrafts, Antiques & Art Several shops along Thanons Samsenthai and Pangkham sell Lao and Thai tribal and hill-tribe crafts. An unmarked shop on Thanon Samsenthai specialises in Hmong embroidery. Several shops along here sell carved opium pipes (the real thing, not the misrepresented tobacco pipes sold in northern Thailand), including Nang Xuan at No 385.

The Kanchana Boutique (☎ 213467) opposite the Hotel Ekalath Metropole on Thanon That Dam carries an extensive selection of such crafts. Lao Phattana Art and Handicrafts Co-op (☎ 212363) at 9 Thanon Pangkham has a fair selection of antique and new handwoven silks and cottons, antique silver, wood carvings and other crafts. Somsri Handicrafts (☎ 216232) at 18-20 Thanon Setthathirat is similar.

Nikone Handicraft Centre (☎ 212191), 1B Thanon Dong Mieng, near the National Circus, specialises in quality handicrafts oriented toward interior decoration.

Champa Gallery (☎ 216299), just northwest of That Dam, features the colourful, well-crafted collages of Monique Mottahedeh as well as works by other local artists. Lao Gallery (☎ 212943), opposite Lao Textiles at 92/2 Thanon Nokeo Kumman, displays contemporary art by Lao and Vietnamese artists.

Jewellery Most of the jewellery shops in Vientiane are along Thanon Samsenthai. Gold and silver are the best deals. Saigon Bijoux at No 369 is supposedly reputable – it sells and repairs gold and silver jewellery and can also make new pieces on request. This shop accepts Visa.

The Indian-owned MM Bari Shop at 366-368 Thanon Samsenthai is one of the few shops that deals in precious stones as well as gold and silver.

The Talaat Sao is also a good place to buy gold and silver jewellery.

Furniture Several workshops around town produce inexpensive custom-designed furniture of bamboo, rattan and wood (eg, teak and Asian rosewood). Phai Exclusive (☎ 214804) at 3 Thanon Thong Tum makes both furniture and accessories of bamboo (plus interesting notecards depicting historic Vientiane architecture).

For rattan furniture, visit the Saylom Rattan Furniture Co (☎ 215860) on Thanon Saylom. Koth Syhavong (☎ 412606), at 257 Ban Jommani Tai, Route 13 south, offers a large selection of both bamboo and rattan. Furniture can be made to order from their catalogue or from custom designs.

Many shops make wooden furniture but the quality can be highly variable. Two shops with good reputations are Lao Wood Industry, Thanon Tha Deua Km 10, and Home Furniture (☎ 314440), 92 Thanon Setthathirat.

Computer Supplies It's not easy finding places to buy hardware and/or software for computers. If you're using DOS/Windows your best bet is Microtec Computer Shop (☎ 213836, fax 212933) at 168-169 Thanon Luang Prabang, a little west of the Hotel New Apollo. Alice Computer (☎ 413740) on Thanon Tha Deua is also good. For Macintosh equipment the only place is Macs (☎ 215515) on Thanon Pangkham.

Fishing Equipment A shop at 275/2 Thanon Setthathirat carries a complete line of fishing rods, lines, nets, lures and other fishing supplies.

Talaat Sao The Morning Market is on the north-eastern corner of the intersection of Thanon Lan Xang and Thanon Khu Vieng. It actually runs all day, from 6 am to 6 pm. The sprawling collection of stalls offer fabric, ready-made clothes, cutlery, toiletry, bedding, hardware, jewellery, watches, electronic goods and just about everything else imaginable.

In the centre of the area is a large building that houses the Vientiane Department Store, which carries mostly imported goods (canned foods, clothes, appliances, handicrafts) from Thailand, China, Vietnam and

Singapore. One section of the department store features a small supermarket that sells soap, local and imported foodstuffs and beer.

Other Markets East of Talaat Sao, just across Thanon Mahasot (or Thanon Nong Bon, as it's labelled on some maps) beyond the bus terminal, the Khua Din Market (Talaat Khua Din) offers fresh produce and fresh meats, as well as flowers, tobacco and assorted other goods. This market has been shifted further east along Thanon Khu Vieng and it's rumoured it will be moved to another location altogether sometime in the future.

A bigger fresh market is Thong Khan Kham Market (Talaat Thong Khan Kham) which is sometimes called the Evening Market since it was originally established to replace the old Evening Market in Ban Nong Duang (which burnt down in 1987). Like Talaat Sao, it's open all day, but is best in the morning. It's the biggest market in Vientiane and has virtually everything. You'll find it north of the town centre in Ban Thong Khan Kham (Gold Bowl Fields Village) at the intersection of Thanons Khan Kham and Dong Miang.

Near this market are a number of basket and pottery vendors. The old Talaat Nong Duang, more commonly known as Talaat Laeng (Evening Market), still has a few vendors.

The That Luang Market is just a little south-east of Pha That Luang on Thanon Talaat That Luang. The speciality here is exotic wildlife foods like bear paws and snakes that are favoured by the Vietnamese and Chinese.

Getting There & Away

Air Vientiane is the only legal port of entry for international flights into Laos. Air departures from Vientiane are straightforward. Upstairs in the airport is a restaurant-lounge area with decent enough food. Departure tax is US$5.

See the introductory Getting There & Away chapter earlier in this book for details on air transport to Laos.

Airline Offices Lao Aviation (☎ 212058) has its main office on Thanon Pangkham around the corner from the Lane Xang Hotel. This office handles international bookings for Lao Aviation and is also an agent for China Southern Airlines, Royal Air du Cambodge, Vietnam Airlines and Air France (Air France does not fly out of Vientiane, but bookings can be made here for flights out of Bangkok). Lao Aviation is open weekdays from 8 am to noon and 2 to 5 pm, and Saturday to 11.30 am. The office for domestic bookings is in a smaller building to one side of the main building. Lao Aviation's phone number at Wattay Airport is ☎ 512028 or 512000.

Lao Air Booking (☎ 215560) at 43/1 Thanon Setthathirat also handles ticketing for Lao Aviation (international only), Royal Air du Cambodge and Vietnam Airlines.

Directly across the street from Lao Aviation is the Thai Airways International (THAI) office (☎ 216143), open weekdays from 8 am to 5 pm, and Saturday until noon.

Road Bus travel beyond Vientiane Prefecture no longer requires any special travel permits. The main bus terminal, built with Japanese aid in 1990, stands next to Talaat Sao on Thanon Khu Vieng.

See table on the following page for bus fares to/from the Talaat Sao terminal.

A second terminal on Route 13 near Km 6 also has buses to the south, eg, Tha Khaek, Savannakhet and Pakse. Fares and departure frequencies are the same. If you plan to travel by interprovincial bus out of Vientiane, it's a good idea to visit the terminal the day before your anticipated departure to confirm departure times, which seem to change every few months. For some of the long-distance buses, eg Savan and Pakse, it may be possible to purchase tickets in advance.

Friendship Bridge For travel across the Thai-Lao Friendship Bridge, see the introductory Getting There & Away chapter. For fare details to and from Vientiane, see taxi and motorcycle taxi details in the Getting Around section further on in this chapter.

VIENTIANE PROVINCE

Bus No	Destination	No of departures per day	Fare (kip)
01	Vang Vieng	3	1300
04	Thalat	3	400
04	Kasi	1	1700
14	Tha Deua & Wat Xieng Khuan (Buddha Park)	every 40 min	200
15	Tha Khaek	2	3500
18	Pakxan	2	1300
19	Somsamai	3	350
22	Ban Keun	3	500
31	Dong Dok	10	100
35	Savannakhet	2	7000
*	Pakse	1	11,000

*no number

Train See the introductory Getting There & Away chapter for information on using Thai trains to reach the Lao-Thai border.

Long-Distance River Ferry A single river route runs north to Luang Prabang along the Mekong river from Vientiane. Foreigners no longer need special permission to board these boats. Boat service to Luang Prabang has become more irregular following improvements to Route 13 north to Vang Vieng and Kasi; most Lao nowadays use road transport since it's faster and cheaper – even if it means risking a shootout around Kasi. The boat is much safer, although slower; if you can't fly to Luang Prabang, we recommend going by boat rather than bus – at least until the 'problem' around Kasi is worked out.

The ferry to Luang Prabang usually takes four or five days upriver, three or four days down, depending on type of boat, cargo load and river height. During the peak dry season ferries can slow considerably, taking as long as a week in either direction. When the river is low, direct Vientiane-Luang Prabang service aboard the large, two-deck ferries may be suspended and passengers must board smaller craft, changing boats at the halfway point in Pak Lai.

Luang Prabang ferries leave from the Kao Liaw Boat Landing (Tha Heua Kao Liaw), which is 7.7 km west of the Novotel Vientiane (3.5 km west of the fork in the road where Route 13 heads north) in Ban Kao Liaw. The usual departure time is between 8 and 9 am and the maximum passenger load for most boats is 20 people. You should go to Kao Liaw the day before your intended departure to make sure a boat is going and to reserve deck space.

The Luang Prabang ferry makes several stops along the way. Passengers typically sleep on the boat except in Pak Lai, where there are a couple of small guest houses.

Destination	Fare (kip)
Huay La	2500
Sanakham	3500
Don Men	5000
Pak Lai	5300
Tha Deua	7000
Luang Prabang	12,000

An entire boat can be chartered to Luang Prabang; the asking price is 230,000 kip but this may be negotiable. Note that women customarily ride inside the ferries – the outside, front and top decks are considered 'improper' places to sit.

Speedboats Faster boat service is available aboard six-passenger *héua wái* (speedboats), which cost 15,000 kip per person to Pak Lai, 22,000 kip to Tha Deua and 30,000 kip to Luang Prabang. Count on a full day to reach Tha Deua or Luang Prabang, four or five hours for Pak Lai. To charter a speedboat you'd have to pay a fee equal to six passenger fares. Like the slower ferries, speedboats leave from the Kao Liaw Boat Landing.

To/From Savannakhet Regular ferry service to Savannakhet has been cancelled, though in rare instances when Route 13 South is flooded (as it was in October 1995), service may be temporarily reinstated. If so, boats to Savan will leave from the old southern ferry pier at Km 4, Thanon Tha Deua.

Getting Around

Central Vientiane is entirely accessible on foot. For explorations in neighbouring districts, however, you'll need vehicular support.

Although traffic in Vientiane has increased steadily along with the ability of Lao residents to afford vehicles, the expected explosion in numbers of vehicles across the Thai-Lao Friendship Bridge has not occurred. Privately owned Thai-registered vehicles face many bureaucratic obstacles in entering Laos; new, unregistered vehicles intended for sale in Vientiane, however, can enter more easily.

Mixed in with all the new Japanese imports you'll see a greying fleet of Citroens, Peugeots and Renaults from the '40s, American Chevys and Fords from the '60s and early '70s, and Volgas and Ladas from the late '70s and early '80s.

To/From the Airport Wattay International Airport is only a 10 minute taxi ride northwest of the city centre. Taxis wait in front of the airport for passengers going into town. The going rate for a jumbo (motorcycle taxi) to the centre of town is 1000 kip, for a car taxi 2000 kip; drivers may ask for more (typically 100B). You would be better off catching a motorcycle taxi on the road in front of the airport, where the fare is only around 15B or about 500 kip. If you're

heading further – say to eastern Vientiane past Wat Si Muang – you'll have to pay around 1500 kip for a jumbo, 2500 to 3000 kip for a car.

There are no public buses direct from the airport, but if you walk the hundred metres south of the terminal to Thanon Luang Prabang, you can catch a bus into town (turn left) for 200 kip.

Going out to the airport from the town centre, a jumbo costs 500 kip, a car 1000 to 2000 kip. You can also catch a Phon Hong bus from the Morning Market for 200 kip.

Bus There is a city bus system but it's not oriented toward the central Chanthabuli district where most of the hotels, restaurants, sightseeing and shopping are. Rather, it's for transport to outlying districts to the north, east and west of Chanthabuli. Fares for any distance within Vientiane prefecture are low – about 200 kip for a 20 km ride.

Taxi A small fleet of car taxis operate in Vientiane, mostly stationed in front of the larger hotels as well as at the airport during flight arrival times. Most taxis in town are old Toyotas; new taxis with 'Taxi Meter' signs on them park next to Talaat Sao but in reality the meters are never used and these are the most expensive type of vehicle you can hire.

For most short trips within town a pedicab or motorcycle is more economical since car taxis are usually reserved for longer trips and for hourly or daily hire. In Vientiane, an older car and driver for the day costs US$20 to 25 as long as the vehicle doesn't leave town. If you want to go further afield, eg to Ang Nam Ngum or Vang Vieng, you may have to pay US$30 to 40 a day.

The standard car taxi from the Thai-Lao Friendship Bridge to the centre of Vientiane is 100B or 4000 kip. This is very reasonable considering that drivers charge the same amount from Wattay Airport into town, though the bridge is about five times further away.

Motorcycle Taxis The standard motorcycle taxi holds two or three passengers; the larger ones (called jumbos or tuk-tuks) have two short benches in the back and can hold four or five, even six passengers. Hire charges are about the same as for samlors (see below) but of course they're much speedier.

A motorcycle taxi driver will be glad to take passengers on journeys as short as half a km or as far as 20 km. Although the common asking fare for Europeans seems to be 1000 kip, the standard local fare for a chartered jumbo should be 400 to 500 kip per person for distances of two km or less, plus 200 kip for each km beyond two; bargaining is mandatory. Share jumbos which run regular routes around town (eg, Thanon Luang Prabang to Thanon Setthathirat or Thanon Lan Xang to That Luang) cost 200 kip per person, no bargaining necessary.

From the Thai-Lao Friendship Bridge to the centre of Vientiane the standard jumbo fare is 1000 kip, though many drivers will ask new arrivals from Thailand for 100 baht (which is what a car taxi should cost). A shared jumbo between the bridge and Talaat Sao is only 300 kip.

You can flag down empty jumbos passing on the street or pick them up at one of the two main jumbo stands, one on Thanon Khu Vieng near Talaat Sao and the other on Thanon Chao Anou at the Thanon Heng Boun intersection.

Motorcycle Hire Vientiane Motor, opposite the fountain on Thanon Setthathirat, rents 100cc motorbikes for US$8 to 10 per day.

Pedicabs Of late sǎam-lâw (samlor) have almost become extinct. Charges are about 300 kip per km (but don't hire a samlor for any distance greater than two or three km).

Bicycle This is the most convenient and economical way to see Vientiane besides walking. Several guest houses rent bikes on a regular basis for around 1000 kip per day. Kanchana Boutique opposite the Hotel Ekalath Metropole on Thanon That Dam also has a few bikes for rent.

Around Vientiane Province

VIENTIANE TO ANG NAM NGUM

Route 13 leads north from Vientiane to Luang Prabang. While road trips all the way to Luang Prabang are not recommended at the moment due to security problems around Kasi, the road is considered safe as far as Vang Vieng (see Dangers & Annoyances in the Facts for the Visitor chapter for details).

Along the way to Ang Nam Ngum (Nam Ngum Reservoir) are a number of interesting stopover possibilities. **Ban Ilai**, in the district of Muang Naxaithong, has a good market for basketry, pottery and other daily utensils. Three waterfalls can also be visited in Muang Naxaithong. The first, **Nam Tok Tat Khu Khana** (also known as Hin Khana), is easy to reach via a 10 km turnoff west from the village of Ban Naxaithong near Km 17. The unsigned turnoff for **Nam Tok Tat Son** is near Ban Hua Khua, 25 km from Vientiane and 100m past the bridge at Ban Hua Khua. The falls here aren't much, really a stepped set of rapids, but there's a picnic area and trails that lead to nearby limestone caves. To reach **Nam Tok Tat Nam Suang**, take the turnoff west off Route 13 near Km 40 (follow the sign for the Lao-Australian Project Centre), between Ban Nakha and Ban Nong Sa. Turn left three km from the highway before a steel bridge; the falls are around 500m from the bridge. A bit farther north along the river is a set of *kâeng* (rapids) and a picnic area with tables.

At Km 52 along the highway is **Talaat Lak Haa-sip Sawng** (Km 52 Market), a large daily market often visited by Hmong and other local ethnic minorities. A bit farther north is the prosperous town of **Phon Hong** at the junction of the turnoff for Thalat and Ang Nam Ngum; Route 13 continues north from here to Vang Vieng. If you're looking for a place to eat lunch, Phon Hong is the best bet anywhere between Vientiane and Vang Vieng.

Vientiane Zoological Gardens, also

known as Thulakhom Zoo, stands alongside Route 13, 60 km from Vientiane. Although this new facility hasn't collected too many different animals yet (with the exception of plenty of deer), the landscaping is good and the zoo seems fairly humane. Entry is 1000 kip, and hours are 8 am to 4.30 pm daily. To reach here by public transport, take a Ban Keun-bound bus (500 kip) and ask to get off at 'Suan Sat Vieng Chan'.

At **Vang Sang**, 65 km north of Vientiane via Route 13, a cluster of five high-relief Buddha sculptures is thought to date to the 16th century, although there are some local scholars who assign it an 11th century Mon provenance (not likely given the absence of any other Mon archaeology in the area). Two of the Buddhas reach over four metres in height. The name means Circle of Elephants, a reference to an elephant graveyard once found in the vicinity. About 20m further on from the main sculptures is another cluster with one large and four smaller images. To reach Vang Sang, take the signed turnoff at Km 63 near Ban Huay Thon, and follow a dirt road 1.8 km to the sanctuary.

Thalat (Thaa Laat), a little more than halfway from Phon Hong to Ang Nam Ngum, is known for its environmentally incorrect market, which sells all kinds of forest creatures – deer, spiny anteaters, rats and so on – for local consumption.

Between the Route 13 turnoff for Thalat and Ang Nam Ngum are a number of pleasant picnic areas along the river.

ANG NAM NGUM ອ່າງນ້ຳງຶ່ມ

Located approximately 90 km from Vientiane, Ang Nam Ngum is a huge artificial lake that was created by damming the Nam Ngum (Ngum river). A hydroelectric plant here generates most of the power used in the Vientiane valley as well as power that's sold to Thailand via high-power wires over the Mekong.

Around 250 sq km of forest were flooded when the river was impounded. Several logging rigs – most of them joint Thai-Lao ventures – are using hydraulic underwater saws to cut submerged teak trees. A Swiss-financed fishing co-op also harvests fish from the lake.

The lake is dotted with picturesque islands and a cruise is well worth arranging. Boats holding up to 20 people can be hired from the main pier in Nakheun at the south end of the lake for US$10 per hour.

Following the 1975 Pathet Lao takeover of Vientiane, an estimate 3000 prostitutes and petty criminals were rounded up and banished to islands on Ang Nam Ngum – men on separate islands from the women – for several years.

Places to Stay & Eat

A trip to Ang Nam Ngum and back could be done in a day, but if you want to spend a night or two, accommodation is available. *Nam Ngum Tour Co* operates a floating hotel with large, clean rooms complete with private hot-water baths and air-con for 10,000 kip per night. The boat is fairly pleasant but rarely leaves the pier except when groups book the entire boat; the dock location is not particularly scenic because of the trashy lumber operations nearby. You can book a room at the hotel in advance at the Nam Ngum Tour Co office at 14/2 Thanon Heng Boun in Vientiane.

A bit away from the lake toward the dam itself is a set of solid, Japanese-built *EDL Bungalows* that formerly housed the Japanese engineers who helped design the dam. These are now open to the public as tourist accommodation for US$15 per night. Each room has hot water and air-conditioning.

A new *hotel* recently opened on Don Dok Khon Kham, an island only 10 minutes by boat from the harbour. This one costs 7000 kip single/double; food is available but running water and electricity only come on in the evening. A shuttle boat to this island costs 1000 kip.

An older *hotel* on Don Santiphap – Peace island, quite a bit farther out in the lake – offers basic bungalows for 4000 kip per person. It's badly decaying; there is no power or running water. The 30 minute boat ride out to this island costs 1500 kip per person.

Next to the floating hotel is a pleasant

floating restaurant where live freshwater fish are kept on tethers beneath the deck. When there's an order, the cook lifts a grill in the deck and yanks a flapping fish directly into the galley.

Getting There & Away

Reaching Ang Nam Ngum by public transport is a fairly simple matter. From the Talaat Sao bus terminal you can catch the 7 am bus all the way to Kheuan Nam Ngum (Nam Ngum Dam) for 500 kip. This trip takes about three hours and proceeds along Route 13 through Thalat. If you don't make the 7 am bus, you'll have to take a bus to Thalat (84 km from Vientiane, 400 kip, 2.5 hours by bus) and then get a pickup or jumbo on to the lake for 400 kip. From Vientiane there are four or five buses daily to Thalat.

Taxis in Vientiane typically charge US$35 to 40 round trip to go to the lake. If you hire one, ask the driver to take the more scenic Route 10 through Ban Keun for the return trip, completing a circle that avoids backtracking. Route 10 is about the same distance as via Thalat. A new toll bridge (700 kip) replaces the Nam Ngum ferry crossing on Route 10.

PHU KHAO KHUAI NBCA
ພູເຂົາຄວາຍ

Off Route 13, west of Thabok, a gravel road leads to Water Buffalo Mountain, a partially pine-forested plateau at around 670m elevation (1026m at its highest point). Surrounded by 2000m peaks and off limits to foreigners for many years following the 1975 Revolution because of the presence of a 'secret' Lao army/air force base, Phu Khao Khuai NBCA (National Biodiversity Conservation Area) offers a cool retreat from the furnace-like heat of Vientiane during the March-to-May hot season. Other times of year it can be misty and cold.

IUCN surveys in 1994 confirmed the presence of wild elephants and gibbons in the area; locals also report such rare species as the gaur, Asiatic black bear, tiger, clouded leopard, Siamese fireback and green peafowl. About 88% of Phu Khao Khuai NBCA is forested, though only 32% has been classified as dense, mature forest. The total NBCA covers 2000 sq km, though a section of 710 sq km toward the west – which contains the army base and several villages – may soon be excised from the NBCA plan to make conservation decrees easier to enforce.

Despite a 600 kip entry fee, there are as yet no visitor facilities. Snacks can be purchased from villages – some of them populated by resettled Hmong – along the way, but it's better to come prepared with your own picnic.

Getting There & Away

Public transport to Phu Khao Khuai is unavailable. It takes around two hours to reach the NBCA from Vientiane via paved Route 13 south and an all-weather gravel road that heads east from Thabok.

The western edge of the NBCA – and the namesake mountain peak itself – can be approached from the south via a winding dirt road from Route 10 east of the Tha Ngon bridge over the Nam Ngum. This route is sometimes impassable in the rainy season; any time of year you'd need a sturdy, high-clearance vehicle to negotiate the road. There are still lots of men in green about in this section – along the way you'll pass a couple of Lao military checkpoints.

LAO PAKO

This unique ecological resort on the banks of the Nam Ngum river offers a relaxing getaway from Vientiane. Built and operated by an Austrian-German couple in a secluded corner of Vientiane Prefecture (about 55 km from the capital), Lao Pako offers quiet country nights along with opportunities for swimming and boating in the river, volleyball and badminton on the property or hiking to nearby villages, wats and waterfalls. The community-oriented proprietors were instrumental in creating a 40-hectare forest preserve on the river's opposite bank; they've also donated money to local village schools.

Lodgings on the landscaped property are built of native materials. A wood-and-bamboo longhouse contains a seven-bed dorm that costs 6000 kip per person, plus three rooms for 15,000 kip single/double. Separate bungalows with private bath are also available for 20,000 kip. There is also an open-air *sala* where you can sleep on the floor for 2000 kip a night. Lao-style buffet meals are served in a separate open-air shelter. Each month the resort puts on a full-moon party with a barbecue and the sharing of *lâo hái* (Lao-style jar liquor). The latter comes from a nearby village, Ban Kok Hai, which is only 15 minutes away by river. Another riverbank village worth visiting is Tha Sang (Elephant Landing), where a local wat houses a large reclining Buddha and classic central Lao-style chedi.

For reservations (advisable on weekends and holidays), call ☎ 216600 in Vientiane, a number which connects with a radio phone at Lao Pako.

Getting There & Away

The best way to reach Lao Pako is to drive or take a 1½ hour bus trip to Somsamai (bus No 19 from Talaat Sao, 350 kip, three times daily at 6.30 am, 11 am and 3 pm) on the Nam Ngum river, whence a local motorised canoe will take you on to the lodge, a 25 minute journey, for 1500 kip.

VANG VIENG ວັງວຽງ

This small town about 70 km north of Phon Hong (160 km north of Vientiane) via Route 13 nestles along a scenic bend in the Nam Song river. The town itself is not without charm, but the main attraction is the karst topography lining the west bank of the river. Honeycombed with unexplored tunnels and caverns, the limestone cliffs here are a spelunker's heaven. Several of the caves are named and play small roles in local mythology – all are said to be inhabited by spirits.

Other than the Chinese-built cement factory just outside of town and a little-used airstrip between Route 13 and the town, Vang Vieng is well removed from modernisation and there are lots of tropical birds in the vicinity. Several monasteries in Vang Vieng district date to the 16th and 17th cen-turies, among them Wat That, Wat Kang, Wat Khua Phan, Wat Sisumang and Wat Phong Phen. Outside of town are a number of Hmong villages, including two which are just four and 10 km west of the Nam Song.

Caves

The most famous of the Vang Vieng caves is **Tham Jang**, a large cavern that was used as a bunker in defence against marauding Chinese Ho (Jiin Haw) in the early 19th century; *thàm* means cave, *jang* is steadfast. A set of stairs lead to the main cavern entrance. Until recently the only method for lighting your way through the cave was by brush or electric torch (flashlight), but lights have since been installed which the caretak-ers will turn on once you've paid the 2000 kip entry fee. From the main room you can look out over the river valley through an opening in the limestone wall; a cool spring at the foot of the cave feeds into the river.

Another cave in the vicinity, **Tham Baat** (Begging-Bowl Cave), contains a rusting iron begging bowl that supposedly belonged to a hermit who lived and died in the caves; you must be fairly nimble to wriggle into this one.

To find these caves and others, ask an angler or boatman along the river to show you the way – most will be glad to guide you to two or three caves for a few hundred kip. Except in the drier months, when you can easily wade across the river, you may also need to hire a boatman to ferry you across the river by pirogue. The section of the river where most of the caves are found is within walking distance (about two km south-west) of the town centre.

Even if you don't plan on any cave explo-ration, a walk along the river can be rewarding. Most of the local fishing pirogues are poled along the river, hence the quiet scenery is unmarred by noisy motors.

Places to Stay & Eat

Two guest houses next to the bus terminal and market, *Phou Bane* and *Saynamsong*, offer basic but clean two-bed rooms for 2000 to 3000 kip per night with shared bath.

Vang Vieng Resort (☎ 214743, radio phone 130440), slightly out of town but near the caves and river, features quiet, comfortable red-tiled cottages for US$15 per room. All rooms come equipped with private toilet and shower.

Several small noodle shops can be found in the vicinity of the guest houses. *Nang Nokkeo* near the Phou Bane serves standard Lao dishes. During the day there are also several food vendors in the market.

Getting There & Away

Route 13 is paved all the way to Vang Vieng. From Vientiane's Talaat Sao terminal catch bus No 1 at 7.30 am, 9.30 am or 1 pm. The fare is 1300 kip and the trip takes about 3½ hours. A good place to break the journey along the way, if you're travelling by private transport, is at the scenic Hin Hoep river junction. The Pathet Lao, Prince Souvannaphouma and Prince Bounome signed a short-lived peace treaty in the middle of the bridge at Hin Hoep in 1962.

Before the road was paved, a common way to cover part of the distance between Vientiane and the town was via ferries across Ang Nam Ngum; timewise, this is no longer a practical way to reach Vang Vieng since it takes nearly five hours just to cross the lake, after which you must continue by road from Tha Heua to Vang Vieng.

KASI ກາສີ

This is little more than a truck stop and staging point for the final road push to Luang Prabang along Route 13. At the moment Kasi is not recommended because of inadequate roads and the danger of guerrilla attacks. In the future – when Route 13 is paved all the way from Vientiane to Luang Prabang and the Kasi area has been 'stabilised' – the road trip should be safer.

At the moment Lao are still using the road for public transport in spite of occasional attacks; because of the national news blackout, no-one really knows how frequent such incidents really are, although some observers estimate 10 to 15 people a year are killed along this road. The most dangerous stretch is the unpaved section north of Kasi on the way to Luang Prabang, so you could go as far as Kasi and turn around – except there's really nothing to see in Kasi.

Should you find yourself in Kasi overnight, the friendly *Van Thong Guest House*, run by a former RLA officer, costs 1500 kip per person in multi-bed rooms, or 3500 kip for a private room. A second choice is the similar *Somchith Guest House*. The on-again, off-again *Mrs Keomany's Guest House* near the Somchith may also have rooms.

Getting There & Away

Kasi is about two hours north of Vang Vieng via paved Route 13. Buses – actually huge truck flatbeds mounted with heavy wooden carriages – cost 700 kip from Vang Vieng.

From here onward to Luang Prabang along the unpaved track is a gruelling eight to 10 hours by truck or bus; when the grading and paving of this final section is complete it should take no longer than five hours. Buses usually do this route at night following the theory that snipers are less likely to be able to hit their target in the dark. All buses carry armaments; drivers proceed slowly to keep an eye out for mines lying in the road.

Northern Laos

Luang Prabang Province ແຂວງຫຼວງພະບາງ

According to the 1995 census the mountainous northern province of Luang Prabang had a total population of 365,000 (down from 434,000 in 1960 – mostly due to refugee emigration) divided among 12 ethnicities, of whom 46% are classified Lao Theung, 40% Lao Loum and 14% Lao Sung. Over 80% of the population are engaged in farming – primarily rice – and of the remaining 17%, who are involved in commerce, most live in the Luang Prabang capital district. Cut off from major markets by a lack of reliable surface transport (even the Mekong is not 100% navigable year-round), the province has developed a small, fragile and largely insular economy of local production and services resting on a traditional subsistence foundation.

History

The area that now encompasses Luang Prabang Province was the site of early Thai-Lao *meuangs* that were established in the high river valleys along the Mekong river and its major tributaries, the Nam Khan, the Nam Ou and the Nam Seuang (Xeuang). The first Lao kingdom, Lan Xang, was consolidated here in 1353 by the Khmer-supported conqueror Fa Ngum. At that time it was known as Meuang Sawa (named after Java, possibly related to the Javanese invasion of Chenla, centred in southern Laos and northern Cambodia, between the 6th and 8th centuries).

In 1357 the name was changed to Meuang Xieng Thong (Gold City District) but sometime after King Fa Ngum accepted a Sinhalese Buddha image called Pha Bang (Large Holy Image) as a gift from the Khmer monarchy, the city-state became known as Luang (Great or Royal) Prabang. Luang

Prabang remained the capital of Lan Xang until King Phothisarat moved the seat of administration to Vientiane in 1545.

But throughout the Lan Xang period, Luang Prabang was considered the main source of monarchical power. When Lan Xang broke up following the death of King Sulinya Vongsa in 1694, one of Sulinya's grandsons established an independent kingdom in Luang Prabang that competed alongside kingdoms in Vientiane and Champasak.

From then on, the Luang Prabang monarchy was so weak that it was forced to pay tribute at various times to the Siamese and Vietnamese, and finally to the French when Laos became a French protectorate in the late 19th century. At this time a French Commis-

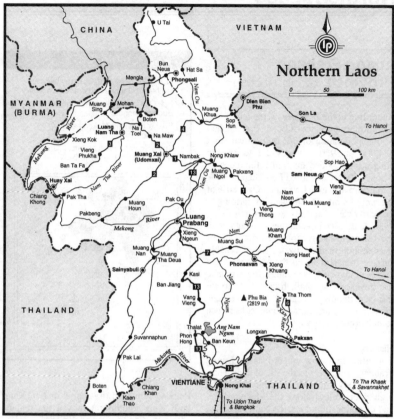

sariat was established in the royal capital. The French allowed Laos to retain the Luang Prabang monarchy, however, as did the fledgling independent governments that followed; it wasn't until the Pathet Lao took over in 1975 that the monarchy was finally dissolved.

The last king and queen of Luang Prabang were imprisoned in a cave in north-eastern Laos where they are thought to have died from lack of adequate food and medical care sometime in the '80s. The Lao PDR government has yet to issue a full report on their whereabouts following the Revolution.

LUANG PRABANG ຫລວງພະບາງ

The city of Luang Prabang (officially 'Nakhon Luang Prabang' but often called simply 'Meuang Luang' locally) is just barely waking up from a long slumber brought on by decades of war and revolution. The population for the entire capital district is 63,000 but the municipality itself has only around 16,000 residents. Few concessions have been made to the modern world save for electricity (subject to frequent power outages) and a growing fleet of cars, trucks and motorcycles; rush hour occurs when school lets out and the streets are filled with bicycles.

Much of this may change when Route 13 is paved through to Luang Prabang from Vientiane, which will allow one-day road travel between the two cities for the first time in Lao history. Another paved highway will eventually link Luang Prabang with the Chinese border, turning the city into a relay point for China-Laos-Thailand commerce. One can only hope that some sort of highway bypass will be constructed so that the highway doesn't run straight through the city – as has so far been proposed.

Orientation
The town sits at the junction of the Mekong and Khan rivers. A large hill called Phu Si (sometimes spelt Phousy) dominates the town skyline at the upper end of a peninsula formed by the confluence of the two rivers. Most of the historic temples are located between Phu Si and the Mekong. Virtually the whole town can be seen on foot in a day or two, though many visitors extend their stay here in order to soak up more atmosphere.

Street names vary widely on city maps and address cards: Thanon Phothisalat may be alternatively known as Thanon Sisavangvong, Navang or Sakkalin! When giving directions, locals almost never quote street names, using well-known landmarks instead.

Easy-to-reach attractions outside of town include the Pak Ou caves to the north-east, reached by river, and the waterfalls of Kuang Si and Taat Sae to the south-east, reached by road.

Guides & Maps An excellent French guidebook to the town, if you can find it, is *Louang Prabang* by Thao Boun Souk (pen name for Pierre-Marie Gagneaux), which was published in 1974 by the now-defunct Bulletin des Amis du Royaume Lao. Local tour guides rely heavily on this little book, though local historians question some of its dates in light of new research.

The LNTA and National Geographic Service released a good bilingual colour map of the city, *Louang Prabang Tourist Map*, in

---

Luang Prabang's Monarchs
Until the reign of King Sai Setthathirat, the Lan Xang Kingdom was based in Luang Prabang, after which the Lan Xang royal seat moved to Vientiane. In 1707 Lan Xang split into the separate kingdoms of Vientiane, Luang Prabang and Champasak. The separate kingdom of Luang Prabang had the following monarchs:

Kitsalat	1707-25
Khamon Noi	1726-27
Inta Som	1727-76
Sotika Kuman	1776-81
Suryavong	1781-87
interregnum	1787-91
Anulat	1791-1817
Manthatulat	1817-36
Sukaseum	1836-51
Tiantha	1851-72
Oun Kham	1872-87
interregnum	1887-94
Sakkalin	1894-1904
Sisavang Vong	1904-59
Sisavang Vatthana	1959-75*

*Official Lao histories claim Sisavang Vatthana was never crowned.

1994 – it's available at the main tourist hotels for around US$2.

Information
Money Lane Xang Bank, 65 Thanon Phothisalat, will change Thai and US currency only – cash or travellers' cheques – for kip. The bank normally won't change in the other direction – kip for either baht or dollars – because of a claimed shortage of these currencies. The rate is a bit lower than in Vientiane (eg 910 kip to the dollar in 1995 for cash, 920 kip for travellers' cheques, versus 920/925 kip in Vientiane). The bank is open Monday to Friday from 8.30 am to 3.30 pm.

Post The old French-built post office has been vacated in favour of a gleaming modern edifice on the corner of Thanons Phothisalat and Kitsalat, opposite the Phousy Hotel. It's open weekdays from 8.30 am to 5 pm.

NORTHERN LAOS

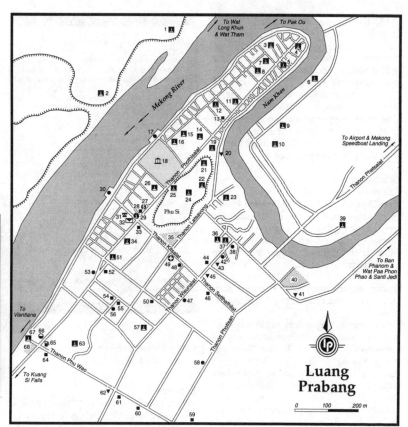

Luang Prabang

0   100   200 m

Telephone A new telephone office around the corner from the post office now offers both domestic and international calls via the country's new satcom system. It's open 7.30 am to 10 pm; as elsewhere in Laos, it's cash only and collect (reverse-charge) calls can't be made.

Luang Prabang's area code is 71.

Medical Services The Provincial Hospital on the western side of Thanon Kitsalat and a Chinese-funded clinic opposite are the only public medical facilities in Luang Prabang to speak of. Neither receive high or even

passing marks from foreign medical observers. Foreign visitors with serious injuries or illnesses are almost always flown back to Vientiane for emergency transit to hospitals in north-eastern Thailand. If flight services between Luang Prabang and Chiang Mai, Thailand, are initiated (rumours say it will happen within the next two years), a direct flight to Chiang Mai would be quicker.

Immigration Luang Prabang immigration is the strictest in the country when it comes to officially checking in and out of the province. If you fly into the city, the *jâeng*

PLACES TO STAY		OTHER		27	Lane Xang Bank
				29	Luang Prabang
13	Villa Santi	1	Wat Chom Phet		Tourism
28	New Luang Prabang	2	Wat Xieng Maen	30	Long-distance
	Hotel	3	Wat Xieng Thong		Ferries
33	Hotel Phousy	4	Wat Pakkhan	31	Telephone Office
44	Rama Hotel	5	Wat Khili	32	Post Office
46	Viengkeo Hotel	6	Wat Sa-at	34	Wat Ho Siang
50	Champa-Lao Hotel	7	Wat Si Bun Heuang	35	Talaat Dala
52	Hotel	8	Wat Si Muang Khun	36	Wat Aham
	Souvannaphoum	9	Wat Paa Khaa	37	Wat Wisunalat
54	Vannida Guest House	10	Wat Phon Song	38	Lao Red Cross
55	Boun Gning Guest	11	Wat Saen	39	Wat Tao Hai
	House	12	Wat Nong	40	Talaat Vieng Mai
59	Phu Vao Hotel		Sikhunmuang	42	Immigration
60	Manoluck Hotel	14	Wat Paa Phai	47	Lao Aviation
61	Muangsua Hotel	15	Wat Xieng Muan	48	Lane Xang Travel
64	Silivongvanh Hotel	16	Wat Chum Khong	49	Provincial Hospital
		17	Boats to Pak Ou	51	Wat That
PLACES TO EAT		18	Royal Palace Museum	53	Provincial Office
		19	Wat Thammo	56	Air Lao
20	Khem Karn Food	21	Wat Pha Phutthabaat	57	Wat Manolom
	Garden	22	Wat Tham Phu Si	58	Talaat Naviengkham
41	Vieng Mai Restaurant	23	Wat Aphai	63	Wat That Luang
43	Visoun Restaurant	24	That Chomsi	65	Petrol Station
45	Young Koun	25	Wat Paa Huak	66	Bus Terminal
	Restaurant	26	Wat Mai	67	Wat Pha Baat Tai
62	Malee Lao Food		Suwannaphumaham	68	Talaat Sao

khào/jâeng àwk procedure is efficiently taken care of at Luang Prabang Airport as at most other Lao airports. If you arrive by road or boat, be sure to check in with immigration on the day of arrival if possible. Officials in Luang Prabang are quick to levy fines – in fact they do so with great gusto – if you delay the procedure for getting your permit checked.

There are small immigration police posts at the slow-boat and speedboat landings for those arriving by river, and one at the bus terminal as well. The main immigration office is on Thanon Wisunalat. Here you'll find a list of all the potential fines you must pay for neglecting to check in or for overstaying your visa; they are the highest in Laos and it's no use arguing that other provincial offices charge less.

As we were going to press I heard unconfirmed rumours that Luang Prabang immigration was requiring all visitors to check in *twice*; once at the port of arrival (ie airport, boat landing or bus terminal) and again at the city immigration office.

Travel Agencies Although the owners of Luang Prabang Tourism, at the corner of Thanons Phothisalat and Kitsalat, would like you to think they still have a monopoly on tourism services in the city (as in the pre-privatisation days), they're just one of several tour agencies in town; others include SODETOUR, Diethelm and Lane Xang. All basically offer the same sorts of one to three-day tours around the province, including visits to hill-tribe villages (though none is as yet permitted to provide overnight village treks). Lane Xang Travel on Thanon Phu Wao seems to be the most receptive to individual travellers looking for something different in the way of travel itineraries.

Walking Tour

If you're in Luang Prabang on your own, a simple walking circuit around the north-east quarter of town will take you to most of the historic and sightseeing spots. You might want to do this circuit in two stages – one part in the coolness of early morning and another in the late afternoon – with time off

NORTHERN LAOS

in between for lunch and a rest. Most of the highlighted sights mentioned below are described in detail later in this chapter.

An easy morning walk might start at the bustling **Dala Market** (Tálàat Dạaláa) at the corner of Thanons Kitsalat and Latsavong. The area surrounding this market is Luang Prabang's commercial nerve centre and you'll find all sorts of interesting and not-so-interesting shops and vendors here. From the market, head south along Thanon Kitsalat, passing the Provincial Hospital on the right and more shops on the left.

At the next big four-way intersection turn left and continue past the Rama Hotel. About 150m past the hotel on the left is **Wat Wisunalat**, one of the city's oldest temples. At the east end of the temple compound is bulbous **That Makmo**, the Watermelon Stupa. Adjacent to the temple's north side is another older temple, **Wat Aham**, known for its two large and venerable banyan trees.

Exiting from the east entrance to Wat Aham, bear left (north) onto the somewhat busy road that connects central Luang Prabang with the airport. Continue north until this road terminates and bear right, following the road that winds its way between the Khan river below on the right and Phu Si (Sacred Hill) above on the left. As you continue north-east along this road you'll pass several views of river life below. If you're hungry, look for the scenic Khem Karn Food Garden on the right overlooking the river; there are also other informal eating places along the river nearby. Or walk up steep, zig-zagging naga stairs to **Wat Thammothayalan** (opposite Khem Karn), one of the few active monasteries on Phu Si, for good views of the Nam Khan.

For the second half of this walking circuit, start at the **Royal Palace Museum** on Thanon Phothisalat. (If you would like to tour the museum, note that it's only open Monday to Friday 8.30 to 10.30 am). From the museum, walk east on Thanon Phothisalat toward the eastern end of the peninsula formed by the junction of the Mekong and Khan rivers. Along this road you'll pass several temples of minor note, including **Wat Saen, Wat Sop, Wat Si Muang Khun** and **Wat Si Bun Heuang**, all lined up along the left (north) side of the street. These are interspersed with a number of charming brick-and-stucco **French colonial buildings** on either side of the street, along with traditional wood-and-mortar houses and hybrid French-Lao brick dwellings. Most of the colonial buildings were built during the '20s and '30s.

When you reach the end of the road, bear left and follow the river bend round to **Wat Xieng Thong**, one of the town's premier temples and one well worth spending some time at. After you've had your fill of this wat, exit toward the river and head west (left) on the river road. On your left you'll pass side streets that lead to small, older temples that the usual guided tour itineraries don't include – **Wat Paa Phai, Wat Xieng Muan** and **Wat Chum Khong**.

When you see the rear side of the Royal Palace Museum on your left, take the next left turn and follow the short road south back to Thanon Phothisalat, where you'll come to **Wat Mai Suwannaphumaham** – noted for its gilded terrace – on your right. On the other side of the street, opposite the front of the Royal Palace Museum, are a set of steps that lead up the north side of Phu Si. To the right of the steps above the road is the abandoned sim of one of Luang Prabang's oldest temples, **Wat Paa Huak**, whose interior murals are not to be missed.

If you're ready for a climb, ascend the steps to the summit of **Phu Si**, where you'll find good aerial views of the town. Sunset vistas from the west side of the hill next to 19th-century **That Chomsi** (Large Stupa) can be superb.

Royal Palace Museum (Haw Kham)
ພິພິທະພັນພະລາຊວັງຂອງ

This is a good place to start a tour of Luang Prabang since the displays convey some sense of local history. The palace (known locally as Haw Kham or Golden Hall) was originally constructed in 1904 – during the early French colonial era – as a residence for King Sisavang Vong and his family. The site for the palace was chosen so that official visitors to Luang Prabang could disembark from their river journeys directly below the palace and be received there.

When Sisavang Vong died in 1959, his son Sisavang Vatthana ascended the throne. According to official Pathet Lao history the 1975 Revolution prevented the prince's actual coronation, though foreign diplomats tell a different story. At any rate after a two-year term as 'Supreme Advisor to the President', King (or Crown Prince) Sisavang Vatthana and his wife were exiled to northern Laos – where they later expired in a cave – and the palace was converted into a museum. An official brochure printed by the Ministry of Information and Culture and distributed at the museum reads, 'On his return to Luang Prabang, Sisavang Vatthana moved to his private residence close to Xieng Thong temple and offered the palace to the Government'.

Architecturally, the building features a blend of traditional Lao motifs and French *beaux arts* styles and is laid out in a double-cruciform shape with the entrance on one side of the lower crossbar. The steps leading to the entranceway are Italian marble. Various royal religious objects are displayed in the large entry hall, including the dais of the former Supreme Patriarch of Lao Buddhism, a venerable Buddha head presented to the king as a gift from India, a reclining Buddha with the unusual added feature of sculpted mourners at his side, an equally unusual Buddha seated with begging bowl (the bowl is usually only depicted with a standing figure) and a Luang Prabang-style standing Buddha sculpted of marble in the 'Contemplating the Bodhi Tree' pose.

In the right front corner room of the palace, which opens to the outside, is a collection of the museum's most prized art, including the Pha Bang. This solid gold standing Buddha is 83 cm tall and is said to weigh either 53.4 kg or 43 kg, depending on which sources you believe. Legend says the image was cast around the 1st century AD in Ceylon (Sri Lanka) and later presented to the Khmer King Phaya Sirichantha, who in turn

gave it to King Fa Ngum in 1359 as a Buddhist legitimator of Lao sovereignty. The Siamese twice carried the image off to Thailand (1779 and 1827) but it was finally restored to Lao hands by King Mongkut (Rama IV) in 1867. Persistent rumours claim that the actual image on display is a copy and that the original is stored in a vault either in Vientiane or Moscow. A new pavilion under construction in front of the museum will house the Pha Bang – a project originally planned before the monarchy was abolished.

Also in this room are large elephant tusks engraved with Buddhas, Khmer-crafted sitting Buddhas and Luang Prabang-style standing Buddhas, an excellent Lao frieze taken from a local temple and three beautiful *saew mâi khán* (embroidered silk screens with religious imagery) that were crafted by the queen.

To the right of the entry hall is the king's former reception room, where busts of the Lao monarchy are displayed along with two large gilded and lacquered Ramayana screens crafted by local artisan Thit Tanh. The walls of the room are covered with murals that depict scenes from traditional Lao life. They were painted in 1930 by French artist Alix de Fautereau; each wall is meant to be viewed at a different time of day – according to the light that enters the windows on one side of the room – corresponding to the time of day depicted.

To the left of the entry hall is a room filled with paintings, silver and china that have been presented to Laos as diplomatic gifts from Myanmar, Cambodia, Thailand, Poland, Hungary, Russia, Japan, Vietnam, China, Nepal, USA, Canada and Australia. The objects are grouped according to whether they're from 'socialist' or 'capitalist' countries.

The next room to the left was once the queen's reception room. Large royal portraits of King Sisavang Vatthana, Queen Kham Phouy and Crown Prince Vong Savang, painted by Russian artist Ilya Glazunov in 1967, are hung on the walls. Also on display in this room are friendship flags from China and Vietnam, and replicas of sculpture from New Delhi's Indian National Museum.

Behind the entry hall is the former throne room where royal vestments, gold and silver sabres, and the king's elephant chair (or saddle) are exhibited. Glass cases hold a collection of small crystal and gold Buddhas that were found inside the That Makmo stupa. Intricate wall mosaics, placed on a deep red background, are a major highlight of the palace art.

Beyond the throne room are halls that lead to the royal family's residential quarters. The royal bedrooms have been preserved as they were when the king departed, as have the dining hall and a room that contains royal seals and medals. One of the more interesting displays in the museum is a room in the residential section that now contains Lao classical musical instruments and masks for the performance of Ramayana dance-drama – just about the only place in the country where you see these kinds of objects on display.

Visiting the Museum The Royal Palace Museum is open Monday to Friday 8.30 to 10.30 am and you're supposed to present an 'invitation' *(bai sanõe)* from a hotel or travel agency to be allowed entry. Hotels and guest houses usually issue these slips of paper to their guests free of charge; some places charge 1000 kip for the slip. You can also try showing up at the museum mid-morning when tour groups are going through; the staff will usually let you fill in the name of the hotel or guest house you're staying at, pay 1000 kip and enter the museum. Travel agencies will ask 3000 kip for the same slip of paper. Shoes and other footwear (socks OK) can't be worn inside the museum, no photography is permitted and you must leave all bags with the attendants.

Wat Xieng Thong ວັດຊຽງທອງ
Near the northern tip of the peninsula formed by the Mekong and Khan rivers is Luang Prabang's most magnificent temple, Wat Xieng Thong (Golden City Temple). It was built by King Saisetthathirat in 1560 and

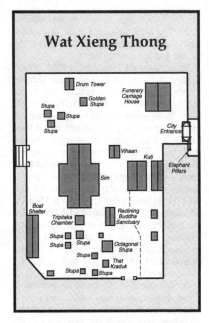

Wat Xieng Thong

remained under royal patronage until 1975. Like the royal palace, Wat Xieng Thong was placed within easy reach of the Mekong. The *hãw tai* (tripitaka library) was added in 1828, the *hãw kawng* (drum tower) in 1961.

The sim represents what is considered classic Luang Prabang temple architecture, with roofs that sweep low to the ground (the same style – part of the Lan Xang-Lanna legacy – is found in northern Thailand as well). The rear wall of the sim features an impressive 'tree of life' mosaic set in a red background. Inside, richly decorated wooden columns support a ceiling vested with *dhammachakkas* (dharma-wheels).

To one side of the sim, toward the east, are several small chapels (actually *hãw*, or hall/building in Lao) and stupas containing Buddha images of the period. The *hãw tai pha sãi-nyàat* or reclining Buddha image building (dubbed La Chapelle Rouge or Red Chapel by the French) contains an especially rare reclining Buddha that dates from the

Luang Prabang

Following the 1995 addition of the city to UNESCO's World Heritage List (a distinction Luang Prabang shares with such architectural treasures as the Taj Mahal and Angkor Wat), Luang Prabang's future now seems relatively assured. The 1994 UNESCO mission pronounced Luang Prabang 'the best preserved city in South-East Asia'.

Luang Prabang has become a tourist attraction because of its historic temples – around 32 of the original 66 built before French colonisation still stand – and because of its lovely mountain-encircled setting, 700m above sea level at the confluence of the Khan and Mekong rivers. In addition to such famous wats as Wat Xieng Thong and Wat Mai, the city is also home to the magnificent Royal Palace Museum. The mix of gleaming temple roofs, crumbling French provincial architecture and multi-ethnic population (Hmong, Mien and Thai tribals are often seen walking around town on their way to and from market) tends to enthral even jaded Asian travellers. ■

JOE CUMMINGS

Above: Detail from a gold relief at Wat Mai

Left: Gilt naga figure at Wat Mai

Below: The impressive 'Tree of Life' mosaic at Wat Xieng Thong

JOE CUMMINGS

JOE CUMMINGS

Right: Temple gable, Wat Mai, Luang Prabang

Below: That Makmo - the Watermelon Stupa, Luang Prabang

JOE CUMMINGS

JOE CUMMINGS

construction of the temple. This one-of-a-kind figure is exquisitely proportioned in classic Lao style (most Lao recliners imitate Thai or Lanna styles), with the monastic robes curling outward at the ankle like rocket fumes. Instead of merely supporting the head, the unique right-hand position extends away from the head in a simple but graceful gesture. In 1931 this image was taken to Paris and displayed at the Paris Exhibition, after which it was kept in Vientiane until its return to Luang Prabang in 1964.

Gold-leaf votives line the upper walls of the Red Chapel on either side of the reclining image. In front of the image are several seated bronze Buddhas of different styles and ages, and on either side of the altar are small embroidered tapestries depicting a stupa and a standing Buddha. A mosaic on the back exterior wall of this chapel was done in the late 1950s in commemoration of the 2500th anniversary of the Buddha's attainment of *parinibbana* (post-death nirvana). The mosaic is unique because it depicts local village life rather than a religious scene.

Near the compound's east gate stands the *hóhng kép mîen* (royal funeral carriage house). Inside is an impressive 12m-high funeral carriage (crafted by local sculptor Thit Tanh) and various funeral urns for each member of the royal family. (The ashes of King Sisavang Vong, the queen and the king's brother, however, are interred at Wat That Luang in the southern end of Luang Prabang). Gilt panels on the exterior of the chapel depict semi-erotic episodes from the Ramayana.

Admission to Wat Xieng Thong is 250 kip.

Wat Wisunalat (Wat Vixoun)
ວັດວິຊຸນນະລາດ

This temple to the east of the town centre was originally constructed in 1513 during the reign of Chao Wisunalat, making it the oldest operating temple in Luang Prabang, but was rebuilt in 1896-8 following an 1887 fire set by marauding Chinese Ho. The original was made of wood, and in the brick and stucco restoration the builders attempted to make the balustraded windows of the sim appear to be fashioned of lathed wood (an old south Indian and Khmer contrivance that is uncommon in Lao architecture). The front roof that slopes sideways over the terrace is also unique. Inside the high-ceilinged sim is a collection of wooden 'Calling for Rain' Buddhas and 15th to 16th century Luang Prabang *sima* (ordination stones). The Pha Bang was kept here from 1507 to 1715 and from 1867-94.

In front of the sim is 34.5m That Pathum (Lotus Stupa), which was started in 1503 by order of Nang Phantin Xieng, wife of King Wisun, and took 19 months to complete. Workmen filled the interior of the stupa with small Buddha images made of precious materials and other sacred items; many of these were stolen when Chinese Ho destroyed the temple (the remainder are on display in the Royal Palace Museum); the stupa underwent reconstruction in 1895. It's more commonly called That Makmo or 'Watermelon Stupa' because of its semi-spherical shape.

Wat Aham ວັດອາຮາມ
Between Wat Wisun and the Nam Khan is Wat Aham, which was formerly the residence of the Sangkhalat (Supreme Patriarch of Lao Buddhism). Two large bodhi trees (pipal or banyan) grace the grounds, which are semi-deserted except for the occasional devotee who comes to make offerings to the town's most important spirit shrine, at the base of the trees.

Wat Mai Suwannaphumaham
ວັດໃໝ່ສຸວັນພູມາຮາມ

Close to the Phousy Hotel and the GPO is Wat Mai (New Temple), which was inaugurated in 1821 (some sources claim it was built in 1797) and was at one time a residence of the Sangkhalat (succeeding Wat Aham). The five-tiered roof of the wooden sim is in the standard Luang Prabang style. The front verandah is remarkable for its decorated columns and sumptuous gold relief walls that recount the legend of Vessantara (Pha Wet), the Buddha's penultimate incarnation, as well as scenes from the *Ramayana* and local village life. To one side of the sim is a shelter where two long racing boats are kept. These are brought out during Lao New Year in April and again in October during the Water Festival.

The Pha Bang, which is usually housed in Luang Prabang's Royal Palace Museum, is put on public display at Wat Mai during the Lao new year celebrations.

Wat That Luang ວັດທາດຫຼວງ

Legend has it that Wat That Luang was originally established by Ashokan missionaries from India in the 3rd century BC. However, there is no physical evidence whatsoever to confirm this and the currently standing sim was built in 1818 under the reign of King Manthatulat. The ashes of King Sisavang Vong are interred inside the large central stupa, which was erected in 1910. A smaller thâat in front of the sim dates to 1820. Inside the huge sim are a few Luang Prabang Buddha images and other artefacts. This temple appears to have the largest contingent of monks in Luang Prabang.

Phu Si ພູສີ

The temples on the upper slopes of 100m Phu Si were recently constructed, but it is likely there were other temples previously located at this important hill site. There is an excellent view of the town from the top of the hill.

On the lower slopes of the hill are two of the oldest (and now abandoned) temples in Luang Prabang. The decaying sim at **Wat Paa Huak** – on the lower northern slope near the Royal Palace Museum – features a splendid carved wood and mosaic facade showing Buddha riding Erawan, the three-headed elephant of Hindu mythology (usually depicted as Lord Indra's mount). The gilded and carved front doors are often kept locked but during the day there's usually an attendant nearby who will open the doors for a tip of a couple of hundred kip. Inside, the original 19th century murals have maintained excellent colour considering the lack of restoration efforts. The murals show historic scenes along the Mekong river, including

visits by Chinese diplomats and warriors arriving by river and horse caravans. Three large seated Buddhas and several smaller standing and seated images date from around the same time as the murals or possibly earlier.

Around on the north-eastern flank of the hill are the ruins of **Wat Pha Phutthabaat**, originally constructed in 1395 during the reign of Phaya Samsenthai on the site of a 'Buddha footprint'. The ruins are of mixed style but are said to show a definite Lanna Thai or Chiang Mai influence with later Vietnamese augmentation.

To continue an ascent all the way to the summit of the hill you are required to pay a 500 kip admission fee, collected at the northern entrance near Wat Paa Huak (you do not have to pay the fee to reach the latter temple, however).

At the summit is 24m **That Chomsi**, which was originally erected in 1804 and restored in 1914. This thâat is the starting point for a colourful Lao new year procession in mid-April. If you continue over the summit and start down the path on the other side you'll come to a small cave shrine called **Wat Tham Phu Si**. Since it's really nothing more than one large, fat Buddha image (a form called Pha Kachai in Lao) and a sheltered area for worshippers, it hardly lives up to its designation as a wat. On a nearby crest is an old Russian anti-aircraft cannon that children use as a makeshift merry-go-round.

Other Temples

In the north-east corner of town near the meeting of the Khan and Mekong rivers is a string of historic, still active temples. Facing Thanon Phothisalat just east of Villa Santi (see Places to Stay) is **Wat Saen** (the name, 100,000 Temple, refers to its founding on an initial 100,000 kip donation), a Thai-style wat built in 1718 and restored in 1932 and 1957. Behind the Villa Santi near the river road, the simple **Wat Nong Sikhunmeuang** was built in 1729, burned in 1774 and rebuilt in 1804.

North-west of the Santi and set back off the street is **Wat Paa Phai** (Bamboo Forest

Temple), whose classic Thai-Lao fresco over the gilded and carved wooden facade is at least a hundred years old; the art depicts scenes from everyday Lao life from the era in which it was painted. Just west of Wat Paa Phai are **Wat Chum Khong** and the older **Wat Xieng Muan**, whose sim dates to 1879. The Buddhist sculpture inside Wat Xieng Muan is better than average and the ceiling is painted with gold *nagas* (water dragons), an uncommon motif in this position – possibly a Thai Lü influence. Both of these wats are known for their elaborate *háang thíen* (candle rails) with nagas at either end.

Wat Si Mahathat (called Wat That for short), two wats west of the Hotel Phousy, is named for a venerable Lanna-style thâat erected in 1548. The sim in front – built in 1910 – is quite ornate, with carved wooden windows and portico, rosette-gilded pillars, exterior *jataka* reliefs and Luang Prabang-style roof lined with temple bells.

West of the Lao Aviation office is **Wat Manolom**, founded in 1375 and once an important local wat that has since faded in importance. The decaying sim held the Pha Bang from 1502 to 1513 and still contains a huge sitting bronze Buddha cast in 1372. This image is approximately six metres high and weighs an estimated two tonnes – it would probably have been moved to another temple by now if anyone could figure out how to move it!

An easy three km walk or bicycle ride south-east of town is **Wat Paa Phon Phao**, a forest meditation wat famous for the teachings of Ajaan Saisamut. Saisamut died in 1992 and his funeral was the largest and most well-attended monk's funeral Laos has seen in decades. The temple's Santi Jedi (Peace Pagoda), built in 1988, has become something of a tourist attraction. This large yellow stupa contains three floors inside plus an outside terrace near the top with a view of the surrounding plains. The interior walls are painted with all manner of Buddhist stories and moral admonitions. Santi Jedi is open daily from 8 to 10 am and 1 to 4.30 pm.

Behind the That Luang Market in town is a modern Vietnamese-Lao Buddhist temple,

Wat Pha Baat Tai (Southern Buddha-Foot Temple). The temple itself is rather garish but behind the temple is a shady terrace overlooking the Mekong; on a hot afternoon this a good place to cool off and watch the sun set.

Across the River

Across the Mekong river from central Luang Prabang are several notable temples in the Xieng Maen District. Xieng Maen itself played an important role as the terminus of the historic road between Luang Prabang and various northern Thai kingdoms (eg, Nan and Phayao).

Wat Long Khun, almost directly across the river from Wat Xieng Thong, is the best place to disembark by boat for Xieng Maen explorations. This wat features a nicely decorated portico of 1937 vintage, plus older sections from the 18th century and a few fading jataka murals. When the coronation of a Luang Prabang king was pending, it was customary for him to spend three days in retreat at Wat Long Khun before ascending the throne. A restoration project, completed in January 1995 by the Dept of Museums & Archaeology with the help of the Ecole Française d'Extrême Orient, has brought new life and beauty to the monastery buildings.

Founded in 1889 and since abandoned, **Wat Tham Xieng Maen** is in a 100m-deep limestone cave (itself known as Tham Sakkalin Savannakuha) a little to the northwest of Wat Long Khun. Many Buddha images from temples that have burned or otherwise fallen into decay are kept here; during Pii Mai Lao (Lao New Year) many local worshippers come to Wat Tham to pay homage and cleanse the images. The large stone-block entrance built around the mouth of the cave displays well-done relief work on stair pedestals, and is flanked by two large, ruined spirit houses and a couple of champa trees. An iron grate across the cave mouth is usually locked; enquire at Wat Long Khun for someone to come and unlock the gate and guide you through the cave. A donation of 500 kip is requested for this service; the cave is very long and dark, and parts of the cave floor are slippery, so it's a good idea to go with a guide. Bring a torch (flashlight). There are several other caves nearby that are easily found and explored with local help, though none is quite as extensive as Tham Sakkalin Savannakuha.

At the top of a hill above Wat Long Khun and Wat Tham is peaceful **Wat Chom Phet** (established 1888), from where there is an undisturbed view of the town and river. A small thâat here contains the bones of Chao Thong Di (wife of King Sakkalin), who died in 1929.

Nearby **Wat Xieng Maen** was founded in 1592 by Chao Naw Kaewkumman, son of Setthathirat, but it fell into ruin and had to be rebuilt in 1927. The newer sim contains a few artefacts dating from the original temple, including the original doors. This spot is especially sacred to Xieng Maen residents because it once housed the Pha Bang – on its way back to Luang Prabang in 1867 following a lengthy stay in Vientiane – for seven days and seven nights.

Getting There & Away Boats can be chartered from Luang Prabang's northern pier to Wat Long Khun for 3000 kip round trip or you can wait for the infrequent ferry boats which charge just 100 kip per passenger.

Markets

Luang Prabang's main marketplace, **Talaat Dala**, stands at the intersection of Thanons Kitsalat and Latsavong. Although not huge by Vientiane standards, it nonetheless features an impressive array of hardware, cookware, dried or preserved foodstuffs, textiles and handicrafts.

The main fresh market, **Talaat Sao**, is at the intersection of Thanon Phothisalat and Thanon Phu Wao near the river and Wat Pha Baat Tai. Also important for fresh produce is **Talaat Vieng Mai** at the north-eastern end of Thanon Photisan. There is also a small morning vegetable and fruit market where Thanon Kitsalat terminates at the Mekong river.

Places to Stay – bottom end

Viengkeo Hotel (☎ 212271) on Thanon Setthathilat is a funky two-storey house that has seven plain two and three-bed rooms with shared bath for 4200 kip (3000 kip for Lao citizens) per room. The staff and mostly local clientele are friendly and welcoming, but virtually no English or French is spoken. An upstairs veranda sitting area overlooks the street.

Around the corner near Wat Wisunalat is the basic but well-run *Rama Hotel* (☎ 212247) where large, clean doubles with fan and private cold-water bath cost 5000/7000 kip single/double a night. The restaurant downstairs becomes a disco at night – for maximum quiet be sure to request a room at the back and top of the hotel.

Vannida Guest House (☎ 212374), 87/4 Thanon Noranarai, is a huge, atmospheric 80-year-old ex-colonial mansion in the quiet residential neighbourhood of Ban That Luang, a few blocks south-west of Talaat Dala. Simple rooms with unscreened windows cost US$8 single, US$10 double. Toilet and shower facilities are shared. Meals are served in a large dining area downstairs.

Less than a block away, on the same side of the street in Ban That Luang, *Boun Gning Guest House* (☎ 212274) offers rooms with screened windows in a modern house for US$6/8 single/double, with shared facilities. All rooms come with floor or ceiling fans plus wall-mounted exhaust fans. Breakfast is available in the small reception area at the front of the house.

Khem Karn Food Garden (see Places to Eat) on the Nam Khan has three basic huts behind the restaurant area for rent for 10,000 kip. Toilet and bathing facilities are shared.

Places to Stay – middle

The friendly, guest house-style *Muangsua Hotel* (☎ 212263) on Thanon Phu Wao has economy fan rooms for US$15, one-bed air-con rooms for US$20 and two-bed air-con rooms for US$25. All rooms come with toilet and hot-water shower. The nearby *Manoluck Hotel* (☎ 212250, fax 212508), recently constructed in the modern Lao style (classic motifs melded with modern function), offers 30 rooms with large mini-fridge, TV, air-con and private hot-water bath for US$25 to 35 depending on number of beds. Most guest rooms are at the back of the building, hence they're protected from street noise, while the restaurant and reception are at the front.

Phousy Hotel (☎ 212292) is well located at the intersection of Thanons Kitsalat and Phothisalat, at the site of the former French Commissariat. Standard rooms equipped with air-con and hot-water bath are US$20/25 single/double, while larger rooms with slightly better furnishings cost US$25/30. The Phousy has an interior restaurant as well as a garden snackbar out front. It's a quiet place to stay in spite of its in-town location; during the cool season small tour groups often use this hotel. The 39-room Phousy is currently being upgraded; when renovations are complete room rates will probably jump to the US$40 to 50 range.

The *New Luang Prabang Hotel* (☎ 212264), next to the office of Luang Prabang Tourism, offers 15 medium-size rooms on three floors, all with air-con, fridge and hot water, for US$30 single/double. It's an OK place, if a bit sterile.

Silivongvanh Hotel, a large cement place on Thanon Phu Wao opposite Wat That Luang, began construction in 1994 but work was suspended in 1995; if completed its major asset will be its proximity to the bus terminal.

Places to Stay – top end

The *Villa Santi* (formerly Villa de la Princesse, ☎ /fax 212267) on Thanon Sakkalin, about midway between the Royal Palace Museum and Wat Xieng Thong, was the first place in Luang Prabang to take advantage of the abundant French-Lao colonial architecture. Formerly the residence of Crown Princess Khampha, the villa was taken over by the national government in 1976 but returned to the princess and her family in 1991. She and her husband extensively remodelled the 120-year-old residence and decorated it with Lao art and antiques.

In 1992 they opened the villa as an 11-room guest house, where comfortable air-con rooms with private bath cost US$40 single/double. A new wing opened in 1995 closely mimics Luang Prabang's classic French-Lao architecture; standard rooms here also cost US$40, while larger suites are available for US$55. Regional cuisine is served in separate upstairs dining rooms in each building; in the old wing there are a few tables and chairs on an adjacent terrace overlooking the street. During the high season (December through February) the Santi is often booked out.

Formerly the official residence of Prince Si Souvannaphoum, the rambling *Hotel Souvannaphoum* (☎ 212200) opposite the Provincial Office on Thanon Phothisalat completed renovations under French supervision in 1995. Spacious, well-decorated air-con rooms cost US$74/79 single/double, larger suites go for US$79/85 and there are a few smaller rooms for US$60/65. A large parlour downstairs is a perfect place to do some quiet reading or postcard-writing; an adjacent dining room serves French and Lao cuisine. A new two-storey wing added to the property contains large air-con rooms with attached bath and private terraces facing a garden for US$52/57 single/double.

Sitting on the crest of Phu Wao (Kite Hill) on the eastern edge of town, the *Phu Vao Hotel* (☎ /fax 212134) has gone by several names, including Ratchathirat, Luang Prabang and Mittaphap. Now under French management, the modern rooms here have air-con, private bath and telephones. There is also a pool, bar and large restaurant. Rates are US$45 to 60 depending on room location (those with city views cost more).

Currently under construction on Thanon Bunkhong, the *Champa-Lao Hotel* is a large two-storey, palace-style place with high-ceilinged rooms and a variety of guest facilities, including a Lao herbal sauna. Rates for the Champa Lao were not yet available as we went to press.

Places to Eat

Luang Prabang has a cuisine all its own. One of the local dining specialities is *jaew bǫng*, a jam-like condiment made with chillies and dried buffalo skin. A soup called áw lám, made with dried meat, mushrooms, eggplant and a special bitter-spicy root, is also a typical Luang Prabang dish (roots and herbs with bitter-hot effects are a dominant force in Luang Prabang cuisine). Other local delicacies include phák nâam, a delicious local watercress that's rarely found outside the Luang Prabang area, and khái pâen, dried river moss fried in seasoned oil and topped with sesame seeds.

Very good and authentic Lao food is available at Malee Lao Food, a rustic wooden eatery run by Malee Khevalat on Thanon Phu Wao. Her house specialties include áw lám, khái pâen, phák nâam, làap (mixed with eggplant in the local style) made with water buffalo, deer or fish, áw pǎa-dàek (fish-sauce curry), tǎm-sôm (green papaya salad), pîng nâam-tók (marinated meat barbecued on skewers), tôm jaew pǎa (spicy fish and eggplant soup), kǎeng awm (a very bitter and hot stew) and sáa (minced fish or chicken salad with lemon-grass and ginger).

Also on hand at Malee are lào-láo, home-distilled liquor darkened with la-sá-bǐi (a herb that's said to be an appetite-sharpener), khào kam (local rice wine) and Lao beer. Prices are very reasonable; three or four people could sit down to a Lao feast at one of the low wooden tables here and share four or five dishes with ample beer or lào-láo for under 10,000 kip. Malee is open daily from 10 am to 10 pm.

More basic but also quite good is the Vieng Mai Restaurant (an English sign reads 'Lao Restaurant'), a small, wooden local Lao restaurant near Talaat Vieng Mai with very tasty làap, tôm yám pǎa (fish and lemongrass soup), jěun pǎa (fried fish) and sticky rice.

Young Koun Restaurant, across the street from the Rama Hotel, makes a good 'Salad Luang Prabang', a savoury arrangement of local watercress, sliced boiled eggs, tomatoes and onions with a unique dressing. Stir-fried long beans here are also good, and tôm yám (lemon-grass soup with fish or chicken) is a house speciality. Two or three doors east of the Young Koun is the equally

good Visoun Restaurant, which serves mostly Chinese food. Both restaurants are open from early in the morning till late at night and have fairly extensive bilingual menus; Visoun serves Chinese khǎo-nóm khuu and other pastries in the early morning.

Further north-east along the same road, the indoor-outdoor Luang Prabang Restaurant caters to a mostly falang clientele with consistent if relatively toned-down Lao and Chinese dishes.

Along the Mekong river are several small thatched-roof, open-air restaurants with passable Lao food, including the View Khaem Khong and Bane Hous. Around the bend on the west bank of the Nam Khan is the semi-posh Khem Karn Food Garden (also called Sala Khem Kane), a larger thatched-roof place with good river views.

A small night market sets up along the river on Thanon Phothisalat near the Vientiane ferry landing, beginning at 5 pm. Illuminating their wares with candlelight after dark, vendors here offer delicious stuffed tomatoes (màak dẹn yat sài) among many other delights; also look for khǎo-nóm bạ-pîng, pancakes made with rice and shredded coconut.

Of the main tourist hotels in town, the Villa Santi offers the best and most authentic cuisine – primarily because the chef is the daughter of Phia Sing, who was the last king's personal chef (and author of the only book on Lao cuisine to be published in English). Breakfast at the Santi is usually a Western-style egg-and-toast affair (though fǒe is available), while lunch and dinner are Lao or Lao-French. French wines are available, but don't miss the house drink called 'Return of the Dragon', a blend of banana liqueur and lào khào kam. Khào kam, a local red, semi-sweet, slightly fizzy wine made from sticky rice, is abundantly and inexpensively available by the bottle in Luang Prabang. It can be very good or very bad depending on the brand.

The dining room at Hotel Souvannaphoum reportedly serves good French food and the decor is superior; the plat du jour costs US$5, while set lunches and dinners are US$9 and US$11 respectively. The restaurants in the *Phousy* and *Phu Vao* hotels are decent for Lao and international food, though like the Luang Prabang Restaurant the Lao food served here is formulated for falang palates. The Phu Vao has the better service and is also a bit of a nightspot – the poolside tables are a popular gathering place and on weekends there is sometimes a live band.

Luang Prabang's first independently owned falang eatery, *Bar-Restaurant Duang Champa*, is housed in a white two-storey colonial near the Nam Khan. The extensive menu includes set meals such as steak frites or poulet grillé et frites for a bargain 3000 to 3500 kip, along with ice cream, pâté, sandwiches, a few Lao dishes and imported French wines by the glass or bottle. It's open daily 9 am to 11 pm.

If you're lucky you may run into a colourful Lao ice cream vendor around town who announces himself in French with 'Les enfants attendent les fies!' ('Children are waiting for fairies!'). His ice cream is only fair, but he speaks good French and a little English.

Entertainment
The only regular nightclub in town is attached to the *Rama Hotel* – it's a very low-key affair with a live band and a loyal Lao clientele who move easily from lam wong to the Electric Slide. Most of Luang Prabang is sound asleep or at least nodding off behind a bottle of khào kam by 10 pm.

Things to Buy
Centrally located Talaat Dala market has the best overall selection of textiles and handicrafts, including several silver vendors who sell a variety of old and new pieces at reasonable prices. For quality silver, visit the workshop of silversmith Thithpeng Maniphone, in Ban Wat That (follow the signs opposite Hotel Souvannaphoum). Thithpeng crafted silverware for Luang Prabang royalty before 1975 (Thailand's royal family are now some of his best customers). He has 15 apprentice silversmiths working under him

to create his designs, but still does the most delicate work himself, including ceremonial swords and spears.

An outdoor gift shop next to the snackbar on the front grounds of the Phousy Hotel offers antique textiles and souvenirs. The Villa Santi and Phu Vao Hotel also have small gift shops with Lao handicrafts. Luang Prabang Gallery, just south of the Provincial Hospital, sells T-shirts, postcards and handicrafts.

Sakura Photo on Thanon Setthathilat near the Rama and Viengkeo hotels has the best selection of films, including Fujichrome 100 slide film. It's also the only place in town with a photocopy machine available to the public.

Getting There & Away
Air Lao Aviation flies daily to Luang Prabang from Vientiane – sometimes twice a day. The flight takes only 40 minutes and the foreigners' fare is US$46 one way. There are four flights per week to/from Phonsavan (35 minutes, US$31) and three flights per week from Huay Xai (50 minutes, US$42), plus one or two flights per week to/from Luang Nam Tha (30 minutes, US$34) and Udomxai (35 minutes, US$25). Flight frequency to/from Luang Nam Tha and Udomxai depends largely on passenger load and availability of aircraft; the only way to find out for sure is to ask at Lao Aviation a day in advance of scheduled departures.

When flying into Luang Prabang, try to get a window seat – the view of the town as the plane descends over the mountains in preparation for landing is excellent.

The US$2 million Thai-assisted upgrading of Luang Prabang airport is due for completion in 1996 so that it can receive larger flights from Vientiane and possibly Chiang Mai, Thailand. The new terminal was designed by Lao architect Hongkad Souvannavong, who also designed the Lao Embassy in Bangkok and the National Assembly in Vientiane.

Airline Offices Lao Aviation (☎ 212172) is on the same road as the Rama Hotel (but west of Thanons Kitsalat/Setthathilat), around the corner from the Viengkeo Hotel on the way to Wat Manolom on the south side of the street. Even if you have a return reservation from Luang Prabang, you should confirm it the day before your scheduled departure.

Bus It is possible but not recommended to travel by road out of Luang Prabang. Many of the roads are dangerous, both due to their poor condition and due to security problems from dissident groups.

To/From Vientiane Luang Prabang can be reached via Route 13 from Vientiane (420 km) but until the road is completely graded and paved – and until the security situation is improved – it's a trip for the foolhardy. So far the road is finished from Vientiane as far as Kasi, roughly two-thirds of the way. See Dangers & Annoyances in the Facts for the Visitor chapter and the Kasi section of the Vientiane Province chapter for important information on bandit/rebel attacks between Kasi and Luang Prabang.

For the record, a direct bus from Vientiane to Kasi leaves Vientiane's Talaat Sao terminal between 6.30 and 7 am, arriving in Kasi around 3.30 or 4 pm; the fare is 1700 kip per person. From this point north, there may be another bus on to Luang Prabang for 5000 to 7500 kip, or you may have to wait for a friendly truck driver going that direction. The last unpaved, rutted 80 km stretch between Kasi and Luang Prabang takes 10 to 12 hours by truck, depending on the number of passengers. This section of the road is twisty and mountainous – not for the squeamish.

From the Luang Prabang end, buses (trucks with wooden carriages) go all the way to Vientiane for 10,000 kip (foreigner price; the Lao pay 7000 kip). To Kasi costs 7500 kip (5000 kip local price) and to Vang Vieng costs 9000 kip (6000 kip local price). Local prices are usually available going north but not heading out of Luang Prabang; in fact virtually all transport out of Luang Prabang follows a two-tier pricing system.

The preceding information on road trans-

port is not meant as a recommendation to travel this route; on the contrary you should avoid travelling on Route 13 between Vang Vieng and Luang Prabang (or vice versa) unless you hear from reliable sources that this section of road is secure.

To/From Other Provinces Luang Prabang is linked with Udomxai Province by road via Nambak (Route 1) and via Muang Xai to Luang Nam Tha Province (Route 2). See the Udomxai Province Getting There & Away section later in this chapter for details. It's also possible to reach Xieng Khuang via Route 7 (which continues east into northern Vietnam), but the road is high and beset with natural and political hazards.

Boat As usual in Laos, river ferries are a major form of transport to other towns. In Luang Prabang the main landing for long-distance Mekong river boats, at the north-west end of Thanon Kitsalat, is called Thaa Héua Méh.

Speedboats use a landing at Ban Don, six km north of Luang Prabang. A jumbo to Ban Don from Talaat Dala can be chartered for 1500 kip. From Ban Don into town foreigners are charged a standard 800 kip for a shared jumbo; to charter one you must pay 4800 kip.

To/From Vientiane Several times a week cargo boats leave Vientiane's Kao Liaw jetty on the Mekong river for the 430 km river trip to Luang Prabang. The duration of the voyage depends on river height, but is typically four or five days upriver, three days down. From Vientiane the fare is 12,000 kip per person.

For downriver (Vientiane-bound) journeys the local boat service charges foreigner prices that are 50% higher than local fare (and 50% higher than those charged in Vientiane): Tha Deua 3600 kip (four to five hours), Pak Lai 9000 kip (11 hours), Vientiane 18,000 kip (two nights, three days). As always, visit the boat landing the day before your intended departure to confirm that there will indeed be a boat.

Speedboat trips downriver to Vientiane take eight or nine hours and cost – including the 'foreigner surcharge' – 47,250 kip. From Vientiane to Luang Prabang speedboats cost 30,000 kip.

See Getting There & Away in the Vientiane section in the Vientiane Province chapter for further information on this route.

To/From Pakbeng & Huay Xai It's also possible to travel by boat along the Mekong river north-west to Pakbeng (160 km) on the Sainyabuli/Udomxai border (for road trips north to Muang Xai) or all the way to Huay Xai (300 km) in Bokeo Province, both of which are now open to foreigners carrying the proper permits.

By slow river ferry the trip to Huay Xai takes two days with an overnight in Pakbeng. The passenger fare is 12,000 kip from Luang Prabang (9000 kip in the reverse direction), only 6000 kip as far as Pakbeng (4000 kip reverse).

Faster and smaller speedboats reach Pakbeng in three hours, Huay Xai in six or seven. The inflated fares out of Luang Prabang are 13,500 kip and 27,000 kip respectively (9000 kip and 18,000 kip downriver until two-tier pricing fever catches on). To charter a speedboat the boat pilots usually ask that you pay the equivalent of six passenger fares but they'll usually go if you pay for four spaces – often they have paid cargo to carry, too. If you want to share the cost of hiring a boat with other passengers it's best to show up at the northern pier the day before you want to leave and see what your prospects are. Then show up again around 6 am the morning of your intended departure to queue up. Speedboat passengers have been required to wear life vests and helmets since a Thai passenger was killed in a boat mishap just south of Pakbeng in 1992.

Speedboat fares are often quoted in Thai baht, though either kip or baht (or US dollars) are acceptable payment.

To/From Nong Khiaw & Muang Khua An alternate way to Luang Prabang from Muang Xai in Udomxai Province is via Nong Khiaw in northern Luang Prabang Province, which is about 127 km by road or along the Nam Ou river. The Nong Khiaw landing is sometimes referred to as Muang Ngoi, the village on the opposite bank of the Nam Ou, or as Nambak, a larger village to the west. Shared speedboats between Luang Prabang and Nong Khiaw cost 8000 kip upriver, 5200 kip downriver, and take around 2½ hours when the water is high enough; during the dry season some stretches of the upper Nam Ou can be treacherous and most pilots won't attempt the trip. From Nong Khiaw it's an hour west to Nambak by passenger truck.

Further upriver from Nong Khiaw are the riverbank villages of Muang Khua (205 km from Luang Prabang) and Hat Sa Neua (265 km), both jumping-off points for Phongsali Province excursions. Speedboats to Muang Khua cost 18,000 per person from Luang Prabang (12,000 kip in the reverse direction) and take four to five hours. To Hat Sa Neua, a short truck ride from Phongsali's capital, speedboats cost 28,500 kip (18,000 kip reverse) and take up to six hours.

Be sure to enquire thoroughly as to river conditions before embarking on a Nam Ou trip; from mid-February on it's not unusual for speedboat pilots to get stranded in Nong Khiaw, unable to bring their boats back till the rains arrive the following May or June.

Once Route 13 north parallelling the Nam Ou between Luang Prabang and Nambak is upgraded and paved, speedboat service along this route will most likely be discontinued.

Getting Around

To/From the Airport Shared jumbos or mini-trucks charge a uniform 1000 kip per foreigner (less for Lao) from the airport into town; in the reverse direction you can usually charter an entire jumbo for the same price.

Local Transport Most of the town is accessible on foot. Jumbos and motor samlor charge around 200 kip per km, with a 300 kip minimum.

The Rama Hotel rents bicycles for 1000 kip per day; Villa Santi has a few bikes available for loan to guests.

AROUND LUANG PRABANG
Pak Ou Caves ถ้ำปากอู

About 25 km by boat from Luang Prabang along the Mekong river, at the mouth of the Nam Ou, are the famous Pak Ou caves (Pak Ou means Mouth of the Ou). The basic attraction here is the two caves in the lower part of a limestone cliff which are stuffed with Buddha images of all styles and sizes (but mostly classic Luang Prabang standing Buddhas). The lower cave, called Tham Ting, is entered from the river by a series of steps and can easily be seen in daylight. Stairs to the left of Tham Ting lead round to the upper cave, Tham Phum, which is deeper and therefore requires artificial light for viewing – be sure to bring a torch (flashlight) if you want to see both caves. Entry to the caves costs 700 kip.

On the way to Pak Ou, you can have the boatman stop at small villages on the banks of the Mekong. Opposite the caves at the mouth of the Nam Ou, in front of an impressive limestone cliff called Phaa Hen, is a favourite spot for local fishers.

Villages near Pak Ou The most common village stop on the way to the caves is **Ban Xang Hai**, which means Jar-Maker Village because at one time that was the local cottage industry here. Nowadays the jars come from elsewhere, and the community of around 70 residents here fills them with lào-l o made in the village. A team of Australian archaeologists has excavated pots beneath the village that may be 2000 or more years old.

At **Ban Thin Hong**, opposite the jar village and close to Pak Ou, a recently excavated cave has yielded artefacts dating back 8000 years, including stone, bronze and metal tools, pottery, skeletons and fabrics. As yet the site hasn't been developed for tourism, but visitors with serious interest can contact Than Thongsa at the Dept of Museums & Archaeology in Vientiane for permission to explore the area.

Opposite Pak Ou on the north bank of the Nam Ou, an arduous path over the limestone ridge leads to a seldom-visited **Hmong village**.

During the late dry season (January to April) local villagers paddle to sandbars in the middle of the Mekong and pan for gold using large wooden platters.

Getting There & Away You can hire boats to Pak Ou from the pier at the back of the Royal Palace Museum. A long-tail boat holding up to 10 passengers should go for US$20 to 25 for the day, including petrol. The trip takes 1½ to two hours upriver, and one hour down. If you stop at villages along the way, it will naturally take longer. Speedboats from Ban Don can cover the distance in half an hour upstream, 20 to 25 minutes down; for one of these you'll have to pay US$25 for a trip of two hours or less. Speedboats can take up to six passengers.

If you go to Pak Ou as part of a guided tour, the guide will most likely stop in at least one village along the way. A picnic lunch is usually brought along to be eaten at the sala between the two caves.

Ban Phanom & Mouhot's Tomb
ບ້ານພະນົມ

This Thai Lü village east of Luang Prabang, around four km past the airport, is well known for cotton and silk hand-weaving. On weekends, a small market is set up in the village for the trading of hand-woven cloth, but you can turn up at any time and the villagers will bring out cloth for inspection and purchase. Even if you don't expect to buy anything, it's worth a visit to see the villagers working on their handlooms. Some of the textile hawkers can be very aggressive.

Between Ban Phanom and the river is the simple tomb of French explorer Henri Mouhot, known as the person who 'discovered' Angkor Wat. Mouhot died of malaria in Luang Prabang in 1861; his engraved tomb was neglected until found by foreign aid staff in 1990. Mouhot's tomb can be found about four km along the Nam Khan from Ban Phanom; follow the road along the river till you see a wooden bench on the left, descend a track opposite toward the river, then walk about 300m along an overgrown path (upriver from the bench) to reach the whitewashed tomb. If this sounds too complicated, ask someone from the village to guide you to the grave for a tip of 500 kip.

Getting There & Away Buses from Luang Prabang to Ban Phanom leave from Talaat Dala several times a day for 200 kip. You can also walk here from town in a half-hour or so.

Kuang Si Falls ນ້ຳຕົກກວາງຊີ
This beautiful spot 29 km south of town features a wide, multi-tiered waterfall tumbling over limestone formations into a series of cool, turquoise-green pools. The lower level of the falls has been turned into a public park with shelters and picnic tables built by a UNDP/FAO project in 1987. Vendors sell drinks and snacks.

A trail ascends through the forest along the left side of the falls to a second tier which is more private (most visitors stay below) and has a pool large enough for swimming and splashing around. A cave behind the falls here goes back 10m. You can continue along a more slippery extension of the trail to the top of the falls for a view of the stream that feeds into it. The best time to visit the falls is between the end of the monsoon in November and the peak of the dry season in April.

On the way to Kuang Si you'll pass Ban Tha Baen, a scenic Khamu village with a cool stream, rustic dam and several miniature waterfalls.

Getting There & Away Guided tours to the falls booked through a local agency cost US$50 to 60 and include transport and lunch at the falls. Freelance guides in Luang Prabang offer trips by jumbo for US$12 to 15; they can take up to six people for this price.

Taat Sae Falls ນ້ຳຕົກຕາດເຊ
A conjunction of the Huay Sae and the Nam Khan, the falls at Taat Sae feature multi-level limestone formations similar to those at

Kuang Si except that the resulting pools are more numerous, the falls are shorter in height, and the site is much closer to Luang Prabang. Popular with local picnickers on weekends, it's almost empty during the week.

A 30 minute jumbo ride south of town will take you to the turnoff from Route 13, then to the pristine Lao village of Ban Aen on the Nam Khan river. Jumbo drivers will go to Ban Aen for 6000 kip return, including waiting time in the village while you visit the falls for a few hours; jumbos can take up to six passengers for the same price. You could also easily reach Ban Aen by bicycle – there's a sign reading 'Tat Se' at the Route 13 turnoff.

From the riverbanks at Ban Aen you can hire a boat to the falls – only five minutes upstream – for 1000 kip each way.

NONG KHIAW (MUANG NGOI)
ໜອງຂຽວ

Anyone travelling by road or river from the capital to Phongsali, Hua Phan or Xieng Khuang provinces stands a good chance of spending some time in Nong Khiaw, a village on the banks of the Nam Ou in northern Luang Prabang Province. Route 1, which extends west to east from Muang Xai to Nam Noen (at the junction with Route 6 in Hua Phan Province), crosses the river here via a steel bridge.

The village of Nong Khiaw (Green Pond) is little more than a haphazard collection of palm thatch and bamboo shacks on the Nam Ou's west bank. Sometimes it's referred to as Muang Ngoi, which is actually the group of shacks on the east bank, and sometimes it's called Nambak, which is actually 23 km west of Nong Khiaw by road.

Places to Stay & Eat
Near the bridge and river landing is an unnamed bamboo *guest house* with very basic three-bed rooms for 1000 kip per person or 2000 kip for the whole room. There's no running water or electricity; you must bathe using buckets of water carried from the river.

A couple of very simple outdoor *cafes*

next to the parking area for passenger trucks offer fish soup, sticky rice and noodles.

A slightly more pleasant wooden *guest house* is available in the larger village of Nambak – let's be generous and call it a town. Water buckets and candlelight do the job as in Nong Khiaw. The selection of places to eat extends to around a half dozen noodle shops.

Getting There & Away

See Getting There & Away in the earlier Luang Prabang section for details on transport to Nong Khiaw from Luang Prabang.

Japanese pickups onward to Muang Xai leave Nong Khiaw roughly three times a day – around 8 to 9 am, 12.30 to 1 pm and 3 to 4 pm. The trip takes five hours and costs 4000 kip.

Similar trucks leave the riverbank terminal every two hours or so to Nambak. This short section of Route 1 is quite good by Lao standards and the 23 km trip takes just a half hour; the fare is 500 kip.

Xieng Khuang Province

ແຂວງຊຽງຂວາງ

Flying into Xieng Khuang Province, one is first struck by the awesome beauty of high green mountains (including the three highest peaks in the country, the loftiest being Phu Bia at 2819m), rugged karst formations and verdant valleys. But as the plane begins to descend, you notice how much of the province is pock-marked with bomb craters in which little or no vegetation grows. Along with Hua Phan, Xieng Khuang is one of the northern provinces that was most devastated by the war. Virtually every town and village in the province was bombed at some point between 1964 and 1973. It has also been the site of numerous ground battles fought over the last 150 years.

The province has a total population of around 200,000 (a surprising increase since the Revolution, probably due to the influx of

Vietnamese), mostly comprised of lowland Lao, Vietnamese, Thai Dam, Hmong and Phuan. The original capital city, Xieng Khuang, was almost totally bombed out, so the capital was moved to nearby Phonsavan (often spelt Phonsavanh due to the Vietnamese influence) after the 1975 change of government. Near Phonsavan is the mysterious Plain of Jars (Thong Hai Hin).

The moderate altitude (average 1200m) in central Xieng Khuang, including Phonsavan and the Plain of Jars, means an excellent year-round climate – not too hot in the hot season, not too cold in the cool season and not too wet in the rainy season. The coldest months are December and January, when visitors should come prepared with sweaters or pullovers, plus a light jacket for nights and early mornings.

History

Although briefly part of the Lan Xang Kingdom in the 14th century, Xieng Khuang has more often than not been either an independent principality or a vassal state of Vietnam called Tran Ninh. From the early 19th century onward central Xieng Khuang – including the Plain of Jars – has been a recurring battle zone. In 1832 the Vietnamese captured the Phuan king of Xieng Khuang, publicly executed him in Hué and made the kingdom a prefecture of Annam, in which the people were forced to adopt Vietnamese dress and customs. Chinese Ho also ravaged Xieng Khuang in the late 19th century, which is one of the reasons Xieng Khuang accepted Siamese and subsequent French protectorship later that century.

Major skirmishes between the Free Lao and the Viet Minh took place in 1945-46, and as soon as the French left Indochina the North Vietnamese began a buildup of troops to protect Hanoi's rear flank. By 1964 the North Vietnamese and Pathet Lao had at least 16 anti-aircraft emplacements on the Plain of Jars, along with a vast underground arsenal. By the end of the '60s this major battlefield was undergoing almost daily bombing by American planes as well as ground combat between the US-trained and supplied Hmong

NORTHERN LAOS

UXO in Xieng Khuang

Contrary to popular belief, the preponderance of unexploded ordnance (UXO) found in the province today was left behind by ground rather than air battles and includes French, Chinese, US, Soviet and Vietnamese materials. Such UXO contamination – munitions, mortar shells, white phosphorous canisters, land mines and cluster bombs – affects over half the population in terms of land deprivation and accidental injury or death. About 40% of the 60 to 80 casualties per year are children, who continue to play with found UXO – especially the harmless-looking, ball-shaped cluster bombs – in spite of public warnings. Several groups have been working to clear the province of UXO, most recently the Britain-based Mines Advisory Group, and a new UN-sponsored UXO trust fund will increase the availability of multilateral aid for this purpose. Among the potential contributors will be the US government, which recently lifted its ban on foreign aid to Laos. ■

---

army and the North Vietnamese-Pathet Lao forces. Among the US military in Laos the area was known as 'PDJ', an acronym for the French term Plaine de Jarres.

A single 1969 air campaign – part of the secret war waged in Laos by the US Air Force and the CIA – annihilated at least 1500 buildings in the town of Xieng Khuang, along with some 2000 more on the Plain of Jars, erasing many small towns and villages off the map permanently. Continuous saturation bombing forced virtually the entire population to live in caves; 'The bombs fell like a man sowing seed' according to one surviving villager.

North Vietnamese troops did their share of damage on the ground, destroying nearby Muang Sing, a city famous for its temples, and towns or villages controlled by the RLA in the western portion of the province.

Now that peace has come to Xieng Khuang, village life is returning to a semblance of normality, although the enormous amount of war debris and undetonated bombs spread across the central and eastern portions of the province are a deadly legacy that will remain for generations.

PHONSAVAN ໂພນສະວັນ

Xieng Khuang's new capital district (pop 57,000) has grown tremendously over the last five years – there's a new airfield, two semi-paved main streets lined with tin-roofed wooden shops, a sprinkling of new concrete structures, two markets, a few government buildings, a bank and several modest hotels. A heavy sense of impermanence remains in the air, however, as if the inhabitants half expected carpet bombing to resume at any time.

Traditionally, the area surrounding Phonsavan and the former capital of Xieng Khuang has been a centre of Phuan language and culture (part of the Thai-Kadai family, like Lao, Siamese and Thai tribals). The local Vietnamese presence continues to increase and you'll hear Vietnamese in the streets almost as frequently as Lao and Phuan.

On some current Lao maps, Phonsavan is labelled 'Muang Pek'; outside the province most Lao (including Lao Aviation) still refer to the capital as 'Xieng Khuang'.

Information

The staff at the Muong Phouan Hotel, Phu Doi Hotel and Auberge de Plaine de Jarres can answer questions on local sights and travel logistics, as well as provide guide services. Lane Xang Travel (☎ Phonsavan 144), which has a branch office near the main dry market, is also a good source of information.

Except for those establishments with their own generators, Phonsavan is electrically powered from 6 to 9 pm only.

Money Opposite the Phu Doi Hotel is a branch of Aroun May Bank but it doesn't seem to keep regular hours. Don't count on cashing any travellers' cheques here – bring plenty of cash to tide you over.

Post & Communications There is now a post office on the main road near the two central markets. Domestic phone service is available here but the sound quality can be very bad; connections with Vientiane often produce unintelligible conversation. With adjustments in the national satcom system, telecommunications should improve in the near future.

Medical Services The Phonsavan hospital, on the road to the new airport, isn't too bad as far as Lao provincial hospitals go, although for any major trauma it's quite handicapped.

Dangers & Annoyances Take care when walking in the fields around Phonsavan as undetonated live bombs are not uncommon. Muddy areas are sometimes dotted with 'bomblets' – fist-size explosives that are left over from cluster bombs dropped in the '70s.

Places to Stay – bottom end
Hay Hin Hotel, a simple wooden place on the main street near the market, has basic two-bed rooms with mosquito nets and shared cold-water bath for 2500 kip per night. Mattresses and walls are thin but the bathrooms are clean. Further east along the same street, the well-maintained *Dorgkhoune Guest House* offers nicer rooms with mosquito nets and better quality mattresses for 3000 kip single/double and 4000 kip triple with shared facilities, or 4000 kip single/double, 5000 kip triple with private shower and toilet.

Continuing east along the same street, the *Muong Phuan Hotel* has similar but more numerous rooms with attached bath for 5000 kip single/double. Those in the back annex are quietest. This hotel also has its own restaurant.

Next door to the Mouang Phouan, the *Vieng Thong Guest House* looks OK from the outside but it's not that well kept inside. Another drawback is the unhelpful all-male staff, who sit around drinking in the lobby nightly. Simple two-bed rooms with shared facilities cost 3000/4000 kip single/double.

Back down toward the market are two more fair choices. The two-storey *Vanhaloun Hotel* charges 4000 to 5000 kip for simple rooms with shared bath, 8000 kip for larger rooms with private shower and toilet. It's very clean and food can be arranged.

Opposite the bus terminal near the main market and Lane Xang Travel, the *Seng Mixay Guest House* has large rooms with two to four beds for 4000 kip, smaller rooms in back for 3000 kip. One of the latter rooms has a small veranda that faces the rear of the property. Toilet and shower facilities are shared. Despite its main street location it's fairly quiet.

A couple of km south-west of the downtown area, toward the airport and the Plain of Jars (Site 1), the *Phu Doi Hotel* (formerly the Mittaphap Hotel) is housed in a two-storey, V-shaped building opposite Aroun May Bank. Ordinary rooms with shared toilet and cold-water shower facilities are overpriced at 8000 kip; the three VIP rooms come with hot-water showers and good mattresses, overall better value at 15,000 kip.

On a ridge above the town and surrounding valley is the relatively new *Auberge de Plaine de Jarres* (also known locally as the Phu Pha Daeng Hotel), a quiet resort with several two-room cabins each with its own fireplace and private hot-water bath. There is also a separate dining/sitting area with a fireplace and picture windows overlooking the valley. The cabins are owned by Vientiane's SODETOUR agency, which usually books them as part of their Xieng Khuang packages. When not part of a package deal, the cabins cost US$40 to 50 a night. During the cool season, when night-time temperatures hover near freezing, the fireplaces and hot-water baths are very attractive.

Places to Eat
The current situation offers more choice than was available two years ago, when it was almost nothing but fõe, meal after meal. Besides the hotels with restaurants (Auberge de Plaine de Jarres, Mouang Phouan Hotel), along the main street through town are several noodle shops and two places regularly serving rice.

The clean and well-run *Sangah (Sa-Nga) Restaurant* near the market and post office offers an extensive menu of Chinese, Thai and Lao food, including good yám, tôm yám, khào khùa and fõe, plus a few Western food

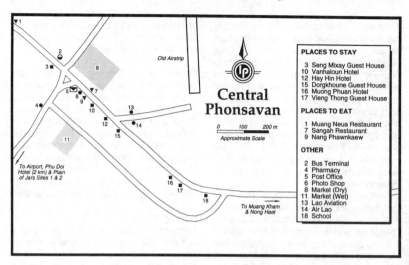

items. Some expats working in Phonsavan have been known to survive on a nightly diet of steak & chips here. Exactly opposite the Sangah, the friendly *Nang Phonkaew* serves the best főe in town.

Further west beyond the bus terminal, look for the *Muang Neua Restaurant*, similar in scope if not quality to the Sangah.

You can also buy food, including fresh produce, in the *wet market* behind the post office.

Entertainment
You might not expect to find any nightlife in this outpost, but a warehouse-like new *disco* near the Phu Doi Hotel, on the road that leads to the Plain of Jars, provides live music nightly for the entertainment of local Lao airmen and anyone else who happens along.

Getting There & Away
Air The Soviet ME-8 helicopters that used to fly to Phonsavan have been replaced by Chinese Y-12 turboprops. Planes fly to/from Vientiane once or twice daily (40 minutes, US$37), and to/from Luang Prabang thrice weekly (35 minutes, US$31). Delays are common on the latter flight. The Lao Avia-

tion office (☎ Phonsavan 103), a wooden shed off the main street in town, is open daily 7 to 11 am and 1.30 to 3.30 pm; these hours are not strictly followed.

Military-owned Air Lao flies biplanes out of Phonsavan to various provincial capitals around the country. Fares are slightly lower than those charged at Lao Aviation, but schedules is highly erratic and the office, which is opposite Lao Aviation, usually stands empty. There is a strong suspicion that Air Lao aircraft are used to fly Lao opium from north-eastern Laos to the Cambodian border.

Road Xieng Khuang Province is best reached by road from the north, ie from Udomxai, northern Luang Prabang (but not southern Luang Prabang) or Hua Phan provinces.

To/From Udomxai & Sam Neua Potholed Route 1 carries passengers east across Udomxai and northern Luang Prabang till the road terminates at Route 7, where a change of buses at the village of Nam Noen continues southward to Phonsavan. It's best to break this journey up by spending the night in Nambak or Nong Khiaw (both in northern Luang Prabang) so that you can get an early start and make it straight from Nambak to Phonsavan in one day – a journey of about 12 hours, including a change of bus in Nam Noen. You're also more likely to find public transport in the early morning; afternoon buses are few and far between in this part of the country. The alternative is to spend the night in the dismal guest house in Nam Noen. Expect to pay about 3000 kip from Nambak (or Nong Khiaw) to Nam Noen, another 3000 kip from the latter to Phonsavan.

To/from Sam Neua, capital of Hua Phan Province, it's a 12 hour, 238 km road trip to Phonsavan via Routes 6 and 7. You must change buses at the junction of Routes 6 and 1 (Nam Noen). Logistically one of the best ways to do this trip is to fly to Sam Neua from Vientiane, then head south by road to Phonsavan. For details see the Sam Neua section.

To/From Vientiane & Luang Prabang It's also possible to reach Xieng Khuang by road from Vientiane or southern Luang Prabang via Route 13 and Route 7 (the junction for the two roads is at Phu Khun, about 38 km north of Kasi). But it's a gruelling two or three day trip along a high mountain road, and western Route 7 is considered unsafe – due to rebel attacks – as far east as Muang Sui. This stretch passes military checkpoints which you're highly unlikely to transit without special permission from the Dept of Defence.

To/From Pakxan Route 6 connects Phonsavan with Pakxan in Bolikhamsai Province but the road is in deplorable condition – especially south of Tha Thom (102 km from Phonsavan), where it's only passable in the dry season. Route 6 south also passes through 'insecure' Saisombun Special Zone.

From February to June it's possible to go by road to Tha Thom, then boat to Pakxan (three days down, five or six up) along the Nam Xan. Although this road-river combination is logistically more feasible than trying to do Route 6 all the way, the danger

of guerrilla attacks in Saisombun preclude either journey as a sensible travel choice until security improves.

Other From the bus terminal opposite the main market, there are public buses to Muang Kham (two hours, 900 kip) and Nong Haet (three hours, 1800 kip), plus larger Russian or Chinese trucks to Muang Sui (two or three hours, 1500 kip) and Nam Noen (six hours, 3000 kip). There are also share taxis – mostly old Volgas or Toyotas – to/from Muang Kham, for 1200 kip per person; this price fluctuates with the availability of petrol from Vietnam, on which Phonsavan depends.

Getting Around
Jumbos are the main form of public transport in town. The standard foreigner price anywhere within a three km radius is 500 kip. You can get a one-way trip to Thong Hai Hin (Plain of Jars, Site 1) for 1000 kip though most drivers want a roundtrip fare of 5000 kip including wait time.

Cars and jeeps can also be hired through the guide services at Lane Xang Travel or Auberge de Plaine de Jarres for jaunts outside of town.

PLAIN OF JARS ທົ່ງໄຫຫິນ
The Plain of Jars is a large area extending around Phonsavan from the south-west to the north-east where huge jars of unknown origin are scattered about in at least a dozen groupings. Site 1 or **Thong Hai Hin** (Stone Jar Plain), 12 km from Phonsavan and the largest of the various sites, features 250 jars which weigh mostly from 600 kg to one tonne each; the biggest of them weighs as much as six tonnes. Despite local myth, the jars have been fashioned from solid stone (a tertiary conglomerate). The stone doesn't seem to have come from the area; a visiting geologist told me he thought it was a type of sandstone that may have come from the mountains dividing Xieng Khuang and Luang Prabang provinces (see the colour section for details).

Many of the smaller jars have been taken away by collectors, but there are still several hundred or so on the plain in the five major sites considered worth visiting. Site 1, the biggest and most accessible, has two pavilions and restrooms that were built for a visit by Thailand's crown prince. This is also where you'll find the largest jar on the plain – it's said to have been the victorious king's and so it's called Hai Jeuam. There's an entrance fee of 1000 kip.

Nearby Site 1 is a Lao air force base which, along with the new pavilions, somewhat mars the jar-viewing atmosphere. Large bottle-shaped clearings on surrounding hill slopes have traps at the 'bottle-top' for snaring sparrows – the birds are apparently attracted by the shape.

Two other jar sites are readily accessible by road from Phonsavan. Site 2, 23 km from town, is known locally as **Hai Hin Phu Salato** and features 90 jars spread across two adjacent hillsides. Vehicles can reach the base of the hills, so it's only a short if steep walk to the jars.

More impressive is 150-jar Site 3, also known as **Hai Hin Laat Khai**. It's 28 km from town on a scenic hilltop near the charming Lao village of Ban Sieng Dii in Muang Kham district, north-east of Phonsavan. The latter contains a small monastery where remains of Buddha images damaged in the war are displayed. The villagers, who live in unusually large houses compared to those of the average lowland Lao, grow rice, sugarcane, avocado and banana. To reach the jar site you must hike around two km along rice paddy dikes and up the hill.

Many smaller sites can also be seen in Muang Kham district, but none contains more than 40 jars or so. Only Sites 1, 2 and 3 can be considered reasonably cleared of UXO. Even at these sites you should take care to stay within the jar areas and stick to worn footpaths.

See colour aside opposite page 208 for more historical and archeological information.

Getting There & Away

You can charter a jumbo from Phonsavan to Site 1 for 5000 kip return. For Sites 2 and 3

your best bet is to arrange a jeep and driver through one of the hotels or Lane Xang Travel. The latter charges US$30 for transport to Sites 2 and 3 for up to four persons, with visits along the way to Ban Sieng Dii near Site 3 and to a Hmong village in the Muang Kham area. The services of an English-speaking guide cost extra.

PHONSAVAN TO NONG HAET

The best road in the province at the moment is Route 7, which links Xieng Khuang with Hanoi via Muang Kham and Nong Haet.

Near Km 27 on the way to Muang Kham (north side of the road) is **Nong Pet**, a large picturesque spring surrounded by rice fields; it's said to be the source of the Nam Ngum river.

A sizeable **Hmong market** is held at 7 am on Sunday about 30 km east of Phonsavan on the way to Muang Kham. Between Muang Kham (55 km from Phonsavan) and Nong Haet (60 km) it's not unusual to see small poppy fields – which typically bloom in January – along the side of the road next to Hmong villages. You may also see Thai Dam funerary shrines – large white tombs with prayer flags, food offerings and a pile of the departed's worldly possessions.

Muang Kham is little more than a rustic highway trading post but there are several jar sites in the vicinity (see the Plain of Jars section earlier). Farther east along the same road, 120 km from Phonsavan, is the market town of **Nong Haet**, which is only about 25 km short of the Vietnamese border.

See the Getting There & Away section under Phonsavan, above, for information on bus and share taxi travel to Muang Kham and Nong Haet.

Mineral Springs ບໍ່ນ້ຳຮ້ອນ

Two hot mineral springs can be visited near Muang Kham. **Baw Yai** (Big Spring) is the larger of the two and lies 18 km from Muang Kham, 51 km from Phonsavan. It has been developed as a resort with bungalows and bathing facilities, and was originally built by Kaysone Phomvihane's wife for visiting politicos. The spring source is in a heavily

---

War Scrap

War junk has become an important part of the local architecture and economy in Xieng Khuang. Torpedo-shaped bomb casings are collected, stored, refashioned into items of everyday use or sold as scrap. Among the most valuable are the 1.5-metre-long casings from US-made cluster bomb units (CBUs), which split lengthways when released and scattered 600 to 700 tennis-ball-size bomblets (each containing around 250 steel pellets) over 5000-sq-metre areas.

Turned on its side, a CBU casing becomes a planter; upright they are used as fenceposts or as substitutes for the traditional wooden stilts used to support rice barns and thatched-roof houses. Hundreds of casings used like this can be seen in Xieng Khuang villages along Route 7, which stretches north-east all the way from Phonsavan to Hanoi, or in villages in the vicinity of the old capital. Aluminium spoons sold in local markets are said to be fashioned from the remains of downed American aircraft.

Farmers from around the province keep piles of war junk – including pieces of F-105 Thunderchiefs, A-1 Skyraiders and other US planes downed during the war – beneath their stilt houses or in an unused corner of their fields, using bits and pieces as needed around the farm or selling pieces to itinerant scrap dealers who drive their trucks from village to village. These trucks bring the scrap to small warehouses in Phonsavan, where it is sold to larger dealers from Vientiane. The going purchase price for scrap in Phonsavan is 100 kip per kilogram. Eventually the scrap is melted down in Vientiane or across the Mekong River in Thailand as a source of cheap metal.

Considering this keen commerce in bits of metal, it is very difficult to believe anyone in Laos could possibly be harbouring live American MIAs (soldiers 'missing-in-action') in the face of US reward offers, which range from US$10,000 for simple information leading to the rescue of any US soldier to millions for anyone who can actually produce a live MIA. ■

---

wooded area where several bamboo pipes have been rigged so that you can bathe nearby.

In a large cleared area farther from the source are a couple of private bathing rooms where hot water is piped in from the spring into American-style tubs; a soak in one of these costs 500 kip. Nearby bungalows cost 1500 kip per night per person. Baw Yai is now open to the public; entry is 750 kip for foreigners, 1000 kip for vehicles.

Baw Noi (Little Spring) is the smaller of the two and feeds into a stream just a few hundred metres off Route 7, a few km before Baw Yai on the way from Muang Kham. You can sit in the stream right where the hot spring water combines with the cool stream water and 'adjust' the temperature by moving from one area to another.

Tham Piu ຖ້ຳປຶວ

When we first visited this cave in 1989 local guides had trouble finding it, but it has since become a standard on Xieng Khuang tour itineraries. The cave is near the former village of Ban Nameun where approximately

400 villagers, many of them women and children, were killed by a single rocket fired into the cave (most likely from a Nomad T-28 fighter plane manned by a Royal Lao Air Force pilot) in 1969. The floor of the large cave, in the side of a limestone cliff, is littered with rubble from the partial cave-in caused by the rocket as well as minor debris left from the two-storey shelter built into the cave. Near the entrance are a few human bones that have been unearthed.

Although Tham Piu is certainly a moving sight, the journey to the cave is the main attraction, since it passes several Hmong and Thai Dam villages along the way and involves a bit of hiking in the forest. From the cave mouth is a view of the forest and plains below. A stream and small irrigation dam at the base of the cliff is picturesque – an undetonated US bomb in the stream almost directly below the mouth of the cave was recently defused and removed. Another cave known as Tham Piu Sawng (Tham Piu 2) can be found a little higher up on the same cliff. This one has a small entranceway that opens up into a large cavern; since it wasn't bombed, the cave formations can be seen in their original state. Don't forget your torch (flashlight).

Tham Piu is just a few km beyond Muang Kham on Route 7.

Getting There & Away You can hire a jeep and driver in Phonsavan for around US$20 to 30 a day for trips to Tham Piu and back.

To get to Tham Piu by public transport, you'd have to take a Nong Haet bus and ask to be let out at the turnoff for Tham Piu. From the turnoff, start walking towards the limestone cliff north of the road until you're within a km of the cliff. At this point you have to plunge into the woods and make your way along a honeycomb of trails to the bottom of the cliff and then mount a steep, narrow trail that leads up to the mouth of the cave. It would be best to ask for directions from villagers along the way or you're liable to get lost; live ordnance is another danger. Better still, find someone in Phonsavan who knows the way and invite them to come along for an afternoon hike.

OLD XIENG KHUANG (MUANG KHUN)
ຂ໌ຽງຂວາງເກົ່າ (ເມືອງຄຸນ)

Xieng Khuang's ancient capital was so heavily bombarded during the 1962-73 war (and ravaged in the 19th century by Chinese and Vietnamese invaders) that it was almost completely abandoned by 1975. Twenty years after war's end the old capital is once again inhabited (population 14,000), though only one of the original French colonial buildings still stands, an old commissariat now used as a social centre. The rubble that was once quaint provincial French-Lao architecture has been replaced by a long row of plain wooden buildings with slanted metal roofs on either side of the dirt road from Phonsavan. Officially the town has been renamed Muang Khun. Many of the local residents are Phuan, Thai Dam or Thai Neua, along with a smattering of lowland Lao and Vietnamese.

Several Buddhist temples built between the 16th and 19th centuries lie in unrestored ruins. The foundation and columns, along with a large seated Buddha, of **Wat Si Phum** are still standing at the east end of town.

That Phuan (also known as That Chomsi), a tall 25 to 30m jedi built in the Lan Xang/Lanna style, and a few isolated Buddha statues, are all of **Wat Phia Wat** that managed to survive the bombing. Sadly the only intact Xieng Khuang-style temples left in Laos today – characterised by striking pentagonal silhouettes when viewed from the front – are in Luang Prabang.

Ban Naa Sii, near Wat Phia Wat, is a sizeable Thai Dam village.

Places to Stay & Eat
The town has one funky wooden *hotel* with rooms for 1500 kip. Near the market in the centre of town are a couple of noodle shops. *Haan Khai Foe* (the English sign reads 'Restaurant') opposite the market is the best choice for lunch.

Things to Buy
If you ask around you may be able to buy antique Thai tribal (especially Phuan, Thai Dam or Thai Neua) textiles in town.

Getting There & Away
Four buses a day ply the bumpy, torturous 36 km route between Phonsavan and Muang Khun for 1000 kip per person. The going rate for a guide and car is around US$60.

MUANG SUI ເມືອງຊຸຍ
Once a city of antique Buddhist temples and quaint provincial architecture, Muang Sui became a Neutralist headquarters and 'Lima Site 108' (a landing site used by US planes) during the Indochina War. The North Vietnamese Army totally wrecked Muang Sui late in the war after running the RLA out of Xieng Khuang Province.

Like Xieng Khuang, the town is now rebuilding and is part of a new district called Phu Kut (population 20,200). Ruins of several older temples can be seen; **Wat Ban Phong**, which still has resident monks, displays a beautiful bronze Xieng Khuang-style Buddha said to hail from the 14th century.

14th century bronze Buddha at Wat Ban Phong

Adjacent to town, a large natural lake called **Nong Tang** is another attraction.

There are no public lodgings as yet in Muang Sui.

Getting There & Away

Large passenger trucks leave Phonsavan's bus terminal daily around 7 am; occasionally there's a second departure around 1 pm. Depending on road conditions and the number of stops along the way, this trip can take anywhere from two to four hours. Route 7 to Muang Sui from Phonsavan is in a very poor state of repair most of the way. The Nam Ngum river crosses the road just east of Muang Sui and during the rainy season you'll have to ferry across by boat.

In Phonsavan you can hire a jeep and driver to Muang Sui and back for 50,000 kip or US$50 through Lane Xang Travel – add US$20 for the services of an English-speaking guide.

Hua Phan Province
ແຂວງຫົວພັນ

The mountainous north-eastern province of Hua Phan, enclosed by Vietnam to the north,

east and south-east, Xieng Khuang to the south-west and Luang Prabang to the west, has a total population of 246,000, of whom around 46,800 live in the provincial capital of Sam Neua ('Northern Sam', a reference to its position toward the north end of the Nam Sam river. Twenty-two ethnic groups make the province their home, predominantly Thai Khao, Thai Daeng, Thai Meuay, Thai Neua, Phu Noi, Hmong, Khamu, Yunnanese and Vietnamese. The Vietnamese influence is very strong as Sam Neua is closer to (and more accessible from) Hanoi than Vientiane; because the province falls on the eastern side of the Annamite Chain, Thai TV and radio broadcasts don't reach here either.

For much of the last half-millennium Hua Phan has been either an independent Thai Neua kingdom or part of an Annamese vassal state known as Ai Lao. It also came briefly under Siamese protectorship as a state called Chao Thai Neua in the 1880s. Except for a two-year interval (1891-93) when the state was exposed to Luang Prabang suzerainty, Hua Phan really only became a Lao national entity under French colonial rule. During the

---

Samana

Hua Phan is perhaps most infamous for the re-education camps established around the eastern half of the province immediately following the 1975 revolution. Such camps, called *samana* in Lao, mixed forced labour with political indoctrination to 'rehabilitate' thousands of civil servants from the old regime. Though most of the camps were closed by 1989, Re-education Camp No 7 is believed to remain in operation somewhere near the Vietnamese border; another camp near the village of Sop Pan also reportedly still retains captives. According to Amnesty International, three political prisoners were sent to Hua Phan from Vientiane in 1992. AI also reports that at Sop Hao at least two camp inductees held since 1975 were only released in 1994. Although as many as 30,000 people were thought to have been interned in 1978-79 – the samana's numeric peak – the Lao government has never issued a statement either confirming or denying the existence of the camps. ■

colonial era the French commissariat at Sam Neua allowed a great deal of autonomy to local Thai Neua meuang chiefs and village headmen. By the end of the Indochina War, all traces of the French presence had been erased.

As a tourist attraction the province's main claim to fame is that Vieng Xai served as the headquarters for the Lao People's Party throughout most of the war years. Textiles in the 'Sam Neua' style – of tribal Thai origins – are another draw. The best textiles are said to come from the areas around Muang Xon and Sop Hao.

SAM NEUA (XAM NEUA) ຊໍາເໜືອ

Tucked away in a long narrow valley formed by the Nam Sam at about 1200m above sea level, Sam Neua is so far one of the country's least visited provincial capitals. Verdant hills, including pointy Phu Luang, overlook the town but other than the natural setting there's not a lot to write home about. District residents are mostly Lao, Vietnamese and Hmong, along with some Thai Dam, Thai Daeng and Thai Lü.

On a rise to one side of town sit the town hall, post office and police station. The latter can be found at the back of a newer building with peaked rooflines and blue trim; this is where you must check in and out of the province. Hua Phan Province has its own tourist office in Sam Neua but the sole staff member does very little except collect his meagre salary and host the occasional LNTA official from Vientiane. The office has no printed handouts or maps, and neither English nor French is spoken.

Things to See & Do

For local residents, Sam Neua boasts what is perhaps the largest and fastest-growing **market** in the region. Consumer products from China and Vietnam line up alongside fresh produce and domestic goods. Sam Neua-style textiles can be found inside the main market building; prices can be very good although quality is generally not up to the standard found in Vientiane. Local

Hmong, Thai Dam, Thai Daeng and Thai Lü frequent this market.

A 1979 **independence monument** mounted by a red star sits on a hill at the north-west edge of town; it's an easy climb, worthwhile for the modest view. From this hill you can continue walking to **Wat Pho Xai**, a distance of around two km from the market. The only monastery in town, with only five monks in residence (the minimum for holding monastic ordination ceremonies), the wat features a small sim that was destroyed during the war and rebuilt in 1983. Two small **thâat** on the way to the independence monument are the only remnants of local prewar temples.

Places to Stay & Eat

Welcome to Laos' rat capital. *Lao Houng Hotel*, near the south end of a bridge spanning the Nam Sam near the market, is a crumbling Chinese/Vietnamese-style place built around a couple of courtyards by the Vietnamese in 1975 – though it looks much older due to the poor concrete engineering used. Until recently under government management, the hotel is now privately managed but is still pretty basic. Ordinary rooms with two beds, mosquito nets, private shower and toilet cost 3500 kip, while suites with spacious sitting rooms and one large bed are 6500 kip. Electricity is available only for a few hours in the evening and there is no running water. The hotel also has a major rat problem – in the middle of the night rats running about in the ceiling sound like children playing football on the roof.

Around the corner from Lao Houng on a perpendicular street up from the market, the *Dokmaidieng Guest House* is a three-storey cube with fairly clean rooms with shared facilities for 1500 kip per bed. Rats, yes, but not as many as at the Lao Houng. Further on along the same road is the *Phou Loung Guest House*, a pleasant two-storey place similar to the Dokmaidieng but with more atmosphere. Rates are 1500 kip per person; the rats are free.

There are only two regular public eating establishments in town, both inside the market compound. For anything other than

NORTHERN LAOS

fŏe you must order in advance. *Joy's Place* is the better of the two and is open daily 6.30 am to 9 pm. *Hin Restaurant* is similar-looking but it's not as clean and service is a little slack.

Getting There & Away
Air Lao Aviation has scheduled flights between Vientiane and the renovated airport at Sam Neua thrice weekly (75 minutes, US$67 one way). The Y-12 landing involves an impressive descent through the narrow Sam Neua valley.

Road Sam Neua can be reached by road from both Xieng Khuang and Udomxai provinces. Route 6 from Xieng Khuang is quite good by Lao standards between Phonsavan and Nam Noen, a small truck stop at the junction of Routes 6 and 1 just north of the Hua Phan Province border. Between Nam Noen and Sam Neua it's a steep, winding, rough but highly scenic dirt road that passes through numerous Lao, Hmong and Khamu villages. It's usually necessary to change buses (actually large converted Russian or Chinese diesel trucks) in Nam Noen; each leg of the journey takes six hours and costs 2500 kip. Occasionally – perhaps once a week – there's a direct passenger truck between Sam Neua and Phonsavan, but total travel time still involves at least 11 hours.

South-east of Sam Neua, Route 6 links with Route 1 from Nambak (Luang Prabang Province) and Muang Xai (Udomxai Province). To/from Muang Xai (Udomxai) involves a similar change of bus in Nam Noen. The Nam Noen to Muang Xai leg costs 7000 kip and involves spending the night in Muang Ngoi. The long section between Muang Ngoi and Sam Neua is a very tough ride. There's a direct truck between Muang Xai and Sam Neua a couple of times a week for 10,000 kip.

The Vietnamese border at Sop Hao is open to Vietnamese and Lao with the proper papers but it is unlikely that a foreigner would be allowed to cross here. The road from Sam Neua to Sop Hao is reportedly quite good, so if the border opens to foreigners Hanoi would become a logical Hua Phan gateway.

AROUND SAM NEUA
A 580 sq km area of forested hills along the Nam Sam between Vieng Xai and Sam Tai in the south-eastern section of the province was named the **Nam Sam National Biodiversity Conservation Area** in 1993. Nam Sam is thought to be a habitat for wild elephant, gaur, banteng, tiger, clouded leopard, various gibbons, Asiatic black bear and Malayan sun bear. Despite the NBCA designation – and even though the area can only be reached by a single 4WD track from Vieng Xai – shifting cultivation by hill tribes and cedar logging by a Yunnanese company threaten the natural forest cover.

Taat Saloei, about 37 km south of Sam Neua off the road to Nam Noen, is a multi-level waterfall said to be very beautiful just after the rainy season. Further south near the town of Hua Muang, about four km off the Sam Neua-Nam Noen road, is **Suan Hin**, a 'stone forest' so-named for its pillar-like rock formations.

The road north-east from Sam Neua to **Sop Hao** on the Vietnamese border passes by several Hmong and tribal Thai villages.

SAM NEUA TO VIENG XAI
If you aren't able to arrange prior admission to the caves at Vieng Xai (see below), the district is still worth wandering about for its scenic beauty. Between Km 11 and 12, coming from Sam Neua, is a sizeable Hmong Lai (Striped Hmong) village called **Ban Hua Khang**. You'll begin seeing **karst formations**, many with obvious cave entrances, after Km 13 along with pretty little valleys terraced in rice. At Km 20 is a three-way intersection; the right fork reaches Vieng Xai after nine km, then continues to Nam Maew on the Vietnamese border (87 km from Sam Neua), while the left fork terminates in 40 km at Paa Haang, also on the Vietnamese border.

Six km before the Vieng Xai turnoff, coming from Sam Neua, is 80m **Nam Neua Falls**. You can walk to the top of the falls straight from a bridge where the road crosses the Nam Neua just after the road forks toward Vieng Xai. For an all-in-one view from the bottom, take the left fork and proceed for two km till you see some terraced rice fields on the right-hand side of the road. A trail winds for a kilometre or so through the fields, along and across a stream and through bamboo thickets before reaching the bottom. You may have to ask locally for directions as the trail isn't particularly obvious. Be sure to apply insect repellent to your feet and ankles in order to keep the ants and leeches at bay. As usual, the falls are most beautiful just after the rainy season, when you can swim in the falls' lower pools.

VIENG XAI ວຽງໄຊ

Originally called Thong Na Kai (Chicken Field) because of the abundance of wild junglefowl in the area, the postwar name for this former Pathet Lao revolutionary headquarters means City of Victory. The district (population 32,800) sits in a striking valley of verdant hills and limestone cliffs riddled with caves, several of which were used to shelter Pathet Lao officers during the Indochina War.

The district capital itself is a small town that seems to be getting smaller as Sam Neua grows larger. The central market is a poor collection of vendors who can't afford transport to the provincial capital, 29 km away.

Caves

There are 102 known caves in the district, around a dozen with war history. The Vieng Xai caves are supposed to be open to the public as a revolutionary memorial and tourist attraction, but in everyday practice the local authorities thus far treat them as if they're some sort of military secret. Although the LNTA in Vientiane will tell you no special permission is needed to enter the caves, visitors aren't allowed in them (nor may they even photograph the cave exteriors) unless they can present special permission from Vientiane to the district officials. The easiest – and most expensive – way to arrange this is to go through a Vientiane travel agency, who will arrange for a guide and letter of introduction. Or you might try bringing a typed, signed and sealed

letter direct from the LNTA – one explaining how you don't really need written permission to enter the caves!

The setting of the caves – inside a narrow and precipitous limestone-walled valley surrounding the town of Vieng Xai– is quite impressive. The PL leadership first starting using them in 1964 because the caves are virtually unassailable by land or air. Today those considered historically the most important are named after the figures who once occupied them. They are within easy walking distance of town.

Tham Thaan Souphanouvong (called Tham Phaa Bong before the war) was deemed fit for royalty and housed Prince Souphanouvong, the so-called 'Red Prince'. Wooden walls and floors, as well as natural cave formations, divided the cavern into a bedroom, meeting room and various other spaces. Souphanouvong eventually built a separate house in front of the cave entrance and today the house is treated with the same combination of fear and respect as the cave.

Tham Thaan Kaysone, the office and residence of the LPP/PL chief – who served as prime minister and president from 1975 till his 1992 death – extends 140m into a cliffside that was scaled by rope before steps were added. Its various rooms included a political party centre, reception room, bedroom, recreation room, meeting room and library. Kaysone also built a handsome house in front of his cave. **Tham Thaan Khamtay**, named for the current prime minister, is an artificial cave dug out of a limestone cliff, similarly divided into various function rooms. One of the deepest caves at 200m is **Tham Xieng Muang**, which was used for hospital facilities. Other caves housed weaving mills, printing presses and other facilities needed by the PL to remain self-sufficient.

Places to Stay & Eat

At the moment you'd do better to stay in Sam Neua rather than in Vieng Xai as there's more choice of accommodation and food.

The Vietnamese-built *Vieng Xai Hotel* (also known as Hotel No 2) at the edge of town near a large pond was even more decrepit than its Sam Neua counterpart, the Lao Houng, when I visited. Though less than 20 years old, the hotel's windows mostly have no glass or bear only a few broken shards, and many of the doors have no latches or locks. A room costs 5000 kip single/double; toilet and shower facilities (no running water) are shared. A Vientiane-based company is currently renovating this hotel to provide a higher standard of accommodation.

Two *föe shops* in the market are the only places to eat. Rice isn't normally available unless you buy it in the market and cook it yourself.

Getting There & Away

Military-owned Air Lao flies between Vieng Xai and Vientiane a couple of times a week but it's nigh impossible to pin down the schedule except by simply showing up at Vieng Xai's minuscule airfield in the morning and asking.

The 29 km journey from Sam Neua to Vieng Xai takes around 45 minutes by private vehicle or about an hour by public bus.

Phongsali Province
ແຂວງພົງສາລີ

Enclosed on three sides by China and Vietnam, and cut off to overland travel from Udomxai and Luang Prabang to the south much of the year, Phongsali is northern Laos' most inaccessible province. Twenty-two ethnicities make up the province's population of approximately 152,000, among them Kheu, Sila, Lolo, Hanyi, Hmong, Pala, Oma, Eupa, Loma, Pusang, Mien, Iko (Akha), Ho, Thai Dam, Thai Khao, Thai Lü, Phuan, Khamu, Phai, Vietnamese and Yunnanese. Phu Noi (easily recognised by their white leggings) form the most numerous ethnicity, followed by Thai Lü, Ho, Akha and Khamu. Prior to the Sino-French Treaty

of 1895, Phongsali was an independent, Thai Lü-controlled principality attached to Xishuangbanna in southern Yunnan.

Phongsali's population density is 9.4 per sq km, the lowest in the country after Sekong and Attapeu. Opium poppy cultivation is widespread among the Hmong, Mien and Lolo in this province. As in Udomxai and Luang Nam Tha the Chinese presence has increased steeply with recent road and construction development.

Phu Den Din, the northernmost NBCA in Laos, covers 1310 sq km in the north-eastern corner of the province along the Lao-Vietnamese border and adjacent to Vietnam's Muong Nhe Nature Reserve. Mountains in this area reach up to 1948m and bear 77% primary forest cover. Many globally threatened or endangered mammals live in the area, including elephant, tiger, clouded leopard, banteng, gaur and Asiatic black bear.

PHONGSALI ພົງສາລີ

Built on the steep slopes of Phu Fa (1625m) at an elevation of around 1400m, Phongsali possesses a year-round cool climate that comes as a welcome relief during the hotter (March to May) season. It can be quite cold during the cool season with temperatures as low as 5° C at night, 10° during the day. Fog and low clouds arc common in the morning any time of year. In the wet season rainfall can be intense.

The capital district (population 25,000) is surrounded by rolling, deforested hills. If you've come expecting to see lots of colourfully garbed minorities in the market or around town, you'll be disappointed unless you arrive during a major holiday like Lao New Year in April, when residents from all around the province visit the capital. The best areas for hill-tribe village exploration are found in the extreme north-west corner of the province where there are no roads. Reaching this area involves walking two or more days.

A small ethnological **museum** established with French assistance and housed in one of the government buildings catalogues the costumes and traditional lifestyles of many of the resident ethnic groups.

Information
Electric power is available 6 to 9 pm only. There is a post office 100m west of the Phongsali Hotel but so far reliable long-distance telecommunications hasn't arrived in the capital.

Money A branch of Lane Xang Bank can exchange cash US dollars, Thai baht or Chinese yuan (but no travellers' cheques) for kip.

Immigration It can be difficult finding someone to provide the jâeng khào/jâeng àwk stamps you're legally supposed to collect when entering and leaving each province. If no-one will perform this task at the Hat Sa boat landing east of town, try the police station in the town itself.

Places to Stay & Eat
Phongsali has three places to stay now. Best is the new and sparkling, Chinese-built *Phongsali Hotel*, a centrally located four-storey building that's the highest structure in the province. The hotel offers 28 plain rooms, most with three beds (good mattresses), all with shared bath and toilet facilities, for 1500 kip per bed. A few rooms with large double beds go for 4500 kip. The staff speak Lao, Phu Noi and Chinese.

Opposite the Phongsali Hotel, the friendly *Laksun Hotel* is a two-storey, metal-roofed wooden structure with a few basic rooms with mosquito nets for 1200 kip per bed. There's a decent restaurant downstairs.

The wooden *Phoufa Hotel*, a former Chinese consulate and military base in the '60s, is another basic place with three beds per room (hard mattresses), mosquito nets and shared facilities for 1200 kip per person. The hotel commands a good view of surrounding area; downstairs is a spartan restaurant.

The three hotel restaurants are reasonably priced. Phongsali Hotel offers the largest menu, mostly Chinese food plus a few Lao dishes. There are several noodle shops on the main street through town toward the market; bowls of fõe are among the cheapest in the country, mostly 200 to 300 kip. Chinese beer is cheap all over town, while Beerlao is relatively expensive. The local lào láo is tinted green with herbs and quite a smooth tipple.

Hat Sa Hat Sa has a *guest house* with multi-bed rooms for 1000 kip per person.

Getting There & Away
Air There is no regular air service to Phongsali; in fact the landing strip at the capital is so small that none of Lao Aviation's turbo-props can safely land on it. Official visitors from Vientiane generally arrive by helicopter.

Road & River From Muang Xai in Udomxai Province it is possible to travel by road as far as Muang Khua in southern Phongsali. Buses leave twice a day (early morning and early afternoon) from either end as long as there are enough passengers; the four hour trip costs 2500 kip per person. The road to Muang Khua from Muang Xai is in fairly good condition – it continues east to Dien Bien Phu in Vietnam.

Once you reach Muang Khua, there is boat transport to Hat Sa in the centre of the province via the Nam Ou river – but only during high-water months (generally June to November, sometimes a month or so later depending on the volume of the annual monsoons).

From Muang Khua boats leave irregularly (in the mornings only) for Hat Sa. The slow boat costs 5000 kip per passenger and takes five to six hours, while speedboats cost just 7000 kip per person (foreigners may be asked for 11,000) and take a comfortable 1½ to two hours.

From Muang Khua a very bad road parallels the river north to the capital but – except for cargo trucks – it's generally used only in the dry months when boat travel is suspended.

Muang Khua and Hat Sa can also be reached by river from Luang Prabang direct along the Nam Ou into the heart of Phongsali Province (except when the river is low). See the Luang Prabang Getting There & Away section for further details.

A new road under construction between Udomxai and Phongsali will begin about 60 km north-east of Muang Xai and leave the current road to Muang Khua at a point about 30 km south-west of the latter, then head directly north – passing through many Lao Sung villages along the way. This new route will beat the current road-and-river trip by at least a day. A Shanghai company is using Chinese labour to build the road at a cost of US$5.7 million.

From Hat Sa From the boat landing at the small town of Hat Sa, passengers share a 4WD vehicle for the 20 km jaunt to Phongsali. Originally built by the French, this rutted and rough dirt track is locally known as the 'buffalo road' since it seems more fit for beast than vehicle. The trip takes 1½ to two hours and costs 1500 kip per person.

From China Another way to reach Phongsali by road is from Luang Nam Tha Province via Yunnan (see Getting There & Away in the Luang Nam Tha Province section later in this chapter for details). If the Yunnan-Phongsali border opens to foreign travel in the near future (it's now open to Chinese and Lao) it will be easier to reach Phongsali from Mengla, Yunnan, than from most points in Laos. Negotiations are currently underway between the provincial governments of Yunnan and Luang Nam Tha to allow foreigners to traverse this stretch of China. The road from the Lao town of Ban Pakha near the Chinese border to Phongsali is relatively good; local buses cost 700 kip per person and take about two hours to reach Bun Neua, where you must change to another bus (another 700B, two hours) for the final leg to the capital. There is a guest house in Bun Neua should you get stranded.

MUANG KHUA ເມືອງຂວາ
This small town sits at the junction of the Nam Ou river – the major north-south trans-port artery in and out of the province – and Route 4, which links Udomxai and Phongsali provinces with Dien Bien Phu in Vietnam.

Lane Xang Bank in Muang Khua can change dollars, baht, yuan – cash only – for kip. There's no electricity in town but individual generators power the town's hotels at night.

Places to Stay & Eat
A four-storey, white-painted *Chinese guest house* without an English or Lao name (look for '1989' incorporated into the 3rd-floor bannister) is the friendliest of the town's three hotels and keeps its generator running longer. Rates are 1200 kip per person in clean three and four-bed rooms. Toilet and bathing facilities are shared.

Nang Aen Kaew Hotel (no romanised sign), named for the friendly Lao lady who runs the place, offers five dark but relatively clean rooms for 2500 kip per room. The shared bathing facilities are not so clean. It's opposite the main bus stop.

Top-end in town is the *Muang Khoua Hotel*, a single-storey white building with a parking area for the self-propelled and fair lodgings for 3000 kip per room. Facilities are shared.

The Muang Khoua has its own Chinese restaurant. There's one other restaurant in town near the Chinese guest house.

Getting There & Away
See the earlier Getting There & Away section for Phongsali for details on transport to Muang Khua. The portmaster in Muang Khua speaks English relatively well.

Udomxai Province
ແຂວງອຸດົມໄຊ

This mountainous northern province is wedged between Luang Prabang to the east, Phongsali to the north-east, Luang Nam Tha to the north-west and Sainyabuli to the south, with a small northern section that shares a border with China's Yunnan Province (less than 60 km from Mengla in Yunnan's Xishuangbanna District). Most of the provincial population of 211,000 is a mixture of some 23 ethnic minorities, predominantly Hmong, Iko (Akha), Mien, Phu Thai, Thai Dam, Thai Khao, Thai Lü, Thai Neua, Phuan, Khamu, Lamet, Lao Huay and Yunnanese Chinese (Ho).

The Yunnanese presence has thickened recently with the influx of Chinese skilled labourers working in the construction industry as well as tradespeople from Kunming, the capital of Yunnan. In the '60s and early '70s the Chinese were well liked in Udomxai because they donated a network of two-lane paved roads radiating throughout the far north, using Udomxai as the central hub. This road system was very important in moving Pathet Lao and NVA troops and supplies around the north during the war. After the 1979 ideological split over Cambodia (China sided with the Khmer Rouge, Laos with Vietnam), the Chinese withdrew all support until rather recently. The new Chinese influx is regarded by many Udomxai inhabitants as economic infiltration since the road-building and construction is no longer foreign aid but paid work for hire, using plenty of imported Chinese materials and labour.

Because Udomxai has a road system of sorts (it has deteriorated considerably since the '70s but is still the best in the north), this province is the most accessible of the country's far northern provinces.

MUANG XAI ເມືອງໄຊ

The capital of Udomxai Province is most commonly called Muang Xai, though some maps label it Udomxai. Before the Indochinese War there wasn't much here but the district became a centre for Chinese troops during the war and today it's still a boomtown riding on imported Chinese wealth.

After roughing it through beautiful countryside along the Mekong river and Route 2 from Pakbeng (or from the east via Nong Khiaw and the Nam Ou) to arrive here, the town can be a bit of a disappointment. Basically it's two long strips of asphalt and dirt where Routes 1 and 2 intersect, flanked by wooden shacks, cement boxes and new construction sites set in the middle of a deforested valley. More traditional thatched-roof houses spread across the rim of the valley toward the base of the surrounding mountain range. If you get off the main street you can find some very picturesque village-like sections. A river flows through town.

The town is roughly 60% Lao Theung and Lao Sung, 25% Chinese and only 15% Lao Loum. Some 4000 Chinese workers may be in the area at any one time, and the Yunnanese dialect is often more commonly heard than Lao in the cafes and hotels. Most of the vehicles in town bear Vietnamese or Chinese licence plates; the town is also a conduit for caravans of new Japanese vehicles assembled in Thailand and being driven to China for resale.

About the only sight of interest is the large day market in the centre of town. A polyglot mix of people from around the province – including many Hmong and tribal Thai – come to buy and sell; most of the products on sale are Chinese or Vietnamese. The most interesting part of the market is in the rear where fresh produce and herbs – brought to market by small farmers – are sold.

Muang Xai has electrical power from 6 to 9 pm only.

Information
Money In town you can spend Chinese yuan, US dollars, baht or kip. Lane Xang Bank, on the edge of town on the road to Phongsali, can give you kip for dollars, baht or yuan but not vice versa. Nor are travellers' cheques yet accepted. Bring cash.

Post & Communications The post office, a large white and mustard-coloured building with a telecom tower about 120m west of the bus terminal, is open Monday to Friday 8 am to 4 pm, Saturday 8 am to noon. A telephone office in the same building is open daily 8 to 11.30 am, 2 to 4.30 pm and 6.30 to 9 pm.

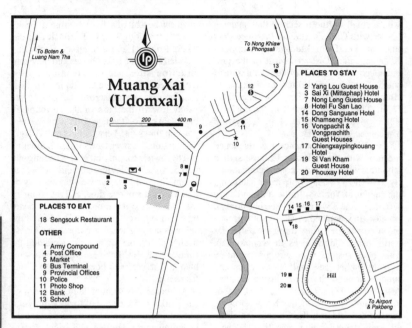

Muang Xai
(Udomxai)

0   200   400 m

PLACES TO STAY
2 Yang Lou Guest House
3 Sai Xi (Mittaphap) Hotel
7 Nong Leng Guest House
8 Hotel Fu San Lao
14 Dong Sanguane Hotel
15 Khamseng Hotel
16 Vongpachit &
   Vongprachith
   Guest Houses
17 Chiengxaypingkouang
   Hotel
19 Si Van Kham
   Guest House
20 Phouxay Hotel

PLACES TO EAT
18 Sengsouk Restaurant

OTHER
1 Army Compound
4 Post Office
5 Market
6 Bus Terminal
9 Provincial Offices
10 Police
11 Photo Shop
12 Bank
13 School

To Boten &
Luang Nam Tha

To Nong Khiaw
& Phongsali

To Airport
& Pakbeng

Hill

Immigration Except at Muang Xai airport, no-one in Udomxai seems interested in stamping your papers in or out of the province – perhaps they're too busy processing all the Chinese migrants. If you want to try, go to the police office, which is about 100m north-east of the bus terminal (rumour says this office may move to a new building across the road). You'll find the immigration department in room No 9.

Places to Stay

The number of places to stay in Muang Xai has expanded rapidly over the last two or three years. Nothing in town so far costs more than 10,000 kip, and most places are under 5000 kip. Virtually all of the hotels and guest houses are owned and operated by Chinese immigrants. Several function mainly as brothels for Chinese workers.

Perhaps the best accommodations in Muang Xai, at least for those who would like to get off the noisy, dusty main streets, are

two places at the end of a dirt road toward the eastern edge of town – the street entrance can be found about 300m east of the bus terminal. Lao Petroleum-owned *Phouxay (Phuxai) Hotel*, in a former Chinese consulate compound off the main street near the south end of town, offers clean two and three-bed rooms with mosquito nets, ceiling fans and shared bath and toilet facilities for 3000 kip per room for foreigners, 2000 kip for Lao. There are also a couple of rooms with private bath and toilet for 5000 kip. The rooms angle around a courtyard with monkeys in cages; there is a dining room that seems to open only for groups.

Next door to the Phouxay the friendly, family-run *Si Van Kham Guest House* (only the words 'guest house' are signed in English) has simple rooms with shared bath for 3000 kip single/double and rooms with attached bath for 5000 kip. There's a sitting area upstairs and operational restaurant downstairs.

Just west of and opposite the road that leads to the Phouxay Hotel and Si Van Kham Guest House is a string of cheap Lao and Chinese-owned lodgings, all similar two- and three-storey places, constructed of cheap materials, with small restaurants downstairs and rooms for 5000 to 10,000 kip a night. From the west, the first is the *Dong Sanguane Hotel*, which has very basic two-bed rooms with shared bath for 1000 kip per person, plus one three-bed room with sitting room and attached bath for 1500 kip per person. Next comes the *Khamseng Hotel*, which has only six rooms and won't accept foreigners – like the aforementioned, it's most likely a brothel for Chinese workers.

Third in the series is the more upscale, Lao-owned *Vongpachit Guest House*, a new place where clean rooms with good beds, vinyl furniture and private bathrooms with showers and tubs (no hot water yet, though the owners say it's coming) go for 5000 kip single/double. Immediately next door is the *Vongprachith Guest House*, owned by the same family as the preceding, which has older, simpler rooms for 2500 kip per person in rooms with shared facilities, or 5000 kip single/double with private bath. The restaurant downstairs is one of the best in the hotel row.

Next comes the scarey-looking *Chiengxaypingkouang Hotel*, a four-storey brown-brick place with a popular disco on the 1st floor. The rooms aren't bad, though there's lots of foot traffic up and down stairs much of the night and very little English or Lao is spoken. One-bed rooms with attached bath cost 3000 kip, two-bed rooms 4000 kip.

Back toward the west end of town near the post office, about 200m west of the bus terminal, stands the Chinese-run *Yang Lou Guest House*. The two-storey white building contains 12 basic but OK two and three-bed rooms which cost 2000 kip per room with shared toilet and shower, 3000 kip with private facilities.

Next door to the Yang Lou, opposite the post office, is the *Mittaphap Hotel* (the Chinese name is Sai Xi Hotel), a four-storey place where relatively clean three, four and five-bed rooms with hard mattresses and shared facilities cost 1000 kíp per bed. Nicer two-bed rooms with good mattresses, fan, air-con and attached bath cost 6000 kip per room. Similar rooms with hot-water showers and mosquito nets go for 10,000 kip. A 4th-floor patio offers good views of town; downstairs are a restaurant and snooker hall. Very little English or Lao is spoken. Choose a room that doesn't face the noisy main street, although things do quieten down between 10 pm and 5.30 am.

Two places almost opposite the bus terminal on the road north out of town are not recommended despite their convenient location. The dingy, three-storey *Hotel Fu San Lao* has three-bed rooms without bath for 1000 kip per bed on the 3rd floor but the bathroom is on the ground floor. The staff try to steer all foreigners toward rooms with fan, mosquito nets, shower and TV for 6000/8000 kip single/double; should you decide to stay here, be sure to check the rooms thoroughly as fans and lights aren't always working. The dimly lit nightclub downstairs supplies male guests with young Yunnanese girls. As usual at the Chinese-owned places in town, very little English or Lao is spoken. The *Nong Leng Guest House*, next to Hotel Fu San Lao, has basic rooms for 3000 kip per single/double, some with attached bath, some without.

On a rise behind the latter lodgings stands *Rich Mountain Hotel*, a massive Chinese hotel complex under construction.

Places to Eat

Sengaloun Restaurant, on the ground floor of the Vongprachith Guest House, is one of the better places to eat. The fare is basic Chinese rice and noodle dishes. The simple, wooden *Sengsouk Restaurant* opposite the Dong Sanguane Hotel offers the best fŏe in town.

A small wooden *cafe* at the entrance to the access road for the Phouxay Hotel and Si Van Kham Guest House has basic Chinese and Lao fare. It's open from around 7 am to 9 pm, though it's basically a lunch place for Chinese working nearby. There are six or seven other ramshackle wooden cafes along the main road in the vicinity of the market.

Getting There & Away

Air Lao Aviation flies between Vientiane and Muang Xai twice a week; the flight takes an hour and 20 minutes and costs US$71 one way for foreigners. Flights to/from Luang Prabang are more frequent – five times a week (one hour, 35 minutes; US$25) – and there are also weekly flights to/from Huay Xai (50 minutes, US$25).

The Lao Aviation office is in a small wooden building on the road to the airfield.

Road The starburst of Chinese-built bitumen roads emanating from Muang Xai are still in fair condition. Japanese pickups handle most of the public interprovincial transport; they park at a dirt area at the main crossroads (the intersection of Routes 2 and 1) in the centre of town. Each truck parks at its own signed (Lao only) stand and waits for a full load of passengers before leaving. The best time to catch a pickup out of town is between 7 and 8 am.

Route 2, the 140 km road between Pakbeng and Muang Xai, takes five or six hours by public transport. One or two pickups a day make the trip in either direction for 4000 kip per person – around 9 am in the morning is the most sure departure in either direction. You can usually charter a truck for 35,000 to 50,000 kip – with no stops along the way a light vehicle can cover the distance in about three hours.

Running east from Muang Xai to Nong Khiaw (129 km) on the banks of the Nam Ou in northern Luang Prabang Province is Route 1, a decent all-weather road with regular transport for 4000 kip per person, charters for 40,000 kip. The trip to/from Nong Khiaw takes four or five hours. It's possible to go on by road to Luang Prabang from Nong Khiaw but this 100 km section of Route 13 is in very poor condition; it's much quicker to go by river – if not via Nong Khiaw then via Pakbeng.

Another road, Route 4, heads north-east from Muang Xai to Muang Khua in southern Phongsali Province, then continues eastward to the Vietnamese border. Passenger trucks to Muang Khua cost 2500 kip per person and take four hours. Heading north from Muang Khua to the Phongsali capital, most people take boats along the Nam Ou rather than use the very bad road that parallels the river. Another way to get to Phongsali is via Luang Nam Tha Province, cutting across the southern tip of China's Yunnan Province from Muang Sing (through Mengla) to Phongsali; this is quicker than going straight from Muang Xai. So far only Chinese and Lao are allowed to do this but who knows what the possibilities will be if the borders are opened on either side?

Boten, now a legal border crossing between Laos and China, can be reached in four hours by public pickup for 3000 kip.

Nam Tha is 117 km north-west of Muang Xai via all-weather Route 2, a fairly easy five hour truck ride for 3000 kip per person (40,000 kip charter).

River See Getting There & Away under Pakbeng later in this section for details on year-round Mekong river transport from Luang Prabang.

When the Nam Ou is high enough (usually June through December and into some portion of January), you can take a speedboat to Nong Khiaw from Luang Prabang for 8000 kip shared or around 45,000 chartered. If the river situation is doubtful, be sure to ask around for several opinions before risking it – river travellers have been known to become stranded between Luang Prabang and Nambak.

If conditions are right, a circle route beginning and ending in Luang Prabang (with Udomxai, Nam Tha and/or Bokeo in the middle) can be accomplished by taking the Nam Ou upriver and the Mekong downriver.

AROUND MUANG XAI

North and south of town are a string of Hmong villages where the tribespeople have come down from higher elevations – either because of mountaintop deforestation due to swidden agriculture, or because they have been pressured by the Lao government to become more integrated into lowland society.

East of town off Route 1 at Km 11 is **Taat Lak Sip-Et** (Km 11 Waterfall), a slender cataract that cascades over a limestone cliff into a Nam Beng tributary. *Baw nãam hàwn* or **hot springs** can be found 28 km from Muang Xai near Muang La, off the road to Phongsali near the banks of the Nam Pak river.

LUANG PRABANG TO MUANG XAI VIA PAKBENG

Although only a trickle of foreign visitors have done it yet, the river-and-road trip from Luang Prabang to Udomxai's capital is an experience in itself. Three hours by speedboat, or a day's travel by river ferry, the Mekong river journey between Luang Prabang and Pakbeng (jumping-off point for the road to Muang Xai) passes craggy stone cliffs, sandy shores, undulating mountains, fishing villages and expanses of both primary and secondary monsoon forest.

Pakbeng itself is worth an overnight if time allows (see the Pakbeng section below), then it's on to Muang Xai via Route 2, an old Chinese-built road that parallels the Nam Beng most of the way. The road is mostly paved but is very rough in spots. Along the way you'll pass Phu Thai, Thai Lü, Hmong, Thai Dam, Lao and Khamu villages, plus primary monsoon forest alternating with secondary growth and slash-and-burn plots.

At Km 90 (about a third of the way to Muang Xai) is **Muang Houn**, the largest village between Pakbeng and Muang Xai and a convenient rest stop. Muang Houn has one guest house with rooms in the 1000 to 2000 kip range, plus plenty of places to eat or stock up on food supplies. Around Km 18 to Km 21 (counting south from Muang Xai) are at least a dozen Hmong villages cultivating poppy.

There are a couple of scenic waterfalls not far from the main road. **Taat Yong** is said to be the largest and is a 12 km hike from Km 87. There are plans to build a vehicle road to the falls eventually. A more fanciful plan bouncing around the province is a tentative series of 'model' villages displaying Lao Loum, Lao Theung and Lao Sung costumes and culture somewhere near Pakbeng (this is the LNTA's idea of 'cultural' tourism).

PAKBENG ປ້ອງແບ່ງ

This rustic town-village at the junction of the Mekong river and the smaller Nam Beng (Pakbeng means Mouth of the Beng) lies about halfway between Luang Prabang and Huay Xai (Bokeo Province). The Mekong here forms the border between Udomxai and Sainyabuli provinces; Pakbeng is on the northern bank and hence belongs to the former.

Basically a market town and transit point for travel to Muang Xai, Huay Xai and Luang Nam Tha, Pakbeng's roughly 500 wooden houses sit along a steep hillside where the mountains of Udomxai slope down to the river. Near the ferry and speedboat piers is a collection of makeshift shops and cafes that get more interesting the farther away from the river you go. Hmong and tribal Thais are frequently seen on the main street. A few vendors along the street sell local textiles and handicrafts.

Two wats of mild interest can be visited in town, both of which are off the east side of the road north, overlooking the Nam Beng. **Wat Khok Kho** is the newer of the two, with a sim of rather recent construction and a wooden *kuti* (monks' quarters).

Farther up the road a series of stairs on the right-hand side lead past a small school to **Wat Sin Jong Jaeng**, an older temple that dates to the early French colonial period or possibly earlier. On the front exterior wall of the small but classic Lao sim is a mural that includes figures with moustaches and big noses – presumably early French visitors. Inside are a number of Buddha images of varying ages. A new Lao-style thâat on the premises was constructed in 1991; it's gilded at the top, and the base is said to contain a cache of *sáksít* (sacred) material (probably small Buddha images of crystal or silver, prayer cloths and rosaries from revered monks). The 80-year-old abbot of Wat Sin Jong Jaeng is highly respected.

Nearby villages might be worth visiting if you can find a guide – ask at the Soukchareun Sarika Hotel.

Places to Stay & Eat

The all-wood *Soukchareun Sarika Hotel*, just up from the pier on the right, has seven basic rooms with tattered mosquito nets for 3000 kip (two beds) and 4000 kip (three beds). Open-sided toilets and showers jut over a cliff out the back of the little hotel and there is a rustic sitting area with a view of the river. All in all, it's not a bad place to spend a day or two. The new *Hotel Sipan Salika* under construction next door will reportedly offer 16 rooms, plus a restaurant and night club.

About 300m up the road towards the centre of town is a distant second choice, the government-run *Phu Vieng Hotel*. The modern, two-storey inn shows potential, but is still usually dirty and deserted.

There are several simple *cafes* along the street leading from the pier, most serving fõe and a few basic Chinese dishes. A day *market* in the centre of town on the left has a few vendors with prepared Lao food. Chinese-made Pabst Blue Ribbon beer is common and cheaper than Lao beer.

Getting There & Away

The slow boat from either Luang Prabang or Huay Xai costs 4000 kip per person (from the Luang Prabang end the boat company may charge 6000 kip, including the 50% 'foreigner tax'). The trip takes eight to 10 hours downriver, 11 to 14 hours upriver.

Shared speedboat taxis from Luang Prabang or Huay Xai take around three hours in either direction and cost a standard 300 baht or 9000 kip per person in either direction, though once again from Luang Prabang you may be charged 50% more. These powerful craft can take up to six passengers (seven including the pilot); if you want to share one you'll have to wait at the pier until six paying passengers turn up. Sometimes when only five passengers show up one of the more affluent passengers will chip in

600B – which should buy a little extra sitting space.

Or you can charter a speedboat for the Luang Prabang to Pakbeng or Huay Xai to Pakbeng routes for 1500 to 1800B; the boats use less fuel to carry one or two passengers rather than six, hence the acceptance (sometimes) of the lower figure. Kip or US dollars are also acceptable, though baht are preferred on this route.

The speedboat ride can be quite thrilling as the shallow craft skip along sections of rapids at 80 kph or more. A Thai passenger was killed in a collision with an unseen rock near Pakbeng in 1992; since then safety helmets and life vests have been required and the Lao authorities are very strict about enforcing the new rule.

Luang Nam Tha Province

ແຂວງຫຼວງນ້ຳທາ

Bordered by Myanmar to the north-west, China to the north, Udomxai to the south and east and Bokeo to the south-west, Luang Nam Tha (Nam Tha for short) is a mountainous province with a high proportion of Lao Sung and other minorities. The province population totals 114,500 made up of 39 classified ethnicities (the largest number in the nation), including Hmong, Iko (Akha), Mien, Samtao, Thai Daeng, Thai Lü, Thai Neua, Thai Khao, Thai Kalom, Khamu, Lamet, Lao Loum, Shan and Yunnanese. As in Udomxai the Chinese presence is increasing rapidly with the importation of skilled labour from Yunnan for construction and road work.

In the early '60s the western half of the province became a hotbed of CIA activity; the infamous William Young, a missionary's son raised in Lahu and Shan villages of northern Myanmar and northern Thailand, built a small CIA-financed, pan-tribal communist resistance army in Ban Thuay, Nam Yu and Vieng Phukha ('Lima Sites' 118A,

Plain of Jars

One of Laos' most enigmatic sights is a plain near Phonsavan littered with stone jars. Various theories have been advanced as to the functions of the jars – that they were used as sarcophagi, as wine fermenters or for rice storage – but no conclusive evidence has yet been uncovered. Stone lids for a few of the jars can be seen lying here and there. The jars are said to be 2000 years old, but in the absence of any organic relics – eg, bones or food remains – there's no reliable way to date them. It is believed that French archaeologists in the '20s or '30s found bone fragments in or near the jars. If true, this would suggest they had been used for funerals.

The local version says that in the 6th century a cruel chieftain named Chao Angka ruled the area as part of Muang Pakan. Sensitive to the plight of Pakan villagers, Lao-Thai hero Khun Jeuam supposedly came down from south China and deposed Angka. To celebrate his victory, Khun Jeuam had the jars constructed for the fermentation of rice wine. According to this version, the jars were cast from a type of cement that was made from buffalo skin, sand, water and sugar cane and fired in a nearby cave kiln. A limestone cave on the Plain of Jars that has smoke holes in the top is said to have been this kiln (the Pathet Lao used this same cave as a tactical shelter during the war).

For details on the Plain of Jars site see page 192. ∎

GLENN BEANLAND

JOE CUMMINGS

Top Right: The function of the jars still remains a mystery to archaeologists.

Left: Looking towards the largest of the jars

JOE CUMMINGS

JOE CUMMINGS

MARK DOWNEY

JOE CUMMINGS

Northern Laos

Top: The ruins of the ancient capital at old Xieng Khuang
Middle Left: A typical Hmong village in Hua Phan Province
Middle Right: Entrance to the lower cave at Pak Ou near Luang Prabang
Bottom: The Buddha-packed interior of the Pak Ou caves

118 and 109). Much of the opium and heroin transported by Air America and other air services either originated in or came through Luang Nam Tha. Westerners still seem to carry a romance for Nam Tha and there is a higher than average number of World Bank, UN, NGO and commercial projects underway in the province.

South of the capital, a 445 sq km piece of monsoon forest wedged between the Nam Ha and Nam Tha rivers was declared the Nam Ha National Biodiversity Conservation Area in 1993. Among the most densely forested regions (96% primary forest cover) in Laos, the Nam Ha NBCA protects a number of rare mammal species. A second, larger piece of land to the west of the Nam Ha is under consideration for similar status.

The Chinese and Lao governments recently opened the border crossing at Boten (pronounced Baw Taen) to foreign travellers, making Luang Nam Tha a new gateway into Laos and ushering in a new era of overland travel between China, Laos and Thailand.

LUANG NAM THA ບ່ວງທາ

Rising from the ashes of war, Luang Nam Tha's capital is expanding rapidly in its burgeoning role as trade entrep"t for commerce between China, Thailand and Laos. There are two town centres, one in the older, southern section of the district near the airfield and boat landing, and a second seven km to the north where the highway comes in from Muang Sing, Boten and Udomxai. The main market is located in the latter section.

Both centres are little more than large clusters of wooden, breeze-block and cement buildings centred around the airfield and market respectively. Like Udomxai this is a town best appreciated by walking well away from the bustling main streets. Near the airfield are two 50-year-old wats, **Wat Ban Vieng Neua** and **Wat Ban Luang Khon**, both of mild interest. Across the river from this area is a Thai Dam village of around 50 families; there's also a large Thai Kalom village in the same area.

The **Nam Tha market** is divided into two major sections, a large dry goods area near

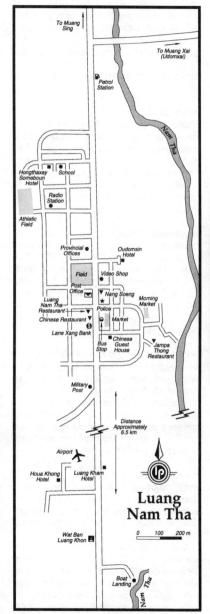

NORTHERN LAOS

Luang Nam Tha

the main north-south street through town, and a fresh produce section a few streets east. The latter opens around 5 am and is finished by 8 am, while the main street market is open 8 am to 4 pm. As Lao markets go, neither is particularly impressive; save your film for Muang Sing.

Information

Tourist Office Luang Nam Tha Travel, a private travel agency with an office at the south end of the main market, has information on places to see around the province. They can also make Lao Aviation bookings with a day's advance notice; this would save you the seven km trip south of town to the airfield.

Immigration Except at the airport (flight departure and arrival times only), it's even harder to get stamped in Luang Nam Tha than in Udomxai. Although there's a small police post next to the market, the police there aren't interested in seeing your papers. If you insist on staying legal, officers at the military post at the edge of town will apply the appropriate red or black stamps.

Money Lane Xang Bank, roughly opposite the main market and bus stop, is open Monday to Friday 8 am to 3.30 pm, Saturday 8 am to 11.30 pm. Travellers' cheques (US dollars only) can be exchanged for kip at a US$3 charge. Cash dollars, baht and yuan are also accepted. For both cash and travellers' cheques, the rates here run about 10 to 15 kip lower than rates in Vientiane.

Places to Stay

North (Market) A no-name *Chinese guest house* near the market has rooms with hard mattresses and mosquito nets, with shared toilet and bath, for 1500 to 2000 kip per room.

About 300m north of the market, a dirt road leads east off the main street to 16-room *Oudomsin Hotel*. Basic three-bed rooms cost 2000 kip with shared shower and toilet, or 4000 kip with private facilities. Nicer two-bed rooms with private facilities cost 5000

kip. There are a restaurant and night club on the premises; once the latter shuts down around 11 pm, nights are quiet.

Similar but slightly more upscale is the 28-room *Hongthaxay Someboun Hotel* (☎ Luang Nam Tha 164), another 500m north and then 150m west of the main street. Three-bed rooms with mosquito nets, private bath and fan cost 3000 kip per person, while two-bed rooms with spring mattresses are 8000 kip single/double. A nightclub in the compound, especially popular on weekends, stops by 11.30 pm, after which it's a reasonably quiet place.

The Thai owners of Vientiane's Tai-Pan Hotel may be building an upmarket hotel in this part of town in the near future.

South (Airfield) *Houa Khong Hotel* (☎ Luang Nam Tha 142), right across from the airfield, features separate bungalows with two or three rooms per unit, some with private bath and fan, some with shared bath, for 3500 kip per person. The bungalows feature large sitting areas with rattan furniture. There's a restaurant on the premises.

Luang Kham Hotel, 150m before the turnoff to the airport on the left, offers 12 rooms with shared bath and no fan for 2000 kip per room, plus rooms with fan and private bath for 5000 kip. It's basically quite OK, though the rooms are a bit dark.

Despite its impressively long menu, the restaurant at the *Houa Khong Hotel* opposite the airfield only serves noodles and fried rice. It's still a good place to eat or have a cup of tea while waiting for approaching Lao Aviation pilots to find a hole in the clouds.

Namo Roughly halfway between Udomxai and Luang Nam Tha you can stay at a wooden *hotel* over a shop in the small town of Namo (Meuang Na Maw), for 1500 kip.

Places to Eat

A small no-name *Chinese restaurant* opposite the police post at the corner of the market has the widest variety of vegetables in town, plus plenty of tofu. The mapo dofu here is guaranteed to make you breathe fire. No Lao or English is spoken.

The *Luang Nam Tha Restaurant*, just a simple wooden place around the corner from the Chinese restaurant, serves OK Lao and Chinese fare. The proprietors give falang customers a copy of the bilingual menu from the Sala Khem Kane Restaurant in Luang Prabang as a reference, although the two restaurants are unrelated. It's generally open from early morning till around 8 or 9 pm.

Nang Soeng, a restaurant just south of Dongsavang Video north of the market, serves basic Lao and Chinese food from 10 am to 8 pm. Down toward the Nam Tha river near the morning market, *Jampa Thong* is a pleasant garden restaurant serving Lao and Chinese.

The restaurant at the *Hongthaxay Someboun Hotel* serves OK Lao and Chinese food. There are a couple of very good fõe places in the market next to the main bus stop.

Getting There & Away

Air Lao Aviation flies a Y-12 to Nam Tha from Vientiane thrice weekly (one hour and 10 minutes, US$80). Flights to/from Luang Prabang are supposed to depart twice weekly (35 minutes, US$34), but in reality the schedule varies with passenger demand. There are also occasional flights to/from Huay Xai (40 minutes, US$36). Although the latest Lao Aviation route map shows a Udomxai-Luang Nam Tha sector, it wasn't operating at all when I visited.

For the less regular flights, ie Luang Prabang and Huay Xai, you should make enquiries at a Lao Aviation or Luang Nam Tha Travel office a couple of days before your desired departure date. Your reservation might make the difference between the company's cancelling or operating a scheduled flight.

Road There are a couple of options for heading north from Nam Tha, and a southward route to Huay Xai.

To/From Muang Xai Nam Tha can be reached via all-weather Route 2 from Muang

Xai (117 km south-east) in four or five hours. Passenger trucks cost 3000 kip per person (40,000 kip charter) and leave in the early morning and early afternoon from either end. The main truck stop in Nam Tha stands in front of the market, not far from the post office and bank.

To/From Huay Xai See under Huay Xai in the Bokeo Province section further on for details of this road.

To/From Boten A side road north off Route 2 about two-thirds of the way to Nam Tha from Muang Xai leads directly to Boten on the Lao-Chinese border. Passenger trucks bound for Boten leave morning and afternoon from Nam Tha (1500 kip, two to three hours on a very poor road).

To/From Muang Sing Two or three trucks a day ply between Nam Tha and Muang Sing, a journey of around two hours (1500 kip).

River When the water level is high enough, passenger boats occasionally run down the Nam Tha river to Pak Tha on the Mekong river for 10,000 kip per person. The latter is about 36 km downstream from Huay Xai. It's reportedly a beautiful trip, but one that will be terminated forever if damming of the river goes through.

Getting Around

A jumbo from the bus terminal/market area to the airport, seven km away, costs 1000 kip. Shared pickups also ply this route several times a day for just 200 kip per person.

MUANG SING ເມືອງສິງ

Lying on the broad river plains of the Nam La north-west of the provincial capital, Muang Sing is a traditional Thai Lü cultural nexus as well as a trade centre for Lao Huay (Lenten), Iko, Hmong, Mien, Lolo and Yunnanese. The entire district numbers 22,500 inhabitants, making it the second most populous district in the province after Luang Nam Tha itself.

From at least the late 16th century until

1803 Muang Sing belonged to the principality of Chiang Khong, after which it came under control of the Nan Kingdom. After a number of Shan princes took refuge from the British Raj here (and in southern Yunnan) in 1885, the British laid claim to the area but finally relinquished pretensions to all lands on the east bank of the Mekong in an 1896 agreement with the French.

Among the buildings left standing from the French era is a 75-year-old brick and plaster garrison which once housed Moroccan and Senegalese troops. It's now used as a small Lao army outpost. One of the arms of the 'China Road' passes through Muang Sing on its way to Mengla, Yunnan, hence the area has come under much Chinese influence since the 1960s.

The main market at Muang Sing – called *talàat nyai* in Lao, *kaat long* in Thai Lü – was once the biggest opium market in the golden triangle, a function officially sanctioned by the French. Perhaps the most colourful market in northern Laos, today it's a venue for fresh produce, meats, and food and clothing staples bought and sold by a polyglot crowd mainly consisting of Thai Lü, Thai Neua, Iko, Yunnanese, Shan, Hmong and Mien. A few traditional textiles – especially the simple, natural-dyed silks and cottons of the Thai Lü – are also sold in the market.

A number of Lao Theung and Lao Sung villages in the vicinity – particularly those of the Iko – can be visited on foot from Muang Sing. Several international NGO employees of German, Japanese and Belgian origins live in town, so the surrounding district is changing rapidly.

Information

Muang Sing has no bank as yet, so bring whatever cash is necessary for the duration of your stay. There is a tiny post office opposite the market.

Although Muang Sing is only 10 km from the Chinese border town of Mohan, you can't legally cross into China here without special advance permission arranged through the LNTA in Vientiane or some other travel agency. Lao border officials will usually allow foreigners to cross for a few hours if you leave your passport with them at the border, however. The contrast between the Lao and Chinese border crossings – a pole stretched across a dirt road on the Laos side, a large gleaming customs building at the end of a smooth-topped dual carriageway on the Chinese – is startling.

That Muang Sing Festival

During the full moon of the 12th lunar month, which usually occurs sometime between late October and mid-November, all of Muang Sing and half the province turn out for the That Muang Sing Festival *(bun thâat meúang sĩng)*. Centred around a Thai Lü stupa on a sacred hill south of town, the festival combines Theravada and animistic elements of worship and includes many of the ceremonies associated with the That Luang Festival in Vientiane (which occurs at the same time).

The thâat itself stands around 10m high and is constructed in the Lanna-Lan Xang style, with a stepped, whitewashed octagonal base and gilded spire. A shrine building to one side contains a row of Buddha images mounted on a sarcophagus-like Thai Lü altar.

The festival begins a few days before the official full moon day as merit-makers climb a broad winding path to the thâat grounds atop the hill and pay their respects by carrying offerings of candles, flowers and incense around the base of the stupa – a tradition called *wíen thíen*. The morning of the full moon Buddhist monks from around the province gather at the stupa for *tàak bàat*, the collection of alms-food. There are also traditional dance performances, carnival-style game booths and lots of food vendors selling khào lãam (sweetened sticky rice baked in bamboo), noodles and other snacks. Many Chinese vendors cross over from Yunnan during the festival to sell cheap Chinese cigarettes, beer and apples. Festival activities spill over into town, where there are nightly outdoor Lao pop music performances with lots of drinking and dancing. Food vendors line the main street at night with candlelit tables.

In spite of its Thai Lü origins, the That Muang Sing Festival is celebrated by virtually all ethnic groups in the area, as much for its social and entertainment value as anything else. This is the biggest event of the year, and is one of the best times for a Muang Sing visit in terms of the variety of people that can be encountered.

Places to Stay & Eat

The *Singthong Hotel*, an atmospheric old two-storey wooden hotel on the main street near the market, offers simple multi-bed rooms with mosquito nets for 2000 kip per bed for foreigners, 1500 kip for locals. Relatively clean toilet and bathing facilities are out back, and there's a restaurant downstairs. The whole building shakes when anyone walks along the upper floor! Rumour says this hotel may close at the end of 1996 when the proprietor's contract runs out – a shame given the history and rustic charm of the place.

Singxai Hotel is a newer concrete establishment behind the market with beds for 1500 to 2000 kip depending on the size of the room. Toilet and bathing facilities are shared. Food is served in a separate building but service is lacking and food quality is poor.

Another older wooden building opposite the Singthong may be converted into a hotel by a Vientiane travel agency. There are also rumours saying a German company may be building a new hotel in town.

Aside from the restaurants at the two hotels, the only places to eat are a few simple *fŏe shops* along the main street and in the market.

Getting There & Away

The winding, partially sealed road from Luang Nam Tha to Muang Sing parallels the Nam Tha, Nam Luang and Nam Sing rivers, crossing them at various points along the way, and passes through strikingly beautiful primary monsoon forest and several hilltribe villages. During the rainy season this road can be difficult, even impassable.

From Luang Nam Tha there are usually

Thai Lü

Thai Lü dominate local culture and commerce in Muang Sing District. Keen traders, they have been unusually successful in maintaining their traditions despite the pressures of outside Lao and Chinese influence, while at the same time enjoying the relative prosperity their district has developed as a Thailand-Laos-China trade centre.

The matrilineal Lü practise a mix of Theravada Buddhism and animism; though traditionally endogamic (tending to marry within one's own clan) they've recently begun marrying outsiders – usually Thai Lü or Thai Neua from other districts. Women are said to enjoy greater political freedom and power than in most ethnic groups in Laos. Typical Thai Lü villages are located on the east bank of a stream or river, with at least one wat at the north end and a cemetery at the west. One of their more distinctive customs includes *su khwan khuay*, a basi (string-tying) ceremony performed for hard-working water buffaloes. ■

A distinctive Thai Lü-style temple

two or three trucks a day, one or two in the morning between 7 and 8, and another in the early afternoon. The fare is 1500 kip per person and the trip takes around two hours.

XIENG KOK ຊຽງກອກ

Roughly 75 km from Muang Sing via a tortuous road that parallels the Nam Ma river much of the way, this Lao village on the Mekong river is Laos' only legally recognised border crossing with Myanmar. Although ostensibly this crossing is open only to Lao and Burmese nationals, we have heard of foreigners who have been able to obtain 28 day Burmese tourist visas at the border for

NORTHERN LAOS

US$30. You might do better to arrange a visa in advance from the Myanmar Embassy in either Vientiane or Bangkok before attempting a crossing here.

If you're successful in entering Myanmar, you can catch a Japanese pickup south-west to meet the road that runs between Thachilek (on the Thai-Burmese border opposite Mae Sai) and Kengtung in the north-eastern Shan State. From Kengtung you can continue into the interior of Myanmar by plane or by bus. The latter mode of transport wasn't legal for foreigners as we went to press, but the surrender of the Mong Tai Army, a large Shan guerrilla army which has been fighting the Yangon government for decades, may mean that the road between Kengtung and Taunggyi will soon be opened to foreigners.

Getting There & Away

Trucks from Muang Sing to Xieng Kok run only two or three times a week; enquire at the truck stop area in front of the Muang Sing market. The 75 km trip takes all day – up to a day and a half under certain road conditions – but may be upgraded in 1996. The fare is 5000 kip.

It is also possible to travel by speedboat to/from Chiang Khong or Huay Xai – three to four hours further south along the Mekong river – for 500 to 600B.

BOTEN ບໍແຕນ

This village on the Chinese border in the north-eastern corner of Luang Nam Tha Province is a major exit point for Japanese cars being smuggled from Thailand to China via Laos. Other than the lines of parked cars, thick with dust, waiting to get into China, there's virtually nothing else to see here.

Now that Boten is a legal border crossing for all nationalities, and with the upgrading of the road to Luang Nam Tha, the village will probably grow into a town of sorts, complete with hotels and restaurants. At the moment a couple of noodle shops and a truck stop are the only services provided. Overnight facilities are available in Mengla on the Chinese side.

The Lao border crossing is open from 8

am to noon and 2 to 4 pm, while the Chinese crossing is open 8 am to 5 pm. The best time of day to cross into Laos from China is the early morning when public transport onward to Luang Nam Tha and Udomxai is most frequently available. See the Luang Nam Tha and Udomxai Getting There & Away sections for details on transport to/from Boten.

Bokeo Province
ແຂວງບໍແຕນ

Laos' smallest and second least populous province, wedged between the Mekong river border with Thailand and Luang Nam Tha Province, has a population of 113,500. In earlier times Bokeo was known as Hua Khong (Head of the Mekong); its current name means Gem Mine', a reference to sapphire deposits in Huay Xai district. The province borders Thailand and Myanmar, and is less than a hundred km from China, hence it's an important focus of the much-ballyhooed 'Economic Quadrangle', a four-nation trade zone envisioned mainly by corporate entities in Thailand and China.

Despite it's diminutive size Bokeo harbours 34 different ethnicities, the second-highest number of ethnic groups per province (after Luang Nam Tha) in the country. They include Lao Huay (Lenten), Khamu, Hmong, Iko (Akha), Mien, Kui, Phai, Lamet, Samtao, Tahoy, Shan, Phu Thai, Thai Dam, Thai Khao, Thai Daeng, Thai Lü, Phuan, Thai Nai, Ngo, Kalom, Phuvan, Musoe (Lahu) and Chinese. Bokeo is the only province with a significant population of Lahu, a hill tribe common in northern Myanmar and Thailand, and is the main provenance of the Lao Huay.

For years the fledgling tourist industry in Laos has been pushing a circular overland itinerary that takes in Luang Prabang, Udomxai, Luang Nam Tha and Bokeo. With the reopening and upgrading of the road between Huay Xai and Nam Tha, this notion

Lao Huay

Also known as Lene Tene, Lenten or Laen Taen (Dressed in Blue), the Lao Huay or Stream Lao are classified by the government as Lao Sung despite the fact they do not – and never have – lived anywhere other than lower river valleys. Ethno-linguistically they do, however, fall within the Hmong-Mien family, most of whom live at higher elevations.

The Lao Huay build their homes – multi-family longhouses of palm and bamboo thatch – alongside rivers or streams from which they irrigate rice fields using simple wooden hydraulic pumps. Unlike the closely related Mien, they do not cultivate opium poppy for trade, only for smoking. Lao Huay women can be identified by the single large coin (usually an old Indochina piastre, sometimes accompanied by several smaller coins) suspended over the part in their long, straight hair and by their lack of eyebrows, which are completely depilated at age 15 according to custom. Both sexes favour dark blue or black clothes – baggy shirts and trousers – trimmed in red.

The Lao Huay use Chinese characters to write their language, often on handmade bamboo paper. Their belief system encompasses a mix of Taoism, ancestor worship and animism, with spirits attached to the family, father house, village, sky, forest, earth, water and birds. Around 5000 Lao Huay live in Laos; in Bokeo Province they're most concentrated in Nam Nyun District. This ethno-linguistic group isn't found in Myanmar or Thailand though there are some Lao Huay villages in Yunnan (China) and north Vietnam. ■

has become a reality; a Thai company recently won the bid for an aid-financed road project which will produce a direct land route from Thailand to China through Laos – including a new bridge over the Mekong between Chiang Khong and Huay Xai.

HUAY XAI ຫວຍຊາຍ

For centuries Huay Xai was a disembarcation point for Yunnanese caravans led by the Hui (Chinese Muslims) on their way to Chiang Rai and Chiang Mai in ancient Siam; today Chinese river barges from Yunnan navigate this far so there is still a brisk trade in Chinese goods. Thailand's Chiang Khong, on the opposite river bank, is also a major source of trade. Speedboats seen along Laos' northern rivers, for example, are imported from Chiang Khong.

Huay Xai today is a bustling riverside town whose main commercial district centres around the vehicle and passenger ferry landings for boats to Chiang Khong. Many new shophouses are under construction along the main street, which curves along the base of a hill overlooking the river.

A set of naga stairs ascends this hillside to **Wat Jawm Khao Manilat**, a thriving temple that overlooks the town and river. Constructed in 1880, the teak Shan-style temple

houses a 1458 stele donated by a former Chiang Khong prince. **Fort Carnot**, built by the French, is now occupied by Lao troops and is off limits to visitors.

Information

Money Lane Xang Bank, 50m off the main street, is open Monday to Friday 8 am to 3.30 pm. Cash or travellers' cheques can be changed for kip here, but the exchange rate is poor compared to Vientiane. You can change cash baht or US dollars at a more favourable rate at Bokeo Travel.

Post & Communications A post and telephone office, a few hundred metres south of the main hotel area, is open daily 8 am to 4 pm; you can make phone calls here till 10 pm.

Immigration Huay Xai is a valid border entry/exit point for any visitor regardless of nationality. You no longer need special permission to cross into Laos here, just a valid visa. Lao visas are available at several agencies in Chiang Khong; the most reliable is Ann Tour, housed in a small booth just north of Ban Tammila Guest House. A regular 15-day Tourist Visa costs 1700B. If you leave your passport (no accompanying

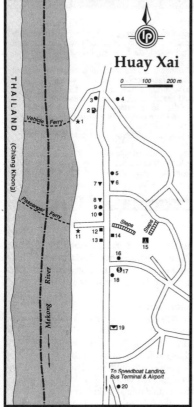

Huay Xai

0   100   200 m

THAILAND (Chiang Khong)

Vehicle Ferry

Passenger Ferry

Mekong River

To Speedboat Landing,
Bus Terminal & Airport

PLACES TO STAY

12 Manilat Hotel
13 Hotel Houei Sai
14 Bokeo Hotel/Bokeo Travel

PLACES TO EAT

6 Savan Bokeo Restaurant & Club
7 Yawt Khawng Coffee Shop
8 Yin Dii Tawn Hap Restaurant

OTHER

1 Customs & Immigration
2 Petrol Station
3 Market
4 School
5 Drinking Water Factory
9 Photo Shop
10 Public Health Office
11 Customs & Immigration
15 Wat Jawm Khao Manilat
16 Lao Aviation
17 Lane Xang Bank
18 School
19 Post Office
20 Telecom Tower

photos necessary) here in the morning at 8.30 am, you can pick it up at 3 pm the same day.

Bokeo Travel, downstairs from Bokeo Hotel in Huay Xai, can arrange trips to nearby villages – including a Lao Huay village 15 km south – or to a sapphire mining area 12 km south. The agency charges a basic rate of 550B a day including car, driver and English-speaking guide.

Places to Stay & Eat
Up from the Mekong ferry landing is the well-run *Manilat Hotel* with basic but clean rooms with fan and private bath for 6000 kip

single/double. There's a very good, inexpensive restaurant downstairs.

The *Hotel Houei Sai*, nearby on the same side of the street, is similar in overall appearance and rates but significantly shabbier. Better is the three-storey *Bokeo Hotel* opposite the other two hotels, where rooms with fan and bath are 6000 kip or 150B.

Cheap noodle and rice plates are available in an open-air shop next to the Bokeo Hotel. A couple of blocks north the *Yin Dii Tawn Hap Restaurant* and *Yawt Khawng Coffeeshop* (the English sign reads only 'Coffeeshop') offer simple Lao and Thai fare plus a variety of cold drinks. Opposite the latter stands the larger and fancier *Savan Bokeo Restaurant & Club*, a popular local night spot with good Lao, Chinese and Thai food.

Getting There & Away
Air Flights between Huay Xai and Luang Prabang operate daily for US$42 each way and take 50 minutes.

There are also weekly flights to/from

Luang Nam Tha (US$36) and Udomxai (US$34). At the moment there are no direct flights between Huay Xai and Vientiane.

Lao Aviation has an office in town opposite Lane Xang Bank; it's open Monday to Saturday open 8 am to 4 pm.

Road This used to be a difficult road because of its poor surface, but upgrading is now underway. However, Hmong guerrilla activity around Vieng Phuka and heroin manufacture and trafficking along the Burmese border means that the area has been unstable for some time, and hence may be dangerous for travellers.

Passenger trucks to Luang Nam Tha, 217 km north-east, cost 8000 kip and currently take 10 hours under good road conditions, though during the rainy season it's often impassable. Once the upgrading and sealing project is completed, the road will be traversable year-round and buses should be able to make the trip in an estimated four to six hours (depending on number of stops). You can stop off in Vieng Phukha (100 km from Huay

Xai) for 6000 kip. A rustic guest house is available in Vieng Phukha.

In Huay Xai the passenger truck terminal can be found near the provincial stadium, about two km south of the Chiang Khong passenger ferry pier. Buses – one a day in both directions – leave from Luang Nam Tha and Huay Xai around 7 am.

River The short ferry ride from Chiang Khong on the Thai side costs 20B each way. On the Huay Xai side, the cross-river ferry landing is just below the Manilat Hotel.

A Thai company has plans to construct a new bridge across the Mekong river from Chiang Khong to Huay Xai by late 1997. Once the bridge is completed, cross-river ferry services will most likely be replaced by a shuttle bus system as in Nong Khai.

Long-distance river ferries down the Mekong to Pakbeng and Luang Prabang cost 4000 kip and 8000 kip respectively. To Pakbeng it's an all-day trip (roughly 8 am to 5.30 pm), while to Luang Prabang it takes a full day and sometimes part of a night

Paa Béuk
The Mekong River stretch that passes Huay Xai is an important fishing ground for the giant Mekong catfish (paa béuk in Lao, Pangasianodon gigas to ichthyologists), probably the largest freshwater fish in the world. A paa béuk takes at least six and possibly 12 years (no-one's really sure) to reach full size, when it will measure two to three metres in length and weigh up to 300 kg. Locals say these fish swim all the way from Qinghai Province (where the Mekong originates) in northern China. In Thailand and Laos its flesh is considered a major delicacy; the texture is very meaty but has a delicate flavour, similar to tuna or swordfish, only whiter in colour.

These fish are only taken between mid-April and May when the river depth is just three to four metres and the fish are swimming upriver to spawn in Lake Tali, Yunnan Province, China. Before netting them, Thai and Lao fishermen hold a special annual ceremony to propitiate Chao Mae Paa Beuk, a female deity thought to preside over the giant Mekong catfish. Among the rituals comprising the ceremony are chicken sacrifices performed aboard the fishing boats. After the ceremony is completed fishing teams draw lots to see who casts the first net, and then take turns casting.

Around 40 to 60 catfish are captured in a typical season. Fishermen sell the meat on the spot for around US$20 per kilo (a single fish can bring up to US$4500 in Bangkok), most of which ends up in Bangkok or Chiang Mai restaurants, since local restaurants in Huay Xai and Chiang Khong can't afford such prices; transport to Vientiane is considered too costly.

Because of the danger of extinction, Thailand's Inland Fisheries Department has been taking protective measures since 1983, including a breed-and-release programme. Every time a female is caught, it's kept alive until a male is netted, then the eggs are removed (by massaging the female's ovaries) and put into a pan; the male is then milked for sperm and the eggs are fertilised in the pan. In this fashion over a million paa béuk have been released into the Mekong since 1983. ∎

(roughly 15 hours) depending on how many stops the boats make.

Speedboats to Pakbeng and Luang Prabang cost 300 to 400B and 600 to 800B (you can pay in kip or dollars but baht are preferred) respectively. The fare differential depends on your bargaining powers; the boat service tries to tack on a 'foreigner surcharge' whenever possible. It's three hours to Pakbeng, six hours to Luang Prabang.

The landings for both the slow boat and speedboats are about two km south of the town centre, near the stadium and passenger truck terminal.

When the new bridge under construction between Chiang Khong and Huay Xai is completed, passenger ferry service will probably be discontinued – if not for all visitors then at least for non-Thai, non-Lao foreigners.

Sainyabuli Province
ແຂວງໄຊຍະບູລີ

This upside-down-L-shaped province between Thailand to the west and both Vientiane and Luang Prabang to the east is one of the most remote provinces in Laos despite its geographic proximity to the nation's capital. The province is quite mountainous (with several peaks higher than 1000m and one as high as 2150m) and devoid of vehicle roads except for one north-south route extending from the provincial capital to the Thai border opposite Thailand's Loei Province. The population totals around 292,000 including Lao, Thai Dam, Thai Lü, Khamu, Htin, Phai, Kri, Iko (Akha) and Mabri; many of these groups migrate back and forth between Sainyabuli and Thailand since the border is fairly unpoliced here.

Sainyabuli (also spelt Sayaburi and Xaignabouri) shares a 645 km border with six different Thai provinces. The northwestern section of the province is considered of major military and commercial importance because Pakbeng – the start of a road

link (Route 2) with northern Udomxai and the Chinese border at Boten – lies less than 50 km from the Thai border on the north bank of the Mekong river.

The province is rich in timber (including teak) and lignite, and is considered the 'rice basket' of northern Laos, since most other northern provinces are too mountainous to produce enough rice to feed the regional population. Other important local crops include maize, oranges, cotton, peanuts and sesame.

The southern reach of the province was the site of a brief but heated border skirmish between the Thai and Lao in 1988. The Lao, using a 1960 American map, claimed the border followed one tributary of the Nam Heuang while the Thai said the border should follow another branch of the river according to a 1908 Siam-France treaty. Laos sent in troops to occupy the disputed 77 sq km territory, and in response Thailand launched air strikes against Laos – a daring move considering that 50,000 Vietnamese troops were deployed in Laos at the time. Over a hundred Thai and Lao soldiers died in battle before an agreement was reached and a compromise border was fixed.

A string of rocky limestone precipices known as **Pha Xang** or Elephant Cliffs (so named because from a distance the grey-white cliffs resemble walking elephants) parallels the Mekong river along the east side of the province. Along the north-west edge of the province is the newly declared **Nam Phoun NBCA**, a 1150 sq km tract of rugged, forested hills thought to sustain elephant, Sumatran rhino, gaur, gibbons, dhole, Asiatic black bear, Malayan sun bear and tiger.

The southern part of the province harbours several scenic waterfalls, including 150m **Nam Tok Na Kha** (three km from Ban Nakha), 105m **Nam Tok Ban Kum** (five km from Ban Kum) and 35m **Taat Heuang** (40 km from Ban Meuang Phae). Unfortunately none of these villages are very accessible by road as yet, and this corner of the province is reputed to be a hangout for smugglers and possibly insurgents. The Vientiane government considers much of the province insecure due to difficulties along the Thai border (specifically eastern Nan Province), including bandits, large-scale cross-border smuggling (especially teak) and the opium-heroin trade.

The 30m **Taat Jaew**, a one km walk northwest of Muang Tha Deua, is a popular local picnic spot.

Other than the fine mountain scenery and waterfalls, there are few attractions for the tourist since Sainyabuli as a region never prospered under the Lan Xang or Vientiane kingdoms, nor did the Khmers reach this far north-west to leave behind any ruins or sculpture. The French had a minor presence in the capital but left little infrastructure behind.

More visitors make it to Pak Lai, a stop on the Mekong river trip between Vientiane and Luang Prabang, than to the capital of Sainyabuli itself.

SAINYABULI ໄຊຍະບູລີ

The capital stands on the banks of the Nam Hung, a tributary of the Mekong river toward the northern end of the province. The surrounding district (population 60,000) contains a large number of Mien, who control the main market and several successful businesses in town.

Other than a couple of wats there is little in town to interest the casual visitor. The grounds of **Wat Si Bun Huang**, south of town past the police station in an adjacent village, contain the brick foundations of Buddhist monuments rumoured to be over 500 years old. In town **Wat Si Savang Vong**, reportedly built by King Sisavang Vong on an older temple site, displays a colourful version of life in Buddhist hell on its front walls.

There is a working **elephant camp** about 45 minutes drive south of Sainyabuli in Phiang district.

Very little English is spoken in Sainyabuli so be sure to pack your phrasebook.

Information
Money Lane Xang Bank, 50m west of Sayaboury Guest House on the opposite side

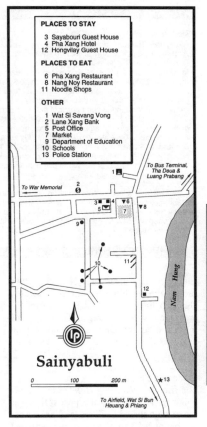

PLACES TO STAY
3 Sayabouri Guest House
4 Pha Xang Hotel
12 Hongvilay Guest House

PLACES TO EAT
6 Pha Xang Restaurant
8 Nang Noy Restaurant
11 Noodle Shops

OTHER
1 Wat Si Savang Vong
2 Lane Xang Bank
5 Post Office
7 Market
9 Department of Education
10 Schools
13 Police Station

Sainyabuli

0   100   200 m

NORTHERN LAOS

of the street, is open Monday to Friday 8 to 11 am and 2 to 4 pm. The bank accepts only cash US dollars – at a lower rate than in Vientiane.

Post & Communications The post office is open Monday to Friday 8 am to 4 pm. Telephone services are available 8 am to 8 pm daily.

Immigration In the not-so-distant past Sainyabuli officials were quite suspicious of foreigners, understandably so in light of the Thai border difficulties and problems with

Mabri

Along the Thai-Lao border in Sainyabuli Province survives a single village of around 60 Mabri (sometimes spelt Mrabri or Mlabri), whom the Lao call *khàa tawng leūang* (Slaves of the Yellow Banana-Leaves). The men wear very little clothing, preferring nothing more than a small piece of cloth to cover the groin, while the women tend to wear castoffs from other hilltribes or from lowlanders. The most nomadic and endangered of all the minority ethnicities in Laos or Thailand, the Mabri customarily move on when the leaves of their temporary huts turn yellow – about every two weeks – hence their Lao name. Their numbers have been greatly reduced (possibly to as few as 250 – around 150 of whom live in Thailand) and experts suspect that few of the Mabri still migrate in the traditional way.

In the past the Mabri were strict hunter-gatherers but many now work as field labourers for the Lao, or for other hill-tribe groups such as the Hmong, in exchange for pigs and clothing. Little is known about the tribe's belief system except that they are animists who believe they are not entitled to cultivate the land for themselves. Their matrilineal social organisation allows serial monogamy; a Mabri woman typically changes mates every five or six years, taking any children from the previous union with her. The Mabri knowledge of medicinal plants is said to be enormous, encompassing the effective use of herbs for fertility and contraception, and for the treatment of snake or centipede poisoning. When a member of the tribe dies, the body is put in a tree top to be eaten by birds.

Unlike in Thailand, where government and non-government agencies are attempting to help the Mabri integrate into the modern social milieu, no-one in Laos has come forth to try and protect the Mabri from becoming a slave society within an increasingly capitalist rural economy. Because of their anti-materialist beliefs, the Mabri perform menial labour for the Hmong and other hill tribes for little or no compensation. ∎

smugglers and insurgents. Nowadays they seem to have loosened up considerably although travel to the southern end of the province is still discouraged. The only place interested in checking and stamping your papers is the police station at the south end of town.

Places to Stay & Eat

The friendly *Pha Xang Hotel*, a two-storey building next door to the post office, has rooms with shared facilities for 2000 kip per person, or 3000 kip per person with attached bath. There's a pleasant balcony sitting area upstairs and a restaurant at the back.

The *Hongvilay Guest House*, south of the market next to the Nam Hung river, has 10 rooms with decent mattresses and shared toilet and bath for 5000 kip single/double. There's an outdoor dance hall at the back, a restaurant and good river views.

The marble-floored *Sayaboury Guest House*, 100m west of the main road and behind the post office, has 10 very nice rooms, a large banquet-style dining room downstairs and an upstairs tea room. At the moment it's reserved for visiting Lao government officials only.

Nang Noy Restaurant, east of the market near the market's main gate, serves a variety of fish, fowl, meat and vegetable dishes – it's the only true restaurant in town outside the hotels and guest houses.

There are several simple *noodle shops* along the main road, some with rice dishes as well. You can also buy take-away food from the market.

Getting There & Away

Air Lao Aviation flies to Sainyabuli from Vientiane thrice weekly. The foreigner fare is US$35 and flights take 45 minutes each way. The airline claims it will establish scheduled flights between Luang Prabang and Sainyabuli in the near future.

Road Incredibly there is still no direct road between Vientiane and Sainyabuli. An all-weather, partially paved road runs south-west from Luang Prabang to Muang Nan on the Mekong's east bank, then connects by ferry with Muang Tha Deua on the west bank and continues south-eastward to the provincial capital. There is a regular passenger ferry to either side of the river for 100 kip.

There is also a road running north to Sainyabuli from Kaen Thao, which is on the Nam Heuang opposite the Thai villages of Ban Pak Huay and Ban Nong Pheu – both are legal crossing points for Thai and Lao, but not for foreigners.

Buses for Luang Prabang (205 km) leave in the morning around 7 or 8 for 2000 kip per person and take four to five hours.

The main bus terminal is two km north of town.

River Regular long-distance ferries between Vientiane and Luang Prabang stop at Pak Lai, for 5300 kip per passenger. From Pak Lai passenger trucks continue the journey to Sainyabuli for 4000 kip. The road trip takes five to six hours under good conditions; during the rainy season the road may be impassable.

By river from Pak Lai to Tha Deua is 145 km. The slow boat takes two days and costs 3500 kip, while speedboats take about four hours and cost 300 to 400B. From Luang Prabang to Tha Deua, speedboats take only an hour and cost 500B per person (including the foreigner surcharge collected by all public transport out of Luang Prabang).

PAK LAI ປາກລາຍ

There isn't much to this small town though more travellers end up staying here than in Sainyabuli simply because it's an overnight stop for Mekong river ferries between Vientiane and Luang Prabang.

A branch of the Lane Xang Bank may be able to change dollars to kip. There's a post office near the Pha Xang Hotel.

Places to Stay & Eat
Pak Lai has two government-run *guest houses*, but the nicer one is reserved for government employees only. The other has no name or sign; it's about a km upriver from the boat landing, just before a sawmill. Look for the last house at the end of the road on the left; it's a two-storey building, wood on top of cement. Basic two-bed rooms with mosquito nets cost 2500 kip per person. Toilet and shower facilities are downstairs. The manager speaks decent English; food can be arranged with advance notice.

Just south of the ferry landing and across from the athletic field are three *restaurants* which serve soups, fried rice and a few Lao dishes. There are also a couple of *noodle shops* in the market a half km north of the landing.

Getting There & Away
Road Pak Lai is inaccessible by road for several months out of the year due to swollen stream and river crossings. Passenger trucks to/from Sainyabuli run from late November to May; the fare is 4000 kip and the trip takes five or six hours. Eventually this road will be upgraded to an all-weather route with faster driving times.

River The slow boat to Pak Lai from Vientiane (216 km) costs 5200 kip and takes 1½ days. Speedboats do the same stretch in four hours for 15,000 kip.

NORTHERN LAOS

Southern Laos

While Vientiane is modernising bit by bit and Northern Laos is almost a country apart with its predominantly hill-tribe and tribal Thai culture, in many ways Southern Laos remains the most traditionally 'Lao' region of the country.

Only two southern provinces, Savannakhet and Champasak, are regularly travelled by tourists. The rural areas of the Mekong river valley are mostly inhabited by lowland Lao who still weave their own cloth, grow all their own food and devoutly practise Lao Buddhism. The southern highlands are populated by a mixture of Thai tribals and various Mon-Khmer groups. Because the ethnic groups of the south aren't as colourfully garbed or flashy as those in the north, the south receives fewer 'hill-tribe gawkers'. Traditions are strong, however, and in the rural south people can still say they do things the way their parents taught them, and the way their parents in turn learned from *their* parents, and so on for many generations.

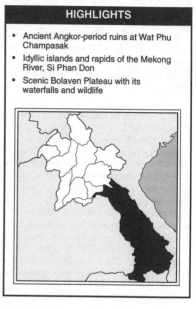

Bolikhamsai & Khammuan Provinces
ແຂວງບໍລິຄໍາໄຊແລະຄໍາມ່ວນ

Bolikhamsai and Khammuan straddle the narrow, central 'neck' of the country, an area of moderately high mountains sloping southwest to meet the Mekong river valley. Lowland Lao, who speak a dialect peculiar to these two provinces, dominate the population followed by lesser numbers of tribal Thais, Phuan, Ta-oy (Tahoy), Kri, Katang, Maling, Tri, Hmong and Mabri.

Khammuan Limestone, a huge wilderness area (1580 sq km) of turquoise streams, verdant monsoon forests and striking karst topography across central Khammuan, was declared a National Biodiversity Conservation Area in 1993. Although much of the NBCA is inaccessible by road, local people have nonetheless managed to reduce key forest-dependent species to very small numbers through hunting, mining and logging. The area is home to the endangered Douc langur, François' langur and several other primate species. If its protected status is properly enforced, the Khammuan Limestone has great potential for wildlife conservation.

Nakai-Nam Theun, the largest NBCA in Laos at 3710 sq km, covers a large portion of eastern Khammuan along the Vietnamese border as well as a smaller section of Bolikhamsai. Forest cover – including extensive stands of wet and dry evergreen, old growth pine mosaic, cypress and riverside forest – totals an estimated 93%, hence Nakai-Nam Theun is an incredibly important

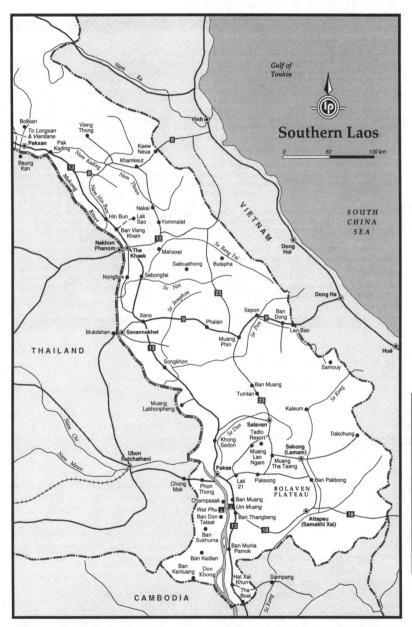

Gulf of
Tonkin

Southern Laos

0   50   100 km

Bolikan
*To Longxan
& Vientiane*
Pakxan
Pak
Kading
Beung
Kan

Vieng
Thong

Vinh

VIETNAM

SOUTH
CHINA
SEA

Kaew
Neua
8
Khamkeut

Nam Ka
Nam Kading
Nam Hin Bun
Nam Theun
13
8

Nakai
Hin Bun   Lak
Sao   Yommalat
Ban Vieng
Kham
**Nakhon
Phanom**   **Tha
Khaek**
12
Mahaxai
Saibuathong   Bulapha
Nongbok   Sebongfai
Se Bang Fai
Dong
Hoi

Se Not
Se Jamphon
23

Xeno
9
Phalan
Sepon
9
Ban
Dong
Lao Bao
Dong Ha

Mukdahan   **Savannakhet**
13
Muang
Phin
Se Pon
Hué

Songkhon
Samouy

THAILAND

Ban Muang
Tumlan   23
Kaleum
Se Kong

Muang
Lakhonpheng

Khong
Sedon
Se Don
Salavan
Tadlo
Resort
Muang
Lao
Ngam
**Sekong
(Lamam)**
Muang
Tha Taeng
Dakchung

**Ubon
Ratchathani**
Pakse
Lak
21
Paksong
Ban Pakbong

Nam Chi

Nam Moun

Chong
Mek
Phon
Thong
Champasak
Wat Phu   Ban Muang
Ban Don   *Um Muang*
Talaat   Ban Thangbeng
Ban
Sukhuma   13
18
**Attapeu
(Samakhi Xai)**
18
BOLAVEN
PLATEAU

Ban Kadian
Ban
Kanluang   Don
Khong
Ban Munla
Pamok
Hat Xai
Khun
Tha
Boel
Siempang
Se Kong

CAMBODIA

Horns of a Dilemma

The 1992 discovery of the *saola* or spindlehorn bovid *(Pseudoryx nghetinhensis)* in Vietnam's Vu Quang Nature Reserve in west-central Vietnam – very near the Laos-Vietnam border – stimulated intense international interest in the potential for finding other large, heretofore-undiscovered mammalian species in the area. Subsequent surveys in 1993 and 1994 confirmed the existence of the spindlehorn in Laos in the northern reaches of the newly decreed Nakai-Nam Theun National Biodiversity Conservation Area (NNTNBCA), a reserve that runs along the eastern portion of Bolikhamsai Province in the Annamite Mountain chain. Its range is now thought to encompass some 4000 sq km of montane evergreen broad-leaved forest between 200 and 2000m above sea level – most frequently at 500 to 1000m – along both sides of the central Lao-Vietnamese border.

Researchers have so far not encountered a live saola in the wild, but physical evidence left behind by local hunts and horn collections suggests the antelope-like animal stands 80 to 90 cm at the shoulder and weighs up to 100 kg. Its distinctively long, slender horns form a slight backwards curve and measure 40 to 50 cm. At the moment there is some disagreement among zoologists as to whether the saola properly belongs in the Bovinae subfamily – which includes wild cattle, spiral-horned antelopes and nilgai – or to the goat-related Caprinae. Total numbers for the spindlehorn are difficult to estimate; the infrequency with which it's encountered even by local hunters confirms the belief that it is an endangered species. In 1994 it was added to the UN Convention on International Trade in Endangered Species (CITES), Appendix 1. Laos reportedly will soon add its imprimatur to the convention.

Hunting in the area poses a continual threat, as virtually every Lao and Vietnamese household in the Annamite Mountains possesses at least one home-fashioned hunting rifle and a set of snare lines; automatic rifles aren't unknown and ammunition is cheap. Logging poses additional threats in the form of further habitat loss in the Nam Theun highlands where the saola makes its home. In spite of the legal protection afforded to the area contiguously covered by the NNTNBCA and Vietnam's Vu Quang Nature Reserve, most of the human activity traditionally practised in the region will continue to degrade the primary forest and its endemic wildlife unless steps are taken to enforce protection of a core area. The saola can be viewed as an indicator species for the region's environmental health; if allowed, its disappearance would darken the outlook for biodiversity in Laos. ■

habitat for the country's forest-dependent wildlife. Over a dozen globally threatened species live in the area, including elephant (one of the country's largest herds), giant muntjac (endemic to this region), gaur, banteng, Asiatic black bear, Malayan sun bear, clouded leopard, tiger and the saola (Vu Quang ox), a horned bovid newly discovered in 1992 in Vietnam's adjacent Vu Quang Nature Reserve. The saola has since been sighted on Laos' Nakai plateau, only a third of which falls within the Nakai-Nam Theun NBCA.

PAKXAN ปากຊັນ

The capital of Bolikhamsai, a town of 35,000 at the mouth of the Nam Xan where it feeds into the Mekong River, functions as a commercial centre and army base but is of little interest to the casual visitor. On the opposite bank of the Mekong from Pakxan is the Thai town of **Beung Kan**, a legal border crossing for Lao and Thai citizens only.

Until recently foreigners were discouraged from spending the night in Pakxan. Several Lao civilians were killed during a bus bombing four years ago and the city was named (in 1979) as the headquarters for the Thai Isan Liberation Party, an anticommunist group led by Thai-Lao trade union activists and two former Thai MPs. The local population are predominantly Phuan, a tribal Thai group; many of them are Christian, which makes them doubly suspicious in the eyes of Lao authorities. With the completion of the highway bed between Vientiane and Pakxan, the area has become considerably more secure.

Places to Stay & Eat

The *Phonesai Guest House* and *Pakxan Phattana Hotel* each have rooms for 4000 kip a single, 5000 kip a double. There are several *noodle stands* near the latter hotel.

Getting There & Away

From the Talaat Sao bus terminal in Vientiane, bus No 18 leaves twice a day (early morning and early afternoon) for Pakxan at a cost of 1300 kip per person; the trip takes around two hours. Buses are also available from a small terminal near Km 6 outside Vientiane. Once the Vientiane-Pakxan section of Route 13 is completely sealed and the various bridges along the way are finished, it shouldn't take any longer than an hour or so to reach Pakxan.

If you're just visiting Wat Pha Baat Phonsan, you won't need to go all the way to Pakxan, as the wat is just over the Vientiane Province line, before Pakxan. Under current road conditions it's one hour from Vientiane by private vehicle, 1½ hours by public bus – hop any Pakxan-bound bus and ask to get off at the wat; catch any Vientiane-bound bus later in the day if you don't intend to stay in Pakxan or continue south.

AROUND PAKXAN
Wat Pha Baat Phonsan

Eighty km north-east of Vientiane via Route 13 south, on the way to Pakxan, is a large *pha bàat* (Buddha-footprint) shrine and important pilgrimage spot for lowland Lao from Bolikhamsai and Vientiane. The highly stylised 'print' – along with a sizeable reclining Buddha figure – sits on a sandstone bluff along with some older monastic structures and stands of bamboo. A well-ornamented 1933-vintage stupa is reminiscent of That Ing Hang in Savannakhet, and the drum tower contains a drum whose head measures two metres in diameter, one of the largest in the country.

Wat Pha Baat Phonsan hosts a large merit-making festival on the full moon of the third lunar month (around July).

Nam Kading

The Kading river, which feeds into the Mekong river 50 km east of Pakxan, is one of the most pristine, least disturbed rivers in Laos. Flowing through a forested valley surrounded by high hills and limestone formations, the wide, turquoise-tinted river provides a great potential for wilderness recreation. (It's coloured thus due to the limestone.) Confirmed animal rarities in the area include elephant, giant muntjac, pygmy slow loris, François' langur, Douc langur, gibbon, dhole, Asiatic black bear, tiger and a large variety of birds.

Dirt roads parallel the Nam Kading upriver some distance, so launching places for canoes, rafts or kayaks are possible. **Taat Wang Fong**, about 60 km from Route 13 by road along the river, is a small waterfall in a very picturesque setting.

Ban Nape

The area around Ban Nape, roughly 200 km south-east of the capital via Routes 13 and 8 near the Vietnamese border, is well known for its scenic limestone formations.

THA KHAEK ທ່າແຂກ

Briefly a farflung outpost of the Mon-Khmer Funan and Chenla empires, when it was known as Sri Gotabura (Sii Khotabun in Lao), this capital of Khammuan Province traces its present-day roots to French colonial construction in 1911-12. The town name means Indian Landing, a reference to its earlier role as a boat landing for Indian and Arab traders. Before the war (and during the war until the NVA and Pathet Lao cut the road north to Vientiane), Tha Khaek was a thriving town and a gambling centre for day-tripping Thais.

Until the revolution the population measured 85% Vietnamese, many of whom had come with the French and/or had fled the Viet Minh movement in North Vietnam. The percentage dipped drastically as many Vietnamese left in the late '70s to seek their fortunes in more favourable business climes. Today Tha Khaek is a quiet transport and trade outpost of 68,300 – mostly lowland Lao, Vietnamese and Thai.

Surviving Franco-Chinese architecture, mixed in with newer structures, is similar to that found in Vientiane and Savannakhet. At

SOUTHERN LAOS

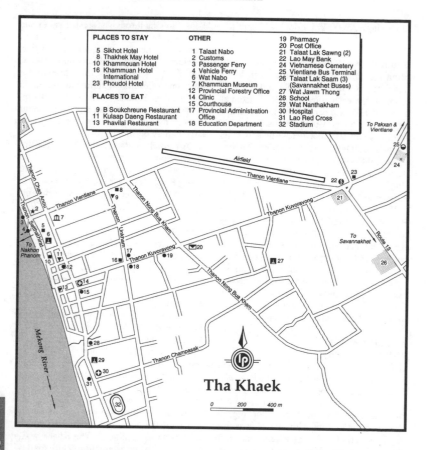

PLACES TO STAY

5 Sikhot Hotel
8 Thakhek May Hotel
10 Khammouan Hotel
16 Khammuan Hotel
    International
23 Phoudoi Hotel

PLACES TO EAT

9 B Soukchreune Restaurant
11 Kulaap Daeng Restaurant
13 Phavilai Restaurant

OTHER

1 Talaat Nabo
2 Customs
3 Passenger Ferry
4 Vehicle Ferry
6 Wat Nabo
7 Khammuan Museum
12 Provincial Forestry Office
14 Clinic
15 Courthouse
17 Provincial Administration
    Office
18 Education Department

19 Pharmacy
20 Post Office
21 Talaat Lak Sawng (2)
22 Lao May Bank
24 Vietnamese Cemetery
25 Vientiane Bus Terminal
26 Talaat Lak Saam (3)
    (Savannakhet Buses)
27 Wat Jawm Thong
28 School
29 Wat Nanthakham
30 Hospital
31 Lao Red Cross
32 Stadium

Tha Khaek

0   200   400 m

the western end of Thanon Kuvoravong near the river is a modest fountain square. Save for the occasional highway project engineer, few foreigners stop over here; for those seeking urban Mekong valley culture, this laid-back, friendly town is worth a couple of days.

Opposite Tha Khaek on the Thai side is Nakhon Phanom, a legal entry/exit point for foreigners. Thai investors have offered to finance a new highway from Tha Khaek to the Vietnamese border to facilitate trade between Thailand, Laos and Vietnam (and beyond via the Gulf of Tonkin). There has

even been talk of building an international bridge across the Mekong river between Nakhon Phanom and Tha Khaek.

Information

A branch of Lao May Bank at the intersection of Thanon Kuvoravong and Route 13 offers foreign exchange services (cash only). The area code for Tha Khaek is 52.

Things to See & Do

In town the large **Talaat Lak Sawng** (Km 2 Market) purveys hardware, clothes, fresh produce and just about everything else the people of Tha Khaek use in daily life. In addition to the usual gold shops there are a large number of vendors selling silverwork.

Khammuan museum near the Sikhot Hotel occupies one room in a government building with no other apparent function. Items on display – some labelled in Lao, some unlabelled – include pottery said to be 2000 years old, basketry, captured French and Japanese rifles, a few antique textiles, pictures of tourist sites in the province and an endless series of snapshots showing provincial officials at various meetings.

Places to Stay

The *Khammouan Hotel* (☎ 212216), a large four-storey, white, curved-front building facing the Mekong, is so far the best all-round deal in town. Landscaped with palm trees, it was probably pretty impressive when it first opened but is now fading a bit; sunset views over the river are still tremendous, however. Large, plain, clean rooms with TV, fridge, air-con, hot water and good mattresses cost 8000 kip single, 10,000 kip double, 12,000 kip triple. The Lao name for this hotel is 'Khammuan Sai Khong', while most samlor drivers know it as 'Sii San' (Four Floors).

If you're looking to economise, the *Thakhek May Hotel* (☎ 212043) a few blocks away from the river on Thanon Vientiane offers simple rooms in a two-storey square building for 3000/4000 kip single/double with shared bath and ceiling fans, 5000 kip single/double with shared bath and air-con. The outside of the building and interior corridors don't look like much but the rooms are quite OK.

The *Khammuan Hotel International* (☎ 212171), a two-storey white building with terraces in front, is run by a young Thai couple and has rooms for 4500/5500 kip single/double with fan, 11,000 kip with air-con, all with private shower and toilet (no hot water). It's a little dilapidated but the friendly staff are an asset.

A little upriver from the Khammouan Hotel stands the *Sikhot Hotel* (☎ 212254, 212225), housed in a former police station

from the French era. The interior of the hotel was redone three years ago in a surreal Art Deco style; the staff are friendly but there's the general feeling that rooms here may be used for assignations with women from the adjacent Sikhot Discotheque. Large, clean rooms in the main building feature high ceilings, air-con, hot water and TV for 13,000 to 16,000 kip depending on the room. A motel-like new building around the back has less expensive rooms costing 6000/8000 kip single/double with fan and hot water.

The *Phoudoi Hotel* (☎ 212048), near the main junction for Route 13 on the east side of town, is a new place where small rooms with two twin beds, TV, air-con, fan and hot-water shower cost 12,000 kip. It's not as good a deal as the Khammouan Hotel and service is slack. Behind is the Baw Phaw Daw Discotheque; the name stands for 'Bolisat Phattanakhet Phu Doi', the name of the military-backed conglomerate that own this hotel and dominates economics and politics in Khammuan Province.

In Lak Sao you can stay at the Baw Pha Daw's second *Phoudoi Hotel* for 14,000 kip a night.

Places to Eat

Although there's no shortage of small restaurants and noodle shops in Tha Khaek, none of them are culinary stand-outs. The *Phavilai Restaurant*, on Thanon Kuvaravong near the river landing and fountain square, serves standard Lao-Chinese rice and noodle dishes; it's open from morning till evening. You'll also find several khào jii vendors on the fountain square in the morning.

Just upriver from the fountain square is a small, unnamed *noodle shop* run by two women who make delicious fõe hàeng, 'dry rice noodles' served in a bowl with various herbs and seasonings but no broth; regular fõe is also available.

The *Kulaap Daeng (Red Rose) Restaurant*, behind the Khammouan Hotel on Thanon Chao Anou, offers Thai, Lao and Chinese ahāan taam sang (food according to order) – it's nothing special but is one of the only enclosed restaurants in town. Better is the *B Soukchreune Restaurant* (☎ 212551) on Thanon Unkham, a clean, nicely decorated place (for a provincial restaurant) with a variety of Lao, Thai and Chinese rice dishes.

There are lots of noodle vendors at Talaat Lak Sawng, plus a smaller cluster of noodle and rice shops near Talaat Lak Saam (Talaat Suksombun) and near the Vientiane bus terminal on Route 13. Look for sweet Tha Khaek watermelons, a local speciality.

Getting There & Away

Air Lao Aviation has had an on-again off-again flight between Vientiane and Tha Khaek costing US$57 each way for foreigners. The American-built runway is currently under renovation and the nearest operating airport is at Lak Sao. The Lao Aviation schedule lists a weekly flight between Vientiane and Lak Sao but in reality the flights go only when at least six passengers make advance bookings – which at the moment isn't very often. The flight takes an hour and 10 minutes and costs US$50.

Road Two direct buses a day leave Vientiane's bus terminal for the 360 km, 10 hour trip to Tha Khaek; the fare is 3500 kip. You can also catch Savannakhet or Pakse-bound buses and get off in Tha Khaek for the same fare. The road between Pakxan and Tha Khaek is in very poor condition much of the way but is undergoing reconstruction. Once the road is brought up to standard the bus trip should take less than six hours.

In Tha Khaek the main terminal for Vientiane and other north-bound buses stands next to a Vietnamese cemetery on Route 13 at the north-east edge of town. Savannakhet and other south-bound buses depart from Talaat Lak Saam (Talaat Suksombun) at Km 3 on Route 13 south. The bus to Savan takes three hours and costs 1700 kip; there are three departures per day in the early morning, late morning and late afternoon.

Flat-bed trucks with wooden carriages ply two basic routes into the Khammuan Province interior, one to Mahaxai (toward the Nakai-Nam Theun NBCA) and the other to Yommalat (vicinity of Khammuan Lime-stone NBCA). There are only two departures per day along both lines, one at 7.30 am and another at noon from the terminal near the cemetery. Mahaxai and Yommalat cost 400 kip; intermediate points are 200 to 300 kip.

River The long-distance river ferry service from Vientiane has been discontinued. If reinstated (not likely except if massive flooding occurs along Route 13 south), the trip from Vientiane will take around eight to 10 hours to reach Tha Khaek, depending on the number of stops along the way.

To/From Nakhon Phanom Ferries cross the Mekong frequently from 8 am to 5 pm weekdays, and to 12.20 pm Saturday. The fare is 35B each way. On the Tha Khaek side, the passenger ferry landing sits 100m north of the Khammouan Hotel; a vehicle ferry landing is directly opposite the hotel.

From Bangkok, Nakhon Phanom is served by express bus.

Getting Around

Jumbos cost 200 kip from the river to Km 2, and 300 kip to Km 3 or the Vientiane bus terminal.

AROUND THA KAEK
Wat Pha That Si Khotabong

Also known as Wat Sikhotabun and Pha That Meuang Kao, this temple, eight km south of town, is a 19th century wat with a large seated Buddha, constructed by order of King Chao Anou. According to local lore this temple was erected on the site of an earlier 10th-century thâat built by King Nanthasen during an era when Tha Khaek was part of a principality called Si Khotabun. Considered one of the most important thâat in Laos, Si Khotabong was restored in the 1950s and augmented in the 1970s. It's visible from the Thai side of the river and is the site of a major temple festival on the full moon of the third lunar month.

Striking limestone formations in the vicinity, especially those along the Se Bang Fai river near **Mahaxai**, 50 km east via Route 12, are the province's drawing card for future

The 19th century Wat Pha That Si Khotabong is considered one of the most important wats in Laos.

fairly undistinguished village, Lak Sao (Kilometre 20) has become the the pet development project of Phattanakhet Phu Doi Co, an enterprise headed by a Lao military general and involved in logging, hotels, construction and cargo transport. The district now boasts a population of 24,000 and is set to become an industrial zone servicing the Vietnam-Laos-Thailand trade along Routes 8 and 12. A market at Lak Sao is known for the sale of wildlife, mostly birds, squirrels, rats, rabbits and reptiles but also rarer and more threatened species.

Savannakhet Province
ແຂວງສະວັນນະເຂດ

Savannakhet is the country's most populous province (671,000, around 15% of the nation's population) and is a very active trade junction between Thailand and Vietnam. The population consists of lowland Lao, Thai Dam, several small Mon-Khmer groups (Lavai, Katang, Pako, Suay, Bru, Mangtong, Kaleung, Chali), Vietnamese and second or third-generation Chinese. The rural villages of Savannakhet are among the most typically Lao, especially those in the Jamphon river valley near Ban Kengkok (south-east of the capital).

Savannakhet is the best place in Laos for seeing the flotsam of the Ho Chi Minh Trail, the main South Vietnam supply route for the NVA during the Indochinese War. It is also the principal gateway for visitors arriving overland from Vietnam via Lao Bao.

About 85 km north of the capital, the 1050 sq km **Phu Xang He National Biodiversity Conservation Area** covers a hilly area of dense evergreen and deciduous forest. IUCN and WCS surveys have suggested the presence of 17 bird species deemed of conservation importance (including the Siamese fireback and red-collared woodpecker), along with animals like elephant, giant muntjac, gaur, banteng, lesser slow loris, Douc langur and tiger.

tourism. Water-sculpted rocks at **Tha Falang** are reachable by pirogue along scenic Nam Don, 14 km east of Tha Khaek via Route 12. Also known as Wang Santiphap, Tha Falang (French Landing) features a wooded area on a stream where French colonials used to picnic.

Well-known limestone caves nearby include **Tham Xieng Liap**, a tunnel intersected by a year-round stream; **Tham Phaa Baan Tham**, a Buddhist shrine cave; **Tham Naang Aen**, a favoured weekend destination for the 'natural air-conditioning' provided by a constant breeze issuing from the cave; and **Tham Phaa Xang**, a large cave complex with separate floors connected by ladders. These caves, as well as hundreds of other unnamed caves, are an important habitat for an extensive variety of bat species. All are accessible from Route 12 between Km 8 and Km 16 along the way from Tha Khaek to Mahaxai; to reach them you'll need your own transport – mountain bike, motorbike or sturdy car/truck – and directions from Tha Khaek.

A road heads east to **Lak Sao** (also spelt Lak Xao) at Ban Vieng Kham, around 30 km north of town on Route 13 halfway between Hin Boun and Tha Khaek. Until recently a

The banteng is one of several species of wild cattle in Laos facing extinction.

SAVANNAKHET ສະວັນນະເຂດ

Officially known as Muang Khanthabuli (but more commonly called Muang Savan or simply Savan), this growing district of 124,000 just across the Mekong river from Mukdahan, Thailand, has become a major relay point for small trade between Thailand and Vietnam. From Savan, Route 9 extends east all the way to the Vietnamese border at Lao Bao, where it continues eastward to the port of Dong Ha on the lower Gulf of Tonkin. Savan is also a lumber centre and there are several lumberyards on the outskirts of town.

Information

Savannakhet Tourism Co (☎ 212733), housed in the Savanbanhao Hotel on Thanon Saenna, has information on local attractions and can arrange tours to Sepon, the Ho Chi Minh Trail, Heuan Hin and other spots outside the city. SODETOUR (☎ (041) 212260) also has a branch in town near the main square.

There is a post office on Thanon Khanthabuli just south of the town centre. You can change money (cash) at the Lao May Bank on Thanon Khanthabuli just west of Thanon Si Muang. Savan's area code is 41.

St Theresa's Catholic Church conducts mass (in Lao) weekdays at 5.30 am, Sundays 7.30 am.

Town Centre

The Vietnamese presence in Savan grew during the French colonial era and, although it diminished during the war, a local Vietnamese school, Mahayana Buddhist temple and a Catholic church testify to a continued Vietnamese influence.

Like Vientiane and Luang Prabang, Savan has a number of French colonial and Franco-Chinese buildings, most of which are found in the small downtown **business district** near the intersection of Thanon Khanthabuli and Thanon Si Muang. Daily activity centres around the cargo and passenger piers for ferries across the river to Mukdahan. Boats are loaded to the gunwales with Chinese and Vietnamese-made goods – particularly ceramics – on their way to Thailand.

Another centre of activity is **Talaat Yai** (Large Market) off Thanon Udomsin. The market runs all day and is visited by a fascinating variety of people.

Along Thanon Phetsalat downtown, in the

PLACES TO STAY

3 Nanhai Hotel
5 Phonepaseut Hotel
8 Hoongtip Hotel
15 Savanbanhao Hotel
18 Savanh I Hotel
20 Mekong Hotel
23 Santyphab Hotel
30 Auberge du Paradis
   (Sala Savanh Guest House)
32 Sayamungkhun Guest House
35 Phonevilay Hotel

PLACES TO EAT

19 Nang Khamweung
21 Four Seasons Restaurant
27 Nang Iam Foe

OTHER

1 Petrol Station
2 Wat Chom Kaew
4 Petrol Station
6 Banque Pour Le Commerce
   Extérieur Lao (BCEL)
7 Talaat Yai
9 Boat Ticket Office
10 Pier for Boats to Vientiane
   & Tha Khaek
11 Pier for Vehicle Ferry
   to Thailand
12 Wat Sainyaphum
13 Kouvoravong Statue
14 Chinese Temple
16 Vietnamese School
17 Vietnamese Consulate
22 Pier for Passenger Ferry to
   Mukdahan (Thailand)
24 Lao May Bank
25 Savannakhet Chinese School
26 Wat Lattanalangsi
28 St Theresa's Catholic Church
29 Petrol Station
31 Wat Sainyamungkhun
33 Cinema
34 Post Office
36 Airport

Savannakhet

0   100   200 m

SOUTHERN LAOS

vicinity of Wat Sainyamungkhun, are two dirt *pétanques* where older Lao and Vietnamese men toss metal balls about in the French game of *boules*.

Wat Sainyaphum

ວັດໄຊຍະພູມ

This temple on the river is Savan's largest and oldest. An unrestored *sim* dates to the 1896 founding of the temple. Also on the grounds is a large, elegantly designed secondary school for monks, which brings the resident monastic population to over 200; among them is the oldest monk in Laos.

Wat Lattanalangsi

ວັດລັດຕະນະລັງສີ

Nearly as large as Wat Sainyaphum, this wat was built in 1951 and houses a monks' primary school. The sim is unique in that it has glass windows (most Lao temple windows are unglazed). Other structures include a gaudy Brahma shrine, a new *sáaláa lóng thám*, and a shelter containing a 15m reclining Buddha backed by *jataka* paintings.

Places to Stay – bottom end

Savan's cheaper hotels were once clustered

in the older part of town toward the ferry piers. Only one is still in operation, the run-down *Santyphab Hotel* (☎ 212277) on Thanon Tha Dan, two blocks east of the main ferry pier. Basic rooms cost 3000/3500 kip single/double with fan or 5000 kip air-con, both with shared bath.

On the river in an old French colonial villa is the Vietnamese-owned *Mekong Hotel* (☎ 212249), with large, high-ceiling rooms, ceiling fans, air-con, tile floors and lots of wood panelling. The musty rooms are in poor condition, however, and the place seems deserted most of the time, except at night when the downstairs nightclub is filled with Vietnamese men and Vietnamese host-esses. Rates are 5000 kip single/double if you don't turn on the air-con, 7500 kip with air-con.

Two slightly more upscale budget places can be found on Thanon Saenna in the middle of town not far from Talaat Yai. Con-sisting of four two-storey houses built around a series of courtyards, the *Savan-banhao Hotel* (☎ 212202) has the largest variety of rooms in town. Large single-bed rooms with air-con and shared hot-water shower cost 5000 kip, similar rooms with private hot-water shower cost 7700 kip and rooms with two beds and a one-channel black & white TV are 8700 kip. The mid-price rooms are very good value. This is also the headquarters for Savannakhet Tourism.

Next door on Thanon Saenna is the similar *Savanh I Hotel*, which since 1993 has been completely taken over by a group of expat geologists for an undetermined period.

Toward the south end of town are two rather recent entries into the accommodation market. The *Phonevilay Hotel* (☎ 212284) at 137 Thanon Phetsalat bears a sign reading 'Hotel-Restaurant-Dancing-Dry cleaning and Administrative' and consists of one and two-storey cottages built around a small courtyard. Rooms come in varying sizes. As the rates climb the rooms increase in size and the mattresses become softer. Simple 3500 kip rooms come with two beds, fan and shared cold-water shower, while 5500 kip buys two beds with air-con and private

shower. Three-bed rooms with air-con and hot-water shower cost 6500/7500/8500 single/double/triple. Slightly larger rooms with TV and fridge and all the rest are 10,000 kip single/double.

Sayamungkhun Guest House (☎ (041) 212426) offers big, spotlessly clean rooms in a big house on Thanon Latsavongseuk for 4000 kip with fan, 8000 to 10,000 kip with air-con, all with private toilet and shower. The only drawback here is its location on a busy street.

If you have an early bus to catch, or if you simply want to stay in the cheapest place in town, there's a *Vietnamese-owned motel* along one side of the bus terminal north of town with bare two and three-bed rooms for 800 kip per person.

Places to Stay – middle & top end
Situated eight blocks north of the airport off Thanon Sisavangvong, the *Phonepaseut Hotel* (☎ 212158) offers clean, modern rooms around a small courtyard and a 25m-long pool across the street – probably the best pool in all of Laos, it's free for guests or 800 kip for visitors. All rooms come with refrig-erator, TV, air-con and private hot water showers, and cost US$15/20 single/double for foreigners. This is where UN staffers and employees of other international aid agen-cies typically stay.

The centrally located *Auberge du Paradis (Salasavanh Guest House)* (☎ 212445) on Thanon Kuvoravong near the main square is housed in a restored 1926 French villa with tile and wood floors throughout. Spacious rooms with air-con, hot water, fan and mos-quito nets cost US$25 single/double. There's a garden at the back with a sitting area where meals can be arranged in advance. SODET-OUR has a branch office here.

The new *Hoongtip Hotel* (☎ 212262), a four-storey neo-gothic place on the corner of Thanons Phetsalat and Udomsin charges US$21 for large modern rooms with air-con and hot water. Built with the cheapest mater-ials, this is the kind of hotel that will probably look very run-down in five years.

There is an attached restaurant and night club, but no lift.

Further north at the edge of town off Thanon Latsavongseuk is the huge six-storey *Nanhai Hotel* (☎ 212371). Built by a Guangdong company, quality is fairly high; rooms with all the mod-cons range from US$34 to 45. Facilities on the premises include a lift, karaoke lounge, restaurant and swimming pool.

Places to Eat

Savan isn't exactly a culinary capital but there are plenty of opportunities to sample Thai, Chinese and Vietnamese food. Local specialities include *sîn sawăn* (a slightly sweet, dried, roasted beef), and *jaew pạadàek*, a thick sauce of mashed chilli, onion, fish sauce and lotus bulb.

In the centre of town are many small Chinese-Vietnamese restaurants, none of them particularly outstanding. Lao food can be difficult to find, but *Nang Khamweung*, a very humble two-table place on Thanon Phetsalat (a block north of Thanon Si Muang) is famous for beef or buffalo lâap and of course sticky rice; it's generally open from noon to 11 pm daily.

Of the many places offering fŏe, local consensus says the best is an unmarked *hâan khăi fŏe* called *Nang Iam* east of the Catholic church near Huay Longkong (third house on the left from Thanon Latsavongseuk). A huge bowl of steaming fŏe here costs 700 kip and comes with a table full of condiments – including saucers of small but incendiary yellow-and-purple-streaked chillies.

Nang Bin cafe and noodle (mii) shop opposite Hoongtip Hotel is good. There are a few more *noodle shops* in the next block north along Thanon Phetsalat. At the south-east corner of Talaat Yai are several *coffee stands* which are good for a cheap breakfast.

A small night market called *Savanhlaty Food Garden*, towards the river from the church in the small town plaza, serves good, inexpensive Lao, Chinese and Thai food. Two side-by-side, hole-in-the-wall *Vietnamese restaurants* a half block north of the square serve around 10 or 11 Thai dishes in

addition to Vietnamese standards. It's 500 kip for any two dishes over rice.

Friendship Restaurant, a small white building with coloured lights and curtained dividers between tables, serves uninspired Vietnamese and Chinese food.

The *Four Seasons Restaurant* (☎ 212792), whose sign merely says 'French Food Restaurant', is housed in an old Chinese shophouse near the river. Run by a friendly Lao-Vietnamese couple who spent many years in France and Thailand, this cozy spot features Lao, Vietnamese and French dishes, including lâap, năem néuang, pizza, steak frites, breakfast and Lao coffee. Prices are reasonable; they also offer bicycles for rent. The charming little building may be razed by the city in its efforts to become more 'modern', so look for a change of location.

One block north of the Lao May Bank is an ice cream shop called *Nang Bunliem*.

The *Phonepaseut, Savanbanhao, Hoongtip* and *Nanhai* hotels have their own restaurants. The Savanbanhao (whose restaurant is actually across the street from the hotel) has quite decent food, although the Phonepaseut is more geared toward serving foreigners. The Hoongtip and Nanhai are a bit pricey.

Entertainment

The *Savanbanhao, Phonepaseut* and *Mekong* hotels have popular discos.

Getting There & Away

Air Lao Aviation flies Y-7 turboprops to Savannakhet daily. The fare for foreigners is US$61 one way and the journey takes one hour and five minutes.

Flights from Pakse leave twice a week when there are enough passengers. This leg costs US$40 and takes 50 minutes.

Road Bus travel to and from Savan will be much faster when the current upgrading project along Route 13 is finished. At the moment travel can be gruelling as the road is in very poor condition except in the immediate vicinity (around 10 km in either direction) of major towns.

Two buses per day leave Vientiane's Talaat Sao bus terminal for the 12 hour ride to Savannakhet. The fare is 7000 kip. In both directions, buses leave around 5 am and 11 am. When the road is fully sealed travel time will probably be cut in half and departures may be more frequent.

To/from Pakse the bus costs 2500 kip and takes around six hours; there are usually two departures between 5 and 7 am each morning, but the only way to know for sure is to show up. As with Vientiane, this trip will be much quicker when Route 13 is finished.

River Long-distance ferry service to Savannakhet from Vientiane has been indefinitely suspended.

To/From Mukdahan, Thailand Ferries frequently cross the Mekong river between Savan and Mukdahan between 8.30 am and 5 pm weekdays and 8.30 am to 12.30 pm Saturday, for 30B from Thailand, 850 kip from Laos.

It's now legal for foreigners to enter and exit the country via Savannakhet; no special permission is needed.

To/From Lao Bao, Vietnam It is legal to enter or exit the country overland via Lao Bao on the Lao-Vietnamese border. From the Savan end, one bus a day goes to the border along unpaved Route 9 at 5 am, arriving around 5 pm for 2800 kip. In the reverse direction the bus leaves around 7 am. The 100 km road is rough going and buses tend to be very crowded. Road travel can be especially difficult during the rainy season from June to October.

Dong Ha, on Vietnam's main north-south highway and railway, is only 75 km east of Lao Bao.

If you don't already have a visa for Vietnam, you can obtain one at the Vietnamese Consulate in Savannakhet or Pakse.

Getting Around

Savan is just big enough that you might want to resort to samlor on occasion. Fares are comparable with those in Vientiane, around 200 kip per km. The Savan equivalent to Vientiane's jumbo is the *sakai-laep* or 'Skylab' – like the famed space lab that lost its orbit and fell to earth.

You can rent bicycles for 1000 kip a day at the Four Seasons Restaurant.

AROUND SAVANNAKHET
That Ing Hang ທາດອິງຮັງ

Thought to have been built in the mid-16th century (about the same time as Vientiane's Pha That Luang and north-eastern Thailand's That Phanom), this well-proportioned, nine metre thâat is the holiest religious edifice in southern Laos. Built on the site where Chao Fa Ngum's forces were based during the liberation of Meuang Sawa, the monument features three terraced bases topped by a traditional Lao stupa and a gold umbrella weighing 40 *baht* (450g).

A hollow chamber in the lower section contains an undistinguished collection of Buddha images (by religious custom, women are not permitted to enter the chamber). Some original stucco decoration on the exterior remains intact but the sculpture in the outside niches is new and not very well executed.

The grounds are surrounded by high cloister walls on three sides and a low wall in front, with ornate gates on all four sides. Some older standing Buddha images in a small sim next to the main thâat are worth seeing if you can get someone to unlock the door.

Behind the That Ing Hang cloister are several wooden temple buildings used by eight resident monks.

On the full moon of February or March there is a big That Ing Hang Festival featuring processions and fireworks.

Getting There & Away That Ing Hang is 12 km north of Savan via Route 13, then three km east on a dirt road. Any north-bound bus passes this turnoff.

Heuan Hin ເຮືອນຫີນ

Located on the Mekong river south of Savan

is this set of Khmer ruins (the name means Stone House), built between 553 and 700 AD. Of interest mainly to Khmer art fanatics, the unrestored ruins are little more than a few walls and piles of laterite rubble.

The best way to get to Heuan Hin is by boat along the Mekong – when the water's high enough it's a 70 km, three hour trip by long-tail boat. By road you must first travel 75 km south via Route 13, then 15 km west along a rough road.

That Phon ທຳ ໄພນ

Said to date from the 16th century, this large, rounded white stupa similar to Luang Prabang's That Makmo (and like Makmo, said to contain a cache of valuable Buddha images) is 65 km south of Savan off Route 13 on the way to Heuan Hin.

SEPON (XEPON) & THE HO CHI MINH TRAIL ເຊໂປນ

The nearest town to the Ho Chi Minh Trail (see box) is Sepon (often spelt 'Xepon', pop 35,600), approximately 170 km east of Savannakhet via Route 9. Sepon was destroyed during the war and is now just another of the many makeshift wooden towns that mark the long-term bombing legacy of eastern Laos.

Sepon is a starting point for visitors to the Trail, the outer edges of which begin some 15 to 20 km to the east. Although there's plenty of debris around, much of it lies in the bush covered by undergrowth. Unless you're prepared to hike some distance from the road (you will need a guide because of the danger of UXO), it's not worth going all the way out to Sepon.

Ho Chi Minh Trail

The infamous Ho Chi Minh Trail – actually a complex network of dirt paths and gravel roads – runs parallel to the Lao-Vietnamese border beginning at a point directly east from the capital of Savannakhet Province.

Though most associated with the 1963-74 Indochina War, the road network was originally used by the Viet Minh against the French in the '50s as an infiltration route to the south. The Trail's heaviest use occurred between 1966 and 1971 when over 600,000 NVA troops – along with 100 tonnes of provisions and a half-million tonnes of trucks, tanks, weapons and ordnance – passed along the route. At any one time around 25,000 NVA troops guarded the Trail, which was honeycombed with underground barracks, fuel and motor repair depots and anti-aircraft emplacements.

The North Vietnamese denied the existence of the Trail throughout most of the war. The USA, on their part, denied bombing it. In spite of 1.1 million tonnes of saturation bombing (begun in 1965 and reaching up to 900 sorties per day by 1969, including outings by B-52 behemoths), traffic along the route was never interrupted for more than a few days. Like a column of ants parted with a stick, soldiers and supplies poured southward with only an estimated 15 to 20% of the cargo affected by heavy bombardment. One estimate says that 300 bombs were dropped for every NVA casualty. The Yanks even tried bombing the Trail with canned Budweiser beer (incapacitation through intoxication!), Calgonite dishwasher detergent (to make the Trail too slippery for travel) and massive quantities of defoliants and herbicides.

The nearest town to the Ho Chi Minh Trail is Sepon (often spelt 'Xepon', pop 35,600), approximately 170 km east of Savannakhet via Route 9. Sepon was destroyed during the war and is now just another of the many makeshift wooden towns that mark the long-term bombing legacy of eastern Laos. From Sepon the outer edges of the Ho Chi Minh Trail are another 15 to 20 km.

A short distance north or south along the Trail, parts of downed helicopters and fighter planes, along with tonnes of other war junk, can be seen. Because of the area's remoteness from scrap metal markets, much of the debris lies untouched. However, near Route 9, the only visible remains are a few bomb craters and a tank wreck or two.

Ban Dong, 34 km west of the Vietnamese border, has a few houses partially built from the scrap metal. Eastern Savannakhet Province (along with Salavan, Sekong and Attapeu farther south) is also one of the primary areas where joint Lao-American teams – under the direction of a US colonel in Vientiane – are searching for the remains of American MIAs. Eighty percent of the American soldiers not yet accounted for in Laos (519 men as of 1993) are thought to have gone down somewhere along the Ho Chi Minh Trail. ■

A few km east is the small village of Ban Dong, and 34 km further on is the Vietnamese border itself, where there is a small market in Vietnamese and Chinese goods.

Places to Stay

Rustic guest house accommodation is available in Sepon, and at least one new hotel is under construction.

Getting There & Away

The bus from Savan to the Vietnamese border stops in Sepon for 2000 kip. Savannakhet Tourism at the Savanbanhao Hotel can arrange car and driver for up to five passengers for around US$200.

Salavan Province
ແຂວງສາລະວັນ

The big attraction in Salavan (often spelt Saravan or Saravane) is the Bolaven plateau, which actually straddles Salavan, Sekong, Champasak and Attapeu provinces. On the Se Set (Set River, a tributary of the Se Don) are several waterfalls and traditional Lao villages. Like the Plain of Jars in Xieng Khuang Province, the Bolaven plateau has an excellent climate. Tourist accommodation is available on the Champasak side of the plateau (see the Champasak Province section for more information).

Among the province's approximately 256,000 inhabitants are a number of relatively obscure Mon-Khmer groups, including Ta-oy (Tahoy), Lavai, Alak, Laven, Katang, Ngai, Tong, Pako, Kanay, Katu and Kado. There are no Lao Sung native to the area.

The province boasts 51% natural forest cover though only one section has thus far received protected status. **Phu Xieng Thong NBCA** covers 995 sq km adjacent to the Mekong river in the western part of the province (about 25 km north of Pakse), the only NBCA in Laos that encompasses the river's typical flats and sandbanks. The opposite bank is protected by Thailand's Pha Taem National Park; both sides are characterised by exposed sandstone ridges and outcroppings (some containing rock shelters with prehistoric cave paintings), interspersed with scrub and mixed monsoon deciduous forest. Rare beasts thought to inhabit this area include elephant, gaur, banteng, Douc langur, gibbon, Asiatic black bear, clouded leopard, tiger and Siamese crocodile.

In the far north-eastern corner of the province is **Samouy**, a district that was part of Savannakhet Province before recent reapportionment. Bordering Vietnam, it's remote and difficult to access, but a 162 km dry-season road will soon be cut to Samouy (and Tahoy) via Route 23 north of the capital. Samouy is an official border crossing – for Lao and Vietnamese only – between Da Lai in Vietnam and this district.

SALAVAN ສາລະວັນ

The provincial capital of Salavan was all but destroyed in the war, when it bounced back and forth between RLG and PL occupation. The rebuilt town is a collection of brick and wood buildings with a population of around 40,000. Only the post office shows evidence of the French era.

The town market was until relatively recently famous for its wildlife products, but this notorious trade seems to have shifted to Lak Sao further north in Khammuan Province.

Information

You can change US dollars or Thai baht for kip (cash only) at the Phak Tai Bank.

Places to Stay & Eat

The government-owned *Saise Guest House* is about two km from the bus terminal. Follow the main road north-east coming from the bus terminal till it ends at a cluster of three buildings near the river. The main building has several rooms with shared facilities for 6000/8000 kip single/double, plus three rooms with two beds, fan and private facilities for 6500/8500 kip. A second building, not quite as nice, has one-bed rooms for 4000 kip, a seven-bed room for 2000 kip per bed and a couple of rooms with two beds for 4500 kip, all with shared facilities. The third building has five rooms with shared bath for 4500 kip single/double or 6000 kip triple.

There are several *noodle shops* in the vicinity of market, plus a small night market along a side street near the main market with pre-cooked Lao food.

The *Ladda Café* serves Lao and Chinese food, although it's best to order in advance to be sure they have what the menu says they have. *Bouavan Ratree* is a restaurant and nightclub with Lao food, live Lao music and taxi dancing.

Getting There & Away
Air Lao Aviation intermittently schedules flights to Salavan, stopping first at Savannakhet and continuing on to Pakse. When flights are operating, the fare is US$91 one way from Vientiane or US$37 from Savannakhet. Service was suspended in 1995 to work on upgrading the American airstrip in Salavan and may resume in 1996 with flights to/from Pakse only.

Road There are regular passenger trucks to Salavan from Pakse in Champasak Province via Khong Sedon between 5 and 10 am. Recently overhauled, the road (Route 20) between these two towns is now quite good – perhaps the best interprovincial road in the country thus far. The 150 km trip takes only three hours (instead of five previously) and costs 1500 kip per person.

Trucks to/from Sekong (90 km) along Route 16 cost 2000 kip and take up to 10 hours; see the Sekong section for details. From Sekong you can continue on to Attapeu.

If you're coming from the north along Route 13, get off in Khong Sedon to connect with the bus to Salavan instead of riding all the way to Pakse. The one-way distance (87 km) is about the same but you save time and money by not having to backtrack. The fare from Khong Sedon to Salavan is 1200 kip.

During the dry season you can take Route 23 north via Tumlan to Route 9 in the Sepon area.

AROUND SALAVAN
The natural lake of **Nong Bua**, 14 km east of town near the source of the Don river (Se Don), is famous for its crocodiles *(khàe* in Lao), which are most abundant during the rainy season. Visible nearby is **Phu Katae**, a 1588m peak.

Nong Kangdong, a lake in Khong Sedon district south-west of the capital, also reportedly has crocs. In this same district stands a decaying 300-year-old stupa, 10m **That Kadaotuk**, an important regional pilgrimage spot.

In **Tumlan**, a Katang village around 40 km north of the capital via Route 23, you can see a 100m, 30-family longhouse and observe local weaving techniques. Katang textiles differ substantially from the well-known textiles of northern Laos, featuring more numerous, narrower bands of colours and patterns.

The **Tahoy** (Ta-oy) district, north-east of Tumlan, is a centre for the Ta-oy ethnic group, who number around 26,000 spread across eastern Salavan and Sekong provinces. The Ta-oy live in forested mountain valleys at 300 to 1000m, often in areas shared by the Katu and other Mon-Khmer groups. Like many Mon-Khmer groups in southern Laos, they practice a combination of animism and shamanism; during village ceremonies, the Ta-oy post diamond-patterned bamboo totems outside the village to warn outsiders not to enter. Ta-oy textiles are valued locally and by collectors in Vientiane. Visitors are only permitted to stay in the district chief's house.

Champasak Province
ແຂວງຈຳປາສັກ

The Champasak area has a long history that began with Kambuja occupation during the Funan (a Chinese mispronunciation of Phanom) and Chenla empires between the 1st and 9th centuries AD. From the 10th to 13th centuries Champasak was part of the

Cambodian Angkor Empire. Following the decline of Angkor between the 15th and late 17th centuries, it was enfolded into the Lan Xang Kingdom but then broke away to become an independent Lao kingdom at the beginning of the 18th century. The short-lived Champasak Kingdom had three monarchs: Soi Sisamut (nephew of Sulinya Vongsa, 1713-37), Sainyakuman (1737-91) and Fai Na (1791-1811).

Today Champasak Province (prior to 1975 three separate provinces – Champasak, Sedon and Sithandon) has a population of around 500,000 that includes lowland Lao (including many Phu Thai), Khmers and a host of small Mon-Khmer groups – Suay, Ta-oy (Tahoy), Lavai, Chieng, Nyaheun, Laven, Kaseng, Katang, Ngai, Inthi, Oung, Katu, Kien, Salao, Tahang and Kate – most of whom live in the Bolaven plateau region.

Timber is the province's main source of income, followed by coffee, tea, cardamom, rattan and other agricultural products. The province is also well known for *mat-mii* silks and cottons that are hand-woven of tie-dyed threads.

PAKSE ປາກເຊ

Founded by the French as an administrative outpost in 1905, Pakse (pop 64,000) is a relatively new town at the confluence of the Mekong and the Don rivers. It is now the capital of Champasak Province but is mainly of interest to the traveller as a point of departure for the Bolaven plateau, the Khmer ruins at Wat Phu Champasak, Si Phan Don (Four Thousand Islands) or Ubon Ratchathani, Thailand. There are only a few colonial-era buildings left standing, most of Franco-Chinese design. One of the better examples is the elaborately ornamented **Chinese Society** building on Thanon 10 in the centre of town.

The large and lively **market** features a very good selection of produce due to Pakse's proximity to the fertile Bolaven plateau. An enclosed market building contains clothes, household goods, preserved foods and gold shops. Trade with Thailand is brisk and the economy is also boosted by the presence of a large pharmaceutical factory four km south of town.

Opposite the ferry pier on the Mekong River's west bank is **Ban Muang Kao**, the beginning of the road journey to Chong Mek on the Thai border. You'll see lots of Thai-land-bound timber being loaded onto barges here.

Short day trips from Pakse can be made to **Taat Sae** waterfall at Km 8 south off Route 13. **Ban Saphai**, a weaving village 15 km north of town, produces distinctive silk and cotton *phàa sálóng*, long sarongs for men.

Many of the town's population are of Chinese or Vietnamese descent – you might want to avoid Pakse during Tet (Chinese and Vietnamese New Year), when the whole town becomes a fireworks battlefield for three days.

Information

Money You can change Thai baht or US dollars (cash) for kip at the BCEL branch near the market and Pakse Hotel. It's open weekdays 8.30 am to 3.30 pm, Saturday 8.30 to 10 am. Phak Tai Bank on Route 13 also changes money, albeit at a lower rate than BCEL.

Post & Communications The main post office is at the corner of Thanons 8 and 1, not far from the river. A new telephone/fax/tele-graph office has opened on Thanon 1, not far from the Champasak Palace Hotel. Pakse's area code is 31.

Travel Agencies You can arrange tours to the Bolaven plateau, Wat Phu Champasak or Don Khong (Khong island) from SODET-OUR (☎ (031) 212122, near the ferry pier), Lane Xang Tour (☎ (031) 212281, next to the Suksamlan Hotel), Inter-Lao Tourisme (☎ (031) 212226, on Route 13 near Phak Tai Bank) or Lao Travel Service (☎ (031) 212503, at Notre Village on Thanon 9).

These agencies can arrange private boats holding up to 20 persons to Wat Phu Champasak for US$40 roundtrip or to Don Khong for US$200

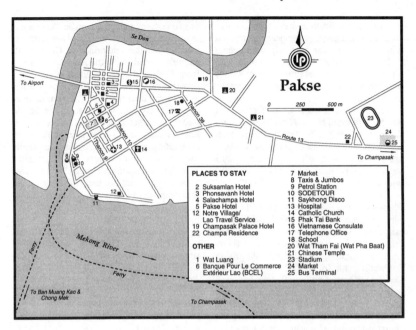

Temples

There are around 20 wats in the city, of which **Wat Luang** and **Wat Tham Fai** (both founded in 1935) are the largest. A monastic school at Wat Luang features highly ornate concrete pillars, heavy carved wooden doors and murals; the whimsy of the artist departs from canonical art without losing the overall traditional effect. Behind the sim is an older monks' school housed in an original wooden building. A thâat on the grounds contains the ashes of Khamtai Loun Sasothith, a former prime minister in the Royal Lao Government before his death in 1959.

Wat Tham Fai, near the Champasak Palace Hotel, is undistinguished except for its spacious wat grounds, which make it a prime site for temple festivals. It's also known as Wat Pha Baat because there's a small Buddha footprint shrine on the premises.

Places to Stay – bottom end

The *Phonsavanh Hotel* (☎ 212842), on the main road crossing the Se Don from the west, has very basic rooms for 4000/5000/6000 kip single/double/triple, all with shared toilet and bath.

Near the downtown market the large *Pakse Hotel* has better rooms starting at 4400 kip for a single/double with ceiling fan and shared bath at the front of the hotel, 6600 kip for a quieter single/double of the same sort toward the back or 8800 kip for a single/double with air-con and private cold-water bath. There are also some singles with bath and air-con toward the front costing 6600 kip.

The clean and friendly *Suksamlan (Souksamlane) Hotel* (☎ 212002) in the same downtown area has decent air-con rooms with private hot-water bath for 300B single, 400B double. Many of the guests at the Suksamlan are Thais doing business in Pakse. The associated *Suksambay Hotel* out near the airport offers similar accommodation.

SOUTHERN LAOS

Lao Travel Service has *Notre Village* (☎ 212503), a guest house near the hospital with five rooms for 5000 kip with shared bath, 7000/10,000 kip single/double with air-con and private facilities. Notre Village may move to an old French mansion nearby on the river.

Next to the Mekong river south of town at Km 5 is *Houyyangkham (Huay Nyang Kham) Guest House* (☎ 212755, fax 212756), a quiet spot with mountain and river scenery. There are 20 rooms in five cottages, each 300B with fan and private hot-water shower, 500B with air-con.

Places to Stay – middle & top end

The *Salachampa Hotel*, two blocks south-east of the Suksamlan in a restored French villa, offers huge rooms with wood floors (tiled downstairs), high ceilings and private hot-water bath for US$25 single/double. One larger corner suite with four beds and two rooms costs US$35, and a medium-size one with three beds is US$30. Breakfast is served on a pleasant terrace overlooking the courtyard. A set of newer rooms alongside the original building lack the charm of the old house and cost US$22. All rooms come with air-con and hot-water shower.

Champa Residence (☎ 212120, fax 212765) at the south-east edge of town, off Route 13 near the bus terminal, consists of three separate modern houses decorated in marble and teak. All rooms come with satellite TV, air-con and hot water; some have bathtubs, some showers only. Rates are US$25/30 single/double. The dining room serves breakfast, lunch and dinner; also on the premises is a small gift shop with some tribal crafts from Attapeu and Sekong. Champa Residence will pay your tuk-tuk fare from the bus terminal, boat landing or airport. It's good value in this range, though it's a bit of a hike from town.

Top end in Pakse is the Thai-owned *Champasak Palace Hotel* (☎ 212263; or (21) 215635, fax 215636 in Vientiane), on Route 13 about a kilometre east of the town centre. Once known in Lao as Wang Nyai Chao Bounome (Prince Bounome Palace),

this five-storey palace on the Se Don served as the former residence of Chao Bounome na Champasak, the last prince of Champasak and prime minister of the Kingdom of Laos from 1960 to 1962. Bounome started construction of the palace in 1968, fled to Paris in 1974 and died in 1978. The Thai renovation isn't bad – it's worth seeing for the tile floors and intact teak fittings on the bottom floor, though most of the interior has been completely redone. Plastic furniture spoils the old-era atmosphere in the dining room/bar – bamboo or rattan would have been better. There are nice views of the Se Don from the terrace and garden in back. Adjacent to the hotel is a steel bridge built by the Soviets in 1990.

Rates for large standard rooms at the Champasak Palace are US$36/40 single/double; larger superior rooms are US$40/44 and palatial VIP suites reach US$144. All rates include American breakfast, tax and service.

Places to Eat

Most of the restaurants and cafes in Pakse serve Chinese and Vietnamese food. Takeaway Lao food is available in the downtown market.

Restaurant Sedone, opposite the BCEL in the market area (near the Pakse Hotel), serves decent noodle soups, rice dishes, breakfast, Lao coffee and stir-fried dishes. It's open early till late and has a Lao/English menu.

Along the same street opposite the Pakse Hotel are several *Vietnamese-owned restaurants* serving noodles, steamed Chinese-style buns and spring rolls. The *Xuan Mai Restaurant*, on the corner opposite the Pakse Hotel, serves good fõe and khào pûn. Excellent mii pét (duck noodles) are available at a nondescript *restaurant* directly opposite the Salachampa Hotel.

The *Paliane* and *Suksamlan* restaurants next door to the Suksamlan Hotel are good and serve mostly Chinese food. The restaurant at the *Champasak Palace Hotel* serves decent Lao, Thai and Chinese food; prices are surprisingly moderate. This hotel also has the only fully stocked bar in Pakse.

Wat Phu Champasak

The site of Wat Phu Champasak was probably chosen by the Hindu Khmers of Angkor because of a spring that flows from near the top of the hill and because the peak is vaguely shaped like a *lingam* or Shiva phallus. Historians say that Phu Pasak was in fact sacred to the pre-Angkor kingdom of Chenla (6th-8th centuries AD) and may have been the site of human sacrifices; some scholars believe that Champasak may have been the capital of Chenla or even the earlier Funan (a Chinese mispronunciation of *phanom*, Khmer for hill). Whatever its provenance, the temple was the site of a cult closely associated with the Indianised monarchies of ancient Indochina, particularly the vast Khmer empire that 200 years later made Angkor its capital.

The layout of the site forms a logical progression through three levels, with a long promenade connecting them; a harmonious ascendance from river to plain to mountain that must have provided a powerful set of symbols for the cult.

For details on the Wat Phu Champasak site see text and plan starting on page 245. ■

JOE CUMMINGS

JOE CUMMINGS

Top Right: Trimurti - the Hindu triumvirate of Shiva, Vishnu and Brahma

Left: A finely-sculptured Parvati relief

Below: The Angkor-period pavilion at Wat Phu

JOE CUMMINGS

JOE CUMMINGS

JOE CUMMINGS

JOE CUMMINGS

JOE CUMMINGS

Southern Laos
Top Left: The 16th century That Ing Hang near Savannakhet
Top Right: The French-era Catholic church in Savannakhet
Bottom Left: Brightly painted local bus in Pakse
Bottom Right: Following the road to market in Don Khon, Si Phan Don

Dok Fang Daeng Restaurant, on Thanon 11 west of the market toward the river junction, is a huge place that serves Lao, Thai, Vietnamese and Chinese. It's open nightly except when reserved by groups.

Entertainment

For a night of modern Lao-style live music and taxi dancing, check out the *Sengtavan Cabaret* (behind SODETOUR near the ferry pier), *Saykhong Disco* (further south-east along the Mekong) or the *disco* downstairs from Suksambay Hotel near the airport.

Getting There & Away

Air Lao Aviation flies Y-7 turboprops to Pakse from Vientiane daily at 7 am. The flight takes an hour and 20 minutes and costs US$95 one way.

Twice a week Lao Aviation also operates flights between Pakse and Savannakhet; the fare is US$40 and flying time is 50 minutes. Flights are also scheduled once a week to/from Don Khong (US$30, 35 minutes), but in actual practice these flights only run when a tour group is on its way to Don Khong.

Once a week there's a flight to/from Attapeu (US$24, 35 minutes).

Pakse-Salavan flights appear on Lao Aviation's current rate sheet (US$29), but with the Salavan airfield in disrepair flights won't be going there for some time.

Lao Aviation used to have Friday flights between Pakse and Phnom Penh for US$35 one way but these were recently suspended.

In Pakse the Lao Aviation office (☎ 212252) is next to the airport, which is a couple of km north-west of town off Route 13. A small restaurant next to the airport opens early and serves good coffee and breakfast.

Road The intercity bus terminal is next to the large Km 2 market (Talaat Lak Sawng) on the south-eastern outskirts of town.

Direct buses between Vientiane and Pakse ply Route 13 once a day for 11,000 kip per person. These leave from either end around 6 am and take a gruelling 16 to 18 hours.

Two buses a day go to/from Savannakhet around 5 and 10 am. These cost 3200 kip per person and take four to six hours.

To/from Champasak there are truck departures at 9 and 11 am and 1 pm. The trip takes two hours and costs 700 kip. You can also hop a passenger truck bound for Don Talaat (12 km south of Champasak), since these stop off in Champasak, for the same fare.

Other departures: Salavan (8 am and 1 pm, two hours, 1500 kip); Sekong (6 am, five to six hours, 3000 kip); Attapeu (5 or 6 am, eight hours, 5000 kip); Paksong (frequently, between 6 am and 2 pm, one or two hours, 1000 kip).

For information on land transport from Pakse to Don Khong, see the Si Phan Don section later in this chapter.

Only a few proper buses leave out of Pakse; most of the public conveyances here are large flatbed trucks with heavy wooden carriages. Generally they're extremely crowded, with cargo piled two metres high on the roof so that they can barely move 15 kph at most. From Km 8 south of town all the way to the Cambodian border, the road is in very bad condition. Consider taking boats south instead; even though they're much slower than passenger trucks, the level of comfort is much higher.

The Asian Development Bank is funding two major roadways through Pakse and across the south to facilitate trade and travel between Thailand, Laos, Vietnam and Cambodia. ADB 6 will go from Chong Mek to Pakse, then on to Attapeu and Yalakhountum on the Vietnamese border; ADB 7 will go from Pakse to Voen Kham on the Cambodian border (basically replacing or enhancing Route 13). The roads are set to begin construction in late 1996. Once these roads south are graded and paved the number of departures will increase, thereby relieving crowding and adding to general comfort.

River Boats to Champasak take about 1½ hours down, 2½ hours up, and cost 500 kip. One or two boats typically leave from the Pakse landing between 7 and 8 am, then again in the afternoon between noon and 1 pm.

For further details on boat travel to Don Khong, see the Si Phan Don section.

To/from Chong Mek, Thailand Ferries run back and forth between the pier at the junction of the Don and Mekong rivers and Ban Muang Kao on the west bank of the Mekong throughout the day. The regular ferry costs 200 kip per person or you can charter a boat across for 2000 kip.

From Ban Muang Kao to the Lao-Thai border you can queue up for a share taxi that carries six passengers for 1000 kip each or hire a whole taxi for 6000 kip (or 200B). The 40 km journey to Ban Mai Sing Amphon on the Lao side of the border takes about 45 minutes. At the border you simply check out through Lao immigration, walk across the line and check in on the Thai side. Passenger trucks on the other side are waiting to take passengers onward to Ubon Ratchathani via Phibun Mangsahan.

Getting Around

There are three kinds of local transport around Pakse: motorised samlor, jumbo and tuk-tuk. The latter differs from the usual jumbo in that it has two rows of bench seats facing forward. Riding any of these vehicles on a shared basis costs 250 kip per person anywhere in town. If you charter one, the standard fares are 500 kip (motorised samlor), 1000 kip (jumbo) and 1500 kip (tuk-tuk).

BOLAVEN PLATEAU ທົ່ງພຽງບໍລິເວນ

Centred in north-eastern Champasak Province, the fertile Bolaven plateau (sometimes spelt Bolovens, known in Lao as Phu Phieng Bolaven) wasn't farmed intensively until the French planted coffee, rubber and bananas here in the early 20th century. Many French planters left following independence in the '50s and the rest followed as US bombardment intensified in the '60s.

Today the Lao have revived the cultivation of coffee beans and both *arabica* and *robusta* are grown in village plots throughout the region. Workers on the coffee plantations tend to come from the Laven tribe, one of the largest ethnic groups native to the plateau (which is named after them – Bolaven means Place of the Laven). Soft world coffee prices have kept production low and small-scale, although Lao coffee fetches among the highest prices of any variety in the world. Other local agricultural products include fruits, cardamom and rattan.

Along with the Laven, the plateau is a centre for several Mon-Khmer ethnic groups, including the Alak, Katu, Ta-oy and Suay. The Katu and Alak arrange their palm-and-thatch houses in a circle and are well-known in Laos for a water buffalo sacrifice which they perform yearly (usually on a full moon in March) in homage to the village spirit. The number of buffaloes sacrificed – typically one to four animals – depends on availability and the bounty of the previous year's agricultural harvest. During the ceremony, the men of the village don wooden masks, hoist spears and wooden shields, and dance around the buffaloes in the centre of the circle formed by their houses. After a prescribed period of dancing the men converge on the buffaloes and spear them to death. The meat is divided among the villagers and each household places a piece in a basket on a pole in front of their house as a spirit offering.

Another unique Katu custom is the carving of wooden caskets for each member of the household well in advance of an expected death; the caskets are stored beneath rice sheds until needed to bury the dead.

Among other tribes, the animistic-shamanistic Suay are said to be the best elephant handlers. Elephants are used extensively in the forests for clearing land and for moving timber. The Alak, Katu and Lawae are distinctive for the face tattoos of their women, a custom that's slowly dying out as Lao influence in the area increases (the Lao government now provides free electricity to many Bolaven villages.)

Several **Katu and Alak villages** can be visited along the road between Pakse and Muang Paksong at the western edge of the plateau. There are also a few within walking distance of the Tadlo Resort (see the following Places to Stay section). In Lao Ngam (not to be confused with Muang Lao Ngam on the road to Salavan), around 40 km east of Pakse, is a large day market frequented by many tribal groups. Other villages can be found by following the dirt road that runs between Paksong and Salavan to the north, especially in the vicinity of Muang Tha Taeng on the border of Sekong and Salavan provinces.

Several waterfalls are linked with the Set river (Se Set), a tributary of the Mekong that drains the plateau. The most commonly visited are **Taat Lo** and **Taat Phan**, both just a few km west of Paksong. Taat Lo (pronounced tàat láw) is only about 10m high but is quite wide; the large, deep pool at its base is suitable for swimming and the adjacent Tadlo Resort offers comfortable accommodation. Taat Phan drops over 120m and is best viewed from a distance – take the turnoff north at Km 38 till it ends and walk down a path to the edge of the small canyon formed by the river to see the falls.

Places to Stay

Tadlo Resort (reservation number in Pakse (031) 212725), next to the Taat Lo waterfall on the Bolaven plateau, is a modest complex of thatched bungalows. Several are owned by the government while a few are privately owned and used by SODETOUR in Pakse. Simple 3rd-class rooms with shared cold-water bath cost 5000 kip, while 2nd-class rooms provide a private cold-water bath for 10,000 kip. At the top end are a couple of well-appointed bungalows that overlook the falls for US$36 a night. The Lodge has large and very pleasant open-air dining room and sitting areas.

In addition to the proximity of Taat Lo and local villages, the lodge offers elephant rides. The typical elephant ride lasts about an hour, plodding through streams, forests and villages; a longer ride to an Alak village can be arranged. If you've booked a Bolaven plateau package through SODETOUR, the elephant ride is included in the deal. You can

purchase your own elephant for around 1,200,000 kip (about the same price as a new Honda motorbike).

To reserve a room at Tadlo Resort in advance (a good idea any time of year except the rainy season), contact SODETOUR in Vientiane or Pakse.

Getting There & Away

Passenger trucks between Pakse and Salavan (passing the entrance to Tadlo Resort) cost 1500 kip per person and take about two hours. Tadlo Resort is 88 km north-east of Pakse and about 1.5 km east of the road to Salavan. The turnoff for Tadlo comes after Lao Ngam, about 30 km before Salavan; you should get off the bus at a bridge over the Se Set. Ask at the pharmacy near this stop for help with your luggage if you can't make the 1.5 km walk.

If you're heading for Paksong, the main centre for the local coffee trade, buses from Pakse cost 1000 kip and take about an hour and 15 minutes. There are also one or two trucks a day between Salavan and Paksong; these take up to five hours (bad road) and cost 1500 kip.

CHAMPASAK ຈຳປາສັກ

This small district of 38,000 on the west bank of the Mekong is a ghost of its former colonial self. An ambitious fountain circle in the middle of the red-dirt main street looks almost absurd, while either side of the street is lined with French colonial homes in various states of disrepair (including one that belonged to Chao Bounome na Champasak), along with a couple of noodle shops, a wooden bank building and a morning market.

The Angkor-period ruins of Wat Phu Champasak lie eight km south-west of town; to reach them you must pass through Champasak. The UNESCO-funded Directorate of Wat Phu Monuments office on the main street (near the market and ferry pier) no longer requires permits to visit the monument. The office is headed by Than Bounlap, who is very knowledgeable about the ruins and can speak English.

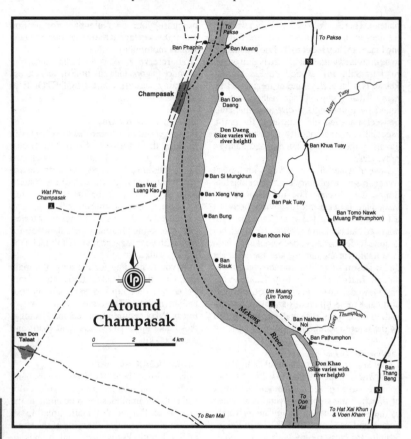

Around Champasak

On Don Daeng, the large river island opposite Champasak, villagers in the year-round settlements of Sì Mungkhun, Xieng Vang, Bung and Sisuk support themselves raising coconuts on the island and fishing in the Mekong.

Places to Stay & Eat

The *Sala Wat Phou*, a reincarnation of the former Champasak Hotel, is housed in a renovated two-storey building next to the provincial offices and near the market. Nine medium-sized rooms with high ceilings, air-con and hot water are priced at US$25/30 per single/double. Meals are available in the hotel dining room.

If you are looking for a less expensive place to stay in Champasak, Than Bounlap at the Monuments office (above) may be able to arrange something.

There are very few places to eat. Try the large *fõe shop* south of the traffic circle on the east side of the street; it's open from 7 am till around 9 pm. This restaurant also does rice dishes and offers cold beer. A smaller *fõe shop* nearer the fountain is open 7 am to 2 pm only. Noodles and fresh produce are also available at the morning market.

Getting There & Away

Ferries from Ban Muang on the east side of the Mekong river to Ban Phaphin (five km north of Champasak) and Champasak on the west side run regularly throughout daylight hours and cost 200 kip per person. During the three-day Wat Phu Festival in February ferries run 24 hours a day. From Ban Phaphin a passenger truck to Champasak costs another 100 kip.

You can also charter a ferry – actually two canoes lashed together with a few planks across the top to create a rustic catamaran – from Ban Muang straight across to the Champasak market landing (near the Sala Wat Phou and fŏe shops) for 1500 to 2000 kip. This means avoiding Ban Phaphin – and the bus – altogether.

Buses to Ban Muang from Pakse run regularly throughout the day for 600 kip per person.

Getting Around

Bicycles can be rented at Sala Wat Phou for riding around town or all the way to Wat Phu Champasak. Jumbos around town are also available at the rate of about 200 kip per kilometre.

WAT PHU CHAMPASAK

ວັດພູຈຳປາສັກ

Literally Mountain Temple, this Khmer temple site is on the lower slopes of Phu Pasak, eight km south-east of Champasak. Though small compared to the Angkor-era sites in Siem Reap, Cambodia, or Buriram, Thailand, Wat Phu is charged with atmosphere. The surviving structures date from as early as the Chenla Kingdom (6th to 8th centuries) to as late as the Angkor period (9th to 13th centuries). The government supposedly has plans to restore the site and establish a national museum in Champasak with international aid. Archaeological research is currently being conducted with the assistance of the Musée Guimet in Paris and some restoration has been carried out.

The archaeological site itself is divided into three main levels which are joined by a long, stepped promenade flanked here and

there by statues of lions and nagas. The lowermost part consists of two ruined palace buildings of 20th century origins – used by recent Lao monarchs to observe the annual Wat Phu festival – at the edge of a large pond used for ritual ablutions and boat races. The naga (dragon) stairway leading to the sanctuary probably dates to the 11th century and is lined with dàwk jàmpaa (plumeria), which is the Lao national tree.

The middle section features two exquisitely carved, rectangular sandstone **pavilions** thought to have been used for gender-segregated worship. The pavilion on the right is in the better condition with regard to surviving sculpture. Wat Phu was converted into a Buddhist temple in later centuries but much of the original Hindu sculpture remains in the lintels, which feature various forms of Vishnu and Shiva as well as Kala, the Hindu god of time and death. The back third of this structure reportedly dates to the 6th century Chenla era while the front two-thirds were probably constructed during the late Angkor period (11th to 13th centuries). Over the main entrance is a relief of Shiva and Parvati sitting on Nandi, Shiva's bull mount, with what appears to be Lakulisa (an obscure, Buddha-like Shiva deity) below. This entranceway is flanked by well-executed reliefs of Parvati.

The remains of a **Nandi pavilion** (dedicated to Shiva's mount) and two galleries flanking another set of laterite steps lead to the next level. Six ruined brick pavilions – only their bases remain – separate the lower two levels from the final and holiest level. Roots and mosses hold the bricks together in some places, and drive them apart in others.

On the uppermost level is the main temple **sanctuary** itself, which once enclosed a large Shiva phallus (linga) that was bathed – via a system of stone pipes – by the sacred spring above and behind the temple complex. A lintel inside the south entrance depicts the story of Krishnavatara in which Krishna kills his uncle Kamsa; this same subject was used for lintels at Prasat Muang Khaek in Nakhon Ratchasima Province and

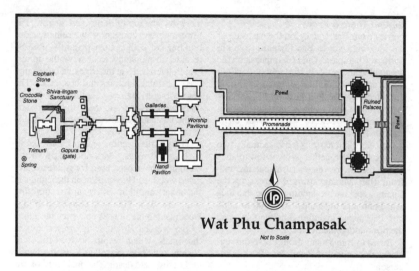

Elephant Stone

Crocodile Stone

Shiva-lingam Sanctuary

Trimurti

Spring

Gopura (gate)

Galleries

Worship Pavilions

Nandi Pavilion

Pond

Promenade

Ruined Palaces

Pond

Wat Phu Champasak

Not to Scale

Prasat Phanom Rung in Buriram Province, Thailand, suggesting that these three temples were ritually linked. Archaeological evidence also indicates that Wat Phu was linked to Khao Phra Wihaan (130 km east on the Thai-Cambodian border), the personal temple of Khmer monarch Suryavarman I during the early 11th century. Reportedly the lingam at Wat Phu was used in ceremonies to 'release' the sacred power of the lingam at Khao Phra Wihaan.

This sanctuary now contains a set of crude, almost clown-faced Buddha images on an altar at one end. Local worshippers have returned pieces of sculpture – mostly stone window bannisters – that had been taken from the ruins, believing that any one who takes a piece of Wat Phu away is in for a run of bad luck.

The upper platform affords a high, wide-angle view of the surrounding plains, and in the evening monkeys cavort in the trees nearby. Behind the upper level is a shallow cave from which the sacred spring flows. Sections of stone pipe that carried the water from the cave to the sanctuary are lying in or near the cave. The spring is still considered sacred – for good luck Lao visitors always dunk their heads under a bamboo spout leading from the spring.

Sculpted into a large boulder behind the topmost sanctuary is a Khmer-style **trimurti**, the Hindu triumvirate of Shiva, Vishnu and Brahma. A few monks reside at a rustic Theravada Buddhist wat nearby. The best view of the plains below are from this wat;

One of the many surviving Hindu lintels at Wat Phu Champasak

the cool, shady grounds are a good spot for a picnic.

Between the Wat Phu complex and the newer wat on the upper level is the so-called **crocodile stone**, a boulder with a deep, highly stylised carving of a croc. This sculpture may have been the site of Chenla human sacrifices.

Information

Hours & Admission The complex is open daily from 8 am to 4.30 pm. Admission (when the admission booth at the gate is occupied) costs 300 kip per person plus 700 kip for a still camera permit or 3000 kip for camcorders. To be sure you're paid and legal, stop in at the Khmer Monuments office in Champasak before heading for the ruins – the office may also be able to help arrange transport.

Festivals

Each June the locals perform a **water buffalo sacrifice** to the ruling earth spirit for Champasak, Chao Tengkham. The blood of the buffalo is offered to a local shaman who serves as a trance medium for the appearance of Chao Tengkham.

Another important local festival is **Bun Wat Phu Champasak** (Wat Phu Champasak Festival), when pilgrims from throughout southern Laos come to worship at Wat Phu in combined Hindu-Buddhist ceremonies. The festival lasts three days during which the large pond at the foot of the hill is used for boat races, young girls in white pray to Shiva and more buffaloes are sacrificed. Other activities include Thai boxing matches, cockfights, music and dancing. The festival is held as part of Magha Puja (Makkha Busaa) during the full moon in February.

Getting There & Away

Wat Phu Champasak is 46 km from Pakse, 13 km from Ban Phaphin and eight km from Champasak. To hire a taxi from Champasak, ask for Wat Phu or 'Muang Kao' ('Old City'); the cost should be around 5000 to 6000 kip round trip, including waiting time at the site. You can also hop a passenger truck or bus bound for Ban Samkha or Don Talaat (200 kip) farther south and ask to be let off at Wat Phu.

See colour aside facing page 240 for more information on Wat Phu Champasak.

UM MUANG ອຸມເມືອງ

Um Muang (more commonly called either Muang Tomo or Um Tomo) is a Khmer temple ruin of the same period as the earliest structures at Wat Phu Champasak (6th to 9th centuries). It's about 45 km south of Pakse off Route 13, in the midst of a forest on a small tributary of the Mekong. The ruins include an esplanade bordered by *lingas* (sacred Shiva phalli), two semi-intact laterite sanctuaries – one with a large vestibule and lintel sculpted with Vaishnava motifs – and a number of sandstone lintels displayed on rocks beneath towering dipterocarps (trees). A large tin shed contains a bronze Sukhothai-style Buddha from Thailand.

Getting There & Away

From Ban Muang (the village opposite Champasak on the Mekong) you can charter a boat to Ban Nakham Noi (the riverbank village nearest the ruins) for 6000 kip round trip (or 2000 kip one way), including waiting time of an hour or so while you locate and tour the ruins. This village is between the southern tip of Don Daeng, a large river island in front of Champasak, and Don Khao, a smaller river island to the south. The village is about one km south of the ruins. At the junction of the river's edge, climb the bank next to the mouth of a tributary stream (Huay Thumphon) to the village, then turn left and walk north along a smaller stream into the forest. When the path forks, stay right and walk about 10 minutes till you see some metal-roof sheds in the forest on your right, then leave the trail and head for the sheds, which shelter parts of the ruins. If you'd rather not test your orienteering skills, children from the village are usually glad to lead you to the ruins.

The ruins can also be reached by motor vehicle from Pakse by turning west at Km 30 at Ban Thang Beng and proceeding to Ban Nakham Noi by road and foot via Ban Pathumphon (just south of Nakham Noi).

BAN PHAPHO & KIET NYONG

ບ້ານຜາໂພແລະກ້ຽດຍ້ອງ

At the nearby Suay village of Ban Phapho (27 km east of Route 13) in Pathumphon district is an elephant training complex, where at any one time around a hundred young elephants may be in training for timber and agricultural work. Many villages in the area keep as many as 15 to 20 working elephants, which are mostly used for carrying bags of rice and other cargo.

In nearby Kiet Nyong, you can contact headman Thaan Nu to arrange half-day elephant treks (overnights aren't permitted by the Lao government). The going rate is 7000 kip per elephant for the half day, and each elephant can take two people. The elephant trek typically goes to the summit of a local hill called Phu Asa, named for a 19th century war hero who fought against the Siamese. From the hillcrest one has a good view of a village, pond and rice fields below. You can also explore the ruins of stone buildings on the hill; the structures date to the 19th century, possibly built in defence of the area.

Getting There & Away

Ban Phapho can be reached by vehicle via a 27 km road that branches east off Route 13 near Ban Thang Beng. For Kiet Nyong, take a Phapho-bound bus about two to three hours from Pakse.

SI PHAN DON (FOUR THOUSAND ISLANDS) ສີ່ພັນດອນ

During the rainy season this scenic 50-km-long section of the Mekong river just north of the Cambodian border reaches a breadth of 14 km, the river's widest girth along its entire 4350 km journey from the Tibetan plateau to the South China Sea. During the dry months between monsoons the river recedes and leaves behind hundreds (or thousands if you count every sandbar) of river islands and islets. The largest of the permanent islands are inhabited year-round and offer fascinating glimpses of tranquil river-oriented village life – 'more detached from time than from the riverbank' as one source has described it. Communities tend to be self-sufficient, growing most of their own rice, sugarcane, coconut and vegetables, harvesting fish from the Mekong and weaving textiles as needed.

Villages on the islands are often named for their relative position toward the upriver or downriver ends. The upriver – usually northern – end of the island is called *hūa* or head, the downriver or south end is called *hāang* or tail. Hence Ban Hua Khong would be a village at the north end of Don Khong, while Ban Hang Som might be a village at the south end of Don Som.

The French left behind a defunct shortline railway (the only railway ever built in Laos), a couple of river piers and a few colonial villas on the islands of Don Khong, Don Det and Don Khon. Other attractions include some impressive rapids and waterfalls, where the Mekong riverbed suddenly drops in elevation at the Cambodian border, and a rare species of freshwater dolphins.

Don Khong (Khong Island)

ດອນໂຂງ

Named for the surrounding river (using the Thai pronunciation *'khõng'* rather than the Lao 'khãwng'), this large island measures 15 km along its north-south axis and eight km at its widest point. The island's 55,000 inhabitants are for the most part concentrated around two villages on either side of the island, Muang Khong on the east shore and Muang Saen on the west; an eight km unpaved road links the two.

Most of the surrounding islands – and parts of the mainland – belong to Don Khong District. As his surname might suggest, the current prime minister of Laos, Khamtay Siphandone, was born on Don Khong; there has been talk that the government may carve the district out of Champasak Province to create a separate province called Si Phan Don.

Things to See & Do A tour of the island can be done by bicycle, available through the Auberge Sala Done Khong and possibly other sources. Another possibility is to hire a jumbo for the whole day, though some of the

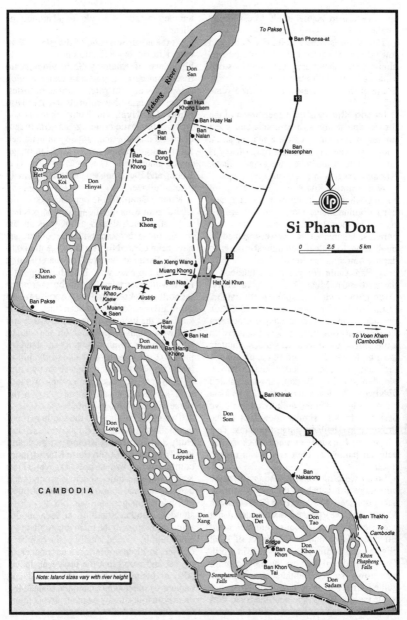

spots described below aren't accessible by jumbo.

The island is quite scenic; rice fields and low hills in the centre and vegetable gardens along the perimeter are punctuated by small villages, most with their own village wats. Some of the wats are over a hundred years old.

Muang Khong is the largest town in the district and features three hotels and guest houses, a few small cafes, a market and a couple of wats. The busiest time of day is around 4 to 6 am when the small Muang Khong market is in full swing.

Wat Phuang Kaew sits in the centre of Muang Khong and features a towering new naga Buddha image facing east toward the river. The local populace believe the abbot here used supernatural powers gained in meditation to defeat communist efforts to depose him after the Revolution.

At Ban Xieng Wang, a neighbourhood at the north end of Muang Khong, is **Wat Jawm Thong**, the oldest temple on the island. Dating to the Chao Anou period (1805-28), the main sim features a unique cruciform floor plan in crumbling brick and stucco with a tile roof. Carved wooden window shutters are a highlight. To the left of the uninteresting cement central Buddha image, an old wooden standing Buddha in one-handed *abhaya mudra* leans in a corner. Some local people say a Khmer architect may have designed this sim; similar floor plans in Nan Province in Thailand suggest possible Thai Lü design. The sandy grounds are shaded by betelnut palms, coconut palms and mango trees.

South-west of Muang Khong, in some hills more or less behind the mayor's office, a foot trail leads to **Tham Phu Khiaw** (Green Mountain Cave). Sacred for decades if not centuries, the cave contains a number of old Buddha images and is the object of local pilgrimages during Lao New Year in April. The remainder of the year the trail becomes overgrown, so you should seek out a local guide for the stiff 30 minute walk up the hill to the cave. East of here near the river, **Wat Ban Naa** is an atmospheric little country temple typical of the style found around the island.

At the north-west end of the island, **Ban Hua Khong** is well known as the 1924 birthplace of Khamtay Siphandone, who rose from being a postman under French rule to his current role as prime minister. Thaan Khamtay has refurbished **Wat Hua Khong Pha Nyai**, which other than one old wooden monastic building has little to recommend it aesthetically. The wat is named for the large cement seated Buddha image in the main sim. The area between Hua Khong and Ban Dong (to the east) is heavily planted in rice.

Muang Saen, on the opposite side of the island from Muang Khong, can be reached on foot, though this is a hot walk in the middle of the day since both sides of the road have been cleared for rice fields. A jumbo to Muang Saen can be hired in Muang Khong for 1500 kip each way. It's a bustling little town with a ferry landing for boats from as far north as Pakse. **Wat Phu Khao Kaew**, on a low hill north of Muang Saen (three or four km from the junction of the north-south and east-west roads), was built on the site of some Khmer ruins. Look for a stand of plumeria trees on the east side of the hill to locate the path to the temple, or better yet hire a guide in Muang Saen for a couple of thousand kip. An unusual bronze gong in the shape of a clock hangs here.

Two smaller villages at the southern tip of the island worth visiting for old wats are **Ban Huay** and **Ban Hang Khong**. At the latter, **Wat Thepsulin Phudin Hang Khong**, more commonly known simply as Wat Hang Khong, features quiet, spacious grounds and a small brick and stucco sim with a collection of Buddha images new and old. A pair of slender wooden standing abhaya mudra Buddhas in front of the main image are obviously highly revered locally as they've been dressed in cloth robes. Smaller images of crystal and wood line the back wall ledge. Also of interest is the nearby carved and painted wooden *wihãan* and the *sãaláa lóng thám* with folk-quality painted tinwork along the eaves. **Wat Silimangkhalaham** in Ban

Huay features similar architectural styles on more neglected grounds.

Festivals A Boat Racing Festival (Bun Suang Heua) is held on Don Khong in early December around National Day. Four or five days of carnival-like activity culminate in boat races next to Muang Khong along the east shore of the island. In former times the islanders celebrated this festival a month earlier at the end of the Buddhist rains retreat (Awk Phansaa), but they now combine the boat races with government-mandated National Day celebrations to save money. Activities at previous festivals have included night-time boxing matches in an outdoor ring.

Places to Stay Prices for accommodation on the island are kept artificially high by the presence of package tour groups. The *Auberge Sala Done Khong* in Muang Khong offers spacious, nicely decorated rooms in an old teak house for US$20 per night with fan only, US$30 if you use the air-con. All rooms come with private toilet and hot-water showers. According to SODETOUR these rates may be raised to around US$45 by 1997. Rooms at the Sala Done Khong may be booked in advance through SODETOUR in Vientiane or Pakse.

Near the ferry landing and next door to Khong's largest noodle shop, *Done Khong Guest House* contains three simple but clean three-bed rooms with shared facilities for 7000 kip per room. Further north toward Ban Xieng Wang, *Souksan Guest House* offers seven cottages, each with two small rooms containing air-con and private cold-water bath for US$30. A separate building further back features dorm-style accommodation – basically just a mattress on the floor – for 2500 kip per bed. The Souksan has a very pleasant restaurant overlooking the river.

The manager of the Auberge Sala Done Khong has double rooms in his own house – *Thongleuam's House* – for US$10. Toilet and bath facilities are shared.

Pakse's Lao Travel Service says it's building a new guest house 200m south of the town centre.

Places to Eat Don Khong is nationally famous for its *lào láo*, often cited as the smoothest in the country. It's available in the market or at any restaurant.

Near the Muang Khong pier are a couple of adequate *hâan kịn dẹum* (eat-drink shops). A large *noodle shop* near the ferry landing also serves khào nĩaw and, with advance notice, khào jâo.

Souksan Guest House has a nice little wooden restaurant overhanging the river. The menu includes vegetarian, Chinese, Lao and falang dishes, plus a variety of breakfasts. Warm beer costs 1500 kip, cold beer 1800 kip! Along the street that leads to the Souksan are several small *cafes* with fõe and Lao snacks.

The dining room at the *Sala Done Khong* is quite good; non-guests may arrange meals here if they order in advance.

Getting There & Away Although located in the far south of the country, Si Phan Don is reasonably accessible.

Air Though scheduled for twice a week, the Lao Aviation flight between Pakse and Don Khong actually only goes when at least six passengers make reservations. Until demand for flights to Don Khong increases, this effectively means the route operates only when a tour group is going. When operative, the flight takes only 30 minutes and costs US$26 one way.

In Pakse, Lao Aviation keeps a 15-passenger Y-7 on hand which can be chartered to/from Don Khong for US$130 (roughly five times a single fare) one way.

The airstrip – built by the US air force as a landing site on their Phnom Penh-Vientiane route during the Indochina War – lies four km from either end of the road between Muang Khong and Muang Saen. The local official in charge of Lao Aviation flights to/from Pakse lives in a house just south of the Auberge Sala Done Khong.

Road From Pakse there are usually two passenger trucks per day to Muang Khong via Hat Xai Khun, directly opposite Muang

Khong on the eastern mainland shore of the Mekong river. The 120 km trip takes at least five or six hours under current road conditions; when the road is paved it will speed up substantially. The 1000 kip fare includes the short vehicle ferry ride across to Muang Khong. From the Pakse end these trucks depart between 7 and 8 am; from Muang Khong they leave around 6.30 and 7.30 am.

If you miss the Khong-bound bus, you can try for trucks going to Khinak (8 am and 1 pm), Nakasong (10.30 am) or Voen Kham (1 pm); all of these trucks stop at Hat Xai Khun along the way.

On *wán sĭn dáp*, days when there's no moon, there may be only one truck a day – even no truck – due to the lack of passengers; the locals believe it's bad luck to travel on such days. On all other days, prepare yourself for possibly the most crowded bus conditions anywhere in Laos.

Hat Xai Khun is about one km west of Route 13. If you're coming under your own power (or have been dropped off in Hat Xai Khun), you can catch the ferry across to Muang Khong for 200 kip per pedestrian or 2500 kip per vehicle. Small boats may be chartered across for 1500 kip to the main landing, 2000 kip to the landing below the Sala Done Khong.

Rumours say the vehicle ferry crossing may move south to Ban Nokhok, opposite Ban Naa on Don Khong, to take advantage of a deeper channel and a slightly shorter distance between mainland and island. If this transpires, small boats will continue to operate from Hat Xai Khun.

River Ferries from Pakse head south around 8 am daily – get to the landing early for space. Be sure to enquire thoroughly before boarding (or the day before) to determine the boat's final destination.

Whether or not the boat goes all the way to Don Khong depends upon river height. During and immediately following the rainy season, boats can make it to the landing at Muang Saen on the west side of Don Khong. This trip requires spending one night on the boat; the fare is 2000 kip.

During dry months large ferryboats can't make it to Don Khong and it really becomes quite an effort to piece together a river voyage all the way there. When the river level descends to intermediate height, boats only go as far as Ban Munla Pamok (1500 kip), roughly 20 km north of the northern tip of Don Khong; from here you may be able to charter a small boat the remainder of the way for around 20,000 kip. There is a guest house in Ban Munla Pamok.

In the late dry season when the river level is particularly low, boats from Pakse may terminate on Don Sai (1000 kip), a large river island roughly two-thirds of the distance between Pakse and Don Khong. Although it's possible to stay overnight on Don Sai, boat travel onward as far as Don Khong usually isn't available, even by charter.

Travel agencies in Pakse or Muang Khong can arrange boat charters between the two towns for around US$200 each way in boats that hold up to 20 persons. Smaller 10-person boats cost less but aren't as comfortable for such a long journey. You may be able to arrange something less expensive directly from one of the boat landings. SODETOUR has plans to establish some sort of regular boat service between Pakse and Don Khong; contact their office in Vientiane or Pakse for more information.

A company called Indocruise (☎ /fax 412740, PO Box 4415, Vientiane), operates a four-day, three-night trip between Pakse and Don Khong aboard the *Vat Phou*, a steel-hull barge topped with wooden cabins, each with two beds and private bath. The all-inclusive fare runs around US$400 per person.

To/From Cambodia From Hat Xai Khun, opposite the east shore of Don Khong, it's 35 km to Voen Kham near the Cambodian border. The crossing between Tha Boei (Lao side) and Phumi Kampong Sralau (Cambodian side) is open to Lao and Cambodians only at the moment but Champasak Province officials are hoping to make this an international access point for foreigners in the near future. The Cambodian side of the river falls roughly on the border of Stung Treng and Preah Vihear provinces, an area known for occasional Khmer Rouge and bandit activity.

Ferries from Muang Saen on Don Khong sail directly to the Cambodian shore of the Mekong at Phumi Kampong Sralau. There are also passenger trucks to Voen Kham from Pakse and Hat Xai Khun.

Getting Around Bicycles can be rented from the Auberge Sala Done Khong for 2000 kip per day; these are quite convenient for seeing the island. Jumbos are also available in Muang Khong and Muang Saen for around 200 kip per km.

Both Sala Done Khong and Souksan Guest House hire large, 20-person boats for 30,000 kip a day or smaller 10-person boats for 18,000 to 20,000 kip. A typical circuit starts with an 8 am cruise to Don Khon, where passengers disembark and walk to Taat Somphamit and the old French bridge; then the boat continues on to Nakasong where motorbike taxis are hired to Khon Phapheng Falls. The boat returns to Muang Khong by 2 or 3 pm.

Don Det & Don Khon
ດອນເດດແລະດອນຄອນ

These two islands south of Don Khong near the Cambodian border were an important transport link for supply lines between Cambodia and Laos during the French colonial era. To bypass the nearby system of rapids and waterfalls in the Mekong river the French even built a 14 km narrow-gauge railway across the two islands, linked by bridge and terminating in concrete piers at either end. The impressive bridge and piers are still intact but much of the rail line has been appropriated by local residents for use as footbridges over streams and gullies around the islands.

Don Khon, the larger of the two islands, is famous throughout Laos for the cultivation of coconut, bamboo and kapok. Some households still make their own incense from the aromatic wood of a local tree, for offering at local temples. In the main village, **Ban Khon**, are several leftover French colonial villas. **Wat Khon Tai**, toward the southwestern end of Ban Khon, is a Lao temple built on the former site of a Khmer temple of undetermined age – possibly Chenla (6th to 8th centuries AD). Large laterite bricks used in the construction of the Khmer temple lie scattered about, along with the foundation and a few pediments and columns. Behind the wooden Lao sim is a 90-year-old Lao jedi next to an ancient Khmer Shiva-lingam on a modern pedestal.

Another 1.5 km west beyond the wat, at the western end of Don Khon, is a raging set of rapids that form a river cascade called **Taat Somphamit** (also known as Li Phi Falls). The falls can also be viewed from Don Xang, a large island north-west of Don Khon.

Railway Hike & Dolphins On Don Khon you can make an interesting five km trek across the island by following the old railbed. Near the start of the trail at the north end of the island is a rusting locomotive and boiler; take care not to brush your bare skin against the thicket surrounding the locomotive, as its fruit produces a rash in some people. Farther along the way you'll pass bits of primary forest, rice fields, small villages and singing birds. The south end of the railbed terminates at the old French pier – across the river to the right is Cambodia.

Irrawaddy dolphins can sometimes be seen off the southern tip of the island in the late afternoon from December to May (during the rainy season the water is too murky and deep). The best dolphin-viewing area is a small sand island a bit farther south of the island coast. Boats can be chartered from the pier area to the sand island for 6000 kip, but ever since a group of Thai tourists were fired upon from the Cambodian side (no-one was injured) in 1994, the sandbar trip has been more or less off limits. This may change if security on the Cambodian side improves. Whether you plan to view from Ban Hang Khon or the sandbar, don't go any earlier than 4 pm; around 5 pm seems to be the best time.

Dolphins Endangered

The rare Irrawaddy dolphin *(Orcaella brevirostris,* called *paa khaa* in Laos) reaches around 2.5m in length at maturity and is native to tropical coastal marine ecosystems as well as freshwater rivers and lakes. In existence since the Holocene epoch, these small, bluish grey-to-black cetaceans swim in small pods of two to three individuals; their bulging foreheads give them a passing resemblance to the much larger Beluga whale.

Although the Irrawaddy dolphin can adapt to either fresh or salt water, it is seldom seen in the sea. It has been recorded in the Brahmaputra river in Bangladesh, Ayeyarwady river in Myanmar, and the Mekong in Laos and Cambodia. The dolphin's continued existence is threatened by gillnetting and bomb fishing in the lower Mekong river and its tributaries (principally the Se Kong, Se Pian and Se Khaman), where its overall numbers have dwindled to an estimated 200 to 300 individuals. In the Don Khong area there may be only 20 to 50 left.

Among the Lao and Khmer, Irrawaddy dolphins are traditionally considered reincarnated humans and there are many stories of dolphins having saved the lives of fishermen or villagers who have accidentally fallen into the Mekong or who have been attacked by crocodiles. Hence neither the Lao nor the Khmer intentionally capture dolphins for food or sport. While using nylon gill nets to catch other fish, Lao anglers may unwittingly entangle a dolphin and then refrain from cutting the net to release the animal in order to save the cost of the net. Unable to reach the surface for air, the entangled dolphin drowns.

The San Francisco-based Earth Island Institute has established a Save the Dolphins project in Laos that raises funds to compensate Lao fishermen on Don Khon and nearby Don Sadam for any nets damaged by cutting free the dolphins. The project is now working with the LPDR's Dept of Forestry & Environment to encourage a return to traditional bamboo fishtraps and small hand nets – along with the creation of deep-water conservation zones – through community-based resource management rather than top-down government prohibition.

Another serious threat to the Mekong dolphin population is the use of explosives for fishing in Cambodia (a practice strictly prohibited in Laos), where hand grenades and other small ordnance are inexpensive and readily available. In this ghoulish practice an explosive charge is detonated beneath the surface of the river, and fish killed by the shock waves float to the surface and are scooped up by fishermen in boats with hand nets. As many as 20 charges a day are detonated in the Cambodian stretches of the Mekong river above Stung Treng – the lower extension of the dolphins' prime habitat.

In an attempt to crush local beliefs and to extract oil for their war machinery, the Khmer Rouge reportedly shot thousands of the dolphins in Tonle Sap, a large lake in northern Cambodia, during their 1970s reign of terror. The future of the dolphin's Mekong river survival continues to rest in Cambodia much more than in Laos.

For more information on the dolphins' plight, or to make a donation to the Irrawaddy dolphin project, write to the Earth Island Institute, PO Box 19, Hua Mak Post Office, Bangkok, Thailand or to EII, Fort Mason Center, E205, San Francisco, California 94123 USA. Be sure to specify your interest in the Lao Community Fisheries & Dolphin Protection Project; you can also write directly to the project staff at PO Box 860, Pakse.

Those concerned about the fate of the Irrawaddy dolphins on the Cambodian side of the lower Mekong can write polite letters to King Sihanouk, Government House, Phnom Penh, Cambodia, asking that the use of nylon gill nets and explosives to catch fish be prohibited and that such prohibitions be enforced. ■

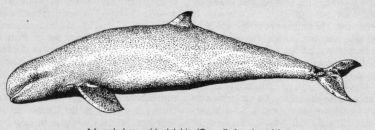

A female Irrawaddy dolphin *(Orcaella brevirostris)*

Although you may hear otherwise, according to Lao immigration and the LNTA the entire island of Don Khon, as part of Khong District, is open to unrestricted foreign travel. As always in rural Laos, do tread lightly in order to help preserve local traditions.

Khon Phapheng Falls
ຄອນພະເພງ

South of Don Khong the Mekong river features a 13 km stretch of powerful rapids with several sets of cascades. The largest, Khon Phapheng, flows between the eastern shore of the Mekong near Ban Thakho (36 km south of Ban Khinak via Route 13). A wooden pavilion on the Mekong shore affords a good view of the falls. A shaky network of bamboo scaffolds on the rocks next to the falls are used by daring fishermen who are said to have an alliance with the spirits of the cascades. Any ordinary mortal who would try getting closer to the falls via these slim bamboo poles would be tempting death.

A Thai-Lao company signed a contract a couple of years ago to build a huge 300 million baht resort near Khon Phapheng falls. International outcries against the project, which would have seriously threatened the local environment since it involved four 18 hole golf courses and a 21 MW hydroelectric plant, have apparently pushed the resort aside – at least for the time being.

On the way to Khon Phapheng you might stop in Ban Khinak to visit the largest market in the Muang Khong District (best in early morning).

Getting There & Away To reach the falls you need to get to Ban Khinak, a riverfront village accessible by boat from Muang Khong on Don Khong island; there are regular ferries between 6 am and noon for 200 kip per person or you can charter a boat for 5000 kip. From Ban Khinak you can hop on a passenger truck to Ban Thakho (a village about three km from the falls) or charter a vehicle direct to the falls. Day trips to the falls can also be arranged through the

Auberge Sala Done Khong and Souksan Guest House.

There are also direct passenger trucks between Ban Khinak and Ban Muang (opposite Champasak).

Sekong Province
ແຂວງເຊກອງ

Although this province in the extreme southeastern corner of Laos, like its neighbour Attapeu, is officially open to tourism, the difficulty of transport has meant that few tourists have yet ventured here.

Laos' least populous province, Sekong numbers only 63,800 people (about 1% of the nation), with a population density of just 8.3 persons per sq km. It's also a very poor province in which nearly a quarter of all children die before the age of five.

Malaria is rampant in the lowland areas of both provinces, especially toward the Vietnamese border where the deadly *falciparum* is the most common variety. Take the appropriate precautions.

Few Lao Loum – either ethnic Lao or tribal Thais – live in this corner of Laos, which is traditionally home to a number of Lao Theung or Mon-Khmer tribes, including the Nyahuene, Chieng, Talieng, Ta-oy (Tahoy), Laven, Katang, Yai Kayon, Ngai, Suay, Ye, Katu, Lawae, Chatong and Kakang. Many of these tribes migrate back and forth between hilly Sekong and the Central Highlands of Vietnam (where they are commonly known as *montagnards*).

Of the several Mon-Khmer ethnicities found in Sekong, the most numerous are the Katu and the Taliang. The latter total around 25,000 and are found only in the district of Dak Chung, north-east of the capital. Both groups tend toward monogamy but tolerate polygyny; their belief systems mix animism and ancestor worship.

It's difficult to get around the province because of the lack of roads. According to the police in Sekong you're supposed to have permission to travel outside the capital despite the national retraction of the permit system. This may simply be a vestige of the old system clung to by local officials or may be because they regard all foreigners as employees of UN and other aid projects, who (under agreements such agencies typically have with the Vientiane government) enjoy slightly less freedom to travel around the country than the average tourist. There is also a danger of UXO in any off-road travel.

SEKONG (MUANG LAMAM) ເຊກອງ

The main reason people generally come to the capital of Sekong – also known as Muang Lamam (pop 18,000) – is to use it as a departure point for river trips down to Attapeu. Carved out of the wilderness less than 10 years ago, Lamam features a phalanx of government buildings in the centre of town, surrounded by residential areas of wood and thatch stilt homes among the cement and wooden ones.

The Se Kong wraps around the town on the south and east sides, while the Bolaven plateau rises precipitously to the west. The pealing bell one hears several times per day comes not from a local wat but from a regional prison across the river from town. This may be another reason why local police are touchy about visitors.

Electric power is available from 6 to 10.30 pm only.

Information

Money Phak Tai Bank changes cash Thai baht and US dollars for kip only. It's open Monday to Friday 8 to 11 am and 2 to 4 pm.

Post The town post office, a block northwest of the hotel, has no public phone system yet. It's open the same hours as the bank.

Places to Stay & Eat

There's only once place to stay in town, the fairly decent 21-room *Hotel Sekong*. Most rooms contain two or three beds with fan and private bath costing 5000/7000 kip per single/double. Two dorm rooms are avail-able for 1500 kip per bed. The manager speaks some French.

Lieng Restaurant, opposite the Hotel Sekong, is a good spot and has Lao and Chinese food. The *Viengthong*, 50m toward the town centre from the Hotel Sekong, isn't bad either, and adds Vietnamese food to the list.

Getting There & Away

Road Passenger trucks from Salavan leave twice daily at around 5.30 am and 10 am; in the reverse direction, departures from Sekong are at 7 am and 12.30 pm. The trip takes 3½ hours and costs 1200 kip. It's another 3½ hours and 2000 kip on to Attapeu from Sekong.

There is also one daily truck between Pakse and Sekong (en route to/from Attapeu), leaving around 6 am from either end, for 3000 kip; this is a journey of around six hours.

In Sekong trucks arrive at and depart from the morning market.

River Boat service down the Se Kong to Attapeu is rather irregular. When running, passenger ferries charge around 4000 kip per person. You can also charter a small boat carrying up to four persons downriver to Attapeu for about 40,000 kip or US$45. The scenic trip takes around eight hours either way; the river parallels the eastern escarpment of the Bolaven plateau most of the way.

Attapeu Province
ແຂວງອັດຕະປື

Rugged, wild, scenic and difficult to get around, the Attapeu/Sekong region harbours many rare animal species. Tigers aren't uncommon, and there's rumoured to be either Javan or Sumatran rhino near the Cambodian border. A recently discovered trout-like fish grows to be 10 kg in the Se Kong, and the Irrawaddy dolphin makes an occasional appearance in the same river. The districts close to the Vietnam border contain thick jungle teeming with birdlife; parrots, parakeets, bee-eaters and other colourful species are often seen.

Both Attapeu and Sekong were heavily bombed during the Indochina War and their already sparse populations have declined further.

Relations between the Attapeu provincial government and its adjacent Vietnamese counterparts are close. Even on Lao National Day, a Vietnamese flag flies alongside the Lao flag at the government guest house in the capital.

ATTAPEU ອັດຕະປື

Officially called Muang Samakhi Xai (pop 19,200), the capital of Attapeu Province is set in a large valley surrounded by mountains and rivers, and is famed in southern Laos as the 'garden village' for its shady lanes and lush flora. The town's location at the confluence of the Se Kong and Se Khaman rivers

makes it perfect for exploration by boat. The flat-topped line of mountains about 1000m over the valley floor to the north and west marks the edge of the Bolaven plateau and offers the country's most dramatic view of this celebrated geographical entity.

The local police aren't used to tourists yet. Passports are scrutinised closely; if your papers aren't in perfect order you could be in for a hassle. They also don't want foreigners travelling around the province without their knowledge, so be sure to check in before heading off to other districts. The southern mountains of Attapeu may be unsafe due to Khmer Rouge or bandit activity; again enquire before venturing in that direction.

Electricity is available from 6 to 10.30 pm only.

Information
Money The Phak Tai Bank (no English sign), about a half km south of the airstrip, can change cash baht or US dollars to kip in

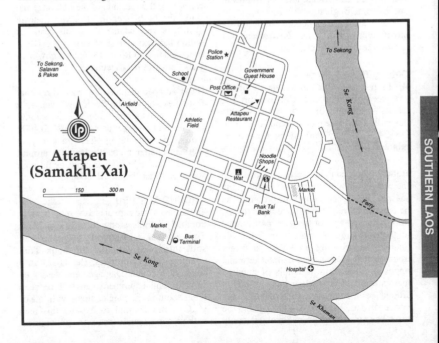

Attapeu (Samakhi Xai)

0   150   300 m

To Sekong, Salavan & Pakse

Police Station
School
Post Office
Government Guest House
Airfield
Athletic Field
Attapeu Restaurant
Noodle Shops
Wat
Market
Phak Tai Bank
Market
Bus Terminal
Se Kong
Hospital
To Sekong
Se Kong
Ferry
Se Khaman

moderate amounts. The overall money supply is very low and depends on weekly deliveries from Vientiane via Lao Aviation.

Post & Communications A post and telecom office stands about 100m north of the government guest house, though there's no telephone service yet, only SSB radio communications.

Places to Stay & Eat

Attapeu has one *government guest house* with six rooms in three buildings inside a walled compound. Rooms come with two or three beds with hard mattresses, mosquito nets and shared toilet and bathing facilities; rates are 2000 kip per room.

A new 30-room hotel of higher standard is currently under construction.

Attapeu Restaurant, in the guest house compound, offers a good variety of reasonably priced rice and noodle dishes. The manager of the restaurant, Ms Maniwan, speaks some English.

There are several noodle shops on the street near a wat. One, *Bualipham*, also serves a few rice dishes.

Getting There & Away

Air Flights from Pakse to Attapeu's airstrip – a weedy field scored with two dirt tyre tracks – operate once or twice weekly depending on passenger demand. The fare is US$24 each way and flying time is 35 minutes.

Road Attapeu can't be reached by road from the rest of Laos during much of the rainy season. During dry months the province can be reached by road along three basic routes. Public transport is for the most part limited to the northernmost road from Pakse via Salavan and Sekong. In Pakse passenger trucks usually leave from a small terminal opposite the stadium a couple of hundred metres north of the regular bus terminal at around 7 am; come early for a seat as it gets very crowded. The fare is 4000 kip and the trip takes nine hours. From Sekong it's only

3½ hours and 2000 kip, from Salavan seven hours and 3200 kip.

The second and most direct route from Pakse goes across the Bolaven plateau via Paksong on Route 28. The road is fairly smooth as far as Paksong (see the earlier Bolaven plateau Getting There & Away section for details) after which it's rather rough. Ordinarily there's no public transport along this road – although it's shorter than the Salavan route there aren't enough potential passengers along the way to make it profitable – but many locals hitch rides on cargo trucks. The drivers usually don't charge locals for this service but may expect a tip from foreigners. We rode to Attapeu along this road on a beer truck – the scenery is spectacular as the road descends along the eastern escarpment of the Bolaven plateau and follows the Se Kong. Driving time is around six to seven hours.

The southernmost road along Route 18 starts from Muang Pathumphon (near Champasak near the east side of the Mekong) and skirts the bottom of the Bolaven plateau. Traffic is very sparse along this road but within the next couple of years the ADB is supposed to turn Route 18 into a highway of sorts that goes into Vietnam.

River Attapeu can also be reached by boat from Sekong via the Se Kong river. July through November there are occasional long-tailed passenger boats for 3000 to 4000 kip per person; during other times of year you can charter a smaller boat for around US$45. The eight hour trip passes through some rapids and beautiful mountain scenery.

AROUND ATTAPEU

To the east of the capital are the most heavily bombed districts along the Ho Chi Minh Trail, **Sansai** and **Phuvong**. Here the Trail split into two, with the Sihanouk Trail heading into Cambodia, the HCM into southern Vietnam. Damaged and destroyed vehicles and equipment can still be seen lying about in the jungle, along with lots of UXO; don't attempt to explore this area without a local guide (ask at the government guest house). It's a three to five-day walk to Sansai District, a beautiful area with many ethnic minorities.

Heavy annual rainfall, combined with the rugged limestone and basalt terrain of the Bolaven plateau, means the north-western part of the province harbours several impressive waterfalls; most are inaccessible by road. A waterfall known as **Nam Tok Katamtok**, off the road to Paksong (Route 28) in a cleft in the Bolaven plateau carved out by the Se Nam Noi river, boasts a spectacular drop of 100m. It's near the split between the Se Nam Noi and Se Katam, between Ban Nong Loi and Ban Kheumkham. **Taat Se Noi**, about 60 km north of Attapeu and 25 km from Sekong (five km west of the point where the Se Nam Noi feeds into the Se Kong), is known locally as 'waterfall of the heads' owing to a WW II incident in which Japanese soldiers decapitated a number of Lao soldiers and tossed their heads into the falls. Though only a short vertical drop of a few metres, the falls is about 100m wide.

The province has one NBCA, **Dong Ampham**, a 1975 sq km area wedged between the Se Khaman and the Vietnamese border. Timber poaching, even in protected/managed forests, threatens to impact the pristine environment negatively; the former governor of Attapeu was recently sentenced to 15 years prison for smuggling timber out of the country. Hydroelectric projects planned for the Se Khaman and Se Su also threaten the NBCA's integrity.

SOUTHERN LAOS

Glossary

aang – tank, reservoir

baht – Thai unit of currency, commonly negotiable in Laos; also a Lao unit of measure equal to 15g

ban – pronounced bâan, the general Lao word for house or village

basi – pronounced 'baa-sĭi', sometimes spelt 'baci'; a ceremony in which the 32 *khwăn* (organ-spirits) are symbolically bound to the participant for health and safety's sake

BCEL – Banque pour le Commerce Extérieur Lao; in English, Lao Foreign Trade Bank

chedi – also spelt 'jedi'; another name for a Buddhist stupa

don – island

falang – from the Lao word *falaang-sèht* or 'French'; any foreigner of European descent

fŏe – rice noodles, one of the most common dishes in Laos

hái – jar

hûay – stream

jâeng khào/jâeng àwk – literally inform enter/inform leave; compulsory rubber stamps put on your departure card by provincial customs or police

jataka – Pali-Sanskrit word for mythological life stories of the Buddha; *sàa-tòk* in Lao

jedi – see chedi

jumbo – a motorised three-wheel taxi, sometimes called 'tuk-tuk'

khào jìi– bread

khào nĭaw – sticky rice, the Lao staple food

khào-nŏm – pastry or sweet; sometimes shortened to *khanŏm*

khwăeng – province

khwăn – see under basi

khŭu baa – Theravada Buddhist monk

kip – Lao unit of currency

làap – a spicy Lao-style salad of minced meat, poultry or fish

lák meuang – city pillar

lào-láo – distilled rice liquor

Lao Loum – 'lowland Lao', ethnic groups belonging to the Lao-Thai diaspora

Lao Sung – 'high Lao', hill tribes who make their residence at higher altitudes, for example, Hmong, Mien

Lao Theung – 'upland Lao', a loose affiliation of mostly Mon-Khmer peoples who live on mid-altitude mountain slopes

lam wong – 'circle dance', the traditional folk dance of Laos, as common at discos as at festivals

lingam – a pillar or phallus symbolic of Shiva, common in Khmer-built temples

LNTA – Lao National Tourist Authority

mae nâam – river (literally, 'mother water'); with river name, shortened to *nâam*, as in Nam Khong (Mekong River)

meuang – pronounced *meúang*, Lao-Thai city state; district; often spelt 'muang'

múan – fun, which the Lao believe should be present in all activities

naga – mythic water serpent common to all Lao-Thai legends and art

NBCA – national biodiversity conservation area, a protective classification assigned to 17 wildlife areas throughout Laos in 1993

nop/wài – Lao greeting, a prayer-like palms-together gesture

paa dàek – fermented fish, a common accompaniment to Lao food

Pathet Lao – literally, Lao Land, a general term for the country and a common journalistic reference to the military arm of the early Patriotic Lao Front (a cover for the Lao People's Party)

pha – holy image, usually referring to a Buddha

phàa nung – sarong, worn by almost all Lao women

phī – spirits; worship of these is the other religion of Laos (and exists alongside Buddhism)

phúu – hill or mountain; also spelt 'phu'

sainyasat – folk magic

sala – pronounced 'sāa-láa'; an open-sided shelter

sāláa long thám – a sala where monks and lay people listen to Buddhist teachings

samana – 'seminar', a euphemism for re-education and labour camps established following the 1975 Revolution

samlor – pronounced 'sāam-lâaw'; a three-wheeled pedicab

sāwng-thâew – literally two-rows; a passenger truck

se – also spelt 'xe', this is the term used in southern Laos to mean river; hence Se Don means Don River, Pakse means *Pàak* (Mouth) of the River

sii – sacred; also spelt 'si'

sim – chapel or sanctuary in a Lao Buddhist monastery where monks are ordained; so

called because of the *sima*, or sacred stone tablets, which mark off the grounds dedicated for this purpose

tàat – waterfall; also *nâam tók*

talàat – market; *talàat sao* is the morning market

thâat – Buddhist stupa or reliquary

thaek-sii – literally taxi: 1) a passenger truck; 2) a three-wheeled motorcycle taxi

tribal Thais – Austro-Thai subgroups closely related to the Lao, who have resisted absorption into mainstream Lao culture

thanŏn – street or road; often spelt thanon

tuk-tuk – see jumbo

wat – Lao Buddhist monastery; depending on the part of Laos you're in, it may be pronounced *vat*

wihāan – from the Pali-Sanskrit *vihara*; a temple building containing important Buddha images and often used by monks for morning and evening chants and/or meditation

Index

MAPS

airfares chart 117
Attapeu (Samakhi Xai) 257
Champasak 244
Huay Xai 216
Laos 10
   northern Laos 170
   provinces 68
   southern Laos 223

Luang Nam Tha 209
Luang Prabang 172
Muang Xai (Udomxai) 204
National Biodiversity
   Conservation Areas 26
Pakse 239
Phonsavan 191
Sainyabuli 219

Savannakhet 231
Si Phan Don 249
Tha Khaek 226
Vientiane 132
   Central Vientiane 136
Wat Phu Champasak 246
Wat Xieng Thong 176

TEXT

Map references are in **bold** type

accommodation 105
agriculture 37
air travel 116-8, **117**
   airline offices 161
   fares 122
   Lao Aviation Offices 118
   to/from Laos 116
   within Laos 122-3
Airport, Wattay International 118
Americans in Laos 20, 188, 209
Ang Nam Ngum 165
animals, *see* fauna
Annamite Chain 24, 50
antiques 114
architecture 44-6, 67
Attapeu 257-9, **257**
Attapeu Province 256-9

Ban Dong 236
Ban Hang Khong 250
Ban Hua Khang 198
Ban Hua Khong 250
Ban Huay 250
Ban Ilai 164
Ban Khon 253
Ban Muang Kao 238
Ban Nape 225
Ban Phanom 186
Ban Phaphin 245
Ban Phapho 248
Ban Saphai 238
Ban Thin Hong 186
Ban Xang Hai 186
bandits 99
bargaining, *see* money
basi (baci) ceremony 57
Baw Noi 194
Baw Yai 193

Beung Kan 224
bicycles 101, 126
Bokeo Province 214-8
Bolaven Plateau 236, 242-3
books 81-3
   history 82
   culture 82
   guidebooks 81
   politics 83
border crossings 118-21
   to/from Cambodia 120
   to/from China 120
   to/from Thailand 118-9
   to/from Vietnam 119-20
Boten 214
boxing, Thai 113
'Buddha Park' (Vientiane) 140
Buddhism, *see* religion
buses & trucks 124
business hours 101

car travel 123-6
   hire 124
   road rules 125
   roads 123-4
carving 114
Champasak 243-4, **244**
Champasak Province 237-55
checkpoints, interprovincial 74
Chiang Khong 119
Chiang Rai Accord 23
children, travel with 98
Chong Mek 119
cinema 112
climate 24
credit cards, *see* money
culture, traditional Lao 50
currency, *see* money
customs 76

dance 48-9, 112
disabled travellers 97
dolphins, Irrawaddy 253
Don Det 253
Don Khon 253
Don Khong 248-53
Dong Ampham 259
dress
   for foreigners 51
   Lao 50
drinks 110-2

ecology 25
economy 34
education 44
electricity 85
embassies 76
environment 25
etiquette 51-2

fauna 28-30
ferries 125
   to/from Thailand 120-1
   to/from Luang Prabang 184
   to/from Vientiane 162
festivals 101-3
fishing 37
flora 27
food 105-10
forestry 37
French in Laos 14-5, 123, 169,
   174, 188, 195, 212, 242
Friendship Bridge 118

gay & lesbian travellers 97
geography 23-4
government 30-4

handicrafts 48, 68, 160
Hat Jommani 118

Hat Sa 201
Hat Xai Khun 252
health 85-96
    malaria 93-4
    precautions 85-7
    problems & treatment 87-96
Heuan Hin 234
highlights 67-9
hiking 101
hill tribes, see people
Hin Boun 229
history 10-23
Hmong 43
Ho Chi Minh Trail 235
holidays 101
hospitals 96
Hua Phan Province 196-200
Huay Xai 215-8, **216**
hydroelectricity 37

investment, foreign 40
Irrawaddy dolphin,
    see dolphins

jewellery 114,160

Kasi 168
kataw 113
Khammuan Limestone NBCA
    222
Khammuan Province 222-9
Khinak 252
Khon Phapheng falls 255
Kiet Nyong 248
Kuang Si falls 187

Lak Sao 229
Lan Xang Kingdom 12, 13, 14,
    23, 46, 52, 59
language 58-65
    courses 104
    dialects 58
    French, use of 64
    other languages 65
    script & tones 59
    useful phrases 65
Lao Bao (Vietnam) 234
Lao Loum 41
Lao Pako 166-7
Lao Sung 42
Lao Thai 41
Lao Theung 42
literature 49-50
logging, see forestry
LNTA (Lao National
    Tourist Authority) 70
Luang Nam Tha 209, 210, **209**
Luang Nam Tha Province 208-14
Luang Prabang 170, **172**

travel to/from 184
history 169
information 171
markets 180
orientation 171
places to eat 181-3
places to stay 180-1
shopping 183
walking tour 173-4
wats 176-80
Xieng Maen District 179
Luang Prabang Province 169-88

Mabri 220
Mahaxai 229
malaria, see health
manufacturing 38
maps 66-7
Mekong river 10, 11, 23, 24, 27,
    124
Mekong River Commission 23
minerals 37
money 77-80
    banking 79
    bargaining 79
    changing money 78
    costs 77
    credit cards 79
    currency 77
Muang Houn 207
Muang Kham 193
Muang Khong 250
Muang Khua 202
Muang Ngoi,
    see Nong Khiaw
Muang Saen 250, 253
Muang Sing 211-3
Muang Sui 195-6
Muang Xai 203-6, **204**
Mukdahan (Thailand) 234
music 48

Nakai-Nam Theun NBCA 222
Nakasong 252
Nakhon Phanom (Thailand) 228
Nam Kading 225
Nam Neua falls 198
Nam Ngum dam, see Ang Nam
    Ngum 165
Nam Phoun NBCA 218
Nam Sam NBCA 198
Nam Tok Ban Kum 218
Nam Tok Katamtok 259
Nam Tok Na Kha 218
Nam Tok Tat Khu Khana 164
Nam Tok Tat Nam Suang 164
Nam Tok Tat Son 164
Nambak 187
Namo 210

National Biodiversity
    Conservation Areas (NBCAs)
    25, 69, 166, **26**
newspapers 83
Nong Bua 237
Nong Kangdong 237
Nong Khiaw (Muang Ngoi) 187
Nong Pet 193

Pak Lai 221
Pak Ou caves 186
Pakbeng 207-8
Pakse 238-42, **239**
Paksong 258
Pakxan 224
Pathet Lao 16
people 41-4
permits, interprovincial, see visas
Pha That Luang (Great
    Sacred Stupa) 145-6
Pha Xang 218
phīi (earth spirit), see religion
Phon Hong 164
Phongsali 200-2
Phongsali Province 200-2
Phonsavan 189-92, **191**
photography 52, 84
Phu Den Din NBCA 200
Phu Katae 237
Phu Khao Khuai NBCA 166
Phu Si (Luang Prabang) 178
Phu Xieng Thong NBCA 236
Phuvong 258
Plain of Jars 192-3
population 40
post 80

religion 52-8
    animism 58
    Buddhism 54-7
    monks & nuns 54
    other religions 58
    spirit cults 52, 57
restaurants 106
river travel 101, 124
road rules, see car travel 125
roads, see car travel 123

Sainyabuli 219, 220, **219**
Sainyabuli Province 218-21
Saisombun Special Zone 33
Salavan 236-7
Salavan Province 236-7
Sam Neua 197-8
Samouy 236
Sansai 258
Savannakhet 230-4, **231**
Savannakhet Province 229-36
sculpture 46-8

Se Set river 236
Sekong (Muang Lamam) 256
Sekong Province 255-6
Sepon (Xepon) 235-6
Si Phan Don 248-5, **249**
Sihanouk Trail 258
soccer 112
Sop Hao 198
spirit cults, *see* religion 57
Suan Hin 198

Taat Heuang 218
Taat Jaew 219
Taat Lak Sip-Et 207
Taat Lo 243
Taat Phan 243
Taat Sae 238
Taat Sae falls 187
Taat Saloei 198
Taat Se Noi 259
Taat Somphamit 253
Taat Wang Fong 225
Taat Yong 207
Tahoy District 237
Talaat Lak Haa-sip Sawng 164
taxis 126
telephone 80-1
textiles 113-4
Tha Boei 252
Tha Falang (Wang Santiphap)
   229
Tha Khaek 225-8, **226**
Tha Na Leng 118
Thai Dam 42

Thai Lü 213
Thalat 165
Tham Phu Khiaw 250
Tham Piu 194-5
That Ing Hang 234
That Kadaotuk 237
That Phon 235
time 85
tipping 79
toilets 96
tourism policy 39
tourist offices 70-1
tours 127-8
train travel 124
travel insurance 75
Tumlan 237

Udomxai Province 202-8
Um Muang 247
UXO (unexploded ordnance) 99,
   189

Vang Sang 165
Vang Vieng 167-8
Vieng Xai caves 199-200
Vientiane 129-64, **132, 136**
   entertainment 157-8
   festivals 143
   transport 163
   history 129
   information 131-3
   markets 160
   orientation 129-30
   places to eat 151-7

   places to stay 146-51
   shopping 158-61
   things to see & do 134
Vientiane Province 129-68
Vietnam, political links with 33
visas 71-3
   interprovince permits 73, 100
   visit 71
   business 71-2
   extensions 72
   journalist 72
   non-immigrant 72
   transit 72
   tourist 71
Voen Kham 252

Wang Santiphap, *see* Tha Falang
   229
Wat Pha Baat Phonsan 225
Wat Pha That Si
   Khotabong 228
Wat Phu Champasak 245-7, **246**
Wat Xieng Thong **176**
water, drinking 87
Wattay International, *see* Airport
weaving 48, 159
women travellers 97
work, for foreigners 104

Xepon, *see* Sepon
Xieng Khuang Province 188-96
Xieng Khuang, Old (Muang
   Khun) 195
Xieng Kok 120, 213-4

LONELY PLANET JOURNEYS

JOURNEYS is a unique collection of travellers' tales – published by the company that understands travel better than anyone else. It is a series for anyone who has ever experienced – or dreamed of – the magical moment when they encountered a strange culture or saw a place for the first time. They are tales to read while you're planning a trip, while you're on the road or while you're in an armchair, in front of a fire.

JOURNEYS books will catch the spirit of a place, illuminate a culture, recount a crazy adventure, or introduce a fascinating way of life. They will always entertain, and always enrich the experience of travel.

ISLANDS IN THE CLOUDS
Travels in the Highlands of New Guinea
Isabella Tree

This is the fascinating account of a journey to the remote and beautiful Highlands of Papua New Guinea and Irian Jaya. The author travels with a PNG Highlander who introduces her to his intriguing and complex world. *Islands in the Clouds* is a thoughtful, moving book, full of insights into a region that is rarely noticed by the rest of the world.

'One of the most accomplished travel writers to appear on the horizon for many years . . . the dialogue is brilliant' – Eric Newby

LOST JAPAN
Alex Kerr

Lost Japan draws on the author's personal experiences of Japan over a period of 30 years. Alex Kerr takes his readers on a backstage tour: friendships with Kabuki actors, buying and selling art, studying calligraphy, exploring rarely visited temples and shrines . . . The Japanese edition of this book was awarded the 1994 Shincho Gakugei Literature Prize for the best work of non-fiction.

'This deeply personal witness to Japan's wilful loss of its traditional culture is at the same time an immensely valuable evaluation of just what that culture was'
– Donald Richie of the Japan Times

THE GATES OF DAMASCUS
Lieve Joris
Translated by Sam Garrett

This best-selling book is a beautifully drawn portrait of day-to-day life in modern Syria. Through her intimate contact with local people, Lieve Joris draws us into the fascinating world that lies behind the gates of Damascus.

'A brilliant book . . . Not since Naguib Mahfouz has the everyday life of the modern Arab world been so intimately described' – William Dalrymple

SEAN & DAVID'S LONG DRIVE
Sean Condon

Sean and David are young townies who have rarely strayed beyond city limits. One day, for no good reason, they set out to discover their homeland, and what follows is a wildly entertaining adventure that covers half of Australia. Sean Condon has written a hilarious, offbeat road book that mixes sharp insights with deadpan humour and outright lies.

'Funny, pithy, kitsch and surreal . . . This book will do for Australia what Chernobyl did for Kiev, but hey you'll laugh as the stereotypes go boom' – Andrew Tuck, Time Out

LONELY PLANET TRAVEL ATLASES

Lonely Planet has long been famous for the number and quality of its guidebook maps. Now we've gone one step further and in conjunction with Steinhart Katzir Publishers produced a handy companion series: Lonely Planet travel atlases – maps of a country produced in book form.

Unlike other maps, which look good but lead travellers astray, our travel atlases have been researched on the road by Lonely Planet's experienced team of writers. All details are carefully checked to ensure the atlas corresponds with the equivalent Lonely Planet guidebook.

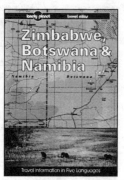

The handy atlas format means no holes, wrinkles, torn sections or constant folding and unfolding. These atlases can survive long periods on the road, unlike cumbersome fold-out maps. The comprehensive index ensures easy reference.

- full-colour throughout
- maps researched and checked by Lonely Planet authors
- place names correspond with Lonely Planet guidebooks
  – no confusing spelling differences
- legend and travelling information in English, French, German, Japanese and Spanish
- size: 230 x 160 mm

Available now:
Thailand; India & Bangladesh; Vietnam; Zimbabwe, Botswana & Namibia

Coming soon:
Chile; Egypt; Israel; Laos; Turkey

LONELY PLANET TV SERIES & VIDEOS

Lonely Planet travel guides have been brought to life on television screens around the world. Like our guides, the programmes are based on the joy of independent travel, and look honestly at some of the most exciting, picturesque and frustrating places in the world. Each show is presented by one of three travellers from Australia, England or the USA and combines an innovative mixture of video, Super-8 film, atmospheric soundscapes and original music.

Videos of each episode – containing additional footage not shown on television – are available from good book and video shops, but the availability of individual videos varies with regional screening schedules.

Video destinations include: Alaska; Australia (Southeast); Brazil; Ecuador & the Galápagos Islands; Indonesia; Israel & the Sinai Desert; Japan; La Ruta Maya (Yucatán, Guatemala & Belize); Morocco; North India (Varanasi to the Himalaya); Pacific Islands; Vietnam; Zimbabwe, Botswana & Namibia.

Coming soon: The Arctic (Norway & Finland); Baja California; Chile & Easter Island; China (Southeast); Costa Rica; East Africa (Tanzania & Zanzibar); Great Barrier Reef (Australia); Jamaica; Papua New Guinea; the Rockies (USA); Syria & Jordan; Turkey.

The Lonely Planet TV series is produced by:
Pilot Productions
Duke of Sussex Studios
44 Uxbridge St
London W8 7TG UK

Lonely Planet videos are distributed by:
IVN Communications Inc
2246 Camino Ramon
California 94583, USA

107 Power Road, Chiswick
London W4 5PL UK .

Music from the TV series is available on CD & cassette.
For ordering information contact your nearest Lonely Planet office.

PLANET TALK

Lonely Planet's FREE quarterly newsletter

We love hearing from you and think you'd like to hear from us.

When...is the right time to see reindeer in Finland?
Where...can you hear the best palm-wine music in Ghana?
How...do you get from Asunción to Areguá by steam train?
What...is the best way to see India?

For the answer to these and many other questions read PLANET TALK.

Every issue is packed with up-to-date travel news and advice including:

- a letter from Lonely Planet co-founders Tony and Maureen Wheeler
- go behind the scenes on the road with a Lonely Planet author
- feature article on an important and topical travel issue
- a selection of recent letters from travellers
- details on forthcoming Lonely Planet promotions
- complete list of Lonely Planet products

To join our mailing list contact any Lonely Planet office.

Also available: Lonely Planet T-shirts. 100% heavyweight cotton..

LONELY PLANET ONLINE

Get the latest travel information before you leave or while you're on the road

Whether you've just begun planning your next trip, or you're chasing down specific info on currency regulations or visa requirements, check out the Lonely Planet World Wide Web site for up-to-the-minute travel information.

As well as travel profiles of your favourite destinations (including interactive maps and full-colour photos), you'll find current reports from our army of researchers and other travellers, updates on health and visas, travel advisories, and the ecological and political issues you need to be aware of as you travel.

There's an online travellers' forum (the Thorn Tree) where you can share your experiences of life on the road, meet travel companions and ask other travellers for their recommendations and advice. We also have plenty of links to other Web sites useful to independent travellers.

With tens of thousands of visitors a month, the Lonely Planet Web site is one of the most popular on the Internet and has won a number of awards including GNN's Best of the Net travel award.

http://www.lonelyplanet.com

LONELY PLANET PRODUCTS

Lonely Planet is known worldwide for publishing practical, reliable and no-nonsense travel information in our guides and on our web site. The Lonely Planet list covers just about every accessible part of the world. Currently there are eight series: *travel guides, shoestring guides, walking guides, city guides, phrasebooks, audio packs, travel atlases* and *Journeys* – a unique collection of travellers' tales.

EUROPE

Austria • Baltic States & Kaliningrad • Baltic States phrasebook • Britain • Central Europe on a shoestring • Central Europe phrasebook • Czech & Slovak Republics • Denmark • Dublin city guide • Eastern Europe on a shoestring • Eastern Europe phrasebook • Finland • France • Greece • Greek phrasebook • Hungary • Iceland, Greenland & the Faroe Islands • Ireland • Italy • Mediterranean Europe on a shoestring • Mediterranean Europe phrasebook • Paris city guide • Poland • Prague city guide • Russia, Ukraine & Belarus • Russian phrasebook • Scandinavian & Baltic Europe on a shoestring • Scandinavian Europe phrasebook • Slovenia • St Petersburg city guide • Switzerland • Trekking in Greece • Trekking in Spain • Ukranian phrasebook • Vienna city guide • Walking in Switzerland • Western Europe on a shoestring • Western Europe phrasebook

NORTH AMERICA

Alaska • Backpacking in Alaska • Baja California • California & Nevada • Canada • Hawaii • Honolulu city guide • Los Angeles city guide • Mexico • New England • Pacific Northwest USA • Rocky Mountain States • San Francisco city guide • Southwest USA • USA phrasebook

CENTRAL AMERICA & THE CARIBBEAN

Central America on a shoestring • Costa Rica • Eastern Caribbean • Guatemala, Belize & Yucatán: La Ruta Maya • Jamaica

SOUTH AMERICA

Argentina, Uruguay & Paraguay • Bolivia • Brazil • Brazilian phrasebook • Buenos Aires city guide • Chile & Easter Island • Colombia • Ecuador & the Galápagos Islands • Latin American Spanish phrasebook • Peru • Quechua phrasebook • Rio de Janeiro city guide • South America on a shoestring • Trekking in the Patagonian Andes • Venezuela

AFRICA

Arabic (Moroccan) phrasebook • Africa on a shoestring • Cape Town city guide • Central Africa • East Africa • Egypt & the Sudan • Ethiopian (Amharic) phrasebook • Kenya • Morocco • North Africa • South Africa, Lesotho & Swaziland • Swahili phrasebook • Trekking in East Africa • West Africa • Zimbabwe, Botswana & Namibia • Zimbabwe, Botswana & Namibia travel atlas

ALSO AVAILABLE:

Travel with Children • Traveller's Tales

MAIL ORDER

Lonely Planet products are distributed worldwide. They are also available by mail order from Lonely Planet, so if you have difficulty finding a title please write to us. North American and South American residents should write to Embarcadero West, 155 Filbert St, Suite 251, Oakland CA 94607, USA; European and African residents should write to 10 Barley Mow Passage, Chiswick, London W4 4PH; and residents of other countries to PO Box 617, Hawthorn, Victoria 3122, Australia.

NORTH-EAST ASIA

Beijing city guide • Cantonese phrasebook • China • Hong Kong, Macau & Canton • Hong Kong city guide • Japan • Japanese phrasebook • Japanese audio pack • Korea • Korean phrasebook • Mandarin phrasebook • Mongolia • Mongolian phrasebook • North-East Asia on a shoestring • Seoul city guide • Taiwan • Tibet • Tibet phrasebook • Tokyo city guide

INDIAN SUBCONTINENT

Bengali phrasebook • Bangladesh • Delhi city guide • Hindi/Urdu phrasebook • India • India & Bangladesh travel atlas• Indian Himalaya• Karakoram Highway • Nepal • Nepali phrasebook • Pakistan • Sri Lanka • Sri Lanka phrasebook • Trekking in the Indian Himalaya • Trekking in the Nepal Himalaya

SOUTH-EAST ASIA

Bali & Lombok • Bangkok city guide • Burmese phrasebook • Cambodia • Ho Chi Minh city guide • Indonesia • Indonesian phrasebook • Indonesian audio pack • Jakarta city guide • Java • Laos • Lao phrasebook • Malaysia, Singapore & Brunei • Myanmar (Burma) • Philippines • Pilipino phrasebook • Singapore city guide • South-East Asia on a shoestring • Thailand • Thailand travel atlas • Thai phrasebook • Thai audio pack • Thai Hill Tribes phrasebook • Vietnam • Vietnamese phrasebook • Vietnam travel atlas

MIDDLE EAST & CENTRAL ASIA

Arab Gulf States • Arabic (Egyptian) phrasebook • Central Asia • Iran • Israel • Jordan & Syria • Middle East • Turkey • Turkish phrasebook • Trekking in Turkey • Yemen

Travel Literature: The Gates of Damascus

ISLANDS OF THE INDIAN OCEAN

Madagascar & Comoros • Maldives & Islands of the East Indian Ocean • Mauritius, Réunion & Seychelles

AUSTRALIA & THE PACIFIC

Australia • Australian phrasebook • Bushwalking in Australia• Bushwalking in Papua New Guinea • Fiji • Fijian phrasebook • Islands of Australia's Great Barrier Reef • Melbourne city guide • Micronesia • New Caledonia • New South Wales & the ACT • New Zealand• Northern Territory• Outback Australia • Papua New Guinea • Papua New Guinea phrasebook • Queensland • Rarotonga & the Cook Islands • Samoa • Solomon Islands • South Australia • Sydney city guide • Tahiti & French Polynesia • Tasmania • Tonga • Tramping in New Zealand • Vanuatu • Victoria • Western Australia

Travel Literature: Islands in the Clouds • Sean & David's Long Drive

THE LONELY PLANET STORY

Lonely Planet published its first book in 1973 in response to the numerous 'How did you do it?' questions Maureen and Tony Wheeler were asked after driving, bussing, hitching, sailing and railing their way from England to Australia.

Written at a kitchen table and hand collated, trimmed and stapled, *Across Asia on the Cheap* became an instant local bestseller, inspiring thoughts of another book.

Eighteen months in South-East Asia resulted in their second guide, *South-East Asia on a shoestring*, which they put together in a backstreet Chinese hotel in Singapore in 1975. The 'yellow bible', as it quickly became known to backpackers around the world, soon became *the* guide to the region. It has sold well over half a million copies and is now in its 8th edition, still retaining its familiar yellow cover.

Today there are over 180 titles, including travel guides, walking guides, language kits & phrasebooks, travel atlases and travel literature. The company is one of the largest travel publishers in the world. Although Lonely Planet initially specialised in guides to Asia, we now cover most regions of the world, including the Pacific, North America, South America, Africa, the Middle East and Europe.

The emphasis continues to be on travel for independent travellers. Tony and Maureen still travel for several months of each year and play an active part in the writing, updating and quality control of Lonely Planet's guides.

They have been joined by over 70 authors and 170 staff at our offices in Melbourne (Australia), Oakland (USA), London (UK) and Paris (France). Travellers themselves also make a valuable contribution to the guides through the feedback we receive in thousands of letters each year.

The people at Lonely Planet strongly believe that travellers can make a positive contribution to the countries they visit, both through their appreciation of the countries' culture, wildlife and natural features, and through the money they spend. In addition, the company makes a direct contribution to the countries and regions it covers. Since 1986 a percentage of the income from each book has been donated to ventures such as famine relief in Africa; aid projects in India; agricultural projects in Central America; Greenpeace's efforts to halt French nuclear testing in the Pacific; and Amnesty International.

'I hope we send the people out with the right attitude about travel. You realise when you travel that there are so many different perspectives about the world, so we hope these books will make people more interested in what they see. These are guidebooks, but you can't really guide people. All you can do is point them in the right direction.'
— **Tony Wheeler**

LONELY PLANET PUBLICATIONS

Australia
PO Box 617, Hawthorn 3122, Victoria
tel: (03) 9819 1877 fax: (03) 9819 6459
e-mail: talk2us@lonelyplanet.com.au

USA
Embarcadero West, 155 Filbert St, Suite 251,
Oakland, CA 94607
tel: (510) 893 8555 TOLL FREE: 800 275-8555
fax: (510) 893 8563
e-mail: info@lonelyplanet.com

UK
10 Barley Mow Passage, Chiswick,
London W4 4PH
tel: (0181) 742 3161 fax: (0181) 742 2772
e-mail: 100413.3551@compuserve.com

France:
71 bis rue du Cardinal Lemoine, 75005 Paris
tel: 1 44 32 06 20 fax: 1 46 34 72 55
e-mail: 100560.415@compuserve.com

World Wide Web: http://www.lonelyplanet.com